U.S. Public Policy in an International Context

Volker Krause

Eastern Michigan University

Zachary A. Smith

Northern Arizona University

Boston   Columbus   Indianapolis   New York   San Francisco   Hoboken
Amsterdam   Cape Town   Dubai   London   Madrid   Milan   Munich   Paris   Montréal   Toronto
Delhi   Mexico City   São Paulo   Sydney   Hong Kong   Seoul   Singapore   Taipei   Tokyo

Editor in Chief: Ashley Dodge
SenioMarketing Coordinator: Jessica Warren
Managing Editor: Denise Forlow
Program Manager: Carly Czech
Project Manager: Amanda Zagnoli, Integra
Senior Operations Supervisor: Mary Fischer
Operations Specialist: Mary Ann Gloriande
Art Director: Maria Lange
Cover Designer: PreMedia Global, Inc.
Cover Image: Anton Balazh/Fotolia
Digital Media Project Manager: Tina Gagliostro
Full-Service Project Management and Composition: Integra/Anandakrishnan Natarajan
Printer/Binder: RR Donnelley-Harrisonburg
Cover Printer: RR Donnelley-Harrisonburg

Credits and acknowledgments borrowed from other sources and reproduced, with permission, in this textbook appear on appropriate page within the text.

Many of the designations by manufacturers and seller to distinguish their products are claimed as trademarks. Where those designations appear in this book, and the publisher was aware of a trademark claim, the designations have been printed in initial caps or all caps.

Library of Congress Cataloging-in-Publication Data

Krause, Volker (Associate professor)
    U.S. public policy in an international context/Volker Krause, Eastern Michigan University, Zachary A. Smith, Northern Arizona University.
        pages cm.
    ISBN 978-0-13-184996-9 (alk. paper)—ISBN 0-13-184996-4 (alk. paper)
1. United States—Politics and government—Textbooks.   2. Comparative government—Textbooks.   I. Smith, Zachary A. (Zachary Alden), 1953-   II. Title.
    JK276.K73 2015
    320.473—dc23

                                                                      2014013280

10 9 8 7 6 5 4 3 2 1

ISBN 10: 0-13-184996-4
ISBN 13: 978-0-13-184996-9

CONTENTS

PREFACE

The purpose of this book is to provide you with an overview of public policies and policy-making processes in the United States as well as a perspective on how the United States compares with other countries in creating effective public policies for a variety of issues of concern to citizens, scholars, and government officials. Our goal is to enhance your knowledge of U.S. public policy not only by writing about public policy making in the United States but also by placing it in an international context with different political, economic, social, and cultural settings. Unlike most traditional public policy textbooks whose primary objective is to educate students about public policy and policy making in the United States,[1] this book will help you understand, appreciate, and evaluate a variety of U.S. public policies from a comparative international perspective.

Most young people know we live in a globalized world. Music, games, messaging, and many other features of social media have been internationalized. People are just as likely to be playing an interactive game with someone from Asia, for example, as someone from Ohio. Most young people do not, however, have a good grasp of how their native country is different or similar to what is happening in other countries. Globalization is here to stay. With globalization has come a sharing of ideas, cultures, and problems in ways that were unthinkable only a couple of generations ago. International communication, the internationalization of markets and values, multinational organizations, transnational networks, and many other features of globalization transcend traditional borders and sovereignty, creating an increasingly interdependent global society. Cultural diversity around the world is facing a process by which human beings are becoming more homogeneous for better or worse.

In a globalized world, it is increasingly imperative that this and coming generations understand their country and how it functions in an international context. Are we in the United States really special and different? If so, how? Do we in the United States do some things better or worse than governments and people in other parts of the world? This book answers these questions while promoting an education that emphasizes global awareness and provides you with important comparative analytical skills to assess the strengths and weaknesses of U.S. public policies in a multicultural global context. The education to which this book contributes will prepare you for the opportunities and challenges in today's era of increased globalization; it is an education that is becoming ever more indispensable for citizens to succeed in the world of the twenty-first century.

Through a comparative perspective identifying similarities and differences in public policy and policy making between the United States and other countries, this text will help you understand how U.S. public policy may inform and be informed by how other countries deal with such policies. By exploring how the United States and other countries may learn from one another to create effective and efficient public policies for elections, criminal justice, healthcare, social welfare, air and water pollution control, alternative energy, and trade, this book seeks to advance global responsibility and good public policy leadership.

There are textbooks that compare public policies and policy making in different countries,[2] but U.S. *Public Policy in an International Context* differs from those in that it considers the United States as the country of reference for comparison. As this book compares the United States with other countries in terms of particular public policies, it combines the field of American public policy with the field of comparative public policy. Although this text is intended mostly for undergraduate and graduate students of comparative politics, comparative government, public policy, and public administration, it may also be used in international business courses exploring how international business may be affected by cross-national variation in public policies.

This book has eleven chapters. The first three chapters provide a foundation for the comparative core. Chapter 1 ("Introduction to Public Policy") defines public policy and provides an overview of public goods, types of public policy, and the process of public policy making. Chapter 2 ("Theoretical and Methodological Approaches") presents various theoretical and methodological approaches to the study of public policy. Chapter 3 ("Setting the Stage") describes the demographic, cultural, social, and institutional contexts of policy making in the United States, introduces the idea of the Dominant Social Paradigm, and examines formal and informal influences on policy making.

Seven chapters make up the comparative core of this book. In each core chapter, we examine a public policy first in the United States and then in a country chosen for comparison with the United States that relates to the policy. Here, we focus on country-specific issues, government agencies and other actors involved in policy making, policy initiatives or current policies, as well as challenges and problems concerning the policy in the United States and the country chosen for comparison. Chapter 4 ("Election Policy") and Chapter 5 ("Criminal Justice Policy") cover public policies regarding fundamental issues of political organizations. Chapter 6 ("Healthcare Policy") and Chapter 7 ("Social Welfare Policy") address public policies regarding major factors associated with human well-being. Chapter 8 ("Air and Water Pollution Control Policy") as well as Chapter 9 ("Alternative Energy Policy") examine public policies regarding vital elements of the environment. Chapter 10 ("Trade Policy") focuses on public policy relating to an important aspect of international economic relations. Throughout the comparative core, we rely mostly on a public policy-making process approach that incorporates elements of a variety of theoretical approaches, such as institutional, incremental, systems, and pluralist theories, and a variety of methodological approaches, such as process and historical methods.

U.S. *Public Policy in an International Context* ends with Chapter 11 ("Conclusion"). After reviewing the purpose and features of this book, the chapter argues that differences in public policies and policy-making processes are, to a large extent, related to differences in political culture and institutional settings.

The selection of countries for comparison with the United States is not random; rather, we chose countries that we deem of particularly strong interest to students of comparative public policy, especially from a U.S. perspective. Our selection rests largely on the importance of these countries and the media coverage and other public exposure they have received regarding their public policies.

Since the promotion of democracy based on free and fair elections is one of the major goals of U.S. foreign policy, India—one of the world's most populous and culturally diverse democracies sitting in one of the most volatile areas of the world with a relatively lower level of economic development—should be of particular relevance when it comes to election policy. China, a major power with over one billion people, has received frequent attention among citizens and policymakers in the United States and other Western democracies due to its violation of human rights in attempts to enforce public order. Thus, China should be of particular relevance when it comes to criminal justice policy—a policy that often reflects a country's balance between public order and respect for human rights.

When it comes to improving healthcare in the United States, there is a tendency to consider Canada's healthcare system for comparison. In order to understand the advantages and disadvantages of Canada's healthcare system, and assess its applicability in the United States, we have focused on healthcare policy in Canada. Sweden often comes to mind as one of the best examples of a social welfare state. Thus, we selected Sweden to study social welfare policy.

Brazil's rainforest is critical to the world's balance of oxygen and carbon dioxide, and its Amazon Basin is one of the world's largest sources of freshwater. Hence, it is important that students look at Brazil to investigate air and water pollution control policy. The Netherlands, a relatively small but highly developed country with a high population density, has been on the forefront in exploring and relying on alternative energy sources to promote efficient and environment-friendly use of energy. Therefore, we chose the Netherlands to examine alternative energy policy.

Japan, one of the world's richest countries, and one of the most important trading partners of the United States and many other countries, has been of particular concern over unfair trade practices, especially in the 1990s. Thus, Japan's role in world trade makes it an interesting case for trade policy.

A comparative approach to learning has a number of wonderful advantages. Knowing the strengths and weaknesses of any policy or government involved in policy making is enhanced by understanding how others are doing things. At the end of each chapter, you will find a list of recommended resources that your professor may require as supplemental readings to the text. We encourage you to explore these suggested readings. We have also provided a list of critical thinking questions to assess your understanding of the text of each chapter. After reading this book, it is our hope that you have a clear understanding of how the United States compares with other countries in specific public policies and policy-making processes.

Notes

1. See, for example, James E. Anderson, *Public Policymaking* (6th ed.) (Boston: Houghton Mifflin, 2006); Clarke E. Cochran, Lawrence C. Mayer, T. R. Carr, and N. Joseph Cayer, *American Public Policy: An Introduction* (8th ed.) (Belmont, CA: Wadsworth, 2005); Thomas R. Dye, *Understanding Public Policy* (11th ed.) (Upper Saddle River, NJ: Prentice-Hall, 2007); Guy Peters, *American Public Policy: Promise and Performance* (7th ed.) (Washington DC: CQ Press, 2006); Christopher A. Simon, *Public Policy: Preferences and Outcomes* (New York: Longman, 2007); and Carter A. Wilson, *Public Policy: Continuity and Change* (Guilford, CT: McGraw-Hill/Dushkin, 2005).
2. See, for example, Jessica E. Adolino and Charles H. Blake, *Comparative Public Policies: Issues and Choices in Six Industrialized Countries* (2nd ed.) (Washington DC: CQ Press, 2011) and Stella Z. Theodoulou, *Policy and Politics in Six Nations: A Comparative Perspective on Policy Making* (Upper Saddle River, NJ: Prentice-Hall, 2002).

ABOUT THE AUTHORS

Volker Krause received his B.A. from the University of Mississippi and his M.A. and Ph.D. from the University of Michigan. He has taught at Eastern Michigan University, Northern Arizona University, and the University of Michigan, and served as co-host for the Correlates of War project's dataset on state system membership. With particular interests in international security and international organization, Krause has published articles in various journals, including *International Politics, Journal of Peace Research, Social Science Quarterly, International Interactions,* and *Conflict Management and Peace Science.* He currently teaches courses in international and comparative politics in the Department of Political Science at Eastern Michigan University.

    Zachary A. Smith received his B.A. from California State University, Fullerton, and his M.A. and Ph.D. from the University of California, Santa Barbara. He has taught at Northern Arizona University, the Hilo branch of the University of Hawaii, Ohio University, and the University of California, Santa Barbara, and served as the Wayne Aspinall visiting professor of political science, public affairs, and history at Mesa State College. A consultant, both nationally and internationally on environmental matters, Smith is the author or editor of over 20 books and many articles on policy and administration. Currently, Smith teaches in the public policy Ph.D. program in the Department of Politics and International Affairs at Northern Arizona University in Flagstaff.

CHAPTER 1

Introduction to Public Policy

LEARNING OBJECTIVES

- Define public policy.
- Explain the difference between public and private goods.
- Explain the types of public policy and the different categories used for public policy.

- Explain the policy-making process.

"A person who knows only one country basically knows no country well."

—SEYMOUR M. LIPSET

This chapter is an introduction to the field of public policy. We have taken a comparative approach to the subject because we believe that it is best to understand the policy-making process in one's country as well as be knowledgeable about how policy is made in other parts of the world. This first chapter begins by defining the concept of public policy according to various scholars who are well known for their studies of the American policy formation system. The common theme in these definitions—and running throughout the text—is how to deal with a problem of public concern. Not surprisingly, there are some differences in describing what public policy is. First, a government, acting on behalf of the public, creates a plan or program to solve the problem. This plan or program is a *public policy;* it is implemented by public administration, and its purpose in solving the problem is to provide a public good. Public policy making is the process of creating public policy.

Second, public policy is conveyed by the government providing public goods. Public goods are defined and distinguished from private goods by two characteristics: nonexcludability and nonrivalness. Public goods are not amenable to being provided by markets; therefore, governments provide and protect public goods. Market failure occurs when people acting to satisfy their self-interest harm society as a whole. Governments help to prevent market failure; they provide public goods such as national security and clean air. This provision and protection of public goods is provided through public policies.

1

Next, the chapter considers various types of public policies: distributive, regulatory, redistributive, substantive, procedural, material, and symbolic policies. Each of these categories and the typologies that encompass them provide different ways of viewing public policies and their purpose. These typologies also provide different views of the role of government. Categories are helpful in understanding public policies by classifying them according to significant distinctive characteristics.

Last, the chapter describes the process of public policy making. This process illustrates different actions that are taken by the government and sometimes the public in the development of public policy. It begins with first identifying a problem and ends with the evaluation of a policy that has been implemented. We will then discuss agenda setting and the two types of agendas. Although some students of public policy disagree with the policy-process approach because it portrays public policy as a linear process, we believe that it is still useful when students are trying to understand the different roles played by government and society when making policy.

The concept of *public policy* may sound abstract and intangible. Yet, public policy affects many areas of our daily lives. Basic civil rights, freedoms and democracy, public safety, justice and order, access to health care, respectable well-being, reliable sources of energy, open trade, and national security—we usually take all these virtuous goods for granted. Millions of people in many parts of the world lack or are deprived of most of these goods, and, even in the United States, not all people equally enjoy all of them. How are such "public goods" provided? How are they allocated? How are they maintained? It is through public policy that we find answers to these questions. Let us now turn to what we mean by public policy.

Defining Public Policy

Many political scientists have tried to understand the roles of governments in providing public goods through appropriate public policies. Crucial to this understanding is what public policy is about.

According to Harold Lasswell, public policy is "a projected program of goals, values, and practices."[1] David Easton views public policy as "impacts of government activity."[2] James E. Anderson notes that (public) policy is "a *relatively stable, purposive course of action followed by an actor or set of actions in dealing with a problem or matter of concern*" (italics in the original).[3] Clark E. Cochran and his associates maintain that public policy is "*an intentional course of action followed by a government institution or official for resolving an issue of public concern*" (italics in the original).[4] Jay M. Shafritz and Christopher P. Borick point out that "[a] public policy is a policy made on behalf of a public by means of a public law that is put into effect by public administration."[5] Thomas A. Birkland refers to public policy as "a statement by government of what it intends to do or not to do."[6] And Thomas R. Dye says that "public policy is whatever government chooses to do or not to do."[7]

Although it looks like there is no single scholarly definition of *public policy*, the definitions quoted from policy scholars converge in the following synthesis: There is a problem of public concern that needs to be dealt with. A government, acting on behalf of the public, creates a plan or program to solve the problem. This plan or program is a public policy; it is implemented by public administration, and its purpose of solving the problem is to provide a public good. Public policy making is the process of creating public policy. This of course means government may decide to do nothing regarding an issue, which also is public policy.

Public Goods

What is "public" about public policy? Why would a government provide for public safety but not produce inexpensive televisions? What is the appropriate role of government in society? What level of government is best suited to deal with what issues? To what extent should governments intervene in markets? Those who study the functions of markets argue that the primary role of government is to promote public interests and maximize social welfare by providing public goods—goods that, if produced, the private sector would produce inefficiently.[8]

So, what are public goods, and why would the private sector not produce them? **Public goods** are defined and distinguished from private goods by two characteristics: nonexcludability and nonrivalness. **Nonexcludability** means a good or service is either difficult or impossible to limit the people who have access to it. Unlike a public good, a private good can be denied to those who have not obtained permission to consume it. This excludability is usually guaranteed by property rights to prevent unauthorized consumption. A public good lacks such excludability; if it is a good for one, it must be a good for all. Then there is the question whether a good is consumed individually or jointly. Whereas bottled water or pizza is consumed individually, clean air or national security is consumed jointly. If a good is consumed individually, consumption by one person makes it less available to others, which implies rivalness. A public good lacks rivalness because it is consumed jointly; it is indivisible among its consumers. **Nonrivalness** means a good cannot be given to only one person. Think of air. No one can say that a certain portion of air is for one person alone; air is all around us, and people can access it freely.

Both nonexcludability and nonrivalness, then, are defining characteristics of public goods consumption. They create problems for the production of public goods, and these problems are subsumed under *market failure*. Since it is impossible to exclude anyone from public goods or to allocate them separately, people can benefit from those goods without contributing to or paying for them. If there were private organizations producing public goods, people could free ride on their products. In other words, if people were asked to pay for public goods produced by private organizations, individual consumers may not pay because they cannot be denied or cut off from those goods. Furthermore, individual consumers may free ride not only on producers but also on other consumers. They may not write a check, for example, because they expect others to pick up the bill.

If people have incentives not to pay for consuming public goods, what incentives are there for the private sector to invest in producing them? The answer is few or none. Private investment is motivated by profit. Without reliable remuneration yielding profit, the private sector is unlikely to invest in costly goods for the public. Thus, in markets, with prices shaped by demand and supply, public goods, if they are produced, are produced insufficiently. Nonexcludability and nonrivalness of public goods therefore lead to market failure.

Market failure occurs when people, through pursuit of their individual interest, harm their collective interest—in other words, when people do what is good for themselves as individuals but bad for themselves as a society. Consuming public goods without contributing to or paying for them, free riding on public goods producers and other consumers, may be in people's individual interest but not in their collective interest when their behavior reduces, or perhaps eliminates, incentives for providing public goods. Markets cannot distribute or provide public goods because those goods are nonexcludable and nonrivalrous. Therefore, public goods will suffer market failures. This is why governments are used to provide public goods.

Consider national security, a costly public good. Once it is available, it is available to everyone within a given society. Nobody can be excluded from it, and it is indivisible. Even those who are unwilling to purchase it can still benefit from national security. They can free ride on its producers and on other consumers expected to pay for it. Although people may see it in their best individual interest not to pay for national security as long as they can expect others to bear the costs for providing it, others may behave correspondingly and also try to free ride. Consequently, if nobody bears the costs for providing national security, it will not be available. Yet, as a society, people are better off with national security than without it.

So how do people protect themselves from behaving in a way that tends to undercut the availability of national security and similar public goods? Confronted with a dilemma between individual interest and collective interest, people facing market failure establish governments to provide for public goods such as national security. Governments produce public goods, paid with taxes, and penalize those who engage in free riding through tax evasion.

Our discussion of market failure has so far considered the production of public goods, but we need to keep in mind that market failure also relates to the preservation of public goods. The point here is that individuals, groups, organizations, or firms, in pursuit of self-interest, may take action with negative and costly consequences or externalities for us all. This may occur through both consumption and production. Consuming energy produced with fossil fuels generates gases that pollute clean air. Those air pollutants are released when consumers use gasoline in driving their cars and when refineries process coal or oil to produce gasoline. Since nobody owns clean air, there is no individual incentive to preserve it. Yet, there is individual interest in consumption of inexpensive gasoline and in earnings from gasoline production. Clean air is a public good. We all benefit from it. It is indivisible and cannot be denied to anyone. Yet, air pollution related to individually beneficial and profitable activities harms our health and affects our climate; it generates significant costs for society as a whole.

It is obvious, then, that a dilemma between individual interest and collective interest exists not only over the production of public goods but also over their preservation. In order to preserve public goods such as clean air, people facing market failure establish governments that regulate consumption and production known to have negative and costly consequences or externalities for us all. Governments preserve public goods with rules and laws, and penalize those who break them. Basically, people create governments to protect themselves from engaging in activities that are harmful to clean air and similar public goods.

Although governments are established to create public policies that produce or preserve public goods under conditions of market failure, the extent of government involvement in markets is a matter of debate guided by several fundamental questions: Can the supply of public goods provide private goods? Does the supply of public goods depend on providing private goods? Should some goods of benefit to the public be private goods rather than public goods?

As mentioned earlier, national security is a public good for a society as a whole; nobody can be excluded from it, and it is indivisible. Yet, speaking at least of the United States, the supply of national security as a public good also provides private goods through contracts to produce the means to protect national security. For instance, national security involves defense against foreign aggression, and such defense requires military preparedness with tanks, ships, and aircraft produced based on government contracts with defense industries in the private sector.

Any public policy to produce or preserve a public good requires a ruling coalition in support of that policy; a ruling coalition represents diverse interest groups. **Interest groups** consist of people who organize around a specific issue in order to advocate for a particular point of view to be reflected in public policy. Examples include pro-environment groups such as the Sierra Club that advocates for environmental protection and pro-labor groups such as the American Federation of Labor and Congress of Industrial Organizations (AFL-CIO) that pushes for workers' rights. In order to create and maintain such support, policymakers tend to rely on issue linkage, logrolling, and side payments providing private goods that satisfy constituencies represented by those interest groups. An example of *logrolling* (trading favors) is establishing permission to drill for oil in districts where constituents are predominantly oil producers in return for their backing of a public policy to improve public education. In other words, if the oil producers do not back public education, then they will not receive permission to drill for oil. This is also an example of *issue linkage*: A private good, oil on private lands, is connected to a public good, education. Neither can move forward alone, but together, both can progress. Oil drilling would be allowed so long as oil producers backed education. Public education, as a policy issue, is dependent on the support of the oil producers.

The question of whether some goods of benefit to the public should be private goods rather than public goods has to do with differences in views regarding the functioning of markets and the appropriate role of government in society, especially the appropriateness of government intervention in markets. An example is whether or not to privatize water. Many regard water as a human right that should be provided by government to ensure access and affordability. When water is privatized, profit, rather than equal access to water that is affordable, is the goal of corporations. Those who advocate more government intervention argue that it is needed to (1) provide public goods that, if produced, the private sector would not produce efficiently due to market failure; and (2) regulate the market because unregulated markets generate socioeconomic inequality and injustice that may fuel political instability.

Returning to the example of water privatization, corporations would focus on generating profits. If the infrastructure supplying water needed repairs, the costs would be passed on to consumers who may not be able to afford higher rates. Consumers who could not afford to pay their water bills would be cut off, meaning they would not have water. This could cause riots, since water is needed in order to sustain life. In fact, this happened in Cochabamba, Bolivia, when a corporation was granted a contract to manage and deliver water. The price of water increased over 200 percent for some consumers,[9] which caused violent protests. Eventually, the delivery and management of water was returned to a public utility company.

Those who oppose more government intervention, or advocate for less government intervention, argue that markets are more efficient with more freedom from government interference. Since prices in free markets are shaped by demand and supply, the more consumer choice among products, and the more producer competition over market shares, the less costly goods are to consumers. An example that works well is cereal in a grocery store. The more different types of cereal, the cheaper each type will be due to competition. Therefore, if goods to the public were private goods rather than public goods, and if markets were as free as possible from government interference, the public could obtain the best possible goods at the lowest possible costs. Furthermore, it is argued that the less government intervention in markets, the more wealth would be generated for everyone, which would ensure greater socioeconomic satisfaction and hence greater political stability. Water delivery systems do not lend themselves to privatization. One system that is connected throughout an entire service area is all that is needed. Competing systems may not be connected to one another and would be wasteful of resources that are often limited.

Within the United States, the Democratic Party has been more supportive of government intervention in markets than the Republican Party. Internationally, Canada, for example, has been more supportive of government intervention in markets than the United States. Besides differences in views within the United States and between the United States and other countries regarding the appropriateness of government intervention in markets, we also need to keep in mind that government involvement through public policy occurs at different levels of government—federal, state, and local in the United States.

In addition to private goods and public goods, there are toll goods and common pool goods. **Toll goods** (e.g., public libraries or toll roads) are characterized

■■■■■■■■■■■■■■ **BOX 1.1** ■■■■■■■■■

Classification of Goods and Services

	Rivalness	Nonrivalness
Excludability	**Private Goods**	**Toll Goods**
	Bottled Water	Public Libraries
	Pizza	Toll Roads
Nonexcludability	**Common Pool Goods**	**Pure Public Goods**
	Common Fish Stocks	Clean Air
	Common Pastures	National Security

Source: Adapted from Charles F. Bonser, Eugene B. McGreagor, Jr., and Clinton V. Oster, Jr., *American Public Policy Problems: An Introductory Guide* (2nd ed.) (Upper Saddle River, NJ: Prentice-Hall), Table 2.2, p. 50.

by excludability and nonrivalness, but **common pool goods** (e.g., common fish stocks or common pastures) are characterized by nonexcludability and rivalness (see Box 1.1).

After placing public policy in the context of governments providing public goods, we need to consider how public policy affects the public as governments create various types of public policies to solve problems of public concern. Thus, it is to typologies or classifications of public policies that we turn in the following section.

Types of Public Policy

In order to understand how public policy may affect the public, it might help to consider typologies of public policies proposed by some prominent political scientists.[10] A "classic" typology is Theodore J. Lowi's classification of public policies as distributive, regulatory, and redistributive policies.[11] **Distributive policies** involve the allocation of services or benefits to particular segments of a population, such as individuals, interest groups, businesses, or communities. Examples include farm subsidies, regional hospitals, schools, and public parks and recreation areas. **Regulatory policies** impose restrictions or limitations on the behavior of individuals, groups, or businesses. Regulatory policy can be categorized into competitive regulatory policies and protective regulatory policies. **Competitive regulatory policies** are designed to limit the supply of goods and services to one or a few designated providers chosen from a larger number of competing potential providers. Examples include regulations of trades and professions such as law, medicine, and engineering. **Protective regulatory policies** are designed to protect the public from negative effects or externalities of private activities. Examples include regulations aimed at tainted food, air pollution, unsafe consumer products, and fraudulent business transactions. **Redistributive policies** intend to manipulate the allocation of wealth, property, rights, or other benefits among social classes or racial groups. The purpose is to provide more benefits to lower income or marginalized groups. Examples include welfare, aid to poor cities or schools, and a progressive tax system where the tax rate increases with the amount of money that can be taxed.

James E. Anderson has classified public policies as being substantive or procedural. This takes into account that there are important differences between policies that provide goods and services expected from government and policies that establish rules for policy making.[12] **Substantive policies** are about what government is set to do or allocate. Examples include construction of highways, payment of welfare benefits, and acquisition of bombers. **Procedural policies** are about how government is set to get something done or take action. These policies create formal processes that must be followed. An example is the federal Administration Procedure Act (APA) of 1947 that tells bureaucracies how they must create rules and regulations.

Murray Edelman proposes a distinction between material and symbolic policies. This takes into account that government allocates various kinds of benefits.[13] **Material policies**, possibly at costs to those adversely affected by them, provide tangible resources or substantive power to their beneficiaries. Examples include welfare payments, housing subsidies, and tax credits. **Symbolic policies** have little material impact on individuals, and there are no real tangible advantages or disadvantages. Rather, they appeal to values held in common by individuals in a given society, values such as social justice, equality, and patriotism. Examples include national holidays that honor patriots, policies concerning a nation's flag, and religion in school. Edelman noted that the rhetoric of a policy goes to one side while the actual decision (tangible benefits) goes to a completely different side. He is referring to the language used in policies. A policy may sound as if it benefits a particular group on the surface, but the substance of the policy benefits an entirely different group. Thus, one side receives a symbol and the other side receives substance.

A typology developed by James Wilson shows how the concentration and diffusion of benefits and costs associated with public policies are related to politics. A combination of benefit concentration and cost concentration is related to interest-group politics, which involves conflict between groups that obtain public policy benefits and groups that bear the costs for them. Here, politics is dominated by lobbying activities as well as strategic interaction among interest groups in zero-sum situations where one group's benefits translate into another group's costs. This occurs with a mandated increase to the federal minimum wage. Lower-paid workers receive the benefits while employers are forced to pay the cost. A combination of benefit concentration and cost diffusion is related to client politics, which involves close clientele relationships between policymakers, regulators, and regulated interests. The military–industrial complex is an example of client politics. This concept describes contracts that occur between private companies for the manufacture of weapons and aircraft that is covered

BOX 1.2

Concentration and Diffusion of Public Policy Benefits and Costs

		Costs	
		Concentration	Diffusion
Benefits	Concentration	Interest-Group Politics	Client Politics
	Diffusion	Entrepreneurial Politics	Majoritarian Politics

Source: Adapted from Thomas A. Birkland, An Introduction to the Policy Process: Theories, Concepts, and Models of Public Policy (Armonk, NY: M. E. Sharpe, 2001), Table 6.2, p. 143.

under defense spending and is sanctioned by Congressmen and women because those same companies contributed to their election campaigns.

A combination of benefit diffusion and cost concentration is related to entrepreneurial politics. This involves attempts by entrepreneurial leaders and their interest groups to persuade policymakers to make regulations that benefit public interests, despite opposition from those who would bear the costs of such regulations. Forcing factories to limit air pollution emissions under the U.S. Clean Air Act is an example of benefit diffusion and cost concentration. The factories pay for the costs of cleaner air that is enjoyed by everyone.

A combination of benefit diffusion and cost diffusion is related to majoritarian politics, which involves efforts by relatively loose groups of people, or those acting on their behalf, to obtain substantive or symbolic public policy statements; this tends to result in public policies that are weak or ambiguous (see Box 1.2).[14] An example is the proposed policy in the United States to use a cap and trade program to limit carbon emissions. A cap, or limit, on the total emissions would be created, and polluting businesses that emitted below their allotted amount could sell the extra credits using a carbon market. Clean air would benefit everyone and the costs would be covered by all energy consumers.

Although no typology of public policies is perfect, attempts to classify public policies may facilitate analysis of public policy in the United States and other countries. We will be discussing the process of public policy making below.

Process of Public Policy Making

Where do public policy proposals come from? How are issues of public concern defined? Why are some issues more likely than others to get on a government's public policy agenda? How do governments make public policy? What perspectives, interests, and stakes are involved in public policy making? How are public policies formulated, adopted, implemented, and evaluated? As we attempt to

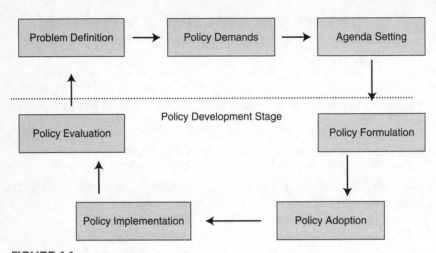

FIGURE 1.1

Process of Policy Making

Source: Adapted from Clarke E. Cochran, Lawrence C. Mayer, T. R. Carr, and N. Joseph Cayer, *American Public Policy: An Introduction* (7th ed.) (Belmont, CA: Wadsworth, 2003), Figure 1–1, p. 8.

answer these questions, we turn to the *process* of public policy making. This process relates to many public policies in the United States and other countries. As we describe the process of public policy making, we consider mostly the United States because it is the country of reference for the comparative perspective adopted in this text. Although we focus on the level of the U.S. national or federal government, the process of public policy making also applies to state and local government levels in the United States.

The process of public policy making is a cyclical process that creates public policies to solve problems of public concern and then provides for feedback about such policies, which leads to another round of public policy making. Specifically, the process of public policy making moves through seven phases: problem definition, policy demands, agenda setting, policy formulation, policy adoption, policy implementation, and policy evaluation; all seven phases are part of two stages: pre-policy development and policy development (see Figure 1.1).[15]

Pre-policy development encompasses problem definition, policy demands, and agenda setting.[16] Before public policies are developed, **problem definition** identifies problems of public concern that government needs to solve with public policies. Problem definition is important because policies are responses to problems. Therefore, if a problem has not been defined, a policy is not likely to be formed. Also, problem definition determines which side groups will take when advocating for or against a policy. As those problems are defined, they form issues that generate contending **policy demands** whose proponents compete for the attention of policymakers in the politics of **agenda setting**; of particular significance in this phase are policy demands generated by national crises or disasters.[17]

Agenda setting is political because it involves various interest and advocacy groups (e.g., business groups, consumer groups, and civil rights groups) wrestling for power to decide what is on the agenda. The likelihood that issues and policy demands get on the agenda depends on their proponents' success in the power struggle for agenda control. Thus, whenever you hear public policies presented in the State of the Union Address, those policies have emerged from a power struggle in the politics of agenda setting. If an issue does not make it on the agenda, it is not addressed. Agenda setting involves calling attention to an issue that people believe the government should address.

Roger Cobb and Charles Elder have noted that there are at least two types of policy agendas: a systematic agenda and an institutional agenda. A **systematic agenda,** or a popular agenda, includes all issues that might be subject to action or that are already being acted on by government. The systematic agenda basically consists of issues being discussed in society. An **institutional agenda,** or a public agenda, includes all issues that are explicitly subject to active and serious consideration by decision-making bodies.[18] Issues being discussed or addressed by a government are part of the institutional agenda. Cobb and Elder argue that an issue gains standing on the institutional agenda after its advocates engage others through issue redefinition.

Problem definition is influenced by moral values, ethical outlooks, and ideological orientations. For example, when asked about their views on abortion, people are divided between positions of pro-life and pro-choice. Conservatives tend to be pro-life, identifying abortion as a practice that ends a human life. Liberals tend to be pro-choice, identifying abortion as a matter of a woman's choice whether or not to terminate her pregnancy. Those who are pro-life are likely to demand a policy to restrict abortion, whereas those who are pro-choice are likely to demand a policy to uphold it. Although pro-life and pro-choice activists want policymakers to deal with abortion, their positions and demands are likely to produce contending policy proposals. Attempting to control agenda setting, pro-life and pro-choice activists compete for political power and the attention of policymakers not only against one another but also against activists who try to get issues other than abortion on the agenda of public policy making. So, pro-life and pro-choice activists need to make sure that (1) abortion becomes an issue on the policy-making agenda and (2) their respective position and demand will determine public abortion policy.

After issues and policy demands have gained the attention of policymakers and a policy agenda has been formed, the process of public policy making moves to **policy development,** which encompasses policy formulation, policy adoption, policy implementation, and policy evaluation. When it comes to **policy formulation,** various political actors—including Congress, the president, government agencies, as well as interest and advocacy groups—are involved in formulating public policies to solve problems of public concern. There are several types of policy solutions that may emerge from this phase: (1) attempts to induce behavior through incentives (e.g., tax credits) or disincentives (e.g., penalties); (2) rules or regulations to manage behavior (e.g., regulations of energy consumption); (3) use of facts or information to persuade people to behave in a certain way (e.g., information about the connection between smoking and lung cancer); (4) rights that provide people with certain entitlements and duties not to violate them (e.g., civil rights); and (5) powers that decision-making bodies are expected to use to enhance decision making (e.g., oversight powers).[19]

After policy formulation, attention turns to **policy adoption**. Here, public policies get formally adopted with legal and financial foundations through formal law-making and budget decisions. Typically, policymakers debate and bargain over alternative policy formulations and then choose an alternative or a combination of alternatives with enough political support for appropriate laws and budgets. In the United States, public policies get adopted when Congress makes laws and approves budgets and the president signs laws made by Congress.

After public policies have been adopted, they need to be implemented to do something practical and effective to solve problems of public concern. As policy making shifts to **policy implementation**, it moves from Capitol Hill and the White House to the government bureaucracy—that is, the departments, agencies, and commissions of the government's executive branch. Policy implementation requires administrative procedures or activities to carry out public policies. Those activities include creating new organizations, assigning new responsibilities to existing organizations, and making rules for effective administration. After the terrorist attacks on the World Trade Center Buildings and the Pentagon on September 11, 2001, implementation of U.S. national security policy involved the creation of the Homeland Security Agency and its subsequent organizational change to the Department of Homeland Security. It also involved assignment of new tasks to existing departments and agencies within the national security establishment. In addition, new rules and regulations were introduced to defend and protect national security.

Implemented public policies are subject to **policy evaluation**. Since public policies are costly, they need to be evaluated to see whether their benefits justify their costs. How effective and efficient are public policies in solving problems of public concern? Do they improve people's lives? Are they providing public goods as they are intended to provide? Do they generate benefits? At what costs? Does spending on them require an increase or a redistribution of taxes, or an increase in public debt and budget deficits? What political capital can be gained from them? These are some of the questions that the legislative and executive branches of government need to consider in assessing the performance and outcomes of public policies, their success or failure in achieving the objectives for which they were made.

Policy evaluation involves internal and external evaluators. In the United States, internal evaluators include the General Accounting Office (GAO), the Congressional Research Service (CRS), and the Congressional Budget Office (CBO) for Congress, the Office of Management and Budget (OMB) for the president, as well as numerous offices in government agencies. External evaluators include private research organizations, the communications media, as well as interest and advocacy groups. The Brookings Institution, the Urban Institute, the American Enterprise Institute, and the Rand Cooperation are all examples of private research organizations.

Policy evaluation leads to decisions on whether to continue public policies, modify them, or terminate them with or without replacement. Policy evaluation leads to updated or new problem definition based on information about the benefits and costs, the performance and outcomes, and the success or failure of public policies formulated, adopted, and implemented to solve what were identified as problems of public concern. There is another round in the cycle of public policy making; thus, public policy making is a cyclical process.

In short, through problem definition, the problems of public concern and the problems that government needs to solve with public policies are identified. Issues are then formed that give rise to contending policy demands whose advocates compete for the attention of policymakers in the politics of agenda setting. After pre-policy development concludes with formation of a policy agenda, policy development gets underway and moves though policy formulation, policy adoption, policy implementation, and policy evaluation to updated or new problem definition, thereby starting another round of the cyclical process of public policy making.

Comparative Public Policy

In a nutshell, comparative public policy is used to help analysts understand how one country's policies relate to those of another country. This is useful when trying to understand the impact of politics and the policy process on a particular country's policies. It also provides insight for improving policies or creating alternative ones.

This book provides an overview of public policies and policymaking processes in the United States and puts them in an international context for a comparison between the United States and other countries in regard to the same policies. Seven core chapters look at four sets of issues of concern to public policymakers: (1) political organization, (2) human well-being, (3) the environment, and (4) international economic relations. Specifically, political culture and institutional settings are integral to understanding how one country's public policies relate to those in another country. The United States is the country that is being analyzed in comparison to others such as India, China, Sweden, and Brazil. We have selected the countries in the book for comparison based on the differences in a country's policy when compared with the United States. Some topics, such as climate change policy, were avoided because they did not provide a good basis for comparison. Not every country used for comparison is exactly like the United States, which is why we explain parliamentary systems as well as other key differences. These differences have an impact on public policies, but they also provide opportunities to better understand specific policies in the United States.

Key Terms

- Agenda setting
- Common pool goods
- Competitive regulatory policies
- Distributive policies
- Institutional agenda
- Interest groups
- Market failure
- Material policies
- Nonexcludability
- Nonrivalness
- Policy adoption
- Policy demands
- Policy development

- Policy evaluation
- Policy formulation
- Policy implementation
- Pre-policy development
- Problem definition
- Procedural policies
- Protective regulatory policies
- Public good
- Redistributive policies
- Substantive policies
- Symbolic policies
- Systematic agenda
- Toll goods

Critical Thinking Questions

- Governments make public policy regarding public goods and services. What is the difference between public and private goods?
- Public policy making is not always a simple and straightforward process. How can policy making be problematic?
- What is the purpose of public policy? Why do government officials make public policies?
- What are the different components of the public policy-making process?
- How have public policies been categorized (i.e., how have scholars distinguished between the different types of public policy)?

Recommended Resources

Anderson, James E., *Public Policymaking: An Introduction* (6th ed.) (Boston: Houghton Mifflin, 2006).

Bickers, Kenneth N., and John T. Williams, *Public Policy Analysis: A Political Economy Approach* (Boston: Houghton Mifflin, 2001).

Birkland, Thomas A., *An Introduction to the Policy Process: Theories, Concepts, and Models of Public Policy* (Armonk, NY: M. E. Sharpe, 2001).

Cochran, Clarke E., Lawrence C. Mayer, T. R. Carr, and N. Joseph Cayer, *American Public Policy: An Introduction* (7th ed.) (Belmont, CA: Wadsworth, 2003).

Dye, Thomas R., *Understanding Public Policy* (12th ed.) (Upper Saddle River, NJ: Prentice-Hall, 2007).

Lester, James, and Joseph Stewart Jr., *Public Policy: An Evolutionary Approach* (2nd ed.) (Belmont, CA: Wadsworth, 2000).

Sabatier, Paul A. ed., *Theories of the Policy Process* (Boulder, CO: Westview, 2001).

Shafritz, Jay M., and Christopher P. Borick. *Introducing Public Policy* (New York: Longman, 2008).

Simon, Christopher A., *Public Policy: Preferences and Outcomes* (New York: Longman, 2007).

Theodoulou, Stella Z., and Matthew A. Cahn, eds., *Public Policy: The Essential Readings* (Englewood Cliffs, NJ: Prentice-Hall, 1995).

Notes

1. Quoted in James P. Lester and Joseph Stewart, Jr. *Public Policy: An Evolutionary Approach* (2nd ed.) (Belmont, CA: Wadsworth, 2000), p. 4.
2. Ibid.
3. James E. Anderson, *Public Policymaking: An Introduction* (6th ed.) (Boston: Houghton Mifflin, 2006), p. 2. *Italics* in original.
4. Clarke E. Cochran, Lawrence C. Mayer, T. R. Carr, and N. Joseph Cayer, *American Public Policy: An Introduction* (7th ed.) (Belmont, CA: Wadsworth, 2003), p. 1. *Italics* in original.
5. Jay M. Shafritz and Christopher P. Borick, *Introducing Public Policy* (New York: Longman, 2008), p. 8.
6. Thomas A. Birkland, *An Introduction to the Policy Process: Theories, Concepts, and Models of Public Policy* (Armonk, NY: M. E. Sharpe, 2001), p. 132.
7. Thomas R. Dye, *Understanding Public Policy* (12th ed.) (Upper Saddle River, NJ: Prentice-Hall, 2007), p. 1.
8. Mancur Olson, *The Logic of Collective Action* (Cambridge, MA: Harvard University Press, 1965) and Steven E. Rhoads, *The Economist's View of The World: Government, Markets, and Public Policy* (Cambridge: Cambridge University Press, 1985).
9. Jim Schultz, "Bolivia: The Water War Widens," NACLA Report on the Americas (2003), pp. 34–37.
10. For a good review, see Anderson, *Public Policymaking: An Introduction* (6th ed.) (2006) and Birkland, *An Introduction to the Policy Process: Theories, Concepts, and Models of Public Policy* (2001).
11. Theodore J. Lowi, "American Business, Public Policy, Case Studies, and Political Theory" *World Politics* 16 (1964): 677–715. A modification of Lowi's typology used here is from Randall B. Ripley and Grace A. Franklin, *Congress, the Bureaucracy, and Public Policy* (3rd ed.) (Homewood, IL: Dorsey, 1984).
12. James E. Anderson, *Public Policymaking: An Introduction* (5th ed.) (Boston: Houghton Mifflin, 2003), pp. 6–7.
13. Murray Edelman, *The Symbolic Use of Politics* (Urbana: University of Illinois Press) and Charles D. Elder and Roger W. Cobb, *The Political Use of Symbols* (New York: Longman, 1983).
14. For Wilson's original typology, see James Q. Wilson, *Bureaucracy* (New York: Basic Books, 1989) and James Q. Wilson, *Public Organizations* (Princeton, NJ: Princeton University Press, 1995).
15. For the United States, see Anderson, *Public Policymaking: An Introduction* (5th ed.) (2007); Clarke E. Cochran, Lawrence C. Mayer, T. R. Carr, and N. Joseph Cayer, *American Public Policy: An Introduction* (7th ed.) (Belmont, CA: Wadsworth, 2003); and James P. Lester and Joseph Stewart, Jr., *Public Policy: An Evolutionary Approach* (2nd ed.) (2000). For Australia, see Peter Bridgman and Glyn Davis, *The Australian Public Handbook* (2nd ed.) (St. Leonards, Australia: Allen & Unwin, 2000). For Canada, see Michael Howlett and M. Ramech, *Studying Public Policy: Policy Cycles and Policy Subsystem* (Toronto: Oxford University Press, 1995).
16. See Roger W. Cobb and Charles D. Elder, *Participation in American Politics: The Dynamics of Agenda-Building* (Baltimore: Johns Hopkins University Press, 1972); John W. Kingdon, *Agenda, Alternatives, and Public Policies* (Chicago: University of Chicago Press, 1984); and David A. Rochefort and Roger W. Cobb eds., *The Politics of Problem Definition: Shaping the Policy Agenda* (Lawrence: University of Kansas Press, 1994).
17. For examples of how national crises and disasters influence agenda setting, current policy change, or new policy development, see Thomas A. Birkland, *After Disaster:*

Agenda Setting, Public Policy, and Focusing Events (Washington, DC: Georgetown University Press, 1997) and *Lessons of Disaster: Policy Change after Catastrophic Events* (Washington, DC: Georgetown University Press, 2006).

18. Cobb and Elder, *Participation in American Politics: The Dynamics of Agenda-Building* (1972).

19. See Deborah A. Stone, *Policy Paradox and Policy Reason* (Glenview, IL: Scott, Foresman, 1988) and Lester and Stewart, Jr., *Public Policy: An Evolutionary Approach* (2nd ed.) (2000), p. 87.

CHAPTER 2

Theoretical and Methodological Approaches

LEARNING OBJECTIVES

- Understand the difference between theoretical and methodological approaches to public policy making.
- Explain eight theoretical approaches to public

  policy making and how they differ.
- Explain eight methodological approaches to public policy making and how they differ.

There are many ways to categorize the theoretical approaches that are used to study public policy making. Theoretical approaches tell us which variables are important when studying public policy making and why to pay attention to those variables. For example, when using pluralist theory, the researcher should pay attention to particular groups surrounding a policy issue, the demands those groups are placing on the policy, and the compromises that result from the various groups in order to pass a policy. Institutional theory requires the researcher to focus on the public policy-making institutions—the executive, legislative, and judicial branches of government as well as the bureaucracy. A researcher using institutional theory would be less likely focus on groups surrounding an issue. Each of these theoretical approaches orders the way researchers analyze the policy-making process. For example, elite theorists would search for elites in society who set the public policy agenda. Pluralists would examine policy formulation for the outcome of competing groups. Feminist theorists would take a particular angle that power relations in the policy process are patriarchal.

These approaches, which reflect the different worldviews regarding politics, are often associated with specific methodological approaches. Researchers usually have a political or philosophical orientation that dictates how they examine public policy, and each methodological approach that is used to study public policy relies on assumptions about what is important to know. Although methodological approaches are often linked to particular theoretical approaches, they are not the same. Methodological approaches tell us how to create or analyze specific public policies.

When conducting comparative analysis, both theoretical and methodological approaches must be the same for every case. For example, you cannot use elite theory to compare the environmental policies of Brazil while using institutional theory to examine the environmental policies in the United States. You would successfully have compared apples and oranges, and your analysis would not be meaningful. The same goes for methodological approaches. Going back to the Brazil and U.S. example, if you use institutional theory for your analysis and decide the historical method is the best way to conduct the analysis, you must use the historical method for both the United States and Brazil.

Theoretical Approaches

In this section, we summarize the following eight theoretical approaches to public policy making:

- Elite theory
- Pluralist theory
- Feminist theory
- Institutional theory
- Rational theory
- Incremental theory
- Systems theory
- Game theory

Elite Theory

According to **elite theory**, public policy is made by and for governing elites. One of the best accounts of elite theory remains to be *The Power Elite* by C. Wright Mills.[1]

Elite theorists argue that a society is governed by a small number of people, or ruling elites, who are from the upper socioeconomic strata of society, including heads of major foundations and corporations, and members of wealthy families. This small group does not argue that ruling elites confer with each other on a regular basis about appropriate policies that government should follow. Rather, they hold that ruling elites share values by virtue of background, education, and worldviews, which obviates their need for collaboration on specific public policy issues. These values include a limited role for government, the preservation and protection of private property, and individual liberty.[2] According to elite theory, the "elites" that the public sees—the politicians and other public actors that we associate with creating and carrying out public policy—are little more than puppets carrying out the wishes of true elites. Beneath a society's political class are its masses—ordinary citizens who think they are influencing public policy but they are largely consumers of propaganda generated by a system designed to keep ordinary citizens complacent and supportive of political actors who carry out the wishes of elites.

One of the strengths of elite theory is that ruling elites are relatively easy to identify. They are the top individuals who oversee a society's major institutions, and political scientists have done a good job of identifying such individuals and their roles in public policy making.[3] Yet, a political system in which elites do not work together to form public policy but fight among themselves over public policy may provide less evidence of elite theory than of pluralist or group theory.

Elite theorists would argue that the U.S. tax system is an example of the power of ruling elites. The system provides loopholes for the wealthy to receive tax relief. It also does not count capital gains as income, which means it is not subject to being taxed. Furthermore, there are university researchers who put forth information that this sort of tax system is beneficial to lower-income groups because the wealth will trickle down, and it is the best way to strengthen an economy.

Pluralist Theory

According to **pluralist theory**, which is also referred to as **group theory**, interest groups interact with each other, sometimes in concert and sometimes in conflict, in ways that influence public policy making, especially by the legislative branch of government. Pluralist theorists argue that individuals contribute to the formulation of public policy, but only as members of and contributors to groups. Groups, through their interaction and influence, work to determine public policy through institutions of government. Groups form and dissolve in response to the growth, development, and importance of issues in society. The strength of particular groups, with regard to public policy making, depends on the importance of issues at a given time and the combination of resources (for example, voting power or campaign contributions) that groups have at their disposal to influence policymakers. Pluralist theorists see elites as ever changing; some groups (and their elite members) gain influence while others become less influential. Policymakers act or react largely in response to pressures placed on them by interest groups that are active and important at any point in the process of public policy making.[4] Critics of pluralist theory point out that a political system works well for individuals who are members of well-organized and resource-rich groups but does not work well for those who have difficulties organizing to influence public policy.

Pluralist theorists would put forth environmental policy as an example of competition between different groups. Environmental policies do not always favor the elite, and often are contrary to interests of large businesses, especially factories that pollute. Environmental policies have been implemented to decrease pollution. However, some older factories are often "grandfathered," meaning they do not have to comply with regulations or have to meet lower pollution standards. Thus, environmental policies regarding pollution can be regarded as the result of compromise between environmental and business interest groups. Most environmental policies have been passed as a result of crises, which caused the environment to become an important issue in society. Such crises allow environmental interest groups to garner enough support and power to push forward environmental policies, meaning that environmental interest groups are not constantly in power.

Feminist Theory

Although there are different definitions of **feminist theory**, there is agreement among feminist theorists that women are, and have been, oppressed due to their gender because of an ideology of patriarchy that permeates society. **Patriarchy**, which recognizes the father or the eldest male as the head of a community, oppresses women through social, economic, political, and other institutions. Throughout history, men have dominated society's public and private sectors. Men have maintained power and control over society based on a system created with obstacles and boundaries that make it prohibitively difficult for women to hold positions of power. This monopoly of power, created and sustained by men, has generated, among other things, policies that reflect dominant male values and that work to the disadvantage of women and the advantage of men.

As an example of how feminist theory applies to public policy, let us consider the environment. Feminist theory applied to environmental policy is usually referred to as *eco-feminist theory*. Eco-feminist theorists argue that male dominance of society, and of women, extends to men's desire to dominate nature. Just as men feel a need to tame and conquer women to establish and maintain power, they also feel a need to tame and conquer the environment to extend their power over nature. Many eco-feminist theorists think that women not only have a greater understanding of nature but also a connection with nature that men do not have. Hence, women have, or should have, a central role in protecting the environment.

Institutional Theory

Institutional theory focuses on formal and legal aspects of public policy making. It deals with political institutions and political actors in the legislative, executive, and judicial branches of government. Institutional theorists are interested in procedural rules and government structures, availability of information, access to policymakers, patterns of interaction between institutions and the public, and connections between institutional arrangements and public policy. All policies are seen as results of inter-institutional arrangements.

An examination of civil rights in the United States could serve as an example of institutional theory. Researchers would examine the role of the U.S. Supreme Court in the foundational case *Brown v. Board of Education of Topeka, Kansas 1954* with ending segregation in schools. They would also examine the role of President Eisenhower who integrated the military and who enforced the Supreme Court's decision by using military force to integrate Central High School in Little Rock, Arkansas, in 1957. Next, institutional theorists would point out the role of Congress when it passed the Civil Rights Act of 1964. Finally, the civil rights movement and how it interacted with each branch of government would be taken into consideration. All of these institutions played an important role in the civil rights movement. Examining civil rights from an institutional perspective is a useful way of understanding how the civil rights movement unfolded.

Rational Theory

According to **rational theory**, all policies are outcomes of optimal decisions. Drawing on microeconomic approaches to the study of human behavior, rational theorists argue that a decision is always rational if no other alternative is better. Rational theorists assume that policymakers are perfectly rational and that they maximize benefits relative to costs by taking the following steps:

* Defining a problem
* Formulating goals
* Identifying policy alternatives
* Examining the benefits and costs of policy alternatives
* Choosing the policy alternative that maximizes benefits and minimizes costs

If policymakers take these steps and make decisions based on rational benefit-cost calculations, rational theorists expect them to generate the best possible policies.[5]

An example of a rational approach to poverty would include defining which members of the population are considered poor. This is done each year in the United States by setting the federal poverty level for income. Next, a goal of ending poverty—or at least lessening poverty—for those members of society would be set. Different methods of poverty alleviation would be considered, such as food subsidies, child-care subsidies, housing subsidies, increased minimum wage, and tax relief or tax credits. Then, policymakers would consider the costs and benefits of implementing any one or combination of the alternatives to alleviate poverty. Last, they would make a decision that allowed for the least cost to society and the maximum amount of benefit.

The assumption of perfect rationality is rejected by Herbert A. Simon, who introduced the notion of **bounded rationality**. According to Simon, it is impossible to gather and examine enough facts to make optimal decisions. Policymakers must make decisions based on a limited amount of information. Rational theory points to ideal policymaking, but Simon's notion of bounded rationality points to policy making that is constrained due to policymakers' limited knowledge and cognitive capacity.[6] Continuing with our poverty alleviation example, policymakers may not consider every possible alternative and every possible benefit and cost. Rather, they would consider some alternatives and the significant benefits and costs.

Incremental Theory

Charles E. Lindblom is credited with introducing the idea of **incremental theory**. According to incremental theory, public policy making is seen as a process of "**muddling through**" or moving in small steps or increments of change.[7] All policy decisions depend on small incremental decisions that tend to be made in response to short-term political conditions, because most decision making is controlled infinitely by events and circumstances rather than by the will of those in policy-making positions. Policymakers move slowly and conservatively when developing new policies. (Rarely are these "new" policies, but rather subtle changes to policies that have already been proposed or enacted.) Due to constraints on public policy making and multiple demands on policymakers with limited resources, making public policy in a nonincremental fashion is difficult, if not impossible. Instead, without the time, money, and intellectual capacity to consider fully all options when making public policy decisions, policymakers do what is easy and take whatever path comes out of bargaining and compromise to satisfy immediate problems. Incremental theory is thought of not only as a descriptive theory of public policy making but also as a normative theory suggesting a good way to make public policy consistent with norms, ideals, and requirements of a democratic political system.

Similar to Simon's notion of bounded rationality, which rejects the assumption of rational theory that policymakers are perfectly rational and make optimal decisions, incremental theory emerged in response to rational theory. According to incremental theory, most policy debates do not end with rational and optimal policy choices. Instead, policy debates continue to evolve over time. Key aspects of *rational decision making* are that (1) all options and means are considered, (2) decisions are products of structured evaluations, (3) major changes can be made on a regular basis, (4) decisions tend to be made proactively, and (5) political pressures should be removed from decisions. By contrast, key aspects of *incremental decision making* are that (1) only few options and means are considered, (2) decisions are products of negotiated settlements, (3) changes are made gradually over time, (4) decisions tend to be made reactively, and (5) political considerations are important in determining policy outcomes (see Table 2.1).

The U.S. federal budget is an example of incremental policy making. There are rarely any drastic changes to appropriations. Instead, small increases or decreases in appropriated amounts are made. This means that the budget from the previous fiscal year serves as a base for the upcoming fiscal year. In other words, when Congress makes decisions for the new budget, it refers to the previous budget.

Systems Theory

Under influence of the post–World War II "behavioral revolution" in political science, David Easton proposed an application of **systems theory** to the study of politics and public policy.[8] According to Easton, in order to improve our understanding of public policy making, we need to understand a political

TABLE 2.1	Key Aspects of Rational and Incremental Decision Making	
Rational Decision Making		**Incremental Decision Making**
• All options and means are considered.		• Only few options and means are considered.
• Decisions are products of structured evaluations.		• Decisions are products of negotiated settlements.
• Major changes can be made on a regular basis.		• Changes are made gradually over time.
• Decisions tend to be made proactively.		• Decisions tend to be made reactively.
• Political pressures should be removed from decisions.		• Political considerations are important in determining policy outcomes.

system. Specifically, a political system is embedded in a political environment created by general socioeconomic conditions, such as economic recession, financial crisis, high unemployment, or international terrorism. The political environment generates demands from individuals or groups, such as demands for economic reforms or counterterrorism measures, which become inputs to the political system. The political system processes these inputs to reach decisions, producing outputs or policies intended to deal with the socioeconomic conditions that created the political environment. As policies are implemented in the political environment, they may lead to outcomes that change the political environment, generating new demands and inputs through feedback on those policies. Unlike institutional theory, which is interested in institutions, actors, procedures, and structures within a political system, systems theory treats a political system as a so-called black box—a generic system without further differentiation (see Figure 2.1).

Systems theory would perceive the calls made from society after the terrorist attacks on 9/11 for increased counterterrorism measures as inputs into the

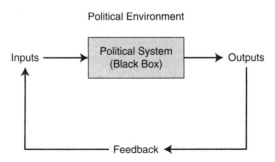

FIGURE 2.1

Inputs-Outputs Model of a Political System

political system. The resulting policies occurred inside the black box. However, once those counterterrorism policies were implemented, they gave way to more demands, such as what should be allowed when interrogating prisoners and what is considered torture. Those demands created a feedback loop that became inputs for new policy considerations.

Game Theory

Although **game theory** is similar to rational theory in the assumption that rational policymakers are trying to reach optimal decisions that maximize their benefits relative to costs, game theory sees decisions as strategically interdependent.[9] More specifically, in bargaining between two policymakers, PM1 and PM2, PM1's decision depends to some extent on what PM2 does, or what PM1 expects PM2 to do. And PM2's decision depends to some extent on what PM1 does, or what PM2 expects PM1 to do. Two general types of games are zero-sum games and non-zero-sum games. In **zero-sum games**, gains for some individuals or groups are losses for others; zero-sum games are winner-loser games. In **non-zero-sum games**, there may not be equal gains for all individuals or groups, but gains for some are not losses for others. Therefore, compromise is more likely in non-zero-sum games than in zero-sum games.

One of the games that game theory commonly applies to the study of public policy making is the **Prisoner's Dilemma**.[10] This game is based on a story of strategic interaction between two criminals. Two suspects who committed a major crime are arrested and placed in separate cells. Although there is enough evidence to convict each of some minor offense, there is not enough evidence to convict either of them with the major crime unless one of them confesses at the expense of the other. If both do not confess, each will be convicted of the minor offense. If one, and only one, confesses, the one who confesses will be free and used as a witness against the other, who will be convicted of the major crime. If both confess, each will be convicted of the major crime, with some leniency for their cooperation with the prosecution.

Let us consider a typical payoff matrix of the Prisoner's Dilemma. According to the previous story, there are two prisoners, Prisoner 1 and Prisoner 2, and each of them can make one of two decisions, A: not confess (and thus, cooperate with the other prisoner), or B: confess (defect against the other prisoner). If Prisoner 1 decides to not confess and Prisoner 2 decides to confess, Prisoner 1 will receive the worst payoff (–10) and be convicted of the major crime, whereas Prisoner 2 will receive the best payoff (0) and be free. Conversely, if Prisoner 2 decides not to confess and Prisoner 1 decides to confess, Prisoner 2 will receive the worst payoff (–10) and be convicted of the major crime, whereas Prisoner 1 will receive the best payoff (0) and be free. If both Prisoner 1 and Prisoner 2 decide to confess, each will receive the second-worst payoff (–8) and be convicted of the major crime, with some leniency for their cooperation with the prosecution. If both Prisoner 1 and Prisoner 2 decide to not confess, each will receive the second-best payoff (–1)

Prisoner 2

		A: not confess (cooperate)	B: confess (defect)
Prisoner 1	A: not confess (cooperate)	−1, −1	−10, 0
	B: confess (defect)	0, −10	−8, −8

FIGURE 2.2
The Prisoner's Dilemma

and be convicted of some minor offense, for which there is enough evidence, but not for the major crime because of the lack of enough evidence without a confession (see Figure 2.2).

It is obvious that Prisoner 1 and Prisoner 2 would be collectively better off if both decided not to confess (−1, −1) than if both decided to confess (−8, −8). Yet, we should keep in mind that the prisoners are placed in separate cells and thus cannot communicate with one another and coordinate their decisions. Neither prisoner can be sure that the other will decide to confess and be free and help the prosecution convict the partner in crime of the major crime; a decision not to confess is very risky ((−10, 0) or (0, −10)). Assuming that the partner in crime will decide to confess rather than not to confess in order to be free rather than convicted of some minor offense, it is rational for each prisoner to decide to confess and avoid being convicted of the major crime. Because Prisoner 1 and Prisoner 2 expect each other to make a decision to maximize their individual payoff, each makes a decision that leaves both collectively worse off ((−8, −8) instead of (−1, −1)).

The Prisoner's Dilemma is used to analyze collective action problems in providing public goods. Although public goods are collective benefits, it is rational to avoid paying the costs to produce them if others can be expected to take a free ride and enjoy the benefits without sharing their costs. Therefore, if everyone tried to maximize their individual payoff by getting benefits without costs to themselves but to others, there would be no incentive for anyone to produce the benefits. Public goods would not exist. In order to ensure that public goods are available, people establish governments that collect taxes to pay for them and to penalize those involved in tax evasion.[11]

Each of the theoretical approaches that have been discussed here contributes to the study of public policy making. Although none of them alone provides an adequate description of how public policy is made, all of them in combination are useful. The same can be said about methodological approaches employed to study public policy making.

Methodological Approaches

In this section, we summarize the following eight methodological approaches to public policy making:

- Process method
- Behavioral method
- Public choice method
- Post-positivist method
- Feminist method
- Discursive method
- Prescriptive method
- Historical method

Process Method

The **process method** focuses on the process of public policy making. Although the process method is often related to institutional theory, it is also associated with elite theory, pluralist theory, and feminist theory. One of the ways in which the process method examines public policy making is an approach that looks at **policy cycles** to describe how policy is made. This approach divides the process of public policy making into several stages, including (1) agenda setting, (2) policy formulation and adoption, and (3) policy implementation.

Since agenda setting involves the listing of items for governmental action, it is a prerequisite to any policy action. Proficiency in agenda setting depends on the ability to get an issue on the list of items to be considered by policymakers. Many groups in society use media as a tool for agenda setting. If an issue can garner enough media attention, it is likely to be addressed by the formal institutions of government.

Policy formulation and adoption may involve action or lack of action on an item placed on a policy agenda. Lack of action is a form of policy formulation and adoption because it is a policy decision to maintain the status quo. Proficiency in policy formulation and adoption depends on the type of policy involved and the location of decision-making authority over a given policy issue.

For the most part, policy implementation is the responsibility of bureaucracies. Bureaucrats or administrators have discretion in implementing policy programs, and discretion is power. Even seemingly minor administrative decisions can have a significant impact on how a general legislative mandate is translated into specific governmental action. For example, a decision on when and where to hold public hearings may have a significant effect on who participates in those hearings. For example, hearings conducted by the U.S. Forest Service for its first Roadless Area Review and Evaluation (RARE 1) to determine the extent and location of wilderness areas on Forest Service lands were held in the Pacific Northwest. Since the hearings were often held close or adjacent to logging communities, a large number of loggers participated in them. As a consequence, the RARE 1 hearings in the region generated an abundance of testimony against establishing additional wilderness areas.

Agenda setting, policy formulation and adoption, and policy implementation are all important stages in the process of public policy making. For a major public policy, such as the Clean Water Act, to be successful, there must be success at each stage. For example, water must become an issue that interests policymakers (specifically members of Congress) in order to place it on a policy agenda. Agreement must then be reached on a policy to deal with the issue. And some organization, such as the Environmental Protection Agency, must have incentives and resources to implement the policy. Failure at any one of these stages will prevent policy objectives from being realized.

Behavioral Method

Not long after World War II, the social sciences in general, and political science in particular, became more "scientific." This was referred to as the "behavioral revolution" in political science. What became known as the scientific or **behavioral method** has been adopted as a major methodological approach to policy analysis. Proponents of the behavioral method, or **positivists**, attempt to follow the dominant methodology employed in the natural and physical sciences by relying on (1) theory and model building, (2) hypothesis testing, and (3) rigorous empirical investigation, with statistical analysis of data collected from surveys, archives, or other sources. Examples of the behavioral method are comparative studies that use a large number of cases. In the United States, this usually occurs with comparing several states to one another to determine how their differences and/or similarities affect their state policies. Analyzing the education policies of every state in the country to determine if different demographic factors impact such policies would be an example of the behavioral method.

Public Choice Method

Because the **public choice method** has adopted the methodology of economics, it is sometimes considered a political economy approach. The public choice method assumes that, motivated by personal gain (primarily economic enrichment), human behavior is rational. Proponents of the public choice method argue that individuals behave in their self-interest, without much attention to the collective outcomes of their decisions. This is seen as a good and rational way to allocate public resources. Policy analysts using the public choice method might, for example, compare the amount of money that people spend on their automobiles with the amount of money that they spend on other forms of transportation, which may lead to the conclusion that the automobile is a preferred means of transportation. More generally, policy analysts using the public choice method may conclude that policies that maximize individual choice and freedom are preferable to policies that maximize collective choice. Such a policy would allow for multiple schools within a city to allow residents to choose the best school. Schools would then compete to attract students by increasing their overall quality; thus improving education through competition.

Post-Positivist Method

In contrast (and response) to the behavioral and public choice methods, the **post-positivist method** focuses more on what is not quantifiable and considers case studies as well as ethnographic and qualitative research more important than scientific rigor.

> Methodologically, these analysts treat each piece of social phenomena as a unique event, with ethnographic and other qualitative indices becoming paramount....(This view)... is described by its concern with understanding rather than prediction, with working hypothesis rather than rigorous hypothesis testing, and with mutual interaction between the inquirer and the object of study rather than detached observation on the part of the analyst.[12]

Policy analysts using the post-positivist method would adopt "a respect for the disciplined employment of sound intuition, itself born of experience not reducible to models, hypothesis, quantification," and hard data.[13]

Whereas positivists and proponents of the public choice method would say that policy analysis could be value-free, post-positivists would claim that all inquiry is inherently value-bound and tied up in the perspectives of analysts. Moreover, positivists and proponents of the public choice method would argue that reality is identifiable, reducible to parts, and understandable through its parts; and post-positivists would assert that there are multiple, holistic, and constructed realities.[14]

The post-positive method questions the idea of cost-benefit analysis as being objective because what is considered a benefit for one group can be considered a cost for another group. An example is the federal minimum wage. Minimum-wage workers would benefit from an increase; however, employers would suffer a cost. Therefore, should an increased minimum wage be considered a benefit or a cost to the public?

Feminist Method

The **feminist method** sees the world as a patriarchy that has dominated public policy by and for the benefit of men, often through the suppression of women. As such, the feminist method also reflects a worldview. The feminist method may be used in conjunction with almost any other method. For example, feminists might use the behavioral method in observing roll-call voting in Congress to examine if there is systematic bias against women's issues.

Discursive Method

The **discursive method**, sometimes referred to the **participatory method**, employs open hearings and meetings involving a broad range of participants—including individuals, interest groups, and government officials—working together to design and redesign public policy. This method is designed to involve far more participants than there are in the process of public policy making. It would include as many interests and stakeholders as can be identified to obtain input that can be useful not only for policy design but also for policy implementation. An example of using the discursive method to analyze policy would be to examine if public hearings for a policy were held in places that were easy to access by everyone and at different times of day in order to include as many people as possible.

Prescriptive Method

The **prescriptive method** is reflected in public policy position papers. It involves argumentation and logic to advance a political position on a particular public policy issue. For example, many people believe that the current federal minimum wage does not provide enough money for a person working full-time to pay for necessities. A person who holds such beliefs would employ the prescriptive method to write a policy proposal that defended a higher minimum wage for workers. Also, this person would consider an increased minimum wage as a benefit, rather than a cost, to the public.

Historical Method

The **historical method** involves providing the history of a particular public policy, or a description of the development of that policy over time. Often, the historical method is part of other methods. An example of the historical method would be tracing the evolution of the Clean Air Act, through its later amendments, to improve overall air quality.

At this point, it should be clear that there are many ways to define, interpret, and understand public policy, as well as many means to analyze public policy. In the following chapter, we will set the stage for our study of U.S. public policy in an international context.

Key Terms

- Behavioral method
- Bounded rationality
- Discursive method
- Elite theory
- Feminist method
- Feminist theory
- Game theory
- Group theory
- Historical method
- Incremental theory
- Institutional theory
- Muddling through
- Non-zero-sum games
- Participatory method
- Patriarchy
- Pluralist theory
- Policy cycles
- Positivists
- Post-positivists method
- Prescriptive method
- Prisoner's Dilemma
- Process method
- Public choice method
- Rational theory
- Systems theory
- Zero-sum games

Critical Thinking Questions

- How are theoretical and methodological approaches different?
- What are the main assumptions for each theoretical approach? In other words, what is considered to be true in order for these different theories to accurately describe policy making?
- How is each method described in this chapter limited? What cannot be examined with the method?
- What is the difference between positivists and post-positivists methods?
- How is rationality different from bounded rationality?

Notes

1. C. Wright Mills, *The Power Elite* (New York: Oxford University Press, 1956).
2. See Thomas R. Dye and Harmon Zeigler, *The Irony of Democracy* (Monterey, CA: Brooks/Cole, 1981).
3. Thomas R. Dye, *Who's Running America: Institutional Leadership in the United States* (Englewood Cliffs, NJ: Prentice-Hall, 1976).
4. See Arthur F. Bentley, *The Process of Government* (Bloomington, IN: Principia Press, 1949); David B. Truman, *The Governmental Process* (New York: Knopf, 1951); Robert Dahl, *Who Governs* (New Haven, CT: Yale University Press, 1961).
5. For a classic discussion of rational decision making, see Graham T. Allison, *Essence of Decision: Explaining the Cuban Missile Crisis* (Boston: Little, Brown, 1971). For a good application of rational theory to policy analysis, see Kenneth A. Shepsle and Mark S. Bonchek, *Analyzing Politics* (New York: Norton, 1997).
6. See Herbert A. Simon, *The New Science of Management Decision* (New York: Harper & Row, 1960) and *Administrative Behavior: A Study of Decision-Making Processes in Administrative Organizations* (New York: Free Press, 1976).
7. See Charles E. Lindblom, "The Science of Muddling Through," *Public Administration Review* 19(2) (1959): 79–88 and *Politics and Markets: The World's Political-Economic Systems* (New York: Basic Books, 1977). For an application of incremental theory to budget processes, see Aaron Wildavsky, *The Politics of the Budgetary Processes* (Boston: Little, Brown, 1964).
8. David Easton, *A System Analysis of Political Life* (New York: Wiley & Sons, 1965).
9. For an introduction to game theory, see Joel Watson, *Strategy: An Introduction to Game Theory* (2nd ed.) (New York: Norton, 2008) and Avinash Dixit and Susan Skeath, *Games of Strategy* (2nd ed.) (New York: Norton, 2004).
10. See Robert Axelrod, *The Evolution of Cooperation* (New York: Basic Books, 1984).
11. For a discussion of collective action problems and government intervention, see Mancur Olson, *The Logic of Collective Action* (Cambridge, MA: Harvard University Press, 1965) and Steven E. Rhoads, *The Economist's View of The World: Government, Markets, and Public Policy* (Cambridge: Cambridge University Press, 1985).
12. See James P. Lester and Joseph Stewart, Jr., *Public Policy: An Evolutionary Approach* (2nd ed.) (Belmont, CA: Wadsworth, 2000), p. 39.
13. Charles J. Fox, "Implementation Research: Why and How to Transcend Positivist Methodologies," *Implementation and the Policy Process*, Dennis J. Palumbo and Donald J. Calista (eds.), (Westport, CT: Greenwood, 1990), pp. 199–212.
14. See Yvonna S. Lincoln and Egon G. Guba, *Naturalistic Inquiry* (Newbury Park, CA: Sage, 1985), p. 37.

CHAPTER 3

Setting the Stage

LEARNING OBJECTIVES

- Define the Dominant Social Paradigm and how it impacts policy making.
- Understand the formal and informal influences on policy making.
- Understand how both the federal system and separation of powers create a decentralized government system and how that decentralization impacts
- policy making and policy implementation.
- Define the differences between presidential and parliamentary democracies.
- Understand short-term bias in the policy-making process.
- Understand how policies can be formed rather quickly in responses to crises and emergencies.

Any examination of public policy and the process of public policy making should start with a description of the demographic, cultural, social, and institutional contexts of policy making in the United States. Demographic characteristics of the United States have changed over time. Such changes have impacted the cultural and social contexts of policies. For example, the United States now has more policies that are meant to benefit minorities than it did in the 1950s before the civil rights movement. It helps to understand how comparisons between other countries and the United States are made and the importance of such comparisons. Thus, in this chapter, we will begin with some demographics and consider the Dominant Social Paradigm (DSP) in the United States. It is important to understand the DSP and its elements because it affects public policy. Briefly, the elements of the DSP include a belief in free market capitalism, limited regulation, and an assumption that economic growth is good. People are individuals, rather than parts of a community, so the good of an individual should come first. Also, there is a strong belief that science and technology can ameliorate problems caused by humans. The DSP makes up part of the cultural and social context of public policy making.

The chapter continues with formal influences on policy making. Specifically, we will look at institutions of government in the United States, summarizing the structures and functions of the legislative, executive, and judicial branches of

31

government. Focusing on representative democracy, which is the classification of democracy that exists in the United States, among different forms of government, we will distinguish between presidential and parliamentary democracies. This is done because every country, with the exception of China, that is discussed here is either a presidential or parliamentary democracy. And finally, we will examine informal influences on policymaking from interest groups, short-term bias, as well as crises and emergencies.

BOX 3.1

Country Profile of the United States

Name of Country: The United States
Conventional Long Form: The United States of America
Type of Government: Constitution-based federal republic

Executive Branch:

Chief of State: President Barack H. Obama (since 20 January 2009); Vice President Joseph R. Biden (since 20 January 2009)

Head of Government: President Barack H. Obama (since 20 January 2009); Vice President Joseph R. Biden (since 20 January 2009)

Legislative Branch:

Bicameral Congress consists of the Senate (100 seats, 2 members elected from each state by popular vote to serve six-year terms; one-third elected every two years) and the House of Representatives (435 seats; members directly elected by popular vote to serve two-year terms)

Judicial Branch:

Supreme Court (nine justices; nominated by the President and confirmed with the advice and consent of the Senate; appointed to serve for life); United States Courts of Appeal; United States District Courts; State and County Courts

Administrative Divisions:

50 states and 1 district; Alabama, Alaska, Arizona, Arkansas, California, Colorado, Connecticut, Delaware, District of Columbia, Florida, Georgia, Hawaii, Idaho, Illinois, Indiana, Iowa, Kansas, Kentucky, Louisiana, Maine, Maryland, Massachusetts, Michigan, Minnesota, Mississippi, Missouri, Montana, Nebraska, Nevada, New Hampshire, New Jersey, New Mexico, New York, North Carolina, North Dakota, Ohio, Oklahoma, Oregon, Pennsylvania, Rhode Island, South Carolina, South Dakota, Tennessee, Texas, Utah, Vermont, Virginia, Washington, West Virginia, Wisconsin, Wyoming

Economic Indicators:

GDP (purchasing power parity): $15.66 trillion (2012 estimation)

GDP Real Growth Rate: 2.2 percent (2012 estimation)

GDP per capita (purchasing power parity): $49,800 (2012 estimation)

Economic Structure: Agriculture 1.2 percent; Industry 19.1 percent; Services 79.7 percent (2012 estimation)

Demographic Indicators:

Population: 316,668,567 (2013 estimation)

Population Growth: 0.9 percent (2012 estimation)

Birth Rate: 13.7 births/1,000 population (2012 estimation)

Infant Mortality Rate: 6.14 deaths/1,000 live births (2012 estimation)

Life Expectancy at Birth: 78.49 years (2012 estimation)

Literacy (age 15 and over can read and write): 99 percent (2012 estimation)

Ethnic Groups: White 79.96 percent, Black 12.85 percent, Asian 4.43 percent, Amerindian and Alaska Native 0.97 percent, Native Hawaiian and other Pacific Islander 0.18 percent, two or more races 1.61 percent (2007 estimation)

Note: A separate listing for Hispanic is not included because the U.S. Census Bureau considers Hispanic to mean persons of Spanish/Hispanic/Latino origin including those of Mexican, Cuban, Puerto Rican, Dominican Republic, Spanish, and Central or South American origin living in the United States who may be of any race or ethnic group (White, Black, Asian, etc.); about 15.1 percent of the total U.S. population is Hispanic

Religions: Protestant 51.3 percent, Roman Catholic 23.9 percent, Mormon 1.7 percent, other Christian 1.6 percent, Jewish 1.7 percent, Buddhist 0.7 percent, Muslim 0.6 percent, other or unspecified 2.5 percent, unaffiliated 12.1 percent, none 4 percent (2007 estimation)

Source: CIA, *The World Factbook on the United States,* available at www.cia.gov/library/publications/the-world-factbook/geos/us.html.

Demographics

Who are we? How educated are we? How religious are we? What is our income? The answers to these questions are what social scientists call *demographics*. In order to answer these questions, let us look at some demographic information about the United States.

The United States has over 350,000,000 people within its borders. It is estimated that, in about 40 years, this total will rise by about one-third.[1] The median age of the U.S. population is 36.8 years, which is 6.8 years older than the median age in 1980. (The median age of females is 38.2 years and the median age of males is 35.4. years.) There are about 4,000,000 more women in the United States than there are men, although they are not evenly distributed throughout the population. There are more men than women under the age of 35 and more women than men above the age of 35. Around 79.5 percent of the U.S. population is white, 15.7 percent is Hispanic, 12.9 percent is black, and 4.5 percent is Asian. By 2050, it is estimated that 72.0 percent of the U.S. population will be white, 24.4 percent will be Hispanic, 14.6 percent will be black, and 8 percent will be Asian.[2] About 80 percent of the U.S. population lives in urban areas.

The United States has a relatively well-educated population. Approximately 30 percent of Americans are college graduates. This is a significant increase from 1970, when about 11 percent of the population were college graduates. The percentage of college graduates among blacks and Hispanics also increased significantly. In 1970, 4.4 percent of blacks and 4.5 percent of Hispanics were college graduates. In 2010, these numbers had increased to close to 20 percent of blacks and 14 percent of Hispanics were graduated from college. The percentages are significantly higher among Asians and Pacific Islanders. In 1970, roughly 20 percent had college degrees. By 2010, this percentage had increased to a little over 52 percent of this group.[3]

Americans are moderately religious. Between 40 and 45 percent of Americans attend church or synagogue. Approximately 75 percent identify themselves as Christian (52 percent as Protestant), about 23 percent as Roman Catholic, and around 2 percent as Jewish.

Per capita income in the United States is around $42,500; that figure ranges from a high of $74,710 in Washington, DC, to a low of $33,073 in Mississippi. Per capita income numbers do not tell us a great deal unless we know how that income is distributed across the population. It is estimated that 12.4 percent of U.S. citizens, and 9.2 percent of families, live in poverty.

Although it varies significantly from state to state and region to region, the country as a whole has a two-party competitive political system. Some states continuously vote for one party. Nationally, both the Democratic and Republican parties have alternated between 40 and 60 percent of the vote since before World War II. Yet, there have been periods when one party has dominated national elections (for example, the Democrats in the 1930s and 1940s and the Republicans in the early part of the twenty-first century).

In some public policy areas, demographics can be very significant. As the population has aged, retired people, and their organized interest groups, have become more influential; this has been felt in the debate on Social Security. Interestingly, various surveys show that about two-thirds of the American population think that government is corrupt.[4] Can one surmise that distrust in government is a function of the demographic profile of the American population? The answer to that question is no. How the public feels about any public policy or politician in power is influenced by a combination of demographics, political debates, and what we call the Dominant Social Paradigm (DSP).

Dominant Social Paradigm

Public policy may be seen as a direct result of this nation's **Dominant Social Paradigm (DSP)**. The DSP constitutes those clusters of beliefs, values, and ideals that influence our thinking about society, government, and individual responsibility. The Dominant Social Program can be defined in various ways but includes acceptance of laissez-faire capitalism, individualism, growth, and progress, and a faith in science and technology. Our DSP has influenced the development of public policy as well as public attitudes toward policies and regulations. Among the most important components of the DSP are free market economics, faith in science and technology, and the growth orientation common in Western democracies.

In the United States, the DSP is rooted in the early history of the country. Political philosophers such as John Locke, Emmerich von Vattel, and Jean-Jacques Rousseau had an important influence on the framers of the U.S. Constitution.

These and other philosophers held that humans had certain **natural rights**—rights we were born with, including the right to life, liberty, and private property. As the Declaration of Independence proclaims, "[W]e hold these truths to be self-evident, that all men are created equal, that they are endowed by their Creator with certain inalienable Rights, that among these are Life, Liberty, and the pursuit of Happiness." The idea of individual freedom and the fight to hold and use one's property is and always has been fundamental to our DSP and our understanding of what American democracy is all about.[5]

Formal Influences on Policy Making

Institutions of Government

The United States is a democratic republic within a federal system. It is a **representative democracy** in that citizen participation in the development of laws and policies is accomplished through elective representatives to government positions. The U.S. Constitution delineates three branches of government that share power in the U.S. political system: the **legislature** (the U.S. Congress); the **executive** (the U.S. President and the federal administration or bureaucracy); and the **judiciary** (the U.S. Supreme Court and various lower-level courts). In addition, the United States has a **federal system**, which means that political power is shared between a federal, central, or national government as well as state governments and local governments. In the United States, states are what may be called provinces or republics in other countries. Given the **separation of powers** between legislative, executive, and judicial branches of government provided by the U.S. Constitution, combined with federalism, political power in the United States is intentionally decentralized.

Members of the U.S. Congress are elected for six-year terms to the U.S. Senate (two U.S. Senators are elected from each state) and two-year terms to the U.S. House of Representatives (U.S. Representatives are elected from congressional districts in each state based on that state's population as of the last census). Thus, one house in Congress has equal representation (Senate) and the other has representation based on population (House of Representatives). The President of the United States is elected for up to two four-year terms, and members of the federal administration or bureaucracy are either political appointees (those at the top of federal departments or agencies) or career civil servants (those who devote their professional lives to working in the federal bureaucracy). Judges in the national court system, including the U.S. Supreme Court, are appointed for life. At the national level, the U.S. Congress originates laws and authorizes programs that are carried out by the president and the federal bureaucracy. Federal courts, including the U.S. Supreme Court, review laws when necessary (e.g., to determine their constitutionality).

For the most part, each state government mirrors the federal government. Forty-nine states have a bicameral legislature, with an upper house (a senate), and a lower house (a house of representatives or an assembly); Nebraska, an exception, has a unicameral legislature. Unlike the national legislature, state legislatures are elected entirely based on population. Although the terms and tenure of state governors vary significantly from state to state, most state governors have significant appointment powers in selecting members of major departments or agencies in state governments. All states have a highest court (usually called a supreme court), but the means of selection and tenure of judges vary significantly from state to state.

State governments can create or eliminate local governments, and delegate to them a wide variety of functions and responsibilities. Often, local governments are responsible for implementing federal laws. States may enact their own laws and regulations pursuant to, and not in conflict with, state and national laws.

Although there is agreement that the federal government is responsible for national defense, there is disagreement over which level of government should take the lead in providing other types of services. In many policy areas, the federal government, state governments, and local governments all play important roles, share jurisdiction, and have multiple and overlapping responsibilities. For example, when it comes to recreational policies, the federal government administers national parks, national forests, and other national lands, whereas state governments administer state parks and other state recreation areas, and local governments administer numerous local recreational facilities. Thus, policy making and policy implementation in the United States are decentralized.

Many policy decisions are made not only by the federal government but also by 50 state governments and a far greater number of local governments. Also, at all levels of government, decision-making power is divided among many departments, agencies, bureaus, committees, boards, and commissions. Thus, decentralization brings with it challenges for policy making. For example, environmental regulatory standards are established by the federal government and enforced by state and local governments, according to federal regulations. This can create problematic management of environmental programs. David Robertson and Dennis Judd trace political conflicts over the creation of a national environmental policy within a federal structure. They point out that state and local governments—charged with enforcement of federal regulations—face many obstacles, including: (1) limited resources to carry out legislative mandates; (2) the need for cooperation among various state and local agencies that deal with such diverse areas as highways, land use, natural resources, and economic development, all of which have environmental impacts; (3) direct economic dependence on local industries to be regulated; and (4) interstate cooperation on environmental problems that cross state boundaries.[6]

In many ways, the decentralized nature of public policy making in the United States affects which groups will be successful in their pursuit of policy goals. Decentralization helps or hurts some organizations and their interests. For example, decentralization may help those with influence in a state legislature but without influence in the U.S. Congress.

Among the countries that we selected for comparison with the United States, six are representative democracies (India, Canada, Sweden, Brazil, the Netherlands, and Japan) and one is a communist state (China). Among the six representative democracies, India, Canada, and Brazil are similar to the United

States in that they also have federal systems. By contrast, Sweden, the Netherlands, and Japan are different from the United States in that they have unitary systems in which most political power is held by a central or national government, while regional and/or local jurisdictions have only limited political power.

Forms of Government

Although one could discuss in great detail the various forms of government in countries around the world, which include monarchy, aristocracy, single-party rule, military dictatorship, and others, we will limit our discussion here to representative democracy. An examination of all the forms of government in all the countries of the world is beyond the scope of this book.

As mentioned in the previous section, the United States is a representative democracy. In early U.S. history, local government was carried out through town hall meetings where citizens would gather and vote on the issue of the day. Such a system is called **direct democracy**. The necessity for representative democracy became clear as the nation's population increased and diversified. **Representative democracy** involves the election of representatives and the delegation of power to those representatives to make public policy, which means that citizens participate in public policy making through elected representatives. The president of the United States is elected indirectly by the Electoral College. States have votes in the Electoral College equal to the number of members they have in both houses of the U.S. Congress.

What makes a representative democracy a "democracy" depends on several factors. There are many definitions of democracy that have roots in ancient Greece, and that have been revised, reformed, and streamlined up to the present. As a baseline, we are going to use a definition of democracy that has been developed by the **Administration and Cost of Elections (ACE) Project**. This joint program was established in 1998 by three international organizations to provide globally accessible information (over the Internet) on the nature, process, and problems associated with organizing and administrating elections. The three organizations that make up the ACE Project are the International Foundation for Elections Systems, the International Institute for Democracy and Electoral Assistance, and the United Nations Department of Economic and Social Affairs. According to the ACE Project, there is no universal definition of democracy.[7]

The practice of democracy differs significantly from country to country. Thus, to define democracy, we must focus on certain attributes such as democratic procedures and participation. A country's practice of democracy depends largely on that country's specific political, social, cultural, and economic circumstances. Although the word *democracy* may mean "rule by the people," the actual application of democracy can mean many different things in many different places. Taking into consideration procedural and normative expectations of participation in a democratic electoral process, the ACE Project has identified "minimum requirements" for a country to be called a democracy. Elections, although important for the practice of democracy, just by themselves do not make a country democratic. For example, although the People's Republic of

China has a regular process of political parties and elections, the communist state of China is not a democracy because it does not meet the minimal criteria that most people would establish for a country to be democratic.

The ACE Project sees the following nine points as minimally necessary for a country to be defined as a democracy. Should any of these points be missing, it is argued that a country is not truly a democracy.

1. Control over government decisions about policy is constitutionally vested in elected representatives.
2. Elected representatives are chosen in frequent and fair elections.
3. Elected representatives exercise their constitutional powers without facing overriding opposition from unelected officials.
4. All adults have the right to vote in elections.
5. All adults have the right to run for public office.
6. Citizens have the right to express themselves on political matters, defined broadly, without the risk of state punishment.
7. Citizens have the right to seek out alternative sources of information, such as the news media, and such sources are protected by law.
8. Citizens have the right to form independent associations and organizations, including independent political parties and interest groups.
9. Government is autonomous and able to act independently from outside constraints (such as those imposed by alliances and blocks).[8]

Representative democracies include presidential and parliamentary democracies, which are distinguished based on (1) whether or not the roles of head of state and head of government are performed by the same individual and (2) whether or not the chief executive is elected directly and separately from members of the legislature. A head of state "symbolizes and represents the people, both nationally and internationally" whereas a head of government has the duty "to deal with the everyday tasks of running the state, such as formulating and executing policy, alongside a cabinet of other ministers who are charged with specific policy areas (such as a minister of foreign affairs or agriculture)."[9]

In a **presidential democracy**, the same individual, a president, is the head of state as well as the head of government. The president is elected directly and separately from members of the legislature. The president has a fixed term and can be ejected from office only if charged with misconduct.

In a **parliamentary democracy**, one individual, a president or a monarch, is the head of state while another individual, a prime minister, is the head of government. The prime minister is elected indirectly through elections of members of the legislature, a parliament. Following a regularly scheduled and direct election of members of the legislature, the prime minister is usually the head of the party with a majority of parliamentary seats or the head of the largest party in a coalition of parties with a majority of parliamentary seats. The prime minister has an unfixed term, which depends on the support of his or her ruling party or coalition of parties, and can be ejected from office through a vote of "no confidence" taken by the legislature.

An advantage of presidential democracies relative to parliamentary democracies is that the president is elected with a direct national mandate for policy making, which means that the president can claim to speak and act on behalf of the whole nation. In addition, it seems that the electorate has more control over the directly elected president in presidential democracies than the electorate has over the indirectly elected prime minister in parliamentary democracies. Since the president is elected separately from members of the legislature and can be from a different party than the legislative majority, the president's power is not directly tied to the legislature. Unlike the prime minister in parliamentary democracies, the president in presidential democracies cannot be dismissed simply by a legislative vote of "no confidence." In presidential democracies, the president and the legislature are clearly more independent of one another than the prime minister and the legislature are in parliamentary democracies. As a result, there is a stronger separation of powers, with stronger checks and balances, between the executive and legislative branches of government in presidential democracies than in parliamentary democracies. As the judiciary may have to settle more policy disputes under a stronger separation of powers, with stronger checks and balances, it may have a more active role in presidential democracies than in parliamentary democracies.

A disadvantage of presidential democracies relative to parliamentary democracies is that they may produce **policy-making gridlock** in the case of divided government, a situation in which the president's party is different from the party that has a majority in the legislature, or at least in one of the chambers or houses of a bicameral legislature. The prime minister's policy agenda in parliamentary democracies may be passed with less executive-legislative conflict than the president's policy agenda in presidential democracies. We also need to keep in mind that, unless charged with misconduct, an unpopular or ineffective president in presidential democracies cannot be dismissed as easily as an unpopular or ineffective prime minister in parliamentary democracies.

The United States is a presidential democracy. However, what about the countries that we selected for comparison with the United States? Although Brazil is similar to the United States in that it is also a presidential democracy, India, Canada, Sweden, the Netherlands, and Japan are different from the United States because they are parliamentary democracies. As we mentioned in the previous section, China is a communist state.

Informal Influences on Policy Making

Policy making is affected not only by formal influences from institutions of government and forms of government but also by informal influences from interest groups, short-term bias, as well as crises and emergencies.

Interest Groups

Although the drafters of the U.S. Constitution had some notion of the role of **interest groups** in society (in 1787, Madison called them "factions" in the Federalist Number 10), they could not imagine how interest groups would develop and prosper. In the modern United States, interest groups have very significant influence on public policy making.[10]

Not all interest groups are equal; some are advantaged over others when attempting to influence public policy. A distinction can be made between types of interest groups by examining their goals and the resources they have available to achieve these goals. Although not all interest groups match exactly one of the following two types, the distinction between them sharpens our analysis and enables us to better understand the advantage that some interest groups have over others in the process of public policymaking.

The first type of interest group is called a **private interest group**; it pursues private benefits, or benefits that the group seeks for its members but that are not available to society at large. Examples of private interest groups are associations of oil and gas producers, steel producers, automobile manufacturers, textile manufacturers, farmers, and ranchers, or any organizations that attempt to regulate businesses or professions in their favor.

The second type of interest group is referred to a **public interest group**. A public interest group pursues public benefits, or collective benefits that cannot be withheld from society at large. Such benefits include clean air, clean water, and the promotion of human rights. Examples of public interest groups are most environmental organizations, consumer associations, and human rights advocacy groups.

In contrast to leaders of private interest groups, leaders of public interest groups, when soliciting contributions, are usually unable to offer specific tangible benefits in return for such contributions; thus, there seems to be little incentive for people to make contributions to public interest groups.[11] When soliciting contributions, leaders of public interest groups may promise collective benefits, such as an expanded national park system; yet, people may realize quickly that these potential benefits may be available irrespective of their contributions. This is a major fund-raising disadvantage of public interest groups. By contrast, given the private nature of their benefits, private interest groups can offer specific tangible benefits in return for contributions to them. For example, the head of an association that represents domestic oil and gas producers can solicit contributions with a promise that these contributions will be used to lobby for additional taxes on imports of foreign oil and gas competing with domestically produced oil and gas. Since contributions to private interest groups are linked directly to specific tangible benefits offered to contributors, private interest groups have a significant fund-raising advantage over public interest groups.

In regard to their ability to raise money, the difference between private and public interest groups is very important. Although interest groups have a variety of resources with varying utility in influencing public policy making, a lot of money is needed for campaign contributions and public relations.

The influence of interest groups on public policy making is even more noteworthy when considering that most of what elected officials do escapes public attention. Although major public policy issues may generate headlines, the details related to these issues are largely ignored by the public. Furthermore, although we may know how elected officials vote from roll calls and voting records, we usually know little about what motivates them to vote one way or another. Many public policy decisions are made outside the public spotlight. Much new legislation or refinement of existing legislation receives very little, if any, attention from anyone other than the parties directly involved in such legislation. The private nature of a large part of public policy making reinforces the fund-raising advantage of private interest groups over public interest groups.

Short-Term Bias

If rational political actors are given a choice between two policy options that will accomplish the same goal over the same time period, they may select the option with the lowest short-term cost. To illustrate, imagine that you are a congress-person considering two competing bills that are designed to deal with a problem over a period of 25 years. The first bill is estimated to cost $5 billion a year for the first 5 years and then $25 billion a year for the next 20 years. The total cost of this bill over 25 years would be $525 billion. The second bill is estimated to cost $25 billion a year for the first 5 years and then $5 billion a year for the next 20 years. The total cost of this bill over 25 years would be $225 billion. If you had to choose between the two bills, the best choice for society might not be the best choice for you. Election cycles—of two years for U.S. Representatives, four years for the U.S. President, and six years for U.S. Senators—require that politicians be responsive to constituents' demands over a relatively short time period. When deciding between two competing bills, one with low short-term costs and high long-term costs and another with high short-term costs and low long-term costs, it may be more politically rewarding to select the bill that is less costly in the short term. This way of thinking may be called **short-term bias.**

Related to short-term bias is the tendency of policymakers and regular citizens to **discount the future** when evaluating current policy options. As a result, policy making is shaped by decisions that defer costs into the future or assume that technological advances or other changes will mitigate any undesired future consequences of decisions made today. Hence, short-term bias is driven not only by politicians' attention to the electoral cycle but also by assumptions about a society's ability to cope with future problems.

Crises and Emergencies

Although policy for the most part is developed and redeveloped in an incremental fashion, **crises and emergency policy making** requires quick decisions and immediate action. The bargaining, compromise, and give-and-take that characterize public policy making during normal times may be suspended during times of crisis or emergency. A notable example is the Great Depression. During President Franklin Roosevelt's first 100 days in office, the policy-making process was streamlined by a sense of urgency and President Roosevelt's personality. In response to North Vietnamese attacks on two U.S. destroyers in the Gulf of Tonkin, the United States swiftly passed the Gulf of Tonkin Resolution, which authorized President Lyndon Johnson to intervene with military force in Southeast Asia, and thus led to an expansion of the Vietnam War. More recently, in response to the terrorist attacks on the United States on September 11, 2001, President George W. Bush acted expeditiously and, by executive order, created the Office of Homeland Security, which later became the Department of Homeland Security.

The Public Policy-Making Stage

By now it should be clear that many factors influence public policy making. Each of these factors plays a specific role in shaping a policy's outcome. The Dominant Social Paradigm provides the overall context of policy making. The system of government and its different branches act as formal influences on policy making, whereas interest groups, short-term bias, and crises act as informal influences. When examining public policy, depending on the theory and methodology being used, certain aspects of the policy-making stage are taken into consideration.

Key Terms

- Administration and Cost of Elections (ACE) Project
- Crisis and emergency policy making
- Direct democracy
- Discount the future
- Dominant Social Paradigm
- Executive
- Federal system
- Interest groups
- Judiciary
- Legislature
- Natural rights
- Parliamentary democracy
- Policy-making gridlock
- Presidential democracy
- Private interest groups
- Public interest groups
- Representative democracy
- Separation of powers
- Short-term bias

Critical Thinking Questions

- The authors discuss the importance of the Dominant Social Paradigm in policy making. What is the Dominant Social Paradigm and how does it affect policy making in the United States?
- The United States has a presidential democracy. Explain how the presidential democracy is different from a parliamentary democracy.
- Policy making in the United States is highly decentralized because of the federal system and separation of powers. How is the concept of a federal system different from separation of powers?
- Interest groups play a role in policy making. What are the two types of interest groups and what is their role in the policy-making process?
- Explain why a short-term bias exists in the policy-making process.
- Normally, policy making in the United States is incremental, meaning it takes place rather slowly and in stages. When does policy making not follow an incremental process?

Notes

1. U.S. Census Bureau, *Statistical Abstract of the United States: 2011* (Washington DC: U.S. Government Printing Office, 2011), http://www.census.gov/prod/www/abs/statab2011_2015.html (accessed February 10, 2012).
2. According to the U.S. Census, a person who is Hispanic may be of any race or ethnicity (white, black, Asian, or other).
3. U.S. Census Bureau, *Statistical Abstract of the United States: 2012* (Washington DC: U.S. Government Printing Office, 2003), p. 151.
4. Harris Survey, "Confidence in Political Institutions, 1967–1995," November 1995, pp. 1–4.
5. If you are confused about how these ideals fit with a U.s. history that includes slavery and the treatment of people as personal property, please remember that earlier notions of equality were not the same as what they are today. As the French philosopher, Paul d'Holbach, wrote at about the time our government was being formed, "[B]y the word people I do not mean the stupid populace…. Every man who can live respectably from the income of his property and every head of a family who owns land ought to be regarded as a citizen." Quoted in George H. Sabine, *A History of Political Theory* (New York: Holt, Rinehart and Winston, 1961), p. 570.
6. David Robertson and Dennis Judd, *The Development of American Public Policy: The Structure of Policy Restraint* (Boston: Little, Brown, and Glenview, IL: Scott, Foresman, 1989), pp. 321–353.
7. See http://www.aceproject.org.
8. Ibid.
9. For the distinction between presidential and parliamentary democracies, see Patrick H. O'Neil, *Essentials of Comparative Politics*, 3rd ed. (New York: Norton, 2010); the information quoted appears on p. 119.
10. Much of the matter in this section has been taken from Chapters through in the Environmental Policy Paradox.
11. See, for example, Mancur Olsen Jr., *The Logic of Collective Action* (Cambridge, MA: Harvard University Press, 1965).

CHAPTER 4

Election Policy

LEARNING OBJECTIVES

- Appreciate regular free and fair elections for the practice of democracy.
- Evaluate people's representation through elections.
- Explain different rules for elections.
- Assess the right to vote in elections and criteria for election candidacy.

- Understand the roles of political parties and campaigns in elections.
- Examine problems and challenges related to election policy.

The United States is the world's most powerful democracy, and the promotion of democracy is a key objective of U.S. foreign policy. One of the major requirements for the practice of democracy is that there are **regular free and fair elections**. The election process in the United States has evolved over time. Through constitutional amendments and legislative acts, the United States has expanded **suffrage** beyond property-holding white males by enfranchising more people from different demographic groups, including African Americans and women.

This chapter is about comparing the election policy between the United States and India. Why do we study India in comparison with the United States? We do so because India has been the world's most populous democracy since it gained independence from Britain in 1947. India's democracy persists in the context of numerous divisions in Indian society, with multiple languages, castes, classes, religions, and regional differences. Although Hindi is the language shared among most Indians, and English is recognized nationwide, there are numerous other languages and dialects used by millions of people across India. The religion that is shared among most Indians is Hinduism. Other religions include Islam, Christianity, Sikhism, and Buddhism. Besides, people in India worship more than 5,000 gods. The social, economic, and cultural differentiation by caste is still one of the most powerful aspects of India's society. Perpetuation of the caste system is a reason for skepticism about India's practice of democracy.

Wondering how democracy is possible in India, Robert A. Dahl notes that democracy is India's "national ideology," and "there is no other. Weak as India's sense of nationhood may be, it is so intimately bound up with democratic ideas and beliefs that few Indians advocate a nondemocratic alternative." Nonetheless, Dahl observes that "India's widespread poverty combined with its acute multicultural divisions would appear to be fertile grounds for the rampant growth of anti-democratic movements powerful enough to overthrow democracy and install an authoritarian dictatorship." Dahl states, "[D]emocracy, it seems, is the only feasible option for most Indians."[1] As a founding member of the **International Institute for Democracy and Electoral Assistance (International IDEA)** in Stockholm, Sweden, India tries to share with other nations its democratic experience and expertise in electoral management, administration, law, and reform.[2]

This chapter utilizes institutional theory to examine the similarities and differences between the United States and India election policy. Election policy is important because it is the formal method of public participation in public policy making. India was chosen because the level of diversity among its population is similar to that of the United States. In both countries, democracy persists, and it is a strong part of national identity. Institutionally, India is somewhat different from the United States because it has a parliamentary system rather than a presidential system. However, both countries have constitutional democracies with federal republics as their system of government. This means they have a federation of states. Power is shared between states and a central government, but the central government is the supreme law of the land. However, India's central government has even more power than the U.S. federal government.

In the following section, we will examine representation through elections, the electorate, criteria for election candidacy, as well as political parties and campaigns with regard to U.S. election policy. Furthermore, we will address some problems and challenges of concern about elections in the United States.

The United States

The United States is a federal republic with a **representative democracy**. Many of its 50 states and thousands of localities may use a referendum—a tool of **direct democracy**—to decide on a specific policy issue (e.g., gay marriage). However, most policies are made by elected representatives, including the U.S. President, members of the U.S. Congress, governors, state legislators, mayors, and members of city or local councils. The framers of the U.S. Constitution intended for the federal government to be run on the basis of representative democracy. States were left to resolve on their own how state governments would be run. Generally, though, state governments emulate the federal government.

Representation through Elections

As a nation, the American people are represented by the President and Vice President of the United States. All registered voters are permitted to vote for them, although both are ultimately elected not directly by the voting population (by popular vote) but indirectly by the **Electoral College** (by electoral vote). Originally, the Electoral College was intended to be comprised of the "most knowledgeable and informed individuals" from each state, appointed by each state legislature and in number equal to the number of that state's U.S. Senators and House of Representatives. The Electoral College is still in effect today, although electors are now chosen by popular vote rather than appointed by state legislatures. There is still a popular vote held for the president and vice president, and it is usually in agreement with the electoral vote, but it is the electoral vote, not the popular vote, that matters in order to win a presidential election.[3]

Each state is represented by two members of the U.S. Senate, which adds up to 100 senators for 50 states. Elections of senators are staggered so that one-third is up for re-election every two years. Each state's registered voters and the senators they elect must be residents of that state. When the U.S. Constitution was passed, it originally granted states the right to appoint their senators. Each senator was given a six-year term that was unlimited pending re-appointment. In 1913, the Seventeenth Amendment to the U.S. Constitution required that senators be chosen by popular vote.[4] Their terms remained the same.

Constituencies are the citizens within a state; the representation of these constituencies in the U.S. Congress is via congressional districts within each state. Each congressional district is represented by one out of 435 members of the U.S. House of Representatives. Originally, each state had at least one representative. Additional representatives were apportioned on the basis of population size determined by the U.S. census every 10 years. By 1910, it was realized that the growing U.S. population would result in an unmanageable number of representatives. Thus, in 1911, the U.S. Congress passed a bill capping the number of representatives at 435. Representatives are up for re-election every two years.

State governments, like the federal government, have three branches, and most state legislatures are bicameral, with a senate and a house of representatives, again like the U.S. Congress. A state's chief executive is called a governor. Governors, state senators, and state representatives are all elected by popular vote. In electing governors, all of a state's registered voters are permitted to vote for their state's gubernatorial candidates. Yet, when it comes to electing state senators and state representatives, registered voters are limited to voting only for candidates running in specific voting districts.

The United States, in almost all elections, follows **single-member district plurality (SMDP)** rules, according to which voters choose among individual candidates competing in single-member districts. Candidates with the largest share of votes are elected to represent those districts. In order to win elections, candidates do not need a majority but only a plurality of votes. For example, let us assume there are three political parties, and each has a candidate competing in an election in a single-member district. If one candidate gets a 40-percent plurality of votes and the other two candidates receive 30 percent of the votes each, that candidate is elected to represent that district even though the other two candidates together obtain a 60-percent majority of votes. In order to win an election in a single-member district, a candidate has to get a share of votes larger than the share of votes obtained by any *one*, not any combination, of the other candidates. Since only one candidate is elected from a single-member district, the candidate with a plurality of votes is elected to represent that district. In the end, votes cast for all other candidates are "wasted."

The Electorate

One of the most important aspects of elections is the **electorate**. The electorate consists of those citizens who have the right to vote in elections. A major requirement for the practice of democracy is that all adults have the right to vote in regular free and fair elections. Although the U.S. Constitution did not specifically disenfranchise any adult citizens when it was signed, states had laws such as **Jim Crow laws** that did. Initially, only property-holding white male U.S. citizens were permitted to vote. Some states required that voters be of a certain religion. Although property ownership as a qualification for voting had disappeared by the 1820s, white male suffrage continued to be the norm. It was not until 1870 that suffrage was extended to African American males with passage of the U.S. Constitution's Fifteenth Amendment, which states that "the right of citizens of the United States to vote shall not be denied or abridged by the United States or by any State on account of race, color, or previous condition of servitude."

The Fifteenth Amendment was more symbolic than effective, however. Jim Crow laws abounded in southern states, and African Americans were kept from the polls through a variety of methods. Grandfather clauses allowed only those to vote whose grandfathers had enjoyed the right to vote. Poll taxes and literacy tests were also used to keep African Americans away from the polls. As a result, the constituency remained mostly white for almost 100 years, until passage of the **Voting Rights Act** in 1965. This act outlawed the use of literacy tests and poll taxes by involving the federal government in the monitoring of state voting registration laws. The act led to the dramatic decline of racial disparity among registered voters.

Women were denied suffrage until 1890, when the Wyoming territory included a "petticoat provision" in its petition for statehood. Many western states followed suit. By the end of World War I, over half of all states had granted women suffrage. In 1920, passage of the U.S. Constitution's Nineteenth Amendment granted the right to vote to all citizens regardless of gender.

States maintained their own laws regarding the minimum voting age, which varied across the union until 1970, when the argument surfaced that, if people at the age of 18 were old enough to go to war, they should also have the right to vote. Passage of the U.S. Constitution's Twenty-Sixth Amendment ensured the right to vote for all U.S. citizens, age 18 or older.

Today, states have laws disenfranchising convicted felons. Most states do not allow felons to vote while they are in prison, on parole, or on probation, but allow them to vote after they are out of the criminal justice system. In some states, convicted felons are permanently disenfranchised.

After a bout with corruption and bribery during what was known as the Gilded Age at the end of the nineteenth century, many states enacted voter registration systems. This enabled many states to enact voter registration qualifications, which perpetuated the disenfranchisement of many eligible voters. Although the Voting Rights Act helped remedy the problem of arbitrary voter registration qualifications, it did not solve the problem. In 1993, the **National Voter Registration Act** was passed to unify voter qualification requirements among states. Although this act is specific to the federal voting system, it applies to state and local districts as well, since no state has a separate voting registration system for state and local elections.

Now that we have examined who gets to vote in the United States, let us take a look at information on who actually votes. In presidential elections, roughly 55 percent of registered voters typically vote. Usually, women turn out to vote in higher numbers than men; older voters vote in higher numbers than younger voters; and Anglos vote in slightly higher numbers than members of racial minority groups. Finally, the wealthy vote in much higher numbers than do the poor.[5]

Election Candidacy

The U.S. Constitution is very clear about who can be **candidates** for the U.S. President, the U.S. Vice President, members of the U.S. Senate, and members of the U.S. House of Representatives. According to the U.S. Constitution (Article II, Section 1),

> No Person except a natural born Citizen, or a Citizen of the United States, at the time of the Adoption of this Constitution, shall be eligible to the Office of President; neither shall any Person be eligible to that Office who shall not have attained to the Age of thirty five Years, and been fourteen Years a Resident within the United States.

Regarding candidates for the U.S. Vice President, the U.S. Constitution's Twelfth Amendment says that "no person constitutionally ineligible to the office of President shall be eligible to that of Vice-President of the United States." The U.S. Constitution (Article I, Section 3) requires candidates for members of the U.S. Senate to be at least 30 years old, to have been U.S. citizens for at least 9 years, and to be inhabitants of the state that they will be chosen to represent. Candidates for the U.S. House of Representatives are required by the U.S. Constitution (Article I, Section 2) to be at least 25 years old, to have been U.S. citizens for at least 7 years, and to be inhabitants of the state that they will be chosen to represent.

Political Parties and Campaigns

The majority of candidates for elected office are affiliated with a **political party**, and voters' political party affiliation has come to influence significantly how they cast their ballots. Furthermore, political parties perform a variety of functions in **election campaigns**, such as organizing events and meetings, raising funds and providing funding to candidates running for office, recruiting and organizing volunteers who want to work for the election of candidates, and purchasing services (e.g., political ads broadcast by television, radio, and other types of media). Throughout most of its history, the United States has had a **two-party system.** Although other political parties exist in the United States, it is very difficult for candidates to win elections unless they are members of one of two dominant political parties: the **Democratic Party** or the **Republican Party.** Political party affiliation is not only present in national elections but, unless it is legally prohibited, it is also present in state and local elections. Currently, Nebraska is the only state to have a state legislature without political party affiliation.[6]

Election campaigns in the United States, especially presidential election campaigns, are very expensive and go through two stages: nomination campaigns and general election campaigns. In *nomination campaigns,* presidential candidates of the same political party compete with one another for delegates who pledge to support them at a national convention where they hope to win their political party's nomination as candidate for president in general elections. The nomination of presidential candidates involves the general public in statewide caucuses and primaries. In *general election campaigns,* presidential candidates of different political parties compete with one another for electors chosen by popular vote on **Election Day,** which is always the Tuesday following the first Monday in November. Throughout both nomination campaigns and general election campaigns, presidential candidates need to raise substantial amounts of money from individual supporters and **political action committees (PACs),** which are organizations that campaign for candidates.[7]

Problems and Challenges

Although the United States has maintained a generally peaceful election process for more than two centuries, its electoral system is not without flaws. We will now address some problems and challenges of concern about elections in the United States. Generally, there are concerns over interference with the fairness of elections, voting rights, and free expression on political matters. Additionally, and perhaps more specifically, there are concerns over campaign financing, time spent on campaigning, the role of the Electoral College in the election process, gerrymandering, and the disproportionate number of white males in elected office.

As mentioned earlier, one of the major requirements for the practice of democracy is that there are regular free and fair elections. Yet, it may be argued that the right to vote in elections is not really held by all adults so long as some states disenfranchise convicted felons, even after they have served their sentence. Furthermore, although voting-age citizens have the right to vote, there may be informal constraints on voting. Recall the discussion of who actually votes: Those with the highest incomes and the highest education are more likely to vote than those with the lower incomes and the lower education levels. It may be argued that people with better jobs, which tend to be reflected in higher incomes and based on higher education levels, are more likely to have an opportunity to vote because they can leave work to vote and may have more reliable transportation to get to and from the polls.

Citizens of the United States have the right to express themselves on political matters without the risk of state punishment, but critics argue that the field for expressing oneself is not level. In order for interests to be conveyed on a mass scale, people must often employ mass media. Costs of doing so can be very prohibitive to most citizens, making access to the electorate a privilege of only a few. Therefore, some opinions and interests are louder while some are never heard. An example is working-class Americans who are paid the minimum wage. They are concerned about raising the federal minimum wage, yet they lack the resources needed to express their concerns and garner national attention.

A specific issue related to general concerns over interference with the fairness of elections is that of campaign financing. Due to the central role of television in campaigns since the 1960s, campaign financing has become an especially important aspect of elections in the United States. With rising costs of TV campaign adds, it is more expensive than ever before to reach enough voters and obtain enough votes to win an election. Thus, wealthy individuals and interest groups with resources to pay for expensive election campaigns have greater influence on who wins elections than those who are less well endowed.

In order to control campaign financing and the growing influence that money can buy in election campaigns, Congress has enacted campaign finance reform measures to reduce the costs of election campaigns, limit financial contributions to individual candidates and political parties, and make campaign financing more transparent and accountable.[8] One of such measures is the **Federal Election Campaign Act (FECA)** of 1971. The goal of the FECA was to limit the influence of wealthy individuals and special-interest groups contributing to the campaigns of specific senators or representatives by mandating the public disclosure of campaign funds by candidates and political parties. In 1974, the FECA was amended to limit the amount of money that could be contributed by individuals, political parties, and PACs. Additionally, public funding was allocated for presidential primaries and general elections. In 1975, Congress established the **Federal Election Commission (FEC)** as an independent regulatory agency to enforce the FECA's provisions, such as those that limit and prohibit campaign contributions. The FEC was also created to reveal campaign finance information and to supervise the public funding of presidential elections.[9]

Despite congressional efforts to regulate campaign financing, unfettered campaign contributions were still allowed in the form of **soft money**. Soft money is money that goes to political parties and political advocacy nonprofit organizations in the form of independent campaign funds that are not contributed directly to a candidate's campaign. In 2002, Congress tried to regulate campaign financing through soft money by passing the **Bipartisan Campaign Reform Act (BCRA)**. The primary objectives of the BCRA were to prevent national political parties and candidates from accepting soft money and to prevent corporations, unions, and other groups from paying for TV or radio ads within two months of a general election.[10] Yet, in 2010, the U.S. Supreme Court ruled in *Citizens United v. Federal Election Commission* that independent election spending by corporations and unions cannot be prohibited because such prohibition would limit political speech, which is protected under the U.S. Constitution's First Amendment.[11]

Besides the issue of campaign financing in relation to the fairness of elections, there is concern that candidates are preoccupied with campaigns for re-election while they are still serving in office. Almost all elected officials seek re-election. Since campaigns are expensive, officials must spend a considerable amount of time raising money for re-election while they are still in office. This means that the majority of incumbents dedicate a lot of time on re-election campaigns, raising money from interest groups that have business before the legislature.

A different challenge is the use of the Electoral College rather than popular vote. The presidential election of November 2000 drew attention to the role of the Electoral College in the election process. In that election, Al Gore received 500,000 more popular votes than George W. Bush, who was elected president by the electoral vote in the electoral college. Although critics contend that the president should be elected by an alternative method, other than by vote of the Electoral College, there are many scholars and policymakers who defend the Electoral College by saying that democracy is upheld because members of the Electoral College (electors) are chosen by popular vote.[12]

Another issue of concern is **gerrymandering**, which involves the manipulation of district lines for electoral gain. Through gerrymandering, district lines are drawn so that votes are in favor of one party over another when they might not be otherwise. Gerrymandering is often performed along racial or ethnic lines. Historically, gerrymandering has been used to draw a district's boundaries so that members of a racial or ethnic group are no longer included as eligible voters in that district. Recently, gerrymandering has been used to redress bias against racial or ethnic groups by drawing district boundaries so that a minority group can be a majority when voting for a candidate, which may have a direct effect on elections. Challenges to drawing district lines, known as **districting**, are usually taken up in the judicial system.[13]

In addition to the concerns addressed so far in regard to elections in the United States, there is concern over the disproportionate number of white males in elected office. It is argued that the interests of females and minorities are not fully represented in elected positions. According to the U.S. Census Bureau, regarding the U.S. population in 2010, 50.8 percent were females and 12.6 percent identified themselves as blacks or African Americans alone.[14] Yet, as a result of the November 2010 congressional election, the 112th U.S. Congress includes 16.6 percent voting females and 7.9 percent voting African Americans.[15] It is obvious that females and African Americans, relative to their percentages of the U.S. population in 2010, are underrepresented in the 112th U.S. Congress. Furthermore, as of the November 2012 presidential election, there has never been a woman elected as President of the United States.

Following the congressional election of November 2006, it was the first time in American history that a female, Nancy Pelosi, became Speaker of the U.S. House of Representatives, advancing to the third-highest position in the U.S. political system. Then, two years later, the outcome of the presidential election of November 2008, the election of an African American candidate, Barack Obama, as U.S. President was clearly a defining event in American history.

So, we have now looked at election policy in the United States; we will devote the next section to election policy in India. We will examine representation through elections, the electorate, criteria for election candidacy, as well as political parties and campaigns in regard to Indian election policy. Furthermore, we will address some problems and challenges of concern about elections in India.

India

India is a federal republic and constitutional democracy with a parliamentary system of government. This means that India's executive functions of head of state and head of government are performed by separate individuals. India's

BOX 4.1

Country Profile of India

Name of Country: India

Conventional Long Form: Republic of India

Type of Government: Federal Republic

Executive Branch:

Chief of State: President Pranab Mukherjee (since 22 July 2012); Vice President Mohammad Hamid ANSARI (since 11 August 2007)

Head of Government: Prime Minister Manmohan SINGH (since 22 May 2004)

Legislative Branch: Bicameral Parliament (Sansad)

The Council of States (Rajya Sabha): 245 members, up to 12 appointed by the president, the remainder chosen by the elected members of state and territorial assemblies; members serving six-year terms

The People's Assembly (Lok Sabha): 545 members, 543 elected by popular vote, 2 appointed by the president; members serving five-year terms)

Judicial Branch:

Supreme Court (one chief justice and 25 associate justices are appointed by the president and remain in office until they reach the age of 65 or are removed for "proved misbehavior")

Administrative Divisions:

28 states and 7 union territories; Andaman and Nicobar Islands*, Andhra Pradesh, Arunachal Pradesh, Assam, Bihar, Chandigarh*, Chhattisgarh, Dadra and Nagar Haveli*, Daman and Diu*, Delhi*, Goa, Gujarat, Haryana, Himachal Pradesh, Jammu and Kashmir, Jharkhand, Karnataka, Kerala, Lakshadweep*, Madhya Pradesh, Maharashtra, Manipur, Meghalaya, Mizoram, Nagaland, Odisha, Puducherry*, Punjab, Rajasthan, Sikkim, Tamil Nadu, Tripura, Uttar Pradesh, Uttarakhand, West Bengal (* refers to union territories)

Economic Indicators:

GDP (purchasing power parity): $4.784 trillion (2012 est.)

GDP Real Growth Rate: 6.5 percent (2012 est.)

GDP per capita (purchasing power parity): $3,900 (2012 est.)

Economic Structure: Agriculture 17 percent; Industry 18 percent; Services 65 percent (2010 est.)

Demographic Indicators:

Population: 1,220,800,359 (July 2013 est.)

Population Growth: 1.312 percent (2012 est.)

Birth Rate: 20.6 births/1,000 population (2012 est.)

Infant Mortality Rate: 46.07 deaths/1,000 live births (2012 est.)

Life Expectancy at Birth: 67.14 years (2012 est.)

Literacy (age 15 and over can read and write): 61 percent (2001 census)

Ethnic Groups: Indo-Aryan 72 percent, Dravidian 25 percent, Mongoloid and other 3 percent (2000)

Religions: Hindu 80.5 percent, Muslim 13.4 percent, Christian 2.3 percent, Sikh 1.9 percent, other 1.8 percent, unspecified 0.1 percent (2001 census)

Source: CIA, *The world Factbook on India,* available at https://www.cia.gov/library/publications/the-world-factbook/geos/in.html (accessed June 22, 2012).

head of state is a president, and its head of government is a prime minister. Among the president's roles are to serve as India's symbolic representative and to appoint the prime minister, elected by the Lok Sabha (House of the People), and members of a Council of Ministers, recommended by the prime minister. The prime minister is the leader of a party or a coalition of parties with the confidence and support of the majority of Lok Sabha delegates. Elected by the Lok Sabha to form a government, the prime minister selects members of the Council of Ministers in charge of all government ministries. The prime minister and all members of the Council of Ministers have seats in the Lok Sabha.

India's federalism was constituted with the **States Reorganization Act** of 1956.[16] The reorganization of states with this act gave linguistic and geographic boundaries to religious, ethnic, and caste divisions. There are 28 states and 7 union territories. States have their own governments, but union territories are ruled by India's central government. Two union territories, Pondicherry and Delhi (i.e., the National Capital Territory of Delhi), have their own legislative assemblies and governments with limited powers. Since elections to the legislative assemblies of Pondicherry and Delhi are included among state assembly elections,[17] this chapter regards these two assemblies as state assemblies.

Although federalism in India looks much like federalism in the United States, India's central government has extensive power relative to state governments when compared to the United States. Specifically, under India's constitution, there are several ways in which the central government can intervene in state jurisdictions. For instance, Article 3 of India's constitution authorizes Parliament, by a simple majority vote, to establish or eliminate states and union territories or change their boundaries and names. Emergency powers granted to the central government by India's constitution enable it, under certain circumstances, to acquire the powers of a unitary state. The central government can also dismiss a state government by presidential rule. Article 249 of India's constitution allows a two-thirds vote of the Rajya Sabha (House of States, or Council of States) to enact legislation that affects any issue subject to state legislation. Articles 256 and 257 of India's constitution require states to comply with laws passed by Parliament, and with executive authority of the central government.

Representation through Elections

As mentioned earlier, one of the major requirements for the practice of democracy is that there are regular free and fair elections. Key elections in India are held for Parliament, a national legislature with two chambers (the Lok Sabha and the Rajya Sabha), state assemblies (Vidhan Sabhas), and the president.[18]

The Lok Sabha, the lower house of Parliament, has 545 members representing Indian constituencies. Almost all of these members, 543 delegates, are elected by voting-eligible citizens based on rules of a **single-member simple plurality (SMSP)** system, which are similar to the single-member district plurality rules for elections in the United States. Two additional members of the Lok Sabha are nominated by the president to represent the Anglo-Indian community. Members of the Lok Sabha serve for terms of five years.

The Rajya Sabha, the upper house of Parliament, has 245 members representing India's 28 and 7 union territories. Most of these members, 233 delegates, are elected by Vidhan Sabhas based on rules of a **single transferable vote (STV)** system, an electoral system designed to grant proportional representation and reduce wasted votes.

What are the rules of a single transferable vote (STV) system? First of all, ballot papers list all candidates standing for election in a multimember constituency, and voters rank individual candidates in order of preference. A threshold, or quota, establishes the number of votes a candidate needs to be elected to a seat in the Rajya Sabha, and the candidate whose number of votes is equal to or greater than the threshold is elected. If the candidate's number of votes is greater than the threshold, and if there is more than one seat to be filled to represent a constituency, the remaining votes are transferred to candidates with the next highest rank in voter preference on each ballot paper. If there is no candidate whose number of votes is at least equal to the threshold, the candidate with the fewest votes is dropped, and, if there is more than one seat to be filled to represent a constituency, that candidate's votes are transferred in the same way as the remaining votes of a candidate above the threshold. The process stops when enough candidates are elected to fill all seats in the Rajya Sabha.

As we saw in our discussion of the electoral system in the United States, it is possible for someone to be elected to Congress, for example, with 40 percent of the popular vote (if there are three people running and two receive 30 percent of the vote). Hence 60 percent of the voters are not represented by someone they supported during the election. In India this situation is somewhat avoided in the Rajya Sabha with the adoption of an STV system.

Members of the Rajya Sabha serve for terms of six years that are staggered so that one-third of its elected membership is up for re-election every two years. The share of members of the Rajya Sabha elected by each state's Vidhan Sabha is roughly proportionate to that state's population relative to India's total population. In addition, 12 members are nominated by the president as representatives of literature, science, art, and social services.

Elections to Vidhan Sabhas, like elections to the Lok Sabha, are carried out according to rules of a single-member simple plurality (SMSP) system. The size of the Vidhan Sabhas depends on the size of the populations represented by these legislatures: Uttar Pradesh has the largest, with 403 members, and Pondicherry has the smallest, with 30 members.

India's head of state is a president elected by an electoral college whose electors include the elected members of the Lok Sabha, Rajya Sabha, and Vidhan Sabhas. Electors from both the Lok Sabha and the Radjya Sabha have the same number of votes as electors from all Vidhan Sabhas. This creates an electoral balance between Parliament at the national level and legislatures at the state level. Electors from more populous states have more votes than electors from less populous states, although an elector from a state represented by more electors has fewer votes than an elector from a state represented by fewer electors. Elections of the president, like elections to the Rajya Sabha, are based on rules of a single transferable vote (STV) system. Yet, since there is only one presidency instead of multiple seats to be filled, presidential elections differ from Rajya Sabha elections in that the threshold or quota to be elected as president requires a candidate to get one more than half the number of votes. Thus, the president is elected with a majority of votes. The president serves for a term of five years and can run for re-election.

In order to maintain regular free and fair elections, India established the **Election Commission,** an independent and quasi-judicial body, under the **Representation of the People Act** of 1950.[19] The Election Commission is completely autonomous and free from any kind of executive interference. It has legal functions in electoral disputes and other matters involving the conduct of elections. The Election Commission supervises all parliamentary and state elections as well as presidential elections under article 324 of India's constitution. The chief election commissioner and other election commissioners are appointed by the president and have tenure for six years, or up to the age of 65 years, whichever is earlier. The chief election commissioner's removal from office can be achieved only through impeachment by Parliament.

Elections to the Lok Sabha and every Vidhan Sabha are normally scheduled every five years. The president can dissolve the Lok Sabha and call a general election before five years are up if a government can no longer command the confidence of the Lok Sabha, and if there is no alternative government to take over. Governments have found it increasingly difficult to stay in power for five years. Under such circumstances, Lok Sabha elections have been held before the end of five years. Regular elections can be stopped only by means of a constitutional amendment and in consultation with the Election Commission; interruptions of regular elections are acceptable only in extraordinary circumstances. When the Lok Sabha is at the end of a five-year term, or when it is dissolved, new elections are called for, and the Election Commission puts into effect the machinery for holding elections. New elections must be held no longer than six months between the last session of the "old" Lok Sabha and the first session of the "new" Lok Sabha.

When the Election Commission makes a final decision regarding an election schedule, it is publicized a few weeks before a formal election process goes into motion. Polling is normally held in different constituencies on different days to enable security forces and election monitors to keep law and order and ensure that an election is fair. Votes are cast by secret ballot. After polling ends, ballots are counted under the supervision of officers appointed by the Election Commission.

The Electorate

All Indian citizens who are age 18 and older, do not have mental problems, and have not been convicted of certain criminal offenses are allowed to vote in elections. The right to vote is irrespective of caste, creed, religion, or gender. Voters are registered at a constituency's electoral registration office. Registered voters are allowed to vote only if they are listed on an **electoral roll**. The electoral roll is revised every year by adding the names of those who are 18 years old as of January 1 of that year or who have moved into a constituency, and by removing the names of those who have died or moved out of a constituency. If you are eligible to vote and are not on the electoral roll, you can apply to an electoral registration officer.

Election Candidacy

Any Indian citizen who is registered as a voter and is 25 years old or older may run as a candidate in elections to the Lok Sabha or Vidhan Sabhas. For the Rajya Sabha, the minimum age is 30; for the president, it is age 35. Candidates for the Rajya Sabha and Vidhan Sabhas should be residents of the same state as the constituency from which they wish to be elected. Generally, candidates have one week to submit their nominations. Each nomination is reviewed by officers appointed by the Election Commission. If a nomination is not found in order, it can be rejected after a summary hearing. Candidates with valid nominations may withdraw within two days after nominations are reviewed.

A candidate's nomination has to be supported by at least one registered voter if it is backed by a registered political party; otherwise, 10 registered voters are required. Also, candidates have to deposit 10,000 rupees (about 2014 $165 American) for Lok Sabha elections and 5,000 rupees for Rajya Sabha or Vidhan Sabha elections; candidates from Scheduled Castes and Scheduled Tribes deposit half these amounts. Deposits are returned if candidates get more than one-sixth of all valid votes in their constituencies. Some of the Lok Sabha and Vidhan Sabha seats are reserved for candidates from the Scheduled Castes or the Scheduled Tribes in approximate proportion to the number of their people relative to each state's total population. In the Lok Sabha, as of 2008, there are 84 seats reserved for the Scheduled Castes and 47 seats reserved for the Scheduled Tribes.[20]

Political Parties and Campaigns

Like the United States, political parties play a very important role in Indian elections. Opinion polls suggest that people tend to vote for political parties rather than for particular candidates. In addition, the costs of campaigning are very high and have grown over time. Political parties have come to dominate election campaigns in India because they provide candidates with various forms of organizational support, including support from broader election campaigns as well as personnel and finance. During election campaigns, political parties put forward candidates as well as proposals with which they hope to persuade people to vote for them and their candidates. When Indians vote for candidates, they usually vote for political parties presenting those candidates.

All political parties must be registered with India's Election Commission, which determines whether a political party is structured and committed to principles of democracy, secularism, and socialism in accordance with India's constitution. Political parties are categorized by the Election Commission based on the length of political activity and success in elections as national or state parties; some political parties may be categorized simply as registered-unrecognized parties.

Through recognition by the Election Commission, political parties may acquire certain benefits for election campaigns. Given the high illiteracy rate among voters, obtaining political party symbols is a very important benefit. The Indian Congress Party, for example, uses the palm of an open hand as its symbol. National political parties may get symbols they may use throughout India, state political parties may get symbols for use throughout states in which they are recognized, and registered-unrecognized political parties may get symbols from a selection of free symbols. In addition to political party symbols, all national and state political parties recognized by the Election Commission may obtain the benefit of free time for political broadcasts through state-owned electronic media (AIR and Doordarshan). Such free time, extending over 122 hours on state-owned television and radio channels, is allocated equitably with a base limit and additional time linked to poll performance of political parties in recent elections.

Official campaigning, which starts after a list of nominated candidates has been completed, lasts for at least two weeks and ends 48 hours before polling closes. (Compare that with presidential elections in the United States, which can last up to two years or even more!) When campaigning, competing political parties and their candidates are expected to follow the guidelines described in a **Model Code of Conduct** prepared by the Election Commission.[21] The Model Code of Conduct, which is based on a consensus among political parties instead of previously established rules, is important to avoid clashes between political parties or their supporters, ensuring peace and order during a period of campaigning. It also provides guidelines for the ruling political party at the national or state level to avoid any complaint that the ruling political party has used its official position unfairly to advance its election campaign.

Like registered political parties in most democracies, all registered political parties in India issue manifestos. In those manifestos, registered political parties can lay out programs they wish to implement in government, and highlight their strengths (positive campaigning) and failures of opposing political parties (negative campaigning). Also, painted slogans are used for popularizing political parties and issues, and pamphlets and posters are distributed throughout each constituency. As in any democracy, during a period of campaigning, rallies and meetings are held throughout each constituency in which candidates persuade their supporters and denigrate their opponents.

Problems and Challenges

Considering that India is the world's most populous democracy, it is important that we not only examine Indian election policy but also address some challenges and problems with elections in India. Generally, there are concerns over **election management** as well as over interference with the fairness of elections, voting rights, and free expression on political matters.

Compared with scheduling elections in the United States, scheduling elections in India is not an easy task. When the Election Commission decides on a schedule, weather conditions are of great concern. If there are winter elections, access to polling stations may be restricted because constituencies are snow-bound. If there are elections during the monsoon season, access to polling stations may be restricted by flooding. In addition to the weather, election planners need to take into account (1) the agricultural cycle for the planting or harvesting of crops; (2) exam schedules, as schools are used as polling stations, and teachers are employed as election officials; and (3) religious festivals and public holidays. Besides, there are logistical difficulties when holding elections, such as sending out ballot boxes, setting up polling booths, and recruiting officials to oversee elections.

A major task in providing for free and fair elections in India is to manage the politicization of social cleavages across the country.[22] After the decline of the **Indian National Congress (INC)** as India's dominant political party, numerous single state-based or single constituency-based political parties have drawn serious attention to social cleavages of caste, class, linguistics, and religion in general elections.[23] Every election campaign tends to heat up toward polling and is often accompanied by massive ethnic violence. Although competition and mobilization by political parties are elements of democratic elections, an observer points out that "parties have not acted as effective agents in evaluating and resolving policy problems and maintaining the stability and coherence of the political system in the long run."[24]

There are also concerns about proper rules and procedures for free and fair elections. In this regard, the Election Commission published 15 electoral reform proposals and seven pending proposals in its 2004 report.[25] Here, we focus on three specific concerns.

This first concern is about the management of elections, especially as it relates to the number of candidates competing in each constituency and the possibility that a candidate may claim more than one seat by running and getting elected in more than one constituency. The Election Commission notes clearly that a large number of candidates are not serious candidates. The second concern is about polls providing information on early voting in elections extending over some time, which may have unfair influence on later voting. Since general elections are scheduled for more than a single day across India, it is possible that voting behavior is influenced by early exit polls. This is also a concern in the United States. The third concern involves the independence, integrity, effectiveness, and conduct of the Election Commission and election officers. Although the Election Commission is an independent authority on elections, every election in India has faced numerous incidents of corruption and political intervention.

Any reforms that are made to India's election policy need to take into account the protection of civil and political rights to ensure that participation and competition in elections is consistent with freedom and equality. India's Election Commission seeks to promote procedural accountability and transparency to prevent electoral fraud, violence, and intimidation against voters, candidates, and parties during elections. But it also needs to be aware of the rights of small political parties to financial support and the mass media as well as the political rights of individual citizens.

Comparison

Ensuring regular free and fair elections is a major requirement for the practice of democracy. According to democratic theorists, two fundamental principles of democracy are (1) popular control over public decision making and decision makers and (2) equality of respect and voice between citizens in the exercise of that control.[26] Participation in elections is an important opportunity for citizens to exercise popular control over public policy making. There have been challenges to this opportunity in both the United States and India, the world's two most populous democracies. We now examine the election policy of the United States and India within the context of a brief comparative study of democracy in the two countries.

The United States operates within an institutional framework of decentralized federalism; strong checks and balances between executive, legislative, and judicial branches of government; and a presidential legislative-executive system. India operates within an institutional framework of centralized federalism; weak checks and balances between executive, legislative, and judicial branches of government; and a parliamentary legislative-executive system.

In the United States, decentralized federalism, where power is divided between a federal government and 50 state governments, influences elections in three distinct ways. First, each state sets its own rules for conducting and participating in elections. Second, each state has its own responsibilities for determining how votes are collected and counted. Each state selects its ballot design, voting machines, and rules for counting ballots. Third, since each state is responsible for holding elections, it decides on the basis of its state constitution how to fill vacant seats for federal office and which nonfederal offices to fill via elections. In India, under centralized federalism, the Election Commission is at the center of all aspects of elections. States do not make independent decisions about elections.

TABLE 4.1 Democracy in the United States and India

	United States	India
Type of State*	Federalism	Federalism
Relationship between Central Government and Local Governments*	Decentralized	Centralized
Legislative-Executive System*	Presidential	Parliamentary
Political Rights**	1	2
Civil Liberties**	1	3
Voice and Accountability***	87.2%	59.2%
Government Effectiveness***	90.0%	55.0%
Rule of Law***	91.5%	54.5%
Control of Corruption***	85.6%	35.9%

Sources:

* Information regarding the type of state, the relationship between the central government and local governments, and the legislative-executive system is from the CIA, *World Factbook,* available at https://www.cia.gov/library/publications/the-world-factbook/ (accessed March 15, 2012).

** Scores for political rights and civil liberties, as of 2011, are from Freedom House's *Freedom in the World 2011 Country Reports,* available at http://www.freedomhouse.org/report/ freedom-world/freedom-world-2011 (accessed March 15, 2012). Scores for political rights and civil liberties range from 1 (most free) to 7 (least free).

*** Percentages regarding voice and accountability, government effectiveness, rule of law, and control of corruption, as of 2010, are from the World Bank's *Worldwide Governance Indicators (WGI),* available at http://info.worldbank.org/governance/wgi/index.asp (accessed March 15, 2012). The indicators range from 0 percent (low) to 100 percent (high).

In the presidential legislative-executive system of the United States, citizens elect their chief executive (the President of the United States) separately from members of their national legislature (the U.S. Congress). In the parliamentary legislative-executive system of India, citizens do not elect their chief executive (India's prime minister) directly but indirectly through elections to the lower house (the Lok Sabha) of their national legislature (India's Parliament).

Next, let's look at the differences between the two countries in terms of freedom and the right to vote. Although the United States is a free country today, it should be remembered that African American males did not have the right to vote until the U.S. Constitution's Fifteenth Amendment was passed in 1870. Yet, despite this constitutional amendment, poll taxes and literacy tests were used to keep African Americans away from the polls until the 1965 Voting Rights Act outlawed such measures and involved the federal government in the monitoring of state voting registration laws. It should be remembered, also, that women across the United States did not have the right to vote until the U.S. Constitution's Nineteenth Amendment was passed in 1920. Even today, concerns remain regarding interference with the fairness of elections, voting rights, and free expression on political matters, as well as campaign financing, time spent on campaigning, the role of the Electoral College in the election process, gerrymandering, and the disproportionate number of white males in elected office. Identity politics related not only to race and gender but also to ethnicity and immigration has notable influence on election policy in the United States.

In India, voting rights have been secured for all Indian citizens who are 18 years old and older, do not have mental problems, and have not been convicted of certain criminal offenses. The right to vote is irrespective of caste, creed, religion, or gender. There have been highly competitive elections despite the country's caste system; vast diversity of ethnic, religious, and linguistic groups; and many people's poor socioeconomic conditions. Yet, it is troublesome that elections with intensive political competition among numerous political parties are often accompanied by massive ethnic violence. India's elections are very competitive because its political spectrum is highly divided. In addition to major political parties, such as the India National Congress (INC) and the **Bharatiya Janata Party (BJP)**, many state-based or special-interest–based political parties run election campaigns for their candidates. As some observers note, India's demographic diversity today might be represented better by the country's diversity of state-based or special-interest–based political parties than by a division between two major nationwide political parties. Yet, because of the rules of a single-member simple plurality (SMSP) system for general elections to the Lok Sabha, many votes for nonelected candidates might be "wasted" despite undeniably competitive elections in each constituency.

The United States clearly grants its citizens significant political rights and civil liberties, but there is room for improvement. In comparison, Indian citizens have more limited political rights and civil liberties than U.S. citizens, which may be due to India's strong caste system, its high levels of poverty and illiteracy, and its discrepancy in poverty and illiteracy between males and females.

There are also important differences between the two countries in terms of their legal systems. Although India has an independent Supreme Court similar to the U.S. Supreme Court, the Indian parliament can reverse Supreme Court decisions by amending the country's constitution. In other words, the rule of law in India can be challenged or subverted. Most analysts also believe there are important differences between the two countries in terms of **political corruption**. Corruption includes bribery, graft, extortion, robbery, patronage, nepotism, cronyism, conflict of interest, and kickbacks. Control of corruption reflects each country's democratic political culture and the integrity of its institutional arrangements.

In the United States, several notable measures have been taken to fight political corruption. In 1971, Congress passed the Federal Election Campaign Act (FECA), which required the public disclosure of campaign funds by candidates and political parties. In 1974, the FECA was amended to limit the amount of money that could be contributed by individuals, political parties, and PACs. Additionally, public funding was allocated for presidential primaries and general elections. In 1975, Congress established the Federal Election Commission (FEC) as an independent regulatory agency to enforce the FECA's provisions, such as those that limit and prohibit campaign contributions. In 1976, the Public Integrity

Section was created within the Department of Justice, and, in 1978, Congress passed the **Ethics in Government Act**.

In India, measures to fight corruption have been rather weak.[27] This may be due to the country's centralized federalism and an economy that has been subject to extensive regulation, protectionism, and public ownership (although India has been moving toward economic liberalization and an open market economy since the early 1990s). It is known that Indian political leaders have used economic policy and national budget distribution as tools of political control.[28] Although India's Election Commission supervises all parliamentary and state elections as well as presidential elections, there have been regular episodes of political intervention and manipulation of election procedures and election results. Protecting the integrity of elections is a key element of electoral reform.

Furthermore, according to the **Right to Information Act**, which the Lok Sabha passed in 2005, government officials are required to release information requested by citizens or face punitive action.[29] Regarding campaign financing, which is controlled predominantly by political parties, a 2002 amendment to the Representation of the People Act was intended to (1) limit each candidate's campaign expenditures, (2) increase the transparency of campaign finance transfers from large and emerging new businesses to political parties, and (3) increase the tax benefit for individual citizens donating private money to campaigns.[30] The amendment has been somewhat effective.[31] As in the United States, efforts to reform election policy in India are still of importance to guarantee regular free and fair elections in the practice of democracy.

By now you should understand the differences and similarities between election policy in the United States and India. Such policy is the foundation of any democracy. Both countries face challenges with ensuring fair elections. However, elections in India are more prone to violent outbreaks, whereas in the United States such violence is an anomaly rather than the norm.

Key Terms

- Bharatiya Janata Party (BJP)
- Bipartisan Campaign Reform Act (BCRA)
- Candidates
- Democratic Party
- Direct democracy
- Election campaigns
- Election Commission
- Election Day
- Election management
- Electoral College
- Electoral roll
- Electorate
- Ethics in Government Act
- Federal Election Campaign Act (FECA)
- Federal Election Commission (FEC)
- Gerrymandering
- Indian National Congress (INC)
- International Institute for Democracy and Electoral Assistance (International IDEA)
- Jim Crow laws
- Model Code of Conduct
- National Voter Registration Act
- Political action committees (PACs)
- Political corruption
- Political party
- Regular free and fair elections

- Representation of the People Act
- Representative democracy
- Republican Party
- Right to Information Act
- Single-member district plurality (SMDP)
- Single-member simple plurality (SMSP)

- Single transferable vote (STV)
- Soft money
- States Reorganization Act
- Suffrage
- Two-party system
- Voting Rights Act

Critical Thinking Questions

- To what extent are regular free and fair elections required for the practice of democracy?
- How are people represented through elections in the United States and India?
- What rules for elections are there in the United States and India?
- What can be said about the right to vote in elections and criteria for election candidacy in the United States and India?
- What are the roles of political parties and campaigns in elections?
- What are the most important problems and challenges related to election policy in the United States and India?

Recommended Resources for U.S. Election Policy

Charles S. Bullock III, *Redistricting: The Most Political Activity in America* (New York: Roman and Littlefield, 2010).

George C. Edwards III, *Why the Electoral College Is Bad for America* (New Haven, CT: Yale University Press, 2004).

Alec C. Ewarld, *The Way We Vote: The Local Dimension of American Suffrage* (Nashville, TN: Vanderbilt University Press, 2009).

Daniel Hays Lowenstein, Richard L. Hasen, and Daniel P. Tokaji, *Election Law: Cases and Materials* (4th ed.) (Durham, NC: Carolina Academic Press, 2008).

Candice J. Nelson, *Grant Park: The Democratization of Presidential Elections, 1968–2008* (Washington, DC: Brookings Institution Press, 2011).

Stephen J. Wayne, *The Roads to the White House, 2012* (9th ed.) (New York: Thomson/Wadsworth, 2011).

Useful Web Sources for U.S. Election Policy

The Election Assistance Commission (EAC)
The Electoral College
The Federal Election Commission (FEC)
Center for Responsive Politic
The International IDEA

Recommended Resources for Indian Election Policy

Pradeep K. Chhibber, *Democracy without Associations: Transformation of the Party System and Social Cleavages in India* (Ann Arbor: University of Michigan Press, 1999).

V. S. Rama Devi and S. K. Mendiratta, eds., *How India Votes: Election Laws, Practice and Procedure* (3rd ed.) (Haryana, India: LexisNexis Butterworths, 2008).

M. S. Gill (Election Commission Chief), *The Electoral System in India*, Election Commission of India.

Robert L. Hardgrave and Stanley A. Kochanek, *India: Government and Politics in a Developing Nation* (6th ed.) (Fort Worth, PA: Harcourt College Publishers, 2000).

Zoya Hasan, ed., *Parties and Party Politics in India* (Oxford: Oxford University Press, 2000).

Niraja Gopal Jayal, ed., *Democracy in India* (Oxford: Oxford University Press, 2001).

Useful Web Sources for Indian Election Policy

Election Commission of India
Indian Election Information
Indian Politics on the Internet: A Resource Guide by Professor Robert L. Hardgrave, Jr.
Association for Democratic Reform (ADR) in India
The International IDEA, *Political Finance Database on India*

Notes

1. All quotes are from Robert A. Dahl, *On Democracy* (New Haven, CT, and London: Yale University Press, 1998), pp. 162–163.
2. For more information on the International IDEA, see http://www.idea.int/ (accessed July 8, 2012).
3. See Lawrence D. Longley and Neal R. Pierce, *The Electoral College Primer, 2000* (New Haven, CT: Yale University Press, 1999).
4. For the Seventeenth Amendment in 1913, which restates the first paragraph of Article I, section 3 of the Constitution and provides for the election of senators by replacing the phrase "chosen by the Legislature thereof" with "elected by the people thereof," see http://www.senate.gov/artandhistory/history/common/briefing/Direct_Election_Senators.htm (accessed March 15, 2012).
5. For an in-depth analysis in this regard, see Andrew Gelman, David Park, Boris Shor, Joseph Bafumi, and Jeronimo Cortina, *Red State, Blue State, Rich State, Poor State: Why Americans Vote the Way They Do* (Princeton, NJ: Princeton University Press, 2008).
6. For a discussion of political parties and party politics in the United States, see Marjorie R. Hershey, *Party Politics in America* (15th ed.) (Upper Saddle River, NJ: Prentice-Hall, 2011).
7. For a discussion of presidential election campaigns, see Stephen J. Wayne, *The Road to the White House 2012* (9th ed.) (New York: Thomson/Wadsworth, 2011).
8. For a brief history of campaign finance regulations in the United States, see "Federal Campaign Finance Laws: A Short History," available at http://www.fec.gov/info/appfour.htm (accessed March 15, 2012).
9. For more information on the Federal Election Campaign Act (FECA), see http://www.fec.gov/law/feca/feca.shtml (accessed July 2, 2012). For the mission and history of the Federal Election Commission (FEC), see http://www.fec.gov/info/mssion.shtml (accessed July 2, 2012).
10. For more information on the Bipartisan Campaign Reform Act (BCRA), see http://www.fec.gov/pages/bcra/bcra_update.shtml (accessed July 2, 2012).
11. See http://www.law.cornell.edu/supct/html/08-205.ZS.html (accessed July 2, 2012).

12. For a discussion of the Electoral College and its problems in the U.S. presidential elections, see George C. Edwards III, *Why the Electoral College Is Bad for America* (New Haven, CT: Yale University Press, 2004).

13. For a discussion of redrawing electoral district lines and its consequences of public policymaking, see Charles S. Bullock III, *Redistricting: The Most Political Activity in America* (New York: Rowman and Littlefield, 2010) and Jonathan N. Katz, *Elbridge Gerry's Salamander: The Electoral Consequences of the Reapportionment Revolution* (Cambridge: Cambridge University Press, 2002).

14. Regarding the percentage of females, see Lindsay M. Howden and Julie A. Meyer, U.S. Census Bureau, "Age and Sex Composition: 2010," C2010BR-03, May 2011, available at http://www.census.gov/prod/cen2010/briefs/c2010br-03.pdf (accessed June 26, 2012). Regarding the percentage of people who identified themselves as black or African American alone, see Sonya Rastogi, Tallese D. Johnson, Elizabeth M. Hoeffel, and Malcolm P. Drewery, Jr., U.S. Census Bureau, "The Black Population: 2010," C2010BR-06, September 2011, available at http://www.census.gov/prod/cen2010/briefs/c2010br-06.pdf (accessed June 26, 2012).

15. Regarding women in the United States Congress since 1917, see Jennifer E. Manning and Colleen J. Shogan, "Women in the United States Congress: 1917–2012," *CRS Report for Congress* RL30261, January 27, 2012, available at http://www.fas.org/sgp/crs/misc/RL30261.pdf (accessed March 16, 2012). Regarding African Americans in the United States Congress since 1870, see Jennifer E. Manning and Colleen J. Shogan, "African American Members of the United States Congress, 1870–2012," *CRS Report for Congress* RL30378, March 6, 2012, available at http://www.fas.org/sgp/crs/misc/RL30378.pdf (accessed March 16, 2012).

16. For a discussion of Indian federalism, see Robert L. Hardgrave, Jr. and Stanley A. Kochanek, *India: Government and Politics in a Developing Nation* (Forth Worth, PA: Harcourt College Publishers, 2000), Chapter 4.

17. See http://eci.nic.in/eci_main1/ElectionStatistics.aspx (accessed July 8, 2012).

18. For a brief description of India's election system and procedures, see Dr. M. S. Gill (Election Commission Chief), *The Electoral System in India*, Election Commission of India, available at http://eci.nic.in/eci_main/eci_publications/books/miscell/ESI-III.pdf (accessed March 18, 2012).

19. For further information about roles of the Election Commission of India, see http://eci.nic.in/eci_main1/index.aspx (accessed March 18, 2012).

20. For the information about the reserved seats for the Scheduled Castes and Scheduled Tribes, see "FAQs-Delimitation of Constituencies," available at http://eci.nic.in/eci_main1/delimitation_faq.aspx (accessed July 9, 2012).

21. For the full text of the Model of Conduct, see http://eci.nic.in/eci_main/Model_Code_Conduct.pdf (accessed March 12, 2012).

22. Regarding ethnic conflict and civic life in India, see Ashutosh Varshney, *Ethnic Conflict and Civil Life: Hindus and Muslims in India* (New Haven, CT, and London: Yale University Press, 2002) and Amrita Basu and Atul Kohli, eds., *Community Conflicts and the State in India* (New Delhi: Oxford University Press, 1998).

23. See Zoya Hasan, ed., *Parties and Party Politics in India* (Oxford: Oxford University Press, 2002).

24. Zoya Hasan, "Introduction: Conflict Pluralism and the Competitive Party System in India" in Hasan (ed.), *Parties and Parties Politics in India* (2002), p. 34.

25. See the Election Commission of India, *Proposed Electoral Reforms,* the Election Commission of India, New Delhi, India, 2004, available at http://eci.nic.in/eci_main/

electoral_ref.pdf (accessed March 15, 2012), and the Association for Democratic Reform (ADR), *ADR/NEW Recommendations for Electoral Reforms,* available at http://adrindia.org/sites/default/files/ADR-NEW%20Recomendations-April20%20 2011-Final.pdf (accessed March 15, 2012).

26. For example, see Robert A. Dahl, *A Preface to Democratic Theory* (Chicago: University of Chicago Press, 1956) and David Beetham, Edzia Carvalho, Todd Landman, and Stuart Weir, *Assessing the Quality of Democracy: A Practical Guide* (Stockholm: International Institute for Democracy and Electoral Assistance, 2008).

27. For update on corruption and anti-corruption efforts in India, see India against Corruption (IAC) website, available at http://www.indiaagainstcorruption.org/ index1.html (accessed March 15, 2012).

28. For example, see Hardgrave and Kochanek, *India: Government and Politics in a Developing Nation* (6th ed.) (Fort Worth, PA: Harcourt College Publishers, 2000).

29. For the details, see the Right to Information (RTI) website, http://www.righttoinformation.gov.in/ (accessed March 15, 2012).

30. For the text, see http://eci.nic.in/eci_main/ElectoralLaws/OrdersNotifications/Order_ Assests_Affidavits.pdf (accessed March 15, 2012).

31. For further information on campaign finance reform in India, see the International IDEA, *Political Finance Database* (2012), available at http://www.idea.int/political-finance/country.cfm?id=105 (accessed March 15, 2012).

CHAPTER 5

Criminal Justice Policy

LEARNING OBJECTIVES

- Evaluate efforts to maintain public order and protect individual rights and liberty.
- Understand goals and procedures of criminal justice policy.
- Explain the institutional framework of criminal justice policy.

- Identify policy actors involved in criminal justice policy making.
- Categorize crimes and penalties.
- Examine problems and challenges related to criminal justice policy.

Across the United States, countless criminal activities around our neighborhoods, cities, and states make headlines every day. The range of reported crimes varies from car accidents, including those involving driving under the influence (DUI) charges, carjacking, drug abuse, murder, sexual assaults (rapes and others), hate crimes (or bias crimes) against certain minority groups, and cybercrimes (e.g., identity theft and cyberbullying) to property crimes as well as business-related crimes. Handling criminal activities daily, this nation's criminal justice institutions and law enforcement authorities work hard toward the establishment of a crime-free and safe society.

In general, wherever there is a criminal justice system in the world, the legislative, executive, and judicial branches of government are the principal agents for criminal justice policy making, and the police, prosecutors, courts, and departments of corrections are the enforcement authorities that implement actual criminal justice policies and programs. The primary goals of criminal justice policies are to (1) serve justice, (2) control crime, and (3) prevent crime in each community; however, there are some variations in practice from one country to another due to different political, economic, and cultural settings. **Doing justice** means that U.S. society establishes the basis for rules, procedures, and institutions of a criminal justice system. **Controlling crime** is to arrest, prosecute, convict, and punish those who defy the laws that society has established. A main restriction for law enforcement authorities to achieve the goal of crime control is that all procedures must be carried out in accordance with criminal laws, which define crimes or illegal activities in society and describe the rights of citizens and procedures for law enforcement. **Preventing crime** means that society's criminal justice institutions take effective measures to prevent and remove risks of crime to individuals, groups, and communities. Prevention methods include, but are not limited to, providing at-risk youth with job skills, after-school activities for youth, neighborhood watch programs, and added security measures.[1]

In this chapter, we will examine different criminal justice policies and practices in the United States and China. We will do this from an institutional perspective. Both the United States and China have the same goals for their criminal justice polices—serve justice as well as control and prevent crime. However, their dominant social paradigms and political systems cause them to go about achieving those goals in different ways. Remember that the United States is a representative democracy, whereas China is under authoritarian rule. This means that their institutions involving criminal justice differ. China was chosen as a comparison to the United States in order to show how these factors result in drastically different criminal justice system.

In the United States, **individual rights and liberty** for all citizens forms a safety net for all criminal laws. It is stipulated that these laws must be in line with the U.S. Constitution's **Bill of Rights** to ensure individual rights and liberties are protected. Essentially, this means that the basic rights of even those convicted of the most heinous crimes are protected and upheld in the process of arrest, adjudication, and incarceration. The Bill of Rights specifies the rights that are protected throughout criminal justice proceedings. Any violation of these rights can be addressed through litigation. The importance of individual rights and liberty is so fundamental to American society that people who may be guilty of crimes are released just because of technical violations of those basic rights.[2] Given the fundamental importance of individual rights and liberty, American legal experts, scholars, and policymakers mention that the U.S. criminal justice system and its policies could be an example for other countries to adopt for their societies. The **United States Congressional-Executive Commission on China (US-CECC)** makes this point in regard to China.[3]

In the United States, policymakers and citizens seek a proper balance between maintaining public order and protecting individual rights and liberty. This is reflected in the dilemma between **crime control** (order as value) and **due process** (law as value). Average Americans believe that protecting individual rights and liberty exceeds maintaining public order. Even after the September 11, 2001, terrorist attacks on the World Trade Center and the Pentagon, and the subsequent passage of the Patriot Act in 2001, most Americans still felt that protecting their individual rights and liberty was their primary concern, rather than maintaining public order.[4]

In contrast, China's policies for maintaining public order are more important than policies protecting individual rights and liberty. Thus, many Western governments and human rights activists have frequently condemned China for major deficiencies in providing for fair criminal justice and human rights protection.[5] According to the U.S. Department of State's 2003 Country Reports on Human Rights Practices, people in China "lacked both the freedom peacefully to express opposition to the Party-led political system and the right to change their national leaders or form of government."[6] Although there is an independent judiciary under China's constitution, "in practice, the Government and the CCP [Chinese Communist Party], at both the central and local levels, frequently interfered in the judicial process and directed verdicts in many high-profile cases."[7] Later, the US-CECC Annual Report 2011 observed that "more people in today's China enjoy an improved quality of life, economic freedoms, and greater access to information via the Internet and other communication technologies. But economic and technological progress has not led to commensurate gains in China's human rights and rules of law record."[8]

In the context of different political systems, policymakers in the United States and China enact different policies. Although the institutional framework of criminal justice in the United States and China may look similar in principle, the two countries clearly differ in regard to policy implementation as well as judicial and prosecutorial practices.

The next section will begin with an illustration of how U.S. law enforcement authorities implement criminal justice policy. Following that, we will look at policy actors in the context of constitutional guarantees of rights to be upheld in criminal justice proceedings. Subsequently, we will consider crimes, penalties, and corrections in the United States. Our exploration of U.S. criminal justice policy will conclude by discussing some problems and challenges.

The United States

In theory, each criminal case in the U.S. criminal justice system is pursued via a progression of 13 steps, with a series of decisions made by four agencies: the police, the prosecutors, the courts, and a correctional system.[9] In reality, criminal procedures for defendants vary from case to case. Also, because of American federalism, the terms and sequence of the 13 steps may differ in some parts from one state to another.

In the United States, all criminal cases must first be reported to the **police** and become the subject of an investigation (step 1). When the police find a possible offender or suspect with enough evidence that the person committed a crime, they put that person physically under arrest, taking him or her into custody pending a court procedure (step 2). An arrest is usually based on a warrant, which is a court order (authorized police action) issued by a judge within a given jurisdiction. Although an arrest is a serious step, it involves a discretionary decision made by the police. Prior to arresting a suspect, police officers are legally obligated to advise the suspected offender of his or her constitutional rights, commonly known as the **Miranda rights**.[10] At a police station, officers photograph a suspect and take his or her fingerprints, and then they interrogate the suspect. Also, a suspect may be placed in a lineup to be identified by a victim or a witness. During the booking process (step 3), a suspect is informed that he or she has the right to counsel and may remain silent.

The next action involves bringing charges against a suspect (step 4). Now, **prosecutors** decide whether there is reasonable cause to believe that (1) an offense was committed and (2) the suspect in custody committed such an offense. Criminal cases are then reinvestigated by prosecutors. After a suspect is charged, she or he must be brought before a judge or magistrate (judicial officer) in an initial appearance (step 5). A suspect is given formal notice of the criminal charge(s) for which the suspect is being held, advised of her or his rights, and informed that she or he may retain counsel. During this initial appearance, the majority of suspects are afforded a chance to post **bail** (money or property pledged to a court or actually deposited with a court for the pretrial release of a suspect from custody). A case will ultimately be dropped if there is not enough evidence that the person committed a crime. If enough evidence exists, there is a preliminary hearing (step 6), which allows a judge to decide whether there is probable cause to believe that (1) a crime was committed and (2) the accused person committed it. At this step, **probable cause**, which is a legal standard based on known facts that a crime has been committed, must be found for a case to continue. If a judge does not find probable cause, a case will be dismissed. If probable cause is found, a case is sent to a **grand jury** (a body of private citizens selected according to law). A grand jury decides whether or not a case will go to trial based on the existence of sufficient evidence (step 7). If sufficient evidence exists, a grand jury submits an indictment to the court, which is a formal written statement (true bill) of the facts of charges against a subject. Misdemeanor cases and some felony cases are processed with an **information**, a formal written accusation submitted to a court by a prosecutor. An information differs from an indictment because it is submitted by a prosecutor rather than a grand jury.

When there is an indictment by a grand jury, an information by a prosecutor, or an arrest warrant by a judge, a suspect is scheduled for an arraignment (step 8), which is the person's first appearance as a defendant before a trial **court**. At an arraignment, a defendant is informed of the charges against him or her, advised of his or her rights as a criminal defendant, and asked to enter a plea to the stated charges. Acceptable pleas include not guilty, guilty, and no contest, or *nolo contendere* (neither admitting nor denying guilt). A plea of guilty must be accepted by a judge who takes into consideration the voluntary action of the plea and the defendant's full knowledge of the consequences of such a plea. When a **guilty plea** is accepted, a judge imposes a sentence without trial. However, a rejected guilty plea (maybe because a judge thinks that the plea is produced through coercion) means that a case goes to trial.

There are times when prosecutors cannot seek a guilty plea. Instead, prosecutors may use **plea bargaining** when their evidence against a defendant is weaker than what is needed to secure a guilty plea. This type of plea is an arrangement between a prosecutor, defendant, and defense counsel in which a defendant agrees to plead guilty to a charge, or a lesser charge, in exchange for a prosecutor's agreement to ask for a less severe sentence. For prosecutors, plea bargaining may result in quick convictions without costly trials. For defendants, plea bargaining may reduce or combine charges, reduce sentences, and lessen defense costs. As a result of guilty pleas and plea bargaining, few criminal cases (10 to 15 percent) go to trial.[11]

The cases that do go to trial are the ones where the defendant pleads not guilty (step 9). Under the Sixth Amendment to the U.S. Constitution, every criminal defendant has the right to a trial by a jury. At either a trial by a jury or a bench trial (a trial for less serious offenses, with judges rather than juries as fact finders), prosecuting and defense attorneys present evidence and question witnesses under procedural law. Although one might think that every trial is held before a judge and a jury, only 5 percent of trials are actually trials by a jury.[12]

A trial results in an acquittal or a conviction on original or lesser charges. An *acquittal* means the defendant has been found not guilty. A *conviction* occurs when evidence proves beyond reasonable doubt that the defendant is guilty as charged. A conviction is followed by sentencing (step 10). Sentences are usually imposed by judges. In some jurisdictions, however, sentences, especially for capital crimes, are imposed by juries. In sentencing, judges or juries have several options, including the death penalty or capital punishment; incarceration in a jail, prison, or any other confinement facility; **probation** (allowing a convicted person to remain at liberty, but subject to certain conditions such as drug testing or drug treatment); restitution (requiring an offender to pay compensation to a victim); and fines (applied mainly as penalties for minor offenses).

Defendants who are found guilty still have a chance to avoid punishment. They may appeal a conviction to a higher court. An **appeal** (step 11) can be based on a claim that a trial court failed to follow proper procedures, or that a defendant's constitutional rights were violated by the police or by a prosecutor, defense attorney, or judge.

Sentences are administered through corrections (step 12) in a **correctional system** that is overseen by departments of corrections and includes prisons, city or county jails, and state or federal penitentiaries. An offender who is incarcerated is eligible for release (step 13) when she or he has served the full sentence imposed by a judge or jury. Under certain conditions, an offender who has served part of her or his sentence may be eligible for **parole** (i.e., conditional release) granted by a parole board. If an offender is released before the full term expires, it is usually because the person has received good-time credit or been granted parole. The offender returns to the community and is then supervised by a parole officer.

In reality, many criminal cases are not pursued via all 13 steps. As noted earlier, there are few trials by a jury. We now understand what steps and decisions are involved in the U.S. criminal justice system. Next, we will examine how criminal justice policy is made and who is involved in criminal justice policy making in the United States.

Policy Actors[13]

The U.S. criminal justice system is framed by laws and legal procedures established by decisions of judges and elected representatives in public offices. Unlike public officials in authoritarian countries such as China, all elected public officials in the United States must make decisions within limits imposed by laws. **Criminal law** authorizes government authorities to punish people for damage they have done to society. In addition to criminal law, there is **civil law** for business deals, contracts, real estate, and so on. Criminal law is composed of two categories: substantive criminal law and criminal procedure law. **Substantive criminal law** provides **penal codes**, which formally define what is considered criminal activity that can elicit punishment by government authorities. These codes are written by elected officials in Congress, state legislatures, or city councils. Penal codes vary from state to state and from city to city. **Criminal procedure law** outlines the rules that law enforcement authorities must follow in all areas of the criminal justice system. The fundamental part of criminal procedure law is defined and written by legislatures, whereas other parts are defined by decisions made by the U.S. Supreme Court as well as state supreme courts.

There are four sources of criminal law: constitutions, statutes, court decisions (case laws), and administrative regulations. Both the *U.S. Constitution and state constitutions* provide basic principles and procedural safeguards for all citizens of the United States. *Statutes* are laws passed by legislative bodies such as the U.S. Congress and state legislatures. Under U.S. federalism, state legislatures write the bulk of criminal law. This leads to many definitions of crimes and procedures varying from state to state. *Court decisions* (or case laws) imply that legal opinions by judges in individual cases have the status of law. For example, the Supreme Court decision in *Wisconsin v. Mitchell* (508 U.S. 476) in 1993 is the benchmark of hate crime legislation.[14] Finally, *administrative regulations* are rules made by federal, state, and local agencies given the power to decide in the public interest on regulations in such areas as health, safety, and the environment (e.g., the Environmental Protection Agency's regulation of air and water pollution). These four sources of criminal law constitute the framework of the U.S. criminal justice system.

The U.S. Constitution and State Constitutions

The U.S. Constitution and state constitutions are the foundation of U.S. criminal law. All laws in the United States must respect the terms of the U.S. Constitution, particularly its first 10 amendments, known as the Bill of Rights (see Table 5.1), which protects all Americans against government actions that might violate basic rights and liberties. Protections against actions by state and local governments were guaranteed in state constitutions only after nationalization of the Bill of Rights through a series of Supreme Court decisions.

The First Amendment (freedom of religion, speech, the press, and assembly) has been a major source of protection of individual liberties and freedom. The Second Amendment (the right to bear arms) has been referred to in the gun control debate. The Fourth through Eighth Amendments are at the heart of an intricate criminal justice system to ensure that individuals are protected under criminal law and its enforcement based on the assumption that any criminal suspect is presumed innocent until proven guilty. In practice, street-level law enforcement officers must gather enough evidence to establish that a suspect committed a crime, and district attorneys must prove guilt beyond reasonable doubt in court. The Fourth Amendment (no unreasonable searches and seizures) forbids law enforcement officers from conducting arbitrary, unreasonable, and general searches and

TABLE 5.1	U.S. Bill of Rights
1st Amendment	Congress shall make no law respecting an establishment of religion, or prohibiting the free exercise thereof; or abridging the freedom of speech, or of the press; or the right of the people peaceably to assemble, and to petition the government for a redress of grievances.
2nd Amendment	A well-regulated militia, being necessary to the security of a free state, the right of the people to keep and bear arms, shall not be infringed.
3rd Amendment	No soldier shall, in time of peace be quartered in any house, without the consent of the owner, nor in time of war, but in a manner to be prescribed by law.
4th Amendment	The right of the people to be secure in their persons, houses, papers, and effects, against unreasonable searches and seizures, shall not be violated, and no warrants shall issue, but upon probable cause, supported by oath or affirmation, and particularly describing the place to be searched, and the persons or things to be seized.
5th Amendment	No person shall be held to answer for a capital, or otherwise infamous crime, unless on a presentment or indictment of a grand jury, except in cases arising in the land or naval forces, or in the militia, when in actual service in time of war or public danger; nor shall any person be subject for the same offense to be twice put in jeopardy of life or limb; nor shall be compelled in any criminal case to be a witness against himself, nor be deprived of life, liberty, or property, without due process of law; nor shall private property be taken for public use, without just compensation.
6th Amendment	In all criminal prosecutions, the accused shall enjoy the right to a speedy and public trial, by an impartial jury of the state and district wherein the crime shall have been committed, which district shall have been previously ascertained by law, and to be informed of the nature and cause of the accusation; to be confronted with the witnesses against him; to have compulsory process for obtaining witnesses in his favor, and to have the assistance of counsel for his defense.
7th Amendment	In suits at common law, where the value in controversy shall exceed twenty dollars, the right of trial by jury shall be preserved, and no fact tried by a jury, shall be otherwise reexamined in any court of the United States, than according to the rules of the common law.
8th Amendment	Excessive bail shall not be required, nor excessive fines imposed, nor cruel and unusual punishments inflicted.

continued

TABLE 5.1 Continued	
9th Amendment	The enumeration in the Constitution, of certain rights, shall not be construed to deny or disparage others retained by the people.
10th Amendment	The powers not delegated to the United States by the Constitution, nor prohibited by it to the states, are reserved to the states respectively, or to the people.

seizures without a court's formal authorization based on probable cause. The Fifth Amendment guarantees protection against double jeopardy, the right not to be compelled to self-incrimination, and due process of law. The Sixth Amendment grants all suspects the right to a speedy and public trial by an impartial jury, the right to be informed of the nature and cause of the charges against them, the right to confront witnesses against them and have witnesses in their favor compelled by a court to testify, and the right to obtain counsel for defense. The Seventh Amendment provides for a trial by a jury in civil cases. The Eighth Amendment prohibits excessive bail and fines as well as cruel and unusual punishment. In short, the U.S. Constitution, the Bill of Rights, and state constitutions are sources of constraints on court decisions and the power of police officers, prosecutors, and judges, all of which may violate individual liberties and freedom.

Criminal Justice Policy Making

Framed by a constitutional presidential system with checks and balances as well as a separation of powers between legislative, executive, and judicial branches of government, the process of criminal justice policy making in the United States involves many government and nongovernment actors, including Congress, the president, criminal justice agencies, courts, interest groups, private enterprises, media, and the public. Historically, state and local governments were the principal authorities to create and implement crime control measures in the United States. With the establishment of the Office of Law Enforcement Assistance in the Department of Justice in 1965, the federal government's responsibility for crime control has expanded gradually through legislation and implementation. However, state and local governments have remained key law enforcement authorities and retained the right to enact criminal justice legislation due to the federalism. Congress, the president, and the Supreme Court have had significant influence at the federal level in regard to contemporary criminal justice policy making.

The Legislative Branch

Primary responsibility for criminal justice legislation rests with Congress, specifically with a variety of committees and subcommittees in the Senate and the House of Representatives. These committees and subcommittees have shaped criminal justice policy by defining the terms of crime and criminal justice procedures; authorizing and reauthorizing criminal justice agencies, programs, and policies; and allocating federal funding for criminal justice agencies and programs. The Senate Judiciary Committee oversees the Department of Justice (DOJ) and its agencies, such as the Department of Homeland Security (DHS) and the Federal Bureau of Investigation (FBI), and it considers executive and judicial nominations.[15] The House Judiciary Committee has jurisdiction over issues concerning the administration of justice through administrative bodies, law enforcement agencies, and federal courts, and it plays a role in impeachment proceedings.[16]

The Executive Branch

Presidents are generally not deeply involved in criminal justice policy making, besides nominating Supreme Court judges and cabinet members such as the Attorney General. Yet, some presidents have taken specific initiatives for national anti-crime legislation and public awareness. The President's Crime Commission created by President Lyndon Johnson in 1965 was a significant contribution to criminal justice policy making. The commission's recommendations informed the Omnibus Crime Control and Safe Streets Act Passed by Congress in 1968, which established the Law Enforcement Assistance Administration (LEAA). In pursuit of a drug-free America, President Ronald Reagan was influential in setting the agenda for a war on drugs. Congress supported this agenda by passing the 1984 Comprehensive Crime Control Act as well as the 1986 and 1988 Anti-Drug Abuse Acts. President George H. W. Bush continued the war on drugs with a primary focus on the demand for drugs in the United States. President William J. Clinton federalized various anti-crime measures, including measures against carjacking, drive-by shootings, and possession of handguns near schools.[17]

Federal Criminal Justice Agencies

The federal government has numerous departments and agencies responsible for criminal justice. The Department of Justice, headed by the Attorney General, is the center of the federal criminal justice system. It hosts numerous agencies that deal with criminal justice; two of those major DOJ agencies include the Federal Bureau of Investigation and the Bureau of Alcohol, Tobacco, and Firearms and Explosives.

State and Local Criminal Justice Agencies[18]

Despite the federal government's responsibility for U.S. criminal justice policy, state and local authorities are the key agencies that implement criminal justice initiatives and programs at the street level. Unlike federal law enforcement, state and local law enforcement can be described as decentralized, with many jurisdictions and law enforcement agencies in counties, cities, and rural towns and villages. State highways and towns with no police force are under the jurisdiction of the state police in each state. Although each state has an attorney general, the power of state attorney generals is rather limited in comparison with the power of the U.S. Attorney General. Most state prosecutions take place at the county level under elected district attorneys. All counties have county jails for handling minor crimes (misdemeanors), and they have probation officers. Convicted felons serve their prison terms in state-run prisons or departments of corrections. State substantive criminal laws are based on federal laws and statutes enacted by the U.S. Congress.

Courts[19]

Under the U.S. Constitution, judicial power is decentralized and divided between a federal court system and 50 independent state court systems. Federal courts largely deal with disputes over federal law, and state courts consider disputes only within their jurisdiction under state law. This dual system in the United States is called **judicial federalism**. It is a unique system in comparison with a single-unitary system of courts in other countries.

The federal court system consists of three levels of courts: the Supreme Court, the Federal District Courts, and the Circuit Courts of Appeal. There are also such special courts as the Court of Claims, the Customs Court, the Patent Court, and the Court of Military Appeals. The Supreme Court presides over the entire judicial system comprising more than 100 Federal District Courts and 11 Circuit Courts of Appeal.

Similar to the federal court system, the state court system is divided into many levels. If an appeal reaches a state supreme court, the decision can be appealed one last time to the U.S. Supreme Court. This is where the two systems converge.

Interest Groups

Similar to many other policies, criminal justice policy is influenced by numerous interest groups. One of the major interest groups in the process of criminal justice policy making is the American Civil Liberties Union (ACLU), whose mission is to "Keep America safe and free." [20] The ACLU is a strong advocate of individual rights. The Anti-Defamation League (ADL) is an important player in combating hate crimes. Its active role in promoting and pressing for hate crime legislation, most notably the Matthew Shepard and James Byrd Jr. Hate Crimes Prevention Act, has been strongly endorsed by the National Organization of Women (NOW), gay rights advocacy groups, and groups representing African Americans, Hispanic Americans, Asian Americans, and others.[21]

In response to domestic violence against women and children, various women's groups such as the National Organization of Women and organized groups of victims of domestic violence have influenced the definition of domestic violence and the development of criminal procedures.[22] Gun control has also been a contentious issue in the public policy-making process. Activists for gun control, such as supporters of the Brady Campaign to Prevent Gun Violence as well as the Coalition to Stop Gun Violence (CSGV), and activists against gun control, such as the National Rifle Association (NRA), have been in competition for influence on legislation.[23]

Crimes, Penalties, and Corrections

Crimes   There are many ways to classify crimes. One method is by the gravity of the harm done. **Felonies** are serious crimes that are punishable by incarceration for more than one year in prison or the death penalty. **Misdemeanors** are less serious crimes that are punishable by jail sentences of less than one year, and/or probation, fines, or other intermediate sanctions.

Others try to categorize crimes by the nature of acts and distinguish among six types of crimes:[24] **Visible crimes** include street crimes or ordinary crimes ranging from shoplifting to homicide. There are three categories of visible crimes: violent crimes, property crimes, and crimes that threaten general social well-being or challenge accepted moral principles. **Occupational crimes** are acts in the context of a legal business or profession. Examples include price fixing, theft of trade secrets, acceptance of bribes by public officials, using insider stock-trading information for personal profit, and embezzlement. **Organized crimes** involve human trafficking, money laundering, and illegal disposal of toxic wastes, illegal development and selling of weapons, and commercial arson. **Victimless crimes** entail willing and private exchanges of goods or services that are in strong demand but illegal; they are offenses against morality. Examples include prostitution, gambling, and drug sale and use. **Political crimes** are acts by the government or against the government that are carried out for ideological purposes. Two remarkable examples are the 1995 bombing of the Oklahoma City federal building and the September 11, 2001, terrorist attacks on the World Trade Center and the Pentagon. **Cybercrimes** are a new category of crimes emerging with new technologies. These crimes occur when people use a computer and the Internet to commit acts against people, property, public order, or morality. Identity theft, computer hacking, and child pornography have become matters of serious concern.

Penalties   After crime offenders are convicted beyond reasonable doubt, they are usually sentenced to (1) fines, (2) restitution, (3) probation, (4) incarceration, or (5) death. Instead of imprisonment with some definite duration, offenders may receive an indeterminate sentence to spend a range of time in prison. When offenders are convicted of two or more separate crimes, sentences may be served consecutively or concurrently. In some cases, offenders have been sentenced to over 200 years in prison because of multiple convictions.

The ultimate punishment to which offenders may be sentenced in the U.S. criminal justice system is capital punishment or the death penalty, which varies among states. Historically, hanging or shooting was commonly used to execute the death penalty. Later, electrocution, the gas chamber, and lethal injection were adopted to execute capital punishment. There are thousands (approximately 3,000 in 2014) of inmates under sentence of death in the United States.[25]

Corrections   There are three types of correction measures. According to a report by the Bureau of Justice Statistics, about 7.1 million people (1 out of every 33 adults) were on probation or parole or incarcerated in jail or prison at the end of 2010.[26] *Probation* is carried out by a system of probation and pre-trial services with officers responsible for investigation, report preparation, and supervision of criminal offenders. *Parole* means that offenders are condition-ally released from prison by discretion of a paroling authority prior to expira-tion of their full sentence.[27] Parolees serve the remaining part of their sentence in the community under supervision of parole officers. If they fail to comply with specific conditions or rules of conduct in the community, parolees can be returned to prison. In 2010, there were nearly 4.9 million people (1 out of every 48 adults) on probation (about 4.1 million) or parole (about 0.8 million) under supervision in the community.[28] **Incarceration** is placing a person inside of a jail or prison to serve his or her sentence. There are federal prisons managed by the Federal Bureau of Prisons (BOP) as well as prisons and jails managed by state and local authorities.[29] In 2010, nearly 2.3 million people (3 in 10) were incar-cerated in federal or state prisons (over 1.5 million) or jails (over 0.7 million).[30]

Problems and Challenges

The U.S. criminal justice system has evolved over time with criminal justice poli-cies being continuously transformed. Elected officials in Congress or state leg-islatures have introduced legislation for crime control and prevention, and fed-eral, state, and local law enforcement authorities have implemented initiatives and programs toward a crime-free and safe society. Still, the U.S. criminal justice system faces a number of problems and challenges. These include continued public concern about crime as well as concerns about a large prison population. Other concerns are increasing prison costs that compete with resources needed for other policy priorities, racial disparity, and the use of capital punishment.

According to the FBI, there were 1.2 million violent crimes and 9.1 million property crimes reported to law enforcement in 2010.[31] With such high num-bers, Americans continue to be concerned about crime. Citizens as well as inter-est groups demand that law enforcement strengthen and exhaust existing crime control mechanisms to create a crime-free and safe society. Realizing that public concern about crime influences votes, elected officials at federal, state, and local levels are motivated to enact numerous criminal codes as well as crime control and prevention measures mandating harsh minimum sentences.

In order to prevent repeated felonies, many states have **three strikes laws.** Under these laws, after three separate felony convictions ("strikes"), where the first two felonies are violent or serious crimes and the third felony is any major or minor crime, offenders are removed from society by giving them long prison sentences, which may be life sentences with the possibility of parole only after many years in prison. Three strikes laws can lead to individuals serving prison sentences for nonviolent or nonserious crimes.[32]

Lengthy incarceration as a result of harsh minimum sentences and three strikes laws contribute to a large prison population in the United States. In fact, according to the World Prison Brief of the International Centre for Prison Studies (ICPS), at the end of 2010, the prison population rate in the United States (730 per 100,000 of national population) was the highest in the world.[33] A prison population of more than 2 million inmates across the United States puts an enormous burden on not only prison administrators but also on federal, state, and local jurisdictions financing incarceration with secure and humane housing for all inmates.

In 2010, for example, the prison budget of the California Department of Corrections and Rehabilitation (CDCR) was $7 billion, and the total cost of California's prisons was $7.9 billion, with an average annual cost per inmate of $47,421.[34] As Solomon Moore wrote in the *New York Times,* "Pew researchers say that as states trim services like education and health care, prison budgets are growing."[35] In order to reduce public spending on prisons, both the federal government and state governments have resorted to the privatization of correctional facilities. In 2010, according to a 2012 report of the Sentencing Project, "private prisons held 128,195 of the 1.6 million state and federal prisoners in the United States, representing eight percent of the total population. For the period 1999–2010, the number of individuals held in private prisons grew by 80 percent, compared to 18 percent for the overall prison population."[36]

Furthermore, there is concern about so-called **racial disparity** in the U.S. criminal justice system. Here, racial disparity means that "the proportion of a racial or ethnic group within the control of the system is greater than the proportion of such groups in the general population."[37] In 2009, African Americans made up 39 percent of those arrested for violent crimes and 30 percent of those arrested for property crimes, although the African American share of the total population was 12 percent. For Americans who are born today, expected incarceration rates are 1 out of every 3 African American males and 1 out of every 18 African American females, 1 out of every 6 Latino males and 1 out of every 45 Hispanic females, and 1 out of every 17 white males and 1 out of every 111 white females.[38] It is obvious from these numbers that someone's likelihood of being incarcerated in their lifetime is higher for nonwhites than for whites, and that it is highest for African Americans.

One of the most controversial issues concerning penalties for crime is about the use of capital punishment or the death penalty. The United States has been criticized internationally and domestically for its continued use of the death penalty.[39] There are several arguments that opponents of the death penalty present for its abolition. It has been a long-standing argument that the disproportion of minorities, particularly African Americans, on death row indicates racial bias in the use of capital punishment. Studies have shown that the death penalty is sought in a disproportionate number of cases involving minorities.

Additionally, the race of the victim is a factor in the difference between those criminals who receive the death penalty and those who do not. Generally, it has been found that a criminal is more likely to receive the death penalty when the victim is white rather than African American, especially if the criminal is African American. Not only is racial bias an issue for those who oppose the death penalty, but studies have shown that the death penalty has no deterrent effect. At best, it is a type of incapacitation, one that many argue is inhumane. Due to improvements in the use of forensics in analyzing evidence, several innocent people have been released from death row in the last several years. There is objection to the use of capital punishment because of the possibility that an innocent person could be executed. Many opponents of the death penalty argue that it is not only immoral but a violation of the U.S. Constitution's Eighth Amendment, which guarantees that citizens will be free of cruel and unusual punishment.

It is evident that there has been a long-standing paradox in criminal justice policy. How do we protect citizens from crime while also protecting the liberties that Americans hold so dear? Although many guilty suspects go free because of technical errors that indicate that their rights were violated, there are still a majority of Americans who would rather have some criminals go free than sacrifice any of their individual freedoms protected by the U.S. Constitution's Bill of Rights. Yet, it is believed by some that there is unfairness in the criminal justice system, unfairness reflected particularly in racial disparity and racial bias. Opponents of the death penalty often argue that to deprive a person of her or his life is the ultimate violation of that person's rights. Even though U.S. criminal justice policy is comparatively still more fair and equitable than other countries' criminal justice policies, it is not without its flaws.

In the next section, we will explore the institutional framework and practice of China's criminal justice policy. We will look at policy actors; examine the history, legal framework, and structure of the criminal justice system; and learn about the people's court system and mediation system to do justice and control crimes. We will also consider crimes, penalties, and judicial administrations. Our study of China's criminal justice policy will conclude with a discussion of some problems and challenges.

China

Until the 1980s, China struggled to create a workable legal system largely due to its chaotic history of civil wars, World War II, and disruptive political campaigns during much of the twentieth century. Arguably most chaotic was the Great Proletarian Cultural Revolution between 1966 and 1976, when virtually

▬▬▬▬▬ BOX 5.1 ▬▬▬▬▬

Country Profile of China

Name of Country: People's Republic of China

Type of Government: Communist State

Executive Branch:

President: President XI Jinping (since 14 March 2013); Vice President LI Yuanchao (since 14 March 2013)

Head of Government: Premier LI Yuanchao (since 16 March 2013); Executive Vice Premier ZHANG Gaoli (since 16 March 2013), Vice Premier LIU Yandong (since 16 March 2013), Vice Premier MA Kai (since 16 March 2013), and Vice Premier WANG Yang (since 16 March 2013) Cabinet: State Council

(appointed by the National People's Congress)

Legislative Branch:

Unicameral National People's Congress or Quanguo Renmin Daibiao Dahui (2,987 seats; members elected by municipal, regional, and provincial people's congresses, and People's Liberation Army to serve five-year terms)

Judicial Branch:

Supreme People's Court (judges appointed by the National People's Congress); Local People's Courts (comprise higher, intermediate, and basic courts); Special People's Courts (primarily military, maritime, railway transportation, and forestry courts)

Administrative Divisions:

23 provinces (sheng, singular and plural), 5 autonomous regions (zizhiqu, singular and plural), and 4 municipalities (shi, singular and plural)

Provinces: Anhui, Fujian, Gansu, Guangdong, Guizhou, Hainan, Hebei, Heilongjiang, Henan, Hubei, Hunan, Jiangsu, Jiangxi, Jilin, Liaoning, Qinghai, Shaanxi, Shandong, Shanxi, Sichuan, Yunnan, Zhejiang; (see note on Taiwan)

Autonomous regions: Guangxi, Nei Mongol (Inner Mongolia), Ningxia, Xinjiang Uygur, Xizang (Tibet)

Municipalities: Beijing, Chongqing, Shanghai, Tianjin

Note: China considers Taiwan its 23rd province; Hong Kong and Macau are considered special administrative regions of China.

Economic Indicators:

GDP (purchasing power parity): $12.38 trillion (2012 est.)

GDP Real Growth Rate: 7.8 percent (2012)

GDP per capita (purchasing power parity): $9,100 (2012 est.)

Economic Structure: Agriculture 34.8 percent, Industry 29.5 percent, Services 35.7 percent (2012 est.)

Demographic Indicators:

Population: 1,343,585,838 (July 2013 est.)

Population Growth: 0.481 percent (2012 est.)

Birth Rate: 12.31 births/1,000 population (2012 est.)

Infant Mortality Rate: 15.62 deaths/1,000 live births (2012 est.)

Life Expectancy at Birth: 74.84 years (2012 est.)

Literacy (people age 15 and over who can read and write): 92.2 percent (2008 census)

Source: CIA, *The World Factbook on China,* available at https://www.cia.gov/library/publications/the-world-factbook/geos/ch.html (accessed March 15, 2013).

all legal institutions in China were abolished. Since 1979, China's legal institutions have been reestablished, albeit with interruption in the aftermath of the 1989 Tiananmen Square Massacre, a violent suppression of a pro-democracy movement and protest in Beijing's Tiananmen Square.[40]

Under domestic and international pressure, China has taken steps to reform its criminal justice system. In 1996, the Chinese government incorporated several fundamental rights and principles, such as access to defense for defendants, in a revision of China's Criminal Procedure Law, and, in 1997, it adopted a revision of China's Criminal Law to fight corruption and deal with challenges due to economic reforms. Furthermore, in 1998, China signed the International Covenant on Civil and Political Rights (ICCPR), and, in 2004, the National People's Congress passed constitutional amendments towards ratification of the ICCPR. Expressing a rather optimistic view of China's progress in reforming its criminal justice system, Ira Belkin, a program officer at the Ford Foundation in Beijing as of 2012, wrote,

> Many sophisticated legal experts both inside and outside the Chinese govern-ment are dedicated to reforming China's criminal justice system to bring it closer to international standards of fairness. As in many areas of reform, China is looking to the West, and in particular to the United States, to gather infor-mation about reforms that may be appropriate.[41]

Yet, observers point out that despite ongoing reforms of its legal and crim-inal justice system, China has difficulties in implementing the rule of law as comprehensively as many Western countries because Chinese Communist Party interests continue to influence judicial reforms as well as all political affairs.[42] Indeed, the US-CECC Annual Report 2011 points out that "the Communist Party exercises control over political affairs, government, and society through networks of Party committees or branches that exist at all levels in government, legislative, and judicial agencies, as well as in businesses, major social groups (including unions), the military, and most residential communities."[43]

Policy Actors[44]

China's Constitution   The People's Republic of China, or PRC (hereafter, we use PRC or China interchangeably), was established as an authoritarian commu-nist state in 1949. A Soviet-style constitution based on ideas of Marxism, Leninism, and Maoism describes China's system of government and spells out the programs and policies of the **Chinese Communist Party**. The preamble to China's constitu-tion makes reference to the Communist Party and defines the PRC as a socialist state with a democratic dictatorship. Despite acknowledgment of democratic prin-ciples, the Chinese Communist Party has the authority to exercise dictatorship over any organization or person that it deems opposed to socialism and the party.

Party   All ruling power in China rests with the Chinese Communist Party (CCP). Based on the organizational principle of democratic centralism, the CCP plays central roles in promoting socialist democracy, developing and strength-ening a socialist legal system, and consolidating public resolve to carry out a program of modernization. The principle of democratic centralism means that members of the CCP can participate in policy deliberations, but all party mem-bers have to support a decision once it is arrived at by a party majority. Within representative and executive party organs, minorities must abide by majority decisions, and lower-level bodies follow orders from higher-level bodies.

The major organs of the CCP are the National Party Congress, the Central Committee, the Politburo (or Political Bureau) of the Central Committee, and the Politburo Standing Committee. For administration, the party relies on secretariats and specific departments under the Central Committee. Of all CCP organs, the National Party Congress (NPC) has the largest membership (2,213 delegates at the17th NPC held in October 2007). Policy debates among its leaders are often shaped by the need to reach a consensus in time to convene the next Congress. Each NPC is held every five years and solidifies central political tasks for the CCP. For example, the 12th NPC in 1982 backed the post-Mao reform effort, the 13th NPC in 1987 legitimized nonstate ownership, and the 14th NPC in 1993 gave a major political boost to a socialist market economy. The NPC held in 2007 under CCP General Secretary Hu Jintao's leadership approved a five-year plan to implement Hu's social economic development doctrine.[45] Since the meetings of the NPC are infrequent, real power in the CCP resides in the **Politburo (Political Bureau)** of the Central Committee and the more exclusive **Politburo Standing Committee.**

Government   One of China's major government organs, the **National People's Congress (NCP)**, formally approves CCP policies and programs. The NPC is at the top of a people's congress system that is arranged hierarchically through provinces, municipalities, rural townships, and so on. Although people's congresses are empowered to supervise the work of government executives at various levels of government, practice is that government executives are ultimately subject to party authorities rather than to people's congresses. The NPC elects and can remove China's president and vice president. On the president's recommendation, the NPC elects China's premier, who is then appointed and can be removed by the president. After the premier's nomination, the NPC elects the members of China's State Council, who are then appointed and can be removed by the president. The NPC also elects the President of the Supreme People's Court as well as the Procurator-General of the Supreme People's Procuratorate. Since the National People's Congress meets once a year for two weeks, the NPC Standing Committee, a permanent organ elected by the NPC, serves as an executive body on behalf of the NPC. Members of China's judiciary are responsible not only to the NPC but also to the NPC Standing Committee, which is composed mostly of party leaders.

The **State Council,** headed by the premier, is the highest executive organ of state administrations; it is equivalent to a cabinet. As of 2012, there are 29 ministries and commissions, including the Ministry of Public Security, the Ministry of State Policy, the Ministry of Justice, and the Ministry of Foreign Affairs. In practice, key decisions of the State Council are made by the premier and vice-premiers.

Although the NPC and the ministries and commissions under the State Council are officially responsible for running China's government, all government institutions are under supervision of the CCP, especially its elite in the Politburo and the Politburo Standing Committee. Nearly all government positions are occupied by party members. Key members of the State Council hold important positions in party organizations, and high-level officials such as the president and the premier are from the top of the party elite. The party decides who gets appointed to or removed from government positions, and it directs the policy-making process by instructing its members in government how to vote on policy proposals. The Chinese Communist Party controls China's government through a centralized political system in which government executive, administrative, legislative, and judicial organs are paired with parallel party organs.[46]

Administrative Divisions[47] China is divided administratively into 23 provinces, five autonomous regions, four municipalities, and two special administrative regions. All administrative divisions have party and government structures identical to those at the national level. China's administrative divisions are organized as follows: Provinces are divided into counties and cities. Under the supervision of county governments, rural political and economic administration is conducted by townships or towns. Each county has, on average, some two dozen townships and towns, with a national total of 33,000 townships and about half that number of towns. There are about 800,000 villages, the lowest-ranked rural administrations, or about two dozen per township. The average village population is a little over 1,000; village populations vary significantly by location.

The Criminal Justice System[48]

History[49] Efforts to establish a contemporary legal and criminal justice system in China began after the CCP seized power in 1949. In the early 1950s, basic criminal laws under the CCP were administrated by the public security, people's procuratorates, and people's courts. A suspected offender would be arrested by a **public security (police)** bureau, formally indicted by a **people's procurator**, and convicted by a hierarchy of **people's courts**. Theoretically, the judiciary was formally independent from the party and state apparatus. Yet, in practice, it remained essentially subordinate to the CCP. At the time, informal or popular justice took precedence over formal or bureaucratic justice, which was most notably reflected in the Great Proletarian Cultural Revolution (1966–1976).

In 1967, all legal organs were objects of rhetorical and physical attack by the Red Guards acting according to the slogan "Smash the public security, courts and procuratorates." The public security and courts continued to exist although their power was weakened. The procuratorates were dissolved, and their prosecutorial functions were taken over by the public security until they were restored in 1977. Although China's criminal justice system was slowly established in accordance with formal and informal Chinese legal traditions during the first 30 years under CCP rule, party policy rather than the rule of law was the major guideline for adjudication. Between 1976 and 1979, core legal institutions were established or reestablished under Deng Xiaoping's leadership.

Criminal Law Framework Extensive reforms of China's criminal justice system were launched at the Second Session of the Fifth National People's Congress in 1979. New laws on courts, procuratorates, crimes, and trials were publicized in the 1979 Criminal Law and Criminal Procedure Law.[50] Effective as of January 1, 1980, reforms reflected the leadership's conviction that, if economic modernization was to succeed, the people—who had suffered through the humiliations, capricious arrests, and massive civil disorders of the Cultural

Revolution—had to be assured that they no longer would be abused or imprisoned due to rumor or illegitimate political pronouncements. The new Criminal Law pronounced that criminal punishments should target all counterrevolutionary and other criminal acts in order to safeguard the people's democratic dictatorship and the smooth progress of socialist construction.

In the aftermath of the Cultural Revolution, political leaders found it important to prevent a possible return of radical policies and a repetition of the era when the Gang of Four ruled by inconsistent party regulations. Aside from establishing a legal code that would be more difficult for corrupt officials to manipulate, new laws made courts responsible for applying all but minor sanctions and made the police answerable to courts. Procuratorates, which had fallen into abandonment during the Cultural Revolution, were reinstated to prosecute criminal cases, review court decisions, and investigate the legality of actions taken by the police and other government institutions. With courts playing a greater role in the criminal justice system, independent investigations were expected to make it more difficult to introduce politically colored testimony into courtrooms.

Between 1980 and 1987, progress was made in replacing "the rule of men" with "the rule of law." Laws originally passed in 1979 and earlier were amended and augmented, and law institutes and university law departments that had been closed during the Cultural Revolution were reopened to train lawyers and court personnel. Important steps had been taken in developing a viable legal and criminal justice system making the government and courts accountable to objective standards. In 1982, the National People's Congress adopted a new constitution that delineates fundamental rights and duties of citizens, including protection from defamation of character, illegal arrest or detention, and unlawful search. This provides the general constitutional foundation of China's contemporary criminal justice system with its public security bureaus, people's procuratorates, and people's courts. Throughout the 1980s and 1990s, the Chinese government kept reforming China's criminal justice system and its criminal laws. The government revised the Criminal Procedure Law in 1996 and the Criminal Law in 1997. Both laws establish the specific legal framework of China's contemporary criminal justice system. As of today, reforms are still in progress.

Structure   China's present criminal justice system is administered by its security apparatus, which includes public security organs (the public police) headed by the Ministry of Public Security, the People's Armed Police, and the People's Liberation Army (PLA). The procuratorial system (people's procuratorates), judicial system (people's courts), and penal system (corrections) fell under the Ministry of Justice.[51]

According to China's constitution, the Standing Committee of the National People's Congress (SCNPC) has legislative and judicial authority; its functions are extensive. The Standing Committee (1) interprets the constitution and various statutes, (2) enacts and amends statutes, and (3) supervises the work of the Supreme People's Court, the Supreme People's Procuratorate, and the State Council. Public security organs (the public police) are responsible for crime investigation, detention of suspects, formal arrest, pretrial custody, and preparatory examination. People's procuratorates are responsible for approving arrests, conducting procuratorial control (including investigations), and initiating public prosecutions. People's courts are responsible for adjudication. Judicial administrative organs under the Ministry of Justice, through corrections, are responsible for the execution of court judgments and decisions.

People's Court System[52]

China's present people's court system is based on 1980 and 1983 revisions of the 1954 Organic Law of the People's Courts and China's 1982 constitution.[53] People's courts handle criminal, civil, economic, administrative, maritime, and other cases prescribed by law. They punish criminals and settle civil and other disputes, and they are expected to educate citizens to be loyal to their socialist motherland and to voluntarily observe China's constitution and laws.

The people's court system has a very centralized and hierarchical structure. Specifically, it consists of (1) a Supreme People's Court, (2) local (higher, intermediate, and basic) people's courts, and (3) special people's courts.

The Supreme People's Court (SPC) is the highest judicial organ and is located in China's capital, Beijing. The SPC has power similar to the Supreme Court in the United States. However, unlike the U.S. Supreme Court, the SPC may take important cases dealing with criminal and other matter directly— rather than act as the last court of appeal—as is the case with the U.S. Supreme Court—when cases deal with matters of greater national importance.

There are local people's courts at various levels of jurisdiction. These courts are divided into higher people's courts, intermediate people's courts, and basic people's courts. Basically, those courts act as either the first court in some jurisdictions or a court of appeals. As such, they are not unlike the court system in the United States where some of the cases are handled by city courts (e.g., parking tickets) or a municipal or superior court for more serious offenses. In both countries there are often avenues to appeal lower-court decisions depending on the jurisdiction and the crime.

As an important supplement to the people's court system, basic people's courts in collaboration with local governments direct a mediation system of **people's mediation committees (PMCs)**.[54] These committees are defined as legally established "mass organizations" for resolving everyday disputes based on the Law on People's Mediation, which was promulgated by China's NPC Standing Committee in 2010 and has been in force since January 2011.[55] People's mediation committees are nongovernmental mediating agencies organized by residents' or villages' committees elected by people who live or work within their local jurisdiction. Each PMC conducts (1) civil mediation, (2) administrative mediation, or (3) arbitration mediation.

Also under supervision of the Supreme People's Court are various special people's courts, including military courts, maritime courts, and railway transport courts. There are three phases in the judicial process in people's court: (1) pre-trial, (2) trial, and (3) post-trial.[56]

Pre-Trial Phase   People's courts try cases in public, except for cases involving state secrets, individual privacy, and crimes committed by minors. The accused in these proceedings are guaranteed full use of rights to defense, including legitimate rights to lawyers and other defenders in legal proceedings.

Trial Phase   Simple civil cases, disputes over economic matters, minor criminal offenses, and cases otherwise prescribed by law may be tried by a single appointed judge, but appeals or protested cases are tried by one to three judges and two assessors (jurors). Assessors are elected by local residents or people's congresses from among citizens or are appointed by courts for their expertise. Trials are conducted so that both judges and assessors play an active part in the questioning of all witnesses. After judges and assessors rule on a case, they pass a sentence. If judicial panel members disagree, their majority view will prevail, although minority opinions will be entered in minutes. Unlike in the United States, judicial decisions do not get precedents.

Post-Trial Phase   Like in the United States, parties who do not agree with judgments or orders can appeal court decisions. Unlike the United States, prosecutors in China can appeal decisions in criminal cases when they disagree with the outcome of the case.

Except for death sentences imposed by the Supreme People's Court, all other capital punishments must be reviewed by higher people's courts and then approved by the Supreme People's Court. The Supreme People's Court may pass on the power of approving death sentences to higher people's courts in regard to crimes that seriously endanger public security and order.

Crimes, Penalties, and Judicial Administrations[57]

Crimes   According to China's 1997 revised Criminal Law, there are 10 types of crimes:

1. Crimes endangering state security, such as treason, espionage, and mass rebellion
2. Crimes endangering public security, such as arson; spreading poison; illegally manufacturing, trading, or transporting guns or ammunition; and causing major accidents
3. Crimes undermining the socialist market economic order, such as smuggling, speculation, and falsely passing off trademarks
4. Crimes infringing on the personal rights or the democratic rights of citizens, such as homicide; bodily injury; rape; forcing women into prostitution; abducting and selling people; unlawfully detaining another person; unlawfully intruding into another person's residence; falsely accusing and framing; defamation, insult, and humiliation; giving false evidence or testimony; and using torture to coerce statements
5. Crimes encroaching on property, such as robbery, stealing, swindling, corruption, and extortion by blackmail

6. Crimes disrupting social order and its administration, such as disrupting public affairs, harboring criminals, concealing stolen goods, hooligan activities, and gambling
7. Crimes endangering the interests of national defense
8. Crimes of bribery and embezzlement
9. Crimes of malfeasance
10. Crimes in violation of military duties[58]

Penalties   In China, 16 is the age of maturity. Individuals who are older are subject to the following penalties when they commit a crime. According to China's 1997 revised Criminal Law, there are five major penalties and three supplementary penalties. The five major penalties are (1) control and supervision, (2) criminal detention, (3) fixed-term imprisonment, (4) life imprisonment, and (5) the death penalty. The three supplementary penalties, which can be imposed independently of the major penalties, are (1) fines (with no specific monetary limit), (2) deprivation of political rights, and (3) confiscation of property. Foreigners who commit crimes may be deported with or without other penalties.

Judicial Administrations[58]   It is worth noting that these crimes and punishments are similar to the activities that are identified as criminal in the United States. One exception is that in the United States the age of maturity is 18.

The next section presents a major departure from anything that would be required in the criminal justice system in the United States. A key responsibility of judicial administrations is to manage reform-through-labor and reeducation-through-labor institutions. **Reform-through-labor (Laogai)** is for offenders sentenced by courts to criminal detention, fixed-term imprisonment, life imprisonment, or the death penalty.[59] **Reeducation-through-labor (Laojiao)** is a nonjudicial, police-administered punishment for offenders sentenced by local *Laojiao* administrative committees, without judicial authority, upon recommendation by public security bureaus under the Security Administrative Punishment Regulations (SAPR). Daily work in labor camps is supposed to educate prisoners and redeem them to become law-abiding citizens. The process of "reform-through-labor" in both juvenile and adult institutions rests on a combination of labor production and political education. The purpose of political education is to rehabilitate and reform. Under political education, prisoners are required to take on legal and moral studies in socialist ideology. Self-criticism and mutual criticism are crucial parts of political education.

Problems and Challenges

China has been involved in reforms of its criminal justice system since 1979. From Western perspectives, however, the pace of China's criminal justice reform seems very slow, which Western leaders attribute to China's CCP-controlled government and a highly centralized legal system. For Chinese leaders, reforming

China's criminal justice system is essential to the preservation of their country's Marxist-Leninist-Maoist constitutional framework and the maintenance of social order under internal and external pressure due to increased globalization and demands for democratization.

Reforms notwithstanding, China's criminal justice system faces a number of problems and challenges. These include government and party interference in court decisions, lack of or obstacles to adequate defense for defendants, new and increasing crimes in the process of economic reforms, and practices such as the death penalty and reeducation-through-labor.

Since China's criminal justice system is still subject to interference by the Chinese Communist Party and government institutions under CCP supervision, officials tend to be immune from the law, engage in corruption, and use the system for political goals. In other words, China's criminal justice system is still characterized more by the rule of the party than by the rule of law.

As the United States Congressional-Executive Commission on China Annual Report 2005 mentions, the independence of judges in China is limited by various forms of government and party interference. "Local governments influence courts through their control over judicial funding and appointments, and frequently use this influence to protect local interests. Party authorities often intervene in politically sensitive cases and routinely screen court personnel decisions." Furthermore, "Since the early 1990s, local people's congresses have exercised increasing influence over court decisions.... Internal administrative practices commonly used in Chinese courts also reduce judicial effectiveness and independence." Assessments of efficiency and decisions on rewards or penalties in China's judicial system are often based on the annual ratio of cases closed over cases filed, which motivates Chinese courts to use frequently "unscrupulous means, including pressuring parties to agree to mediated outcomes and refusing to accept cases late in the year." Since judges can be disciplined "for a range of errors, including appellate reversals for legal error," they tend to "rely on advisory requests" to seek "advance guidance from higher court authorities about how to decide cases in order to avoid punishment." This hurts fairness in China's judicial system "by separating actual court decisions from trials, and by making subsequent appeals (to the same entity that responded to the request for review) a formality."[60]

Fairness in China's judicial system is further impaired by extensive shortages of trained legal experts. Most prosecutors are not even college graduates, let alone law school graduates; the situation is similar in regard to judges and lawyers. Until adoption of the 1982 Provisional Regulations (on Lawyers in China), China had seen no legal profession for over 20 years. In the early 1980s, China had only 1,300 legal advisory offices and 4,800 lawyers. According to the 1982 Provisional Regulations, lawyers were not required to pass bar examinations to be qualified to practice. Instead, agencies of the Ministry of Justice approved applicants who qualified with minimum education and experience. Since 1988, there have been biannual bar examinations.

Ministry of Justice practices under the 1982 Provisional Regulations were overtaken by the 1997 Law on Lawyers; the responsibility for lawyer qualification was moved from the Ministry of Justice to the All China Lawyers Association.

The US-CECC Annual Report 2004 states, "The Chinese bar has grown, from 43,533 registered lawyers in 1989 to 122,585 in 2001." Yet, the report continues, "Relative to the population as a whole, their numbers remain low by Western standards. At present, there is roughly one lawyer for every 10,000 individuals in China, compared to a ratio of about 1 to 550 in the United States."[61]

Although Chinese courts handled about 6 million cases in 1999, most defendants could not get any legal representation. Since the 1990s, the Chinese government has shown commitment to establish a legal aid system to promote the rule of law by increasing the ability of average citizens to use China's legal aid system.[62] Yet, the expansion of China's legal aid system has faced significant shortages of legal aid workers with a legal education and a lawyer's license.

When lawyers do their work and provide legal aid, they face obstacles and intimidation. Specifically, "Lawyers have long complained about the 'three difficulties' that they face in criminal defense work: (1) the difficulty in obtaining permission to meet with a client, (2) the difficulty in accessing and reviewing the prosecution's evidence, and (3) the difficulty in gathering evidence in support of the defense." Furthermore, "it is increasingly dangerous for Chinese defense lawyers to carry out their work, especially in high-profile or politically sensitive cases." This is so because "law enforcement officials sometimes resort to intimidating lawyers who defend these cases, charging or threatening to charge them with crimes such as 'evidence fabrication' under Article 306 of the Criminal Law." This practice is a problem that "persists and has become more damaging to China's legal system in the face of unchecked police power."[63]

Criminal trials result in convictions at extremely high rates in China's criminal justice system. As the US-CECC Annual Report 2008 explains, "Extremely high conviction rates in criminal cases are due in part to the lack of fairness of criminal trials, and the 'three difficulties' that hinder criminal defense lawyers' ability to defend their clients." Defendants are denied counsel and kept in long pre-trial confinement as public security officers subject them to coercion or torture to extort confessions. Public security officials also detain and intimidate witnesses in order to get statements. "There is a strong presumption of guilt in criminal cases, and a guilty verdict is a virtual certainty in politically sensitive cases."[64]

Realizing the need for modernization in an era of globalization, and seeking success of economic reform, China's leaders have adopted policies to accelerate economic growth and progress by moving toward a socialist market economy. Concomitant with this move, however, China is challenged by rising economic inequality that is considered a source of new crimes, including drug smuggling, money laundering, trafficking of women and children, and cyberspace terrorism. Also, crimes have grown to a magnitude that did not exist under more totalitarian communist rule. There are currently more cases of public corruption, economic crime, computer crime, narcotics trafficking, robbery, and murder than there were one or two decades earlier.[65] According to statistics released by the Supreme People's Court, 30,788 officials prosecuted in 2004 were involved in economic crimes; 20,435 suspects were arrested for economic crimes, and 21,449 suspects were prosecuted for crimes like smuggling, tax evasion/dodging, and financial fraud.[66]

China's economy continues to grow in conjunction with an extreme urban–rural income divide and a sharp rise in urban crime rates. As it appears, due to extreme delays in handling cases and due to extensive shortages of legal experts, China's criminal justice system has not been very successful in dealing appropriately with new crimes and their circumstances.

Human rights advocates are concerned about several practices used in China's criminal justice system. These include the death penalty and reeducation-through-labor. According to the 2010 Amnesty International report, China "continued to use the death penalty extensively against thousands of people for a wide range of crimes that include nonviolent offences and after proceedings that did not meet international fair trial standards." Yet, in 2010, the Supreme People's Court gave new guidelines to Chinese courts making it clear that the "death penalty should be 'resolutely' handed down to those who have committed 'extremely serious' crimes, but that the punishment should be reserved for the tiny minority of criminals against whom there is valid and ample evidence." Also, the Supreme People's Court, together with the Supreme People's Procuratorate, the Ministry of Public Security, the Ministry of State Security, and the Ministry of Justice, announced new regulations "enhancing legal procedures regarding the collection, examination, verification and determination of legality of evidence in death penalty cases."[67]

A significant problem with reeducation-through-labor (RTL) is that, unlike court-ordered reform-through-labor for major crimes, it is used as punishment for minor crimes with great discretion for public security officers in detaining individuals without effective guarantees of rights to an appeal or a fair trial.[68] Reeducation-through-labor has been used frequently to intimidate political activists and prevent public demonstrations. An administrative punishment, RTL has been subject to criticism because there is no judicial process involved, its scope is vague and arbitrary, punishment under it is severe, it has been included as an extrajudicial and convenient procedure in local regulations, and there are abusive conditions in its facilities.[69]

Comparison

An essential goal of criminal justice policy is to do justice and to control and prevent crime. No matter whether we look at the United States or China, or possibly any other country, criminal justice policy exists to protect individuals and societies against crime. In both the United States and China, crime control and prevention rests more or less on some combination of deterrence, justice, incapacitation, and rehabilitation. In both the United States and China, monetary fines, incarceration, and the death penalty are used to implement some form of deterrence and justice, and incarceration in both countries is a widely used method of incapacitation. Although incarceration may be seen as a method of rehabilitation or corrections, rehabilitation in the United States is commonly implemented through parole and probation, whereas rehabilitation in China is a justification for reform-through-labor and reeducation-through-labor.

There is some optimism that criminal justice reforms in China will change Chinese criminal justice policy in ways that would make it more similar to criminal justice policies found in Western countries, especially in the United States. Respect for the rule of law and guarantees of fundamental rights and principles, such as access to defense for defendants, need to be demonstrated not only on paper but also in practice. It is in this regard that China still has quite a way to go to make sure that its reforms not only remain statements to placate domestic and international critics of its human rights record but also get put into practice. Any right to legal assistance or due process is an empty shell so long as defense lawyers face obstacles and intimidation to prevent them from defending their clients and so long as defendants are denied counsel and tortured until they confess.

Despite their common goal of controlling and preventing crime, the U.S. and Chinese criminal justice policies exhibit significant differences in their practices and related assumptions, values, and institutions. Of particular concern are fundamental differences between the United States and China with regard to the rule of law and the importance of individual rights and liberty.

In the United States, all laws, including criminal laws, must respect the U.S. Constitution and its amendments. Even if the U.S. Congress and the U.S. President were controlled by the same party, and even if the majority of U.S. Supreme Court justices were sympathetic to that party, the U.S. Supreme Court, through judicial review, can be expected to strike down any law that is found unconstitutional, no matter how much support it has from the dominant party. No person or party is above the law; the ultimate law is the United States Constitution and its amendments. Thus, U.S. criminal justice policy, like any other policy adopted and implemented in the United States, is bound by the rule of law and constitutionality. Its system is embedded in institutions with checks and balances based on a separation of powers provided by the U.S. Constitution.

Although China is formally ruled under a constitution, for all practical purposes it is the Chinese Communist Party that rules in a centralized political system of an authoritarian communist state. Under such authoritarian rule, political power is not institutionalized according to a Western notion of the rule of law. Although China's political system distinguishes between executive, administrative, legislative, and judicial organs, all government institutions are under supervision of the CCP. Government organs are paired with parallel party organs, and the party decides who gets selected for government positions and how votes are cast on policy proposals.

In both the United States and China, criminal justice systems operate at different levels of jurisdiction. The United States has (1) three levels of federal courts (the U.S. Supreme Court, Federal District Courts, and Circuit Courts of Appeal); (2) special courts; and (3) state and local courts. China has (1) the Supreme People's Court; (2) local (higher, intermediate, and basic) people's courts; and (3) special people's courts. The United States has a highly institutionalized process from arrest to appeal, with the U.S. Supreme Court as the highest and final court to adjudicate appeals. In principle similar to the United States, China provides for the possibility to appeal court judgments and orders, and, in principle, China's Supreme People's Court is the highest and final court for appeals to be adjudicated.

In practice, however, the fairness of China's judicial system, including independent and effective adjudication of appeals, is restricted and undermined due to interference by the CCP and government institutions under CCP supervision.

One of the key values held in the United States is the importance of individual rights and liberty. The U.S. criminal justice system protects individuals and society not only against crimes committed by other individuals but also against crimes committed by the government through arbitrary use of the criminal justice system. While preventing crime, the U.S. criminal justice system is bound by the rule of law, specifically by the U.S. Constitution's Bill of Rights, to respect, uphold, and protect individual rights and liberty throughout criminal justice proceedings. Given the presumption that criminal suspects are innocent until proven guilty, convictions must be based on proof of guilt beyond reasonable doubt. Defendants have rights to a lawyer, due process of law, a speedy and public trial by an impartial jury, protection from self-incrimination, reasonable bail if arrested and detained, and fair and just punishments if convicted. The U.S. Constitution's Bill of Rights upholds individual liberty by protecting people's freedom from arbitrary arrest, unfair trials, convictions based on extortion of confessions under coercion and torture, excessive fines and bail, and punishments that are considered unusual and cruel. Criminal justice practices that people in the United States are protected against continue in China's criminal justice system despite official reforms and Chinese statements to the contrary.

In China, individual rights and liberty tend to be of lesser importance than social order, the country's socialist system, and the CCP. Thus, it is not surprising that at least 6 of 10 types of crimes identified by China's 1997 revised Criminal Law involve crimes against the collective (state security, public security, the socialist market economic order, social order and its administration, national defense, and military duties).

Critics of the U.S. criminal justice system point out that it involves discrimination against minorities, especially against African Americans. Efforts to address and reduce racial disparity and racial bias are important to maintain and raise confidence in the rule of law and fairness of the U.S. criminal justice system.

China's criminal justice system is criticized not only for discrimination against minorities and the death penalty, which is used far more extensively in China than in the United States, but also for a disturbing record of systematic human rights violations. As China is exposed to increasing globalization, with more integration in the international economic system, and as China seeks greater respect and influence as one of the world's major powers, it is likely to face further domestic and international pressure for economic, political, and judicial reforms. There will be further pressure on China to promote economic liberalization, democratization, respect for human rights, as well as change toward a criminal justice system that is based on the rule of law and commitment to fairness, not only in principle but also in practice. A critical challenge for China is to do all this while trying to maintain public security and social stability and to preserve its socialist system, perpetuate one-party rule under the CCP, and deal with rising economic inequality and new crimes unleashed in the process of economic reform.

Ultimately, China's leadership has to decide whether their interests, the interests of the CCP, and the interests of their country remain best served by human rights violations and a criminal justice system whose practice continues to defy Western standards.

Key Terms

- Appeal
- Bail
- Bill of Rights
- Chinese Communist Party
- Civil law
- Controlling crime
- Correctional system
- Courts
- Crime control
- Criminal law
- Criminal procedure law
- Cybercrimes
- Doing justice
- Due process
- Felonies
- Grand jury
- Guilty plea
- Incarceration
- Individual rights and liberty
- Information
- Judicial federalism
- Miranda rights
- Misdemeanors
- National People's Congress (NCP)
- Occupational crimes
- Organized crimes
- Parole
- Penal codes
- People's courts
- People's mediation committees (PMCs)
- People's procuratorates
- Plea bargaining
- Police
- Politburo (Political Bureau)
- Politburo Standing Committee
- Political crimes
- Preventing crime
- Probable cause
- Probation
- Prosecutors
- Public security (police)
- Racial disparity
- Reeducation-through-labor (*Laojiao*)
- Reform-through-labor (*Laogai*)
- State Council
- Substantive criminal law
- Three strikes laws
- United States Congressional-Executive Commission on China (US-CECC)
- Victimless crimes
- Visible crimes

Critical Thinking Questions

- What should be an appropriate balance between maintaining public order and protecting individual rights and liberty?
- What are the goals and procedures of criminal justice policy in the United States and China?
- How does the institutional framework of criminal justice policy in the United States differ from the institutional framework of criminal justice policy in China?
- What policy actors are involved in criminal justice policy making in the United States and China?

- How can crimes and penalties be organized?
- What are the most important problems and challenges related to criminal justice policy in the United States and China?

Recommended Resources for U.S. Criminal Justice Policy

George F. Cole and Christopher E. Smith, *The American System of Criminal Justice* (12th ed.) (Belmont, CA; West/Wadsworth, 2010).

Nancy E. Marion, *A Primer in the Politics of Criminal Justice* (2nd ed.) (New York: Criminal Justice Press, 2007).

Nancy E. Marion and Willard M. Oliver, *The Public Policy of Crime and Criminal Justice* (2nd ed.) (Upper Saddle River, NJ: Prentice-Hall, 2011).

Frank Schmalleger, *Criminal Justice: A Brief Introduction* (8th ed.) (Upper Saddle River, NJ: Prentice-Hall, 2011).

The Sentencing Project, *Reducing Racial Disparity in the Criminal Justice System: A Manual for Practitioners and Policymakers* (Washington DC, 2000).

Barbara Ann Stolz, *Criminal Justice Policy Making: Federal Roles and Process* (New York: Praeger, 2001).

Useful Web Sources for U.S. Criminal Justice Policy

Federal Court Website

Department of Justice Agencies Index

Office of Justice Program at the Department of Justice

Bureau of Justice Statistics

Kathleen Maguire, ed. *Sourcebook of Criminal Justice Statistics* [Online]. U.S. Department of Justice, Bureau of Justice Statistics

Recommended Resources for Chinese Criminal Justice Policy

Chen Jianfu, *Chinese Law: Towards an Understanding of Chinese Law, Its Nature and Development* (The Hague: Kluwer Law International, 1999).

Ronald C. Keith and Zhiqiu Lin, *New Crime in China: Public Order and Human Rights* (London: Routledge, 2006).

Stanley B. Lubman, *Bird in a Cage: Legal Reform in China after Mao* (Stanford, CA: Stanford University Press, 1999).

Harold M. Tanner, *Strike Hard! Anti-Crime Campaigns and Chinese Criminal Justice, 1979–1985* (Ithaca, NY: East Asia Program, Cornell University, 1999).

Richard J. Terrill, "China," in *World Criminal Justice Systems: A Survey* (6th ed.) (Newark, NJ: Lexis Nexis, 2007), chapter 7 (pp. 575–677).

Ronald J. Troyer, John P. Clark, and Dean G. Rojek, eds., *Social Control in the People's Republic China* (New York: Praeger, 1989).

Useful Web Sources for Chinese Criminal Justice Policy

Chinese government Internet information center in English
The Supreme People's Court in China
The Ministry of Justice in China
The Ministry of Public Security in China
U.S. Congress-Executive Commission on China official website

Notes

1. United Nations Office on Drugs and Crime. "Tenth United Nations Conference on the Prevention of Crime and the Treatment of Offenders: Preventing Crime and Cutting Costs," available at http://www.un.org/events/10thcongress/2088c.htm (accessed April 25, 2013).

2. A discussion balancing between individual rights and social order in the United States can be found in criminal justice textbooks such as George F. Cole and Christopher E. Smith, *The American System of Criminal Justice* (12th ed.) (Belmont, CA: West/ Wadsworth, 2010) and Frank Schmalleger, *Criminal Justice: A Brief Introduction* (8th ed.) (Upper Saddle River, NJ: Prentice-Hall, 2011).

3. The US-CECC consists of nine senators, nine members of the House of Representatives, and five senior administration officials appointed by the president. It has been a powerful force for U.S. foreign policy toward China in terms of the rule of law and protection of human rights in China. See the US-CECC website at http://www.cecc.gov/ (accessed February 16, 2012).

4. Darren W. Davis and Brian D. Silver, "Civil Liberties vs. Security: Public Opinion in the Context of the Terrorist Attacks on America," *American Journal of Political Science* 48(1) (2003): 28–46.

5. See Victor Dawes and Sheung Lai Tse, "Evaluating the Chinese Criminal Justice System under International Human Rights Standards," *Asian Pacific Law Review* 7 (1999): 19–44 and Jianfu Chen, *Chinese Law: Towards an Understanding of Chinese Law, Its Nature and Development* (Hague: Kluwer Law International, 1999). Also see Ann Kent, "States Monitoring States: The United States, Australia, and China's Human Rights, 1990-2001," *Human Rights Quarterly* 23 (2001): 583–624, and Steve Chan, "Human Rights in China and the United States: Competing Visions and Discrepant Performances," *Human Rights Quarterly* 24 (2002): 1035–1053.

6. See the United States Department of State's 2003 Country Reports on Human Rights Practices, available at http://www.state.gov/g/drl/rls/hrrpt/2003/27768.htm (accessed April 25, 2013).

7. Ibid. (accessed February 16, 2012).

8. The quote is from the executive summary of the US-CECC Annual Report 2011, available at http://www.cecc.gov/pages/annualRpt/annualRpt11/AR11Exec.pdf (accessed February, 16, 2012), p. 1.

9. A detailed discussion of these steps can be found in the U.S. Department of Justice's "The Justice System," available at http://bjs.ojp.usdoj.gov/content/justsys.cfm (accessed February 16, 2012), as well as George F. Cole and Christopher E. Smith, *The American System of Criminal Justice* (11th ed.) (Belmont, CA; West/Wadsworth, 2007), Chapter 3, and Frank Schmalleger, *Criminal Justice: A Brief Introduction* (4th ed.) (Upper Saddle River, NJ: Prentice–Hall, 2001), chapter 1.

10. This is the famous Supreme Court decision of *Miranda v. Arizona*. See http://www.law. cornell.edu/supct/html/historics/USSC_CR_0384_0436_ZS.html (accessed February 16, 2012).

11. The figure is reported in Cole and Smith, *The American System of Criminal Justice*, p. 86.

12. The figure is reported in Ibid.

13. For a detailed discussion of policy actors, politics, and the policy-making process regarding criminal justice policy in the United States, see Nancy E. Marion, *A Primer in the Politics of Criminal Justice* (2nd ed.) (New York: Criminal Justice Press, 2007); Nancy E. Marion and Willard M. Oliver, *The Public Policy of Crime and Criminal Justice* (2nd ed.) (Upper Saddle River, NJ: Prentice-Hall, 2011); and Barbara Ann Stolz, ed., *Criminal Justice Policy Making: Federal Roles and Process* (New York: Praeger, 2001).

14. For a review of the *Wisconsin v. Mitchell* case, see http://www.law.cornell.edu/supct/ html/92-515.ZO.html (accessed February 16, 2012).

15. For the Senate Judiciary Committee, see http://judiciary.senate.gov/ (accessed February 16, 2012).

16. For the House Judiciary Committee, see http://judiciary.house.gov/ (accessed February 16, 2012).

17. See Nancy Marion, "Presidential Agenda Setting in Crime Control" in Marion and Oliver, *The Making of Criminal Justice Policy in the United States* (2008).

18. For a brief discussion of the criminal justice system and practices of state and local authorities in the United States, see Kevin B. Smith, Alan Greenblatt, and Michele Mariani, *Governing States and Localities* (2nd ed.) (Washington, DC: CQ Press, 2008), Chapter 8. Because of American federalism, state criminal justice systems and practices vary from state to state.

19. See http://www.uscourts.gov/FederalCourts.aspx (accessed February 16, 2012).

20. For missions and activities of the American Civil Liberties Union (ACLU), see http://www.aclu.org/ (accessed February 16, 2012).

21. For missions and activities of the Anti-Defamation League (ADL), see http://www. adl.org/combating_hate/ (accessed February 16, 2012). For a summary of hate crimes and politics in the United States, see James B. Jacobs and Kimberly Potter, *Hate Crimes: Criminal Law and Identity Politics* (Oxford and New York: Oxford University Press, 1998).

22. For missions and activities of the National Organization of Women (NOW), see http://www.now.org/ (accessed February 16, 2012).

23. For the politics of gun control in the United States, see Robert J. Spitzer, *The Politics of Gun Control* (4th ed.) (Washington, DC: CQ Press, 2007) and Harry L. Wilson, *Guns, Gun Control, and Elections: The Politics and Policy of Firearms* (Lanham, MD: Rowman & Littlefield, 2007).

24. The following descriptions of different types of crimes are based on George F. Cole and Christopher E. Smith, *The American System of Criminal Justice* (11th ed.) (Belmont, CA: West/Wadsworth, 2007) and Frank Schmalleger, *Criminal Justice: A Brief Introduction* (4th ed.) (Upper Saddle River, NJ: Prentice-Hall, 2001).

25. See the Bureau of Justice Statistics, *Capital Punishment 2010-Statistical Table*, available at http://bjs.ojp.usdoj.gov/content/pub/pdf/cp10st.pdf (accessed February 21, 2012).

26. See the Bureau of Justice Statistics, *Correctional Populations in the United States, 2010*, available at http://bjs.ojp.usdoj.gov/content/pub/pdf/cpus10.pdf (accessed February 22, 2012).

27. For information about probation and parole services in the U.S. court system, see http://www.uscourts.gov/FederalCourts/ProbationPretrialServices.aspx (accessed February 22, 2012).

28. See the Bureau of Justice Statistics, *Correctional Populations in the United States, 2010*, available at http://bjs.ojp.usdoj.gov/content/pub/pdf/cpus10.pdf (accessed February 22, 2012) and *Probation and Parole in the United States 2010* at http://bjs.ojp.usdoj.gov/content/pub/pdf/ppus10.pdf (accessed February 22, 2012).

29. See http://www.bop.gov/ (accessed February 22, 2012).

30. See the Bureau of Justice Statistics, *Correctional Populations in the United States, 2010*, available at http://bjs.ojp.usdoj.gov/content/pub/pdf/cpus10.pdf (accessed February 22, 2012), and *Probation and Parole in the United States 2010*, available at http://bjs.ojp.usdoj.gov/content/pub/pdf/ppus10.pdf (accessed February 22, 2012).

31. See FBI, *Crime in the United States 2010*, available at http://www.fbi.gov/about-us/cjis/ucr/crime-in-the-u.s/2010/crime-in-the-u.s.-2010 (accessed February 16, 2012).

32. For example, see Emily Bazelon, "Arguing Three Strikes" *New York Times*, May 21, 2010, available at http://www.nytimes.com/2010/05/23/magazine/23strikes-t.html?pagewanted=all (accessed February 22, 2012). Also, see the Stanford Three-Strike Project for three strikes laws in California, available at http://www.law.stanford.edu/program/clinics/threestrikesproject/ (accessed February 22, 2012).

33. See the World Prison Brief of the International Centre for Prison Studies, available at http://www.prisonstudies.org/info/worldbrief/wpb_stats.php (accessed May 21, 2012).

34. See *The Price of Prisons*, available at http://www.vera.org/priceofprisons (accessed May 22, 2012).

35. See Solomon Moore, "Prison Spending Outpaces All but Medicaid," *New York Times*, March 2, 2009, available at http://www.nytimes.com/2009/03/03/us/03prison.html (accessed February 22, 2012).

36. See the Sentencing Project, *Too Good to be True: Private Prisons in America* (Washington, DC, 2012) available at http://sentencingproject.org/doc/publications/inc_Too_Good_to_be_True.pdf (accessed May 22, 2012).

37. See the Sentencing Project, *Reducing Racial Disparity in the Criminal Justice System*: *A Manual for Practitioners and Policymakers* (Washington DC, 2000), available at http://www.sentencingproject.org/doc/publications/rd_reducingracialdisparity.pdf (accessed February 22, 2012), p. 1.

38. See Marc Mauer, "Addressing Racial Disparities in Incarceration," *Prison Journal* 91(3) (2011): 87–101.

39. For example, see *US Death Penalty Facts* compiled by Amnesty International USA, available at http://www.amnestyusa.org/our-work/issues/death-penalty/us-death-penalty-facts (accessed February 22, 2012).

40. For a treatment of the background of the 1989 Tiananmen mass movement, see Nan Lin, *The Struggle for Tiananmen: Anatomy of the 1989 Mass Movement* (Westport, CT: Praeger, 1992).

41. Ira Belkin, "China's Criminal Justice System: A Work in Progress," *Washington Journal of Modern China* Vol. 6 (2) (2000): 62.

42. For example, see J. Chen, Y. Li, and J. M. Otto, *Implementation of Law in the People's Republic of China* (The Hague: Kluwer Law International, 2002),

43. The quote is from the US-CECC Annual Report 2011, available at http://www.cecc.gov/pages/annualRpt/annualRpt11/AR2011final.pdf, p. 36 (accessed February, 16, 2012).

44. This section is based on information available in English at the Chinese government Internet information center, http://www.china.org.cn/english/Political/25060.htm (accessed February 23, 2012). For a discussion of politics and policy-making in China, see Kenneth Lieberthal, *Governing China: From Revolution through Reform* (2nd ed.) (New York and London: Norton, 2003); Tony Saich, *Governance and Politics of China* (3rd ed.) (New York: Palgrave Macmillan 2010); and John Bryan Starr, *Understanding China: A Guide to China's Economy, History, and Political Structure* (3rd ed.) (New York: Hill and Wang; 2010). For a summary of stages and processes of law making in China, see Murray Scot Tanner, "How a Bill Becomes a Law in China: Stages and Processes in Lawmaking" in Stanley Lubman, ed., *China's Legal Reforms* (Gloucestershire, England: Clarendon, 1996), pp. 39–64, and Murray Scot Tanner, *The Politics of Lawmaking in Post-Mao China* (Gloucestershire, England: Clarendon, 1999).

45. See the 18th NPC special report by the CCP's Xinhuanet (CCP's official media) in English at http://news.xinhuanet.com/english/2007-10/15/content_6883135.htm (accessed February 22, 2012).

46. See "The Central Administrative System," available at http://www.china.org.cn/english/MATERIAL/28847.htm (accessed February 22, 2012).

47. See "The Local Administrative System," available at http://www.china.org.cn/english/Political/28842.htm (accessed February 22, 212).

48. The following section relies on information available to the authors in English. For updated information on China's Judiciary, see http://www.china.org.cn/english/Judiciary/25025.htm (accessed February 22, 2012).

49. To understand the history of China's criminal justice system and its practice, see Chen Jianfu, *Chinese Law: Towards an Understanding of Chinese Law, Its Nature and Development* (The Hague: Kluwer Law International, 1999); Harold M. Tanner, *Strike Hard! Anti-Crime Campaigns and Chinese Criminal Justice, 1979–1985* (Ithaca, NY: East Asia Program, Cornell University, 1999); Ronald C. Keith and Zhiqiu Lin, *New Crime in China: Public Order and Human Rights* (London: Routledge, 2006); Stanley B. Lubman, *Bird in a Cage: Legal Reform in China after Mao* (Stanford, CA: Stanford University Press, 1999); Richard J. Terrill, "China" in *World Criminal Justice Systems: A Survey* (6th ed.) (Newark, NJ: Lexis Nexis, 2007), Chapter 7 (pp. 575-677); and Ronald J. Troyer, John P. Clark, and Dean G. Rojek, eds., *Social Control in the People's Republic China* (New York: Praeger, 1989).

50. An English version is available at http://www.cecc.gov/pages/selectLaws/criminalJustice/index.php (accessed February 22, 2012).

51. For more information, see http://www.china.org.cn/english/Judiciary/25025.htm (accessed February 22, 2012); Yingyi Situ and Weizheng Liu, "The Criminal Justice System of China," Zheng Wang, "The Police System in the People's Republic of China," and Robert Davidson and Zheng Wang, "The Court System in the People's Republic of China with a Case Study of a Criminal Trial" in Obi N. Ignatius Ebbe (ed.), *Comparative and International Criminal Justice Systems: Policing, Judiciary, and Corrections* (Boston: Butterworth-Heinemann, 2000); Zou Keyuan, "Towards the Rule of Law: An Overview of China's Legal Reform" in Wang Gungwu and John Wong (eds.), *China: Two Decades of Reform and Change* (Singapore: Singapore University Press, 1999); Jianan Guo et al., "World Factbook of Criminal Justice Systems: China" (1993) from the U.S. Department of Justice website, available at http://bjs.ojp.usdoj.gov/content/pub/ascii/WFBCJCHI.TXT (accessed February 22, 2012).

52. The following discussion draws mostly on Lubman, *Bird in a Cage* (1999), Davison and Wang, "The Court System in the People's Republic of China" (2000), Tanner,

Strike Hard! (1999), and Ronald C. Brown, *Understanding Chinese Courts and Legal Process: Law with Chinese Characteristics* (Boston: Kluwer Law International, 1997).

53. An English version of revisions of the Organic Law of the People's Courts is available at http://www.novexcn.com/organic_law.html (accessed February 23, 2012).

54. See "Mediation System," available at http://www.china.org.cn/english/Judiciary/31185.htm (accessed February 23, 2012).

55. For information on the Law on People's Mediation, see the U.S. Library of Congress, "China: New Law on Mediation," available at http://www.loc.gov/lawweb/servlet/lloc_news?disp3_l205402221_text (accessed February 22, 2012), and the section "Mediation as a Vehicle To Maintaining Social Stability" in the US-CECC Annual Report 2011, available at http://www.cecc.gov/pages/annualRpt/annualRpt11/AR11Exec.pdf (accessed February, 16, 2012), pp.182–183.

56. For a description of China's trial system, see http://www.china.org.cn/english/Judiciary/31280.htm (accessed February 22, 2012) and Chen, *Chinese Law* (1999), Lubman, *Bird in a Cage* (1999), and Davidson and Wong, "The Court System in the People's Republic of China" (2000).

57. This section relies on Chen, *Chinese Law* (1999). An English version of the 1997 revised Criminal Law is available at http://www.cecc.gov/pages/newLaws/criminal-LawENG.php (accessed February 23, 2012).

58. "Laws of the People's Republic of China," available at http://www.asianlii.org/cn/legis/cen/laws/clotproc361/ (accessed April 23, 2014).

58. The following description relies on Dorothy H. Bracey, "Corrections in the People's Republic of China," in Troyer, Clark, and Rojek (eds.), *Social Control in the People's Republic of China* (1989), as well as Tanner, *Strike Hard!* (1999) and "System for Judicial Administration," available at http://www.china.org.cn/english/Judiciary/31137.htm (accessed February 23, 2012).

59. For a study of China's hard labor camps, see Harry Hongda Wu, *Laogai: The Chinese Gulag* (Boulder: Westview, 1992).

60. See the US-CECC Annual Report 2005, available at http://www.cecc.gov/pages/annualRpt/annualRpt05/CECCannRpt2005.pdf (accessed May 22, 2012), p. 89.

61. See the US-CECC Annual Report 2004, available at http://www.cecc.gov/pages/annualRpt/annualRpt04/CECCannRpt2004.pdf (accessed May 22, 2012), p. 75.

62. See Lubman, *Bird in a Cage* (1999), pp. 156–157, and the US-CECC Annual Report 2004.

63. See the US-CECC Annual Report 2007, available at http://www.cecc.gov/pages/annualRpt/annualRpt07/CECCannRpt2007.pdf (accessed May 22, 2012), p. 47.

64. See the US-CECC Annual Report 2008, available at http://www.cecc.gov/pages/annualRpt/annualRpt08/CECCannRpt2008.pdf (accessed May 22, 2012), p. 39.

65. See the US-CECC Annual Report 2004, available at http://www.cecc.gov/pages/annualRpt/annualRpt04/CECCannRpt2004.pdf (accessed May 22, 2012).

66. "China Prosecutes 30,788 officials in 2004." *China Daily*, March 9, 2005, available at http://www.chinadaily.com.cn/english/doc/2005-03/09/content_423329.htm (accessed May 22, 2012).

67. See Amnesty International, *Death Sentences and Executions 2010*, available at http://www.amnesty.org/en/library/asset/ACT50/001/2011/en/ea1b6b25-a62a-4074-927d-ba51e88df2e9/act500012011en.pdf (accessed February 2012), p. 19.

68. See Human Rights Watch, "Reeducation through Labor in China," available at http://www.hrw.org/campaigns/china-98/laojiao.htm (accessed February 22, 2012).

69. For more detail regarding this criticism, see Human Rights in China, "Reeducation through Labor (RTL): A Summary of Regulatory Issues and Concerns," available at http://hrichina.org/sites/default/files/oldsite/PDFs/Reports/HRIC-RTL.pdf (accessed May 25, 2012), pp. 3–5.

CHAPTER 6

Healthcare Policy

LEARNING OBJECTIVES

- Evaluate access to healthcare.
- Identify policy actors involved in healthcare policy making.
- Differentiate between health-care programs.
- Understand the implementation of healthcare policy under federalism.

- Compare the Patient Protection and Affordable Care Act with the Canada Health Act.
- Examine problems and challenges related to healthcare policy.

Healthcare policy is considered globally to be one of the foremost policy areas of concern. A World Bank study shows that there are generally two urgent healthcare policy concerns around the world.[1] First, there is concern about the need for policies to provide urgent treatments for an uncountable number of physical health problems caused by newly emerged or discovered epidemics and other kinds of diseases, including various types of cancers, HIV/AIDS, bird flu pandemic, and so forth. This concern is on healthcare agendas not only in poorly industrialized countries in Sub-Saharan Africa and South Asia, but also in industrialized countries such as the United States, Canada, and Japan. Second, there is concern about the need for policies to address healthcare crises that are associated with sharply rising healthcare costs and the declining quality of access to medical services. This concern appears often in public discussions in countries such as the United States, Canada, and Japan, for example.

In this chapter, we explore the latter concern focusing on skyrocketing healthcare costs and the declining access to high-quality medical treatments in the United States and Canada.[2] As frequently stated in public debates over healthcare reform, Americans have the most expensive healthcare system in the world; total annual expenditures on healthcare in 2012 reached $8,895 per person (47.7 percent from government revenues and 52.3 percent from private insurance and out-of-pocket), or 17.4 percent of the gross domestic product (GDP). Canadians paid only $4,363 per person (70.6 percent from government revenues and 29.4 percent from private insurance and out-of-pocket), or 11.4 percent, of GDP in 2009.[3] The average for the 30 members of the Organization for Economic Cooperation and Development (OECD) was $3,361, or 8.03 percent of GDP, in 2009 (72.2 percent from government revenues and 27.8 percent from private insurance and out-of-pocket).[4] Since the American healthcare system is the most expensive in the world, healthcare cost reduction has been one of the largest concerns in the United States.

In addition, there is concern in the United States about equal access to healthcare and fair coverage of health insurance for all Americans.[5] A 2009 CBS News/New York Times Poll reports that 85 percent of Americans felt that the American healthcare system needs fundamental changes (51 percent) or to be completely rebuilt (34 percent). The same study unveils that 65 percent of Americans saw "providing coverage for uninsured" as a more serious issue than "keeping health care costs down."[6] According to the U.S. Census Bureau, in 2010, more than 256.2 million Americans (83.7 percent) had some healthcare coverage either through tax-subsidized employer-based insurance, other individual-paid private insurance, or publicly funded insurance such as Medicare or Medicaid; 49.9 million Americans (16.3 percent) were uninsured.[7] As we shall discuss in the following section, there are two distinct policy issues related to uninsured and underinsured populations. Although the equity problem for uninsured Americans has generated larger policy demands for a universal healthcare system with much attention focused on the Canadian healthcare system as a possible model to follow. In fact, in recent surveys, 49 percent of Americans favored the Canadian healthcare system, and 34 percent considered the American healthcare system better than the healthcare systems in European countries or Japan.[8]

Interestingly, the majority of Canadians continue to prefer the Canadian healthcare system despite persistent dissatisfaction with a number of issues, such as increasing healthcare costs and declining quality of and accessibility to publicly funded healthcare services under the **Canada Health Act (CHA)**.[9] Such views are consistent with the Canadian government's concern about healthcare reform, one of its policy priorities.[10] In the debate over reforming Canada's healthcare system, Canadian policymakers and experts have examined American-style healthcare policy (i.e., flexible private insurance) as one of their alternatives; nevertheless, it seems that Canadians do not favor the American healthcare system in comparison with European healthcare systems.[11] As we shall discuss later, the reasons for Canadians' choice regarding their future healthcare system are deeply embedded in Canadian history, culture, and political and economic settings. Similarly, Americans' choice of managed care and other programs (e.g., Medicare and Medicaid) is deeply rooted in American history, culture, and political and economic settings. Thus, it is difficult to say which healthcare policy is better.[12]

This chapter uses both the historical and institutional perspectives to compare the U.S. and Canadian healthcare systems and policies. Underlying both of these perspectives are certain elements of their respective dominant social paradigms. Specifically, the United States has a much stronger stance toward free market capitalism and individuality. Thus, the U.S. system is based mostly on private companies providing insurance and services. Canada has less of a stance toward free market capitalism and is more about providing services for everyone, rather than just individually. Therefore, we see the Canadian system strives for universal coverage and healthcare that is provided by public and nonprofit entities.

We will also deal with contemporary issues regarding both the American and Canadian healthcare systems, identify policy actors involved in policymaking for both systems, look at the healthcare programs for each country, and address some problems and challenges related to healthcare policy in the United States and Canada. The chapter will conclude with a comparison of the healthcare systems of both countries.

The United States

As noted earlier, in 2010, 83.7 percent of Americans had some healthcare coverage ranging from tax-subsidized employer-based insurance and other **individual-paid private insurance** to **publicly funded insurance** such as Medicare or Medicaid, while 16.3 percent, including women and children, were uninsured. Although much public attention focuses on extending health-care access to those who do not have insurance, issues regarding publicly funded universal health insurance are very complex. As we shall discuss in the following section, Medicare and Medicaid as a single payer and publicly funded health insurance have provided extensive health insurance coverage for Americans (the elderly, poor, and disabled) who meet certain criteria. This is one of the reasons why governmental healthcare spending has been extremely high in the United States. The majority of ordinary Americans have 'limited' access to a variety of healthcare services under a **managed healthcare** system providing **tax-subsidized, employer-based insurance**. There are variations in obtaining healthcare services and prescription drug coverage because of the diversity in different types of managed care systems. Privately funded health insurance is very expensive, yet it does not cover eye care, dental care, some specialist services, and so forth.

Before examining publicly funded insurance and various types of managed healthcare insurance that are publicly controlled but privately paid, we will briefly illustrate how so-called ordinary workers with managed healthcare insurance have access to healthcare in daily life. Although it is difficult to generalize about the "ordinary," or the "average," worker in the United States, we illustrate the case of standard employees who work for one of the three major automobile companies.

In the United States, those who have full-time employee status with an automobile manufacturer can obtain an employer-paid health insurance. Although healthcare packages vary from time to time because of prior-negotiated deals between the automobile makers and the United Auto Workers (UAW), each employee must select one health insurance plan from the prior-negotiated deals and pay some premium for her or his selected insurance plan beyond the employer-paid cost.

When employees or members of their families need medical treatment, they first must meet their family practitioner who is their **primary care physician (PCP)**. The employees present their health insurance card issued by their insurance company to their PCP, who serves as a gatekeeper within the insurance network that the employees selected. When they receive a service from their PCP, they must make a co-payment that is determined by their selected insurance plan for insured services. If their PCP determines that they need access to some specialists, hospitals, diagnostic testing, or prescription drugs, then the insured employees may choose those services or drugs among those specified within their selected insurance network.

For example, when patients have severe back pain, they first must see their PCP for screening. After diagnosis by X-ray or any other method, which occasionally requires going to another facility, their PCP may prescribe pain relief medication that needs to be obtained from a registered drugstore as well as two weeks of physical therapy at still another facility. In the case of physical therapy, patients must contact a physical therapist within their insurance network and present their PCP's prescription and insurance card to the physical therapist's office. Although patients can see a physical therapist outside their insurance network, their insurance company will most likely reject their request for coverage or reimbursement of any cost that patients paid to the therapist as **fee-for-Service (FFS)** out-of-pocket. For advanced and expensive diagnosis of severe back pain, a PCP may prescribe highly advanced tests such as magnetic resonance imaging (MRI) or cat scan (CT) at a nearby hospital within a patient's insurance network. Sometimes, patients may need to provide a co-payment for an advanced diagnosis, which depends on their insurance package.

When patients need some urgent care during holidays, they are asked to visit the emergency room (or urgent care center) in a hospital located nearest to their home. In the hospital, they must present their insurance card and be registered in the hospital medical system. After getting necessary treatment, they are asked to pay at an accounting department some cost that their insurance does not cover. In most cases, if patients are visiting another state or country when they need emergency care, they have a certain amount of time to notify their local PPC in order to be eligible for their insurance coverage. Although uninsured individuals may receive treatment at any public or private emergency room, the cost of treatment is higher in private hospitals than it is in public hospitals.

As ordinary automobile workers have employer-paid health insurance, they can benefit from highly advanced (and expensive) medical care in the United States. Yet, there are limits. For instance, patients with employer-paid insurance have limited access to fair and adequate services, including some specialists or advanced treatments, and there are other restrictions.

The situation that we described for full-time employees who are fully insured and have a certain level of access to healthcare also applies to healthcare services for the elderly, poor, and disabled Americans under Medicare or Medicaid. One of the most intensive current concerns in regard to healthcare policy, however, was the growing lack of accessibility to healthcare services for uninsured Americans.

In order to deal with healthcare costs and unequal access to healthcare, discussion focused for years on needed changes in the American healthcare system. Advocates of a business approach to healthcare argued that, in order to reduce healthcare costs, managed healthcare benefited more Americans than the fee-for-Service (FFS).[13] Unlike the FFS, managed healthcare is designed to control healthcare expenditures, provide efficient services, and introduce a customer service orientation to healthcare. Yet, managed healthcare did not benefit uninsured Americans because it presupposed that patients had some sort of employer-paid health insurance.

There has been public debate over universal healthcare for uninsured Americans through public funding since the 1960s.[14] The heart of this debate centered on whether healthcare should be a purely public good provided by the government when private mechanisms fail to deliver it equitably. Americans were reluctant to accept a universal government-provided healthcare system because traditionally they were skeptical of any government interference with their individual rights and freedoms. According to 2000 National Election Studies data, 56 percent of Americans said they were uncertain about or objected to health insurance provided by the federal government.[15] Interestingly, almost 10 years later, this uncertainty seemed to change. According to a 2009 CBS News/New York Times Poll, 72 percent of Americans were in favor of a government-administered health insurance plan, similar to Medicare, as an option to compete with private health insurance plans, whereas 20 percent were opposed to it. Also, 50 percent and 59 percent of Americans, respectively, said that the government would do better in "providing medical coverage" and "holding down costs" than private insurance companies. Furthermore, 85 percent of Americans thought that the American healthcare system needed serious reform.[16]

Recognition of the need for healthcare reform led to the **Patient Protection and Affordable Care Act (PPACA)** that President Barack Obama signed into law in 2010. Yet, despite increased public healthcare spending and coverage under the PPACA, many Americans who have no employer-based insurance and cannot afford private insurance remain uninsured because they are not eligible for any publicly funded insurance.[17] As of this writing, 7 million Americans have signed up for what is often referred to as "Obamacare."

Next, we will identify policy actors involved in American healthcare policymaking. We then will look at American healthcare programs and address some problems and challenges related to those programs.

Policy Actors

Historically, healthcare in the United States was delivered via public and private institutions without central planning or coordination. There are many actors who have been significantly involved in shaping contemporary healthcare policy.[18] These include Congress, every president as well as his aides in the White House, and bureaucracies at the federal level, state and local authorities, and various interest groups such as the American Medical Association (AMA) and drug and medical equipment industries.

The process of healthcare policy making, like any other policy-making process in the United States, is framed by a constitutional presidential system with checks and balances as well as a separation of powers between legislative, executive, and judicial branches of government. Furthermore, it is shaped by the dynamics of federalism, which divides authority between the federal government and state governments.

The Legislative Branch   With regard to healthcare policy making, the legislative branch performs an important role in adopting and rejecting healthcare policy proposals and in evaluating programs such as Medicare and Medicaid. As Woodrow Wilson wrote, "Congress in its committee-rooms is Congress at work."[19] Committees and subcommittees in both the Senate and the House of Representatives are major actors in the policy-making process. Congressional committees are very influential with regard to legislative agendas and decisions on policy proposals. Their influence tends to extend beyond the legislative branch through congressional oversight or review of policies and programs as they are implemented by the executive branch—by federal departments, agencies, and commissions. There are a total of eight committees and six subcommittees with significant influence on healthcare legislation.

Key members on these committees and subcommittees exercise considerable power in reviewing, reevaluating, revising, rewriting, and adopting or rejecting policy proposals sponsored by members of Congress. When it comes to healthcare legislation, 171 organizations and interest groups, such as the American Medical Association and the American Association of Retired Persons (AARP), are very active in healthcare advocacy and work to influence committee decisions.[20] For instance, a major reason for the failure of the Clinton Administration's American Health Security Act was "the biggest-scale lobbying effort that has ever been mounted on any single piece of legislation—both in terms of dollars spent and people engaged" by coalitions of numerous healthcare interest groups, including the AMA.[21]

The Executive Branch   The primary responsibility for the promotion of public health in the United States rests with the **Department of Health and Human Services (DHHS)** and the **Department of Veterans Affairs (DVA)**. The DHHS is a core federal agency in charge of healthcare policy provisions. The main objectives of the DHHS are to deal with (1) diseases and health conditions; (2) safety and wellness; (3) drug, food safety, and dietary issues; (4) disaster and emergencies; (5) families and children; (6) aging; and (7) specific populations. In order to achieve these goals, the DHHS houses 11 agencies.[22] The Social Security Administration (SSA) was an agency under the DHHS until 1995.[23] On August 15, 1994, President Clinton signed legislation to make the SSA an independent agency, which took effect on March 31, 1995.

Among the 11 agencies under the DHHS, our discussion on health insurance will focus on the Centers for Medicare and Medicaid Services (CMS).[24] Besides the CMS, we often hear about the Food and Drug Administration (FDA),[25] whose main function is to set safety standards on food and medicine.

Established as an agency within the Department of Agriculture by the Pure Food and Drug Act of 1902, the FDA has been under the DHHS since 1980.

Another important agency under the DHHS is the National Institutes of Health (NIH).[26] Founded in 1887 and consisting of 25 separate institutes and centers, the NIH is responsible for conducting federal health science research. The main purpose of research conducted by the NIH and its affiliates is to determine the causes and cures of diseases as well as prevention methods. The NIH relies on universities, schools, and other nonfederal institutes to assist in conducting research through grants.

The Centers for Disease Control and Prevention (CDC), established in 1946, is the primary agency responsible not only for research but more importantly for the prevention and control of infectious diseases and epidemics, including HIV/AIDS and sexually transmitted diseases (STDs).[27] The mission of the CDC has expanded over the years to include efforts to prevent job-related hazards and environmental health threats, among other things.

The Department of Veterans Affairs (DVA), through the Veterans Health Administration (VHA), provides services to more than 23 million veterans. It operates the Veterans Healthcare System (VHS) comprising 152 medical centers and nearly 1,400 community-based outpatient clinics, as well as community living centers, Vet Centers, nursing homes, and residential rehabilitation treatment programs.[28] The purpose of the VHS is to provide low-cost healthcare to war veterans in need of medical and social services. Those with disabilities and diseases acquired while in the armed forces receive medical care that is typically free of charge. Also, dependents of veterans who died or were disabled during military service can receive healthcare through the VHS. The Veterans Health Care Eligibility Reform Act of 1996 expanded health benefits for veterans. Besides the VHS, the Department of Defense (DoD) has provided a healthcare program for active duty personnel, retired service members, National Guard/Reserve members, and their families, survivors, and others entitled to DoD medical care. [29] More specifically, since February 1998, the TRICARE Management Activity (TMA) leadership has managed the **TRICARE** healthcare program.[30] TRICARE is the most important benefit for military personnel and their family members because it provides comprehensive healthcare coverage. It also offers healthcare programs for retired service members, including TRICARE Pharmacy, TRICARE Dental (United Concordia), and TRICARE Life.

State Governments   Since the 1980s, when the federal government faced a massive fiscal constraint with a budget deficit of 3 trillion dollars, state governments have become significant policy actors in healthcare.[31] Not only are state governments responsible for health departments, hospitals, and mental health institutions, but they also have discretion in delivering Medicaid and the State Children's Health Insurance Program (SCHIP) as well as setting eligibility standards for prescription drug coverage under the 2003 Medical Modernization Act. In addition, state governments have regulated managed care organizations (MCOs) to enhance healthcare provisions for working-age families. Every state has passed legislation for controlling and monitoring the managed healthcare system. As of today, state legislators are trying to reform healthcare programs such as Medicaid and Managed Care through new legislation for minimizing the federal government's role in healthcare while introducing free market principles of consumer choice and competition.[32]

Interest Groups   Interest groups are powerful actors that shape healthcare policy in the United States. From 1997 to 2002, there were 171 organizations and groups actively involved in the healthcare policy-making process, seeking influence through lobbying and financial contributions to specific parties or individuals.[33] Today, the number is undoubtedly higher. The most powerful healthcare lobbying group in the United States is the **American Medical Association (AMA),**[34] the principal agent for protecting physicians' rights and benefits. When Medicare was passed by Congress in 1964–65, the AMA spent $1.2 million to fight against it because it would introduce federal control over healthcare delivery. Similarly, when the Clinton Administration sent their comprehensive healthcare reform plan to Congress, the AMA, joined by other lobbying groups, mounted significant resistance to the proposal.

The **American Association of Retired Persons (AARP)** has become a powerful healthcare lobbying group advocating enhanced insurance benefits for elderly citizens under Medicare.[35] The AARP put in significant effort to make sure that prescription drug coverage for people at the age of 65 and above would be included in the 2003 Medicare Modernization Act (MMA). Given the growing population of elderly citizens in the United States, the AARP's role in healthcare policymaking can be expected to increase.

Another significant actor in health policymaking is the **Pharmaceutical Research and Manufacturers of America (PhRMA)**, which represents drug manufacturers in the United States.[36] The PhRMA and companies it represents opposed the bill for the 2003 Medicare Modernization Act because they feared price controls and monitoring by the Centers for Medicare and Medicaid Services and the Food and Drug Administration. Through massive campaign contributions to elected officials, the PhRMA had successfully pushed for the elimination of various regulations when the MMA took effect in 2005.

Healthcare Programs

American public policy delivery of healthcare services relies primarily on the market. A variety of private businesses (i.e., private healthcare facilities, insurance companies, drug companies) offer numerous services to customers. For several decades, the U.S. government has been increasingly involved in the delivery of healthcare by creating rules or allocating financial resources in pursuit of three objectives: (1) to make healthcare accessible to the poor, young, and elderly—populations that are unable to receive employer-paid health insurance or themselves pay for their healthcare; (2) to ensure high-quality healthcare for those who cannot pay as well as those who can pay; and (3) to support research on innovative healthcare solutions and technological improvements that might take much longer without government initiatives supporting research. In this section, we will focus on pursuit of the first objective through publicly funded health insurance programs known as Medicare and Medicaid.[37]

Medicare   Medicare began in 1965 as a supplement to the Social Security Act of 1935. Directly under federal administration, Medicare provides prepaid hospital insurance and low-cost voluntary medical insurance for the elderly. Since its inception, Medicare has been broadened to include coverage for anyone of any age with a permanent disability, diabetes, or advanced kidney disease, which is also known as end stage renal disease. In 2010, 43.3 million U.S. citizens (14.5 percent) were enrolled in a Medicare program.[38]

After several incremental reforms and extensions since 1965, Medicare currently consists of four parts.[39] Hospital insurance (Part A), the standard provision of Medicare, covers a broad range of hospital and post-hospital services, excluding ordinary nursing home or routine home care, with some deductible and coinsurance. A *deductible* is a set dollar amount that a patient must pay directly before insurance benefits begin; *coinsurance (co-pay)* is a percentage of a medical bill that a patient must pay directly after meeting the deductible. Medical insurance (Part B) provides supplemental insurance for seniors age 65 and older. Services covered include physicians' services, outpatient hospital services, home healthcare, and other medical services.

Medicare Advantage Plans (Part C) were created by the Balanced Budget Act of 1997. These plans are available to people covered under Medicare Parts A and B. Among the plans that eligible Medicare beneficiaries can choose from to receive all their Medicare healthcare coverage, including coverage for prescription drugs, are Medicare Health Maintenance Organizations (HMOs), Preferred Provider Organizations (PPOs), Private Fee-for-Service Plans, and Medicare Special Needs Plans.

In 2003, the Medicare Prescription Drug, Improvement, and Medicare Modernization Act (MMA), passed amid much concern about increasing costs of prescription drugs, created the prescription drug coverage program (Part D). Fully implemented in January 2006, this program offers comprehensive prescription drug coverage and subsidies for low-income citizens who have no other coverage for prescription drugs.

Medicaid   Medicaid was established under Title XIX of the Social Security Act of 1965 to provide health insurance and medical services to low-income individuals and families. Medicaid enrollments grew from about 43 million in 2000 to about 62 million in 2009, and payments increased from $168 billion to $318 billion.[40] As of this writing, with the passage of the Affordable Care Act, precise Medicaid enrollment figures are difficult to determine. Unlike Medicare, Medicaid is a federal–state cooperative healthcare program, which means that the federal government sets general standards for healthcare available under Medicaid while states and local authorities determine eligibility and benefit levels. According to federal standards, Medicaid is available to:[41]

- Low-income families with children
- Recipients of Supplementary Security Income (SSI)
- Infants born to Medicaid-eligible pregnant women for up to the first year of life

- Children under the age of 6 and pregnant women whose income is at or below 133 percent of the federal poverty line
- Certain Medicare beneficiaries

Guided by federal standards, state governments can establish their own criteria for Medicaid eligibility; decide on benefits packages and determine the type, amount, duration, and scope of services; set provider payment rates; and administer their own Medicaid programs. Thus, it is not surprising that states not only differ in their Medicaid enrollments and payments but also in their payments per individual enrolled in Medicaid. For instance, in 2009, 1,588,000 people in Arizona were enrolled in Medicaid, with $8,617 million paid, but in Michigan, 1,890,000 people were enrolled in Medicaid, with $10,171 million paid.[42]

As a supplement to Medicaid, the **State Children's Health Insurance Program (SCHIP)** took effect in 1997 to provide medical coverage for children who might not be eligible under prevalent Medicaid provisions. Funded mostly by the federal government, the SCHIP is designed and administered by states. In 2010, the SCHIP paid $7,913 million covering healthcare for 7.7 million children.[43]

The Managed Healthcare System   In order to reduce medical costs and to increase fairness and efficiency in U.S. healthcare, policymakers have been trying to design and implement new programs, make new rules, and establish/reorganize government agencies. Of particular interest in such healthcare reforms has been a managed healthcare system.[44] The idea of managed healthcare emerged in the United States as part of a national health insurance proposal under the Nixon Administration. This idea became policy when Congress passed the **Health Maintenance Organization (HMO) Act of 1973** creating a managed healthcare system with health maintenance organizations (HMOs). The HMO Act makes it possible to obtain grants and loans to start or expand HMOs, removes some state restrictions on HMOs, and requires employers with 25 or more employees to offer, on request, certified HMO options. Under the managed healthcare system, the federal government, employers, and private insurers attempt to hold down medical costs by using selective contacting—requiring patients to see only certain providers—through **health maintenance organizations (HMOs), preferred provider organizations (PPOs)**, or **independent practice associations (IPAs)**.

There are two ways in which HMOs and PPOs are expected to hold down medical costs. First, HMOs and PPOs create networks of preferred gatekeepers (hospitals and doctors) who have been prepaid for medical services. This eliminates the fee-for-service system in which professional healthcare providers established their own office, saw only their own patients, and charged a separate fee for each individual service performed. If a patient saw more than one provider, the patient would receive a separate bill for each service from each provider. Unlike professional healthcare providers under the FFS system, preferred gatekeepers or primary care physicians must see patients first to give a referral for patients to see specialists. This strategy is supposed to reduce medical costs by limiting the utilization of costly and unnecessary specialists. Second, as costs are prepaid under insurance coverage through HMOs and PPOs, there is no incentive for doctors or hospitals to perform unnecessary services or tests. This strategy is supposed to reduce medical costs by improving efficiency.

Implementing the managed healthcare system has raised several concerns.[45] Although managed healthcare helps to slow down the rapid rise of healthcare costs for some insurance providers, it limits the quality of healthcare by restricting the choice of specialists whom consumers can meet besides their PCPs and prepaid healthcare providers under their HMOs or PPOs. Individual primary care physicians limit the number of patients because prepaid insurance removes the fee-for-service incentive for physicians. Consequently, many patients who have relatively minor illnesses or injuries but need urgent treatment are delivered to emergency rooms before meeting their PCPs, and those in emergency rooms have to wait in long lines to receive necessary treatments. Some patients who need intensive treatments can see only specialists on a predetermined and restricted list of specialists within a given provider network under HMO and PPC insurance coverage. Thus, despite what they want or need, patients lose the opportunity to get proper treatments from their physicians of choice even though they have adequate insurance.

Some of the issues raising concern about managed healthcare became worse throughout the 1980s and 1990s. In response, many states passed a patient and provider "bill-of-rights" to address alleged abuses by physicians and insurance companies.[46] Bills discussed in Congress in 2004 to protect consumers under managed healthcare plans and other healthcare coverage, specifically the Bipartisan Patient Protection Act in the Senate and the Patients' Bill of Rights Act in the House of Representatives, never became law.[47]

Because managed healthcare is based on employer-subsidized health insurance, there has been concern about the loss of health insurance coverage for those who leave or lose their jobs. Such concern has led to policies to continue and protect health benefits for employees and their families under the Consolidated Omnibus Budget Reconciliation Act (COBRA), passed in 1986,[48] and the Health Insurance and Portability Accountability Act (HIPAA), passed in 1996.[49]

The Clinton Healthcare Reform Proposal of 1993   One of the most ambitious attempts to reform the American healthcare system was the Health Security Act (HSA), a proposal that the Clinton Administration submitted to Congress in 1993.[50] The Clinton proposal, which failed to win congressional support to be passed into law, was a very complex 1,342-page bill intended to cover all Americans under universal healthcare with mandatory enrollment in health plans regulated by a huge centralized bureaucracy. Key elements of the Clinton proposal included a standardized government health benefit package, employer mandates to provide the standardized package while paying 80 percent of the costs, fee controls for doctors and caps on public and private health insurance spending, as well as a national health board to oversee the system.[51]

Although officials claimed that the proposal would certainly work and save money, many Americans thought that the Clinton proposal was overwhelmingly complex and tried to change the entire healthcare system regardless of whether or not the proposed reforms were going to be workable and effective. Many Americans worried that the Clinton proposal asked them to pay more for minimal benefits because it limited their choice of health services and imposed caps on insurance coverage. Reinforcing public worries, Donna E. Shalala, Secretary of Health and Human Services under the Clinton Administration, testified before the Senate Finance Committee that "under the Clinton Plan 40 percent of all Americans with insurance would be paying more for their health care premiums."[52] Due to the complexity and unpopularity of the Clinton proposal, along with a large campaign against it that was organized by coalitions led by the AMA and other interest groups, committees in both the Senate and the House of Representatives neglected the proposal, letting it die in committee. In the aftermath of the Clinton Administration's failed attempt at fundamental and comprehensive healthcare reform, the federal government made incremental changes to ongoing healthcare programs, insurance plans, and managed healthcare.[53]

The Patient Protection and Affordable Care Act (PPACA) of 2010

Healthcare reform was a key part of Barack Obama's 2008 presidential campaign, and the expansive PPACA is the product of over a year of deliberations between the president, members of Congress, and special-interest groups and lobbyists. It was signed into law by President Barack Obama in 2010. The goals of the PPACA are to improve the quality of healthcare in the United States, lower skyrocketing healthcare costs, and expand healthcare coverage to all Americans. The PPACA consists of ten titles and relies on staggered implementation, which means that reforms are spread out, with some taking place immediately after the act was passed, and others not taking effect until 2014.

The PPACA is very extensive and will affect many facets of healthcare in the United States. Challenged mainly over its mandate that all U.S. citizens and legal residents, with few exceptions, have health insurance and can be subject to a tax penalty for noncompliance, the PPACA was upheld by the U.S. Supreme Court in June 2012.

Problems and Challenges

In the United States, healthcare reform remains a top national priority expressed in public debate and policy proposals. As we think about healthcare reform, let us consider some key problems and challenges of concern regarding the contemporary U.S. healthcare system.

The three most important policy concerns in regard to healthcare are costs, access, and quality. Higher costs can make access difficult, yet high-quality standards increase costs. The challenge for policymakers is to balance all of these concerns. Because age projections indicate that one-third of the American population will reach the age of 65 within the next 30 years, and healthcare costs are expected to continue rising, there is significant concern about the future of Medicare and Medicaid funding. Furthermore, a 2010 study found that, in comparison with six other countries (Australia, Canada, Germany, the Netherlands, New Zealand, and the United Kingdom), the United States had the highest health expenditures per capita but ranks second-lowest in regard to quality care.[54]

Critics of Medicare claim that it provides only a minimal amount of healthcare coverage. Benefits such as vision and dental care are usually not offered to Medicare enrollees. Although Medicare pays for a limited time of care in hospitals or nursing homes, there are still significant costs for patients who need long-term hospital or nursing home care. As mentioned earlier, there are a deductible and coinsurance for hospital care, and expenses for ordinary nursing home or routine home care are not covered.

For Medicaid, coordinating efforts to contain rising healthcare costs and reducing healthcare fraud and abuse is complicated by variations in the funding and implementation of Medicaid across states. As noted before, under general standards set by the federal government, state governments can decide on their own criteria for Medicaid enrollments and payments.

Evaluations of both Medicare and Medicaid point to fraud and abuse by medical offices. According to the DHHS, over $100 billion is estimated to be lost annually due to fraud and abuse of Medicare and Medicaid.[55] Fraud and abuse come in the form of practitioners charging for unnecessary procedures or for procedures that were never done. Additionally, evidence indicates that Medicare and Medicaid have been billed by providers not qualified for the services they are charging for and for patients not eligible for services provided. This is in spite of the 1982 Tax Equity and Fiscal Responsibility Act that created Peer Review Organizations (PROs) designed to monitor quality of care and detect fraud. After HIPAA was passed in 1996, the **Health Care Fraud and Abuse Control (HCFAC) program** was created in 1998 to combat fraud and abuse of Medicare and Medicaid.[56] The HCFAC program is designed to coordinate federal, state, and local law enforcement activities with respect to healthcare fraud and abuse.

Education about proper nutrition and regular exercise is another challenge to healthcare. Although a central objective of healthcare reform under the PPACA (Obamacare) is to provide comprehensive and affordable healthcare services for all Americans, it also needs to be realized that people's health may benefit significantly by changing their diet and exercising. Everyone could have access to free healthcare anytime they want it, but this still might not save people from obesity-related deaths. In a similar vein, we know that smoking cigarettes may reduce a human life span by 20 to 30 years. So spending money to keep teenagers from smoking would be an excellent healthcare investment. Yet this kind of preventative measure is rarely included in health policy legislation. Campaigns and initiatives by the DHHS and other agencies and actors, including local governments, to prevent health hazards that may require expensive medical treatment are significant contributions to reducing healthcare costs while creating a more efficient and effective healthcare system.[57]

In addition to costs, access to high-quality healthcare is of major concern to policymakers in the United States. According to the U.S. Census Bureau, in 2010, when 83.7 percent of Americans were covered by some form of health insurance, 16.3 percent of Americans were still uninsured. [58] There is a large disparity between those who have access to it and those who do not. Despite programs like Medicare and Medicaid, people who are older or poor, and especially those who live in rural areas or in low-income urban households, may not receive high-quality healthcare. With rising costs and declining benefits, many Americans are facing a reduction in adequate health services. Yet, attempts to move in the direction of a national health insurance plan have been met with much opposition.

Opposition to nationalized health insurance, such as that in Canada, rests to a large extent on the view that making more people eligible for health insurance will lead to rising healthcare costs that will be shifted to taxpayers. Healthcare costs are already on the rise for several reasons. As medical technology and various types of surgical techniques become more sophisticated, greater capital investments are needed. In addition, medical services (e.g., intensive hospital care and long-term nursing home/facilities care) are afflicted by a shortage of qualified medical personnel, resulting in higher labor costs to attract medical service professionals. Furthermore, healthcare costs increase with rising administration costs in private clinics and large hospitals. Attempts to minimize healthcare costs may conflict with attempts to provide equal access to high-quality healthcare under a national health insurance plan if it is expected that such a plan will require more government bureaucracy and more government spending funded by increased taxation. Adding to worries about rising healthcare costs are concerns that a national health insurance plan, through more government control over healthcare delivery, will reduce freedom (a key American value) in regard to choices of healthcare coverage and providers.

Canada

When asked about universal access to publicly funded health insurance, many Americans think of the Canadian healthcare system as a possible model for reforming the U.S. healthcare system. Although many politicians and experts have referred to the Canadian healthcare system as a good example of "no-user fees" and "cost-sharing," it is not well known how the Canadian **single-payer healthcare system** was established and why such a system would work or not work in the United States. In the next section, we will take a closer look at Canadian healthcare policy.

The American healthcare system evolved on the basis of different legislative acts and incremental changes to existing legislation, and therefore looks like a patchwork. Canadian healthcare policy, however, was completely designed and implemented under the **Canada Health Act (CHA)**. Operating under federalism (like the United States), Canada has a **decentralized healthcare system** that divides healthcare delivery between the federal government and local governments.[59] For instance, the primary role of the federal government is to shape

BOX 6.1

Country Profile of Canada

Name of Country: Canada

Type of Government: Constitutional monarchy, parliamentary democracy, and federation

Independence: July 1, 1867 (Union of British North American colonies); December 11, 1931 (Independence Recognized by the United Kingdom)

Executive Branch:

Head of State: Queen ELIZABETH II (since 6 February 1952); represented by Governor General David JOHNSTON (since 1 October 2010)

Head of Government: Prime Minister Stephen Joseph HARPER (since 6 February 2006)

Cabinet: Federal Ministry chosen by the prime minister usually from among the members of his own party sitting in Parliament.

Legislative Branch: Bicameral Parliament

Senate (Senat): 105 senators, appointed by the Governor General with the advice of the prime minister and serving until 75 years of age

The House of Commons (Chambre des Communes): 308 members, elected by direct popular vote to serve a maximum of four-year terms

Judicial Branch:

Supreme Court of Canada (judges are appointed by the governor general on the recommendation of the prime minister); Federal Court of Canada; Federal Court of Appeal; Tax Court of Canada; Provincial/Territorial Courts (these are named variously Court of Appeal, Court of Queen's Bench, Superior Court, Supreme Court, and Court of Justice)

Administrative Divisions:

10 provinces and 3 territories*; Alberta, British Columbia, Manitoba, New Brunswick, Newfoundland and Labrador, Northwest Territories*, Nova Scotia, Nunavut*, Ontario, Prince Edward Island, Quebec, Saskatchewan, Yukon Territory*

Economic Indicators:

GDP (purchasing power parity): $1.77 trillion (2012 est.)

GDP Real Growth Rate: 1.9 percent (2012 est.)

GDP per capita (purchasing power parity): $41,500 (2012 est.)

Economic Structure: Agriculture 1.8 percent, Industry 28.6 percent, Services 69.6 percent (2012 est.)

Demographic Indicators:

Population: 34,568,211 (July 2013 est.)

Population Growth: 0.784 percent (2012 est.)

Birth Rate: 10.28 births/1,000 population (2012 est.)

Infant Mortality Rate: 4.85 deaths/1,000 live births (2012 est.)

Life Expectancy at Birth: 81.48 years (2012 est.)

Literacy (people age 15 and over who can read and write): 99 percent (2003 est.)

Ethnic Groups: British Isles origin 28 percent, French origin 23 percent, other European 15 percent, Amerindian 2 percent, other, mostly Asian, African, Arab 6 percent, mixed background 26 percent

Religions: Roman Catholic 42.6 percent, Protestant 23.3 percent (United Church 9.5 percent, Anglican 6.8 percent, Baptist 2.4 percent, Lutheran 2 percent), other Christian 4.4 percent, Muslim 1.9 percent, other

and unspecified 11.8 percent, none 16 percent (2001 census)

Source: CIA, The World Factbook on Canada, available at https://www.cia.gov/library/ publications/the-world-factbook/geos/ca.html (accessed April 30, 2013).

the rules of the relationship between providers and patients by regulating the healthcare sector. To design and implement healthcare services and insurance programs, the federal government and provincial/territorial governments must work together on important arrangements such as shares of financial transfers. The primary agents carrying out healthcare policy are 10 provincial and 3 territorial governments.

Before considering healthcare policy institutions, we will briefly sketch how each Canadian citizen accesses Canada's healthcare system in daily life.[60] Under the CHA, the Canadian healthcare system relies extensively on primary care physicians (i.e., general or family practitioners) who account for about 58 percent of all practicing physicians in Canada. These physicians usually establish initial contact with the formal healthcare system as first-contact clinical service; they arrange for access to most specialists, hospital admissions, diagnostic testing, and prescription drug therapy as secondary care or additional care services.

When Canadians need medical treatment, they first meet their family practitioner or local clinic and present a health insurance card issued by their province/territory. If a family practitioner arranges for access to specialists, hospitals, diagnostic testing, and prescription drug therapy, patients can go to an insured hospital operated as a private nonprofit entity and run by a community board of trustees, voluntary organization, or provincial health authority. Costs are paid through national health insurance.

Most doctors in Canada are private practitioners who work in independent or group practices, whereas some doctors work in community health centers, have hospital-based group practices, or work in affiliation with hospital outpatient departments. Thus, like the traditional practice in the United States, when Canadian patients receive medical treatment by their family practitioner, they must pay on a fee-for-service basis and then submit their service claims directly to a **provincial/territorial health insurance plan** for payment. Physicians in other practice settings may also be paid on a FFS basis but are more likely to be salaried or remunerated through an alternative payment scheme.

Canada spent around $4,363 per capita in 2009 on healthcare; 70.6 percent was funded publicly and 29.4 percent was funded through private health insurance or out-of-pocket payments, which covers otherwise noninsured healthcare services such as dental care, eye care, and prescription drugs.[61] Canadians' spending on private insurance and out-of-pocket payments has increased nearly 30 percent throughout the last two decades.[62]

Many Canadians think that their single-payer healthcare system needs to be reformed because of reduced quality of healthcare delivery and service availability as well as rising healthcare spending.[63] In comparison with six other countries (Australia, Germany, the Netherlands, New Zealand, the United Kingdom, and the United States), Canada has the second-highest health expenditures per capita but ranks lowest in regard to quality care.[64]

In public debate, many experts in Canada say that the declining quality and quantity of healthcare provisions are closely related to the lack of economic motivation in regard to centralized and bureaucratized healthcare programs. They argue that meaningful reform needs to introduce a pluralistic market-oriented (or market-maximized) healthcare system such as the private or managed healthcare system that exists in the United States, or the universal private health insurance system that exists in Switzerland.[65]

Next, we will identify policy actors involved in Canadian healthcare policy making. Then, we will look at the history of Canadian healthcare policy and address some related problems and challenges.

Policy Actors

Before considering government agencies and other actors involved in Canadian healthcare policy making, we need to keep in mind that policy making in Canada is embedded in the institutional setting of a parliamentary system. In order to understand the Canadian policy-making process, let us see how a bill becomes a law in Canada.

Legislative Process[66]   Under Canada's constitution, every policy on the agenda to become a federal law must pass through a formal legislative process. Although Canada's Senate has the right to submit a legislative proposal or bill, almost all legislative proposals are first introduced in the Canadian House of Commons by Cabinet members or other members of the House. After a bill is read in detail without debate in the House of Commons, it is printed. This process is called a *first reading*. In a *second reading*, the principles of a bill are debated and voted on. If a bill is approved in a second reading, it is sent to a committee, which listens to testimony, examines a bill, and submits a report to the House of Commons, recommending that it be accepted as it is, accepted with amendments, or scrapped. Amendments are debated and voted on in the House of Commons. In a *third reading*, the House debates and votes on the final draft of a bill. If a bill passes in the House, it is sent to the Senate, where a bill is treated in the same way as in the House. If a bill also passes in the Senate, it is given Royal Assent and becomes a law.

Commissions of Inquiry   The Canadian government frequently organizes commissions of inquiry to aid in the process of policy making. Some commissions are intended to determine the facts of a specific event or policy issue. Others examine a policy area and make recommendations for new policies that the government should consider implementing. For instance, in 2001, the government set up the Royal Commission on the Future of Health Care in Canada for healthcare reform. The commission issued a report titled "Building on Value" and released the report to the public in 2002, which contributed to establishing a new framework for Canadian healthcare policy based on the CHA.

Healthcare Policy-Making Process   As noted earlier, healthcare policy in Canada is carried out primarily by 10 provincial and 3 territorial governments, although the federal government plays an important role by providing financial resources to provincial/territorial governments. Under Canada's federalism, healthcare policy making is, to a large extent, a power game between the federal government and provincial/territorial governments.[67] Furthermore, within provincial/territorial jurisdictions, ultimate decisions on the allocation of healthcare services are based on arrangements or agreements between provincial/territorial governments and healthcare providers.[68]

Health Canada   Various actors are involved in Canadian healthcare policy making. For instance, the Prime Minister, in reaching policy decisions and monitoring healthcare programs, and the Ministry of Finance, in implementing finance policy that may affect healthcare delivery, are important actors in the process of healthcare policy making. The heart of Canadian healthcare policy design and implementation, however, is **Health Canada**, Canada's federal health department.[69] The head of this department is Canada's Minister of Health, supported by a Deputy Minister and an Associate Deputy Minister. Through regional presence, Health Canada implements healthcare policy in every province and territory.

Each of the branches, offices, and bureaus in Health Canada has an important role in the administration of Canadian healthcare policy. For instance, the Health Products and Food Branch deals with access to safe and effective health products and provides food information for healthy choices. The Healthy Environments and Consumer Safety Branch focuses on reduced health and environmental risks from products and substances as well as on safer living and working environments. The First Nations and Inuit Health Branch focuses on improving health outcomes and reducing health inequalities between the First Nations and other Canadians.

In its mission statement, Health Canada asserts that its obligation is to improve the lives of Canadians and make them among the healthiest people in the world.[71] In pursuit of its mission, Health Canada has the following core roles:

* *Leader/Partner:*   Through administration of the Canada Health Act.
* *Fund Provider:*   Supporting policy for the federal government's Canada Health and Social Transfer (CHST), replaced in 2004 by the Canada Health Transfer (CHT). Health Canada also transfers funds to First Nations and Inuit organizations and communities to deliver community health services and provides grants and contributions to organizations that reinforce Health Canada's objectives.

- *Guardian/Regulator:* Through stewardship that protects Canadians and facilitates the provision of products vital to Canadians' health and well-being. Health Canada regulates and approves the use of thousands of products, including biologics, consumer goods, food products, medical devices, natural health products, pesticides, pharmaceuticals, and toxic substances.
- *Information Provider:* Through high-quality science and research to support policy development, regulate increasingly sophisticated products, and provide services, information, and management essential to affordable and world-class healthcare for Canadians.

Furthermore, Health Canada has responsibilities in the areas of environmental health protection, substance abuse, tobacco policy, workplace health, and safe use of consumer products. Health Canada also monitors and tracks diseases and takes action to prevent or control them.

Provincial/Territorial Governments   Most of Canada's healthcare services are administered by provincial/territorial governments that decide on the allocation of healthcare services in negotiations with healthcare providers. All provincial/territorial health insurance plans are expected to meet national principles set under the Canada Health Act. The primary department responsible for healthcare in each province/territory is a provincial/territorial ministry of health headed by a health minister. All provincial/territorial health ministers meet with Canada's Minister of Health at a conference to coordinate provincial/territorial healthcare programs.

Interest Groups   Although there are numerous special-interest groups involved in Canada's healthcare policy-making process, the most influential organization is the **Canadian Medical Association (CMA)**. The CMA serves all Canadian physicians and is the key national advocate for the highest healthcare standards.[70] The CMA has played an important role in first establishing and then protecting Canada's publicly funded single payer health insurance. The CMA was created in Quebec City in October 1867 with 164 physicians who recognized the need for a national medical body. Since then, CMA membership has grown to more than 60,000 physicians, medical residents, and medical students. Although the CMA is located in Ottawa, its network extends all over Canada.

Healthcare Policy History

How did Canada establish its publicly funded single-payer health insurance? How did it evolve into its contemporary form? In response to these questions, let us look at the history of Canadian healthcare policy, with a focus on key events in Canadian health insurance legislation, from 1945 through 2004.[71]

Stage I: Establishing a Universal Health Insurance Program (1945–1972)   In 1947, the Saskatchewan government introduced a provincewide and universal hospital services plan, which became a major trigger for establishing a comprehensive health insurance program in Canada. Following Saskatchewan, both British Columbia and Alberta launched a similar health insurance program in 1949.

In 1957, the federal legislature passed the Hospital Insurance and Diagnostic Services Act (HIDSA), which offered reimbursement of one-half of provincial/territorial costs for specified hospital and diagnostic services. The HIDSA provided for publicly administered universal coverage for specific services under uniform terms and conditions. By 1961, despite opposition from medical and health profession lobbying groups across Canada, all provincial/territorial governments passed bills for hospital insurance and entered into cost-sharing agreements with the federal government. The Canadian Medical Association tried to protect its members' interests by avoiding major governmental intervention in healthcare practices.

Following a universal and provincewide medical insurance bill initiated by the government of Saskatchewan, provincial governments—including those of Ontario, British Columbia, and Alberta—developed medical insurance plans based on the principle of voluntary insurance. Then, in 1964, the Royal Commission on Health Services released a report that provided the federal government with a Health Charter for Canadians and stressed the need for government-sponsored, comprehensive, and universal health services for all Canadians. In order to protect the freedom and interests of healthcare providers, the Hall Commission recommended basing medical insurance on the freedom of choice of providers and the autonomy of physicians.

In 1966, the federal legislature passed the **Medical Care Insurance Act (MCIA)**, which offered reimbursement or cost-sharing of one-half of provincial/territorial costs for medical services provided by doctors outside hospitals. The MCIA was established with four key principles: universality, comprehensiveness, public administration, and portability. By 1972, all Canadian provinces/territories had universal health insurance plans for physician services.

Stage II: Financial Struggle and Passage of the Canada Health Act (1972–1990) The basic concept of a national universal health insurance plan (Medicare) was that, while the federal government covered almost half of provincial/territorial health expenditures, Medicare would attempt to harmonize provincial/territorial health systems and ensure that relatively similar services would be provided across Canada. However, while operating Canada's national Medicare program, the federal government was confronted with the need to control healthcare costs, yet the provincial/territorial governments made all healthcare spending decisions. Moreover, provincial/territorial governments thought that federal funding destroyed provincial/territorial healthcare priorities by covering only hospital and medical care.

These concerns led to new federal provincial/territorial negotiations that resulted in the 1977 Federal-Provincial Fiscal Arrangements and Established Programs Financing (EPF) Act. Under this act, insured healthcare was no longer supported with federal funding linked to provincial/territorial spending but with federal cash and tax transfers. Cash transfers were made through block funding, and tax transfers were made by reducing federal tax rates to give federal/territorial governments some tax room to raise their own tax rates without any net change for taxpayers.

In 1979, the federal government decided to review Canada's publicly funded healthcare system by creating the Health Services Review, with Emmett Hall appointed as Special Commissioner. Specifically, the Health Services Review was created to evaluate the use of federal money for healthcare services in provinces/territories and to determine whether extra billing by doctors and user fees by hospitals were deteriorating access to health services. The Health Services Review eventually recommended ending extra billing and user fees because they might erode public health insurance by generating a two-tier healthcare system.

Recommendations from the Health Services Review became the basis of healthcare reform proposals considered in the federal legislature. The House of Commons established an all-party Health Care Task Force whose conclusions focused on (1) expanding federal funds for healthcare, (2) continuing conditional funding transfers, (3) articulating the role of the federal government in healthcare provisions, and (4) merging all existing health insurance legislation into a single act. Following the conclusions of the Health Care Task Force, the Federal Minister of Health, Monique Bégin, presented a report titled "Preserving Universal Medicare," including guarantees of access to healthcare services.

In 1984, the Canada Health Act was passed. In addition to consolidating existing hospital and medical acts into one single legislative act, the CHA lays out five principles for healthcare in Canada: (1) universality of coverage, (2) comprehensiveness of insured services, (3) portability of benefits across provincial/territorial boundaries, (4) public administration by provincial/territorial agencies, and (5) accessibility to insured services on uniform terms and conditions. Compliance with these five principles is required for provincial/territorial health insurance plans to be funded with federal money, and there is a mechanism through which the federal government can impose financial sanctions on provinces/territories for noncompliance.

Eventually, all provinces/territories accepted the Canada Health Act. Although the CHA was well implemented and operated when it took effect, it soon became apparent that it was difficult to maintain universal and comprehensive healthcare coverage under the CHA at times of economic recession. When Canada experienced economic recession in the 1980s and 1990s, it faced serious constraint on federal and provincial/territorial public spending, including spending on healthcare.

Stage III: The Lost Decade and the Erosion of National Healthcare (1991–2000) Throughout the 1990s, the Canadian government tried to reduce public spending and revive Canada's economy. In order to decrease the fiscal burden due to rising healthcare costs driving up federal healthcare spending, the federal government declared that Established Programs Financing transfers from the federal government to provincial/territorial governments would be frozen for five years after 1990. In fact, the proportion of provincial/territorial healthcare expenditures covered by EPF transfers declined from 30.6 percent in 1980 to 21.5 percent in 1996.[72] Although no amendment was made to the CHA, the federal government as well as provincial/territorial governments were under such massive fiscal constraint that support for the CHA, at least in idea, began to erode.

Under pressure to reduce public spending by controlling healthcare costs, the federal government shifted its healthcare spending dramatically in favor of home-based care and prescription drugs rather than care based in hospitals. At the same time, the federal government initiated a major cost-cutting campaign on nationalized hospital services. In trying to reduce its fiscal burden, the federal government further increased an already rising fiscal burden on provincial/territorial governments and created gaps in universal and comprehensive healthcare services across Canada's provinces/territories.

The 1990s were years of exhaustive fiscal constraint for provincial/territorial governments. Under the CHA, 9 of Canada's 10 provincial governments attempted to cut healthcare funding by introducing a variety of measures to rationalize healthcare services (reductions of hospital beds, merging and closure of hospitals, restrictions of salary for physicians, and public sector downsizing affecting nurses and other healthcare workers). There were also several new initiatives, including the regionalization of healthcare services, the expansion of community care and public health programs, and innovations through telephone health information.

In October 1994, Prime Minister Jean Chrétien announced that the federal government would form a National Forum on Health (NFH).[73] The NFH was a new federal initiative for healthcare reform. Out of concern that the NFH might replace federal–provincial/territorial negotiations on healthcare matters, many provincial governments boycotted the NFH. As a result, the NFH was solely a federal initiative. Still, provincial/territorial officials, members of provincial/territorial government advisory bodies, and "informal" observers sent by provincial/territorial governments participated in NFH meetings.

The purpose of the NFH was to find new and innovative ways to improve Canada's healthcare system. In 1997, the NFH released a two-volume final report, *Canada Health Action: Building on the Legacy*, which solidly endorsed Canadian Medicare by restating key features of Canada's healthcare system: public funding for medically necessary services, the "single-payer" model, the five principles of the CHA, and a strong federal–provincial/territorial partnership. In order to preserve Canada's national Medicare program under the CHA and adjust it in light of new realities, the report suggested that it was important to expand publicly funded health services, which would encompass all medically necessary services, pharmacare (drugs), and home care.

Another major federal attempt at healthcare reform under the CHA was the 1995 Canada Health and Social Transfer (CHST), which combined Established Program Financing (EPF) with the Canada Assistance Plan (CAP). Under the CHST, provincial/territorial governments received federal block transfer funding to spend on healthcare and post-secondary education (formerly supported with EPF funding) as well as on social services (formerly supported with CAP funding).

Many provincial/territorial leaders were concerned not only about allocation of healthcare funding but also about autonomy in healthcare policy making. Throughout the 1990s, concerns about the role of the federal government in Canada's healthcare system motivated attempts to build a social union. By 1999, the federal government and all provincial/territorial governments, except Quebec, entered into the **Social Union Framework Agreement (SUWA)** for a collective approach to social policy, including policy on healthcare.

Throughout the 1990s, provincial/territorial governments began to reexamine their healthcare systems and to question the status quo. Although provincial/territorial healthcare systems have, for the most part, been preserved, many provincial/territorial governments realized that people have been directly affected by longer wait-times for services, overcrowding in emergency rooms, and the exclusion of previously insured services and new technologies from public health insurance coverage. Furthermore, Canadians have become more concerned about the increased personal burden of healthcare costs, as well as about the viability of public health insurance due to unprecedented growth in the private market for diagnostic labs and services, such as home care, and increased costs of outpatient prescription drugs.

Stage IV: Demands for a New Healthcare System under Canadian Values (2000–2004) Throughout the 1990s, the federal government rebalanced its budget and reached an agreement on healthcare with provincial/territorial government leaders (or first ministers). The agreement established key reforms in primary healthcare, management of pharmaceuticals, health information and communications technology, and health equipment and infrastructure. The agreement also announced that the government would substantially increase cash and tax transfers in support of healthcare under the CHST. Even with increased funding, serious concerns about fiscal capacity remained among provincial/territorial leaders. Several provinces such as Alberta, Saskatchewan, and Quebec held a provincial commission on healthcare to address such concerns. The commission reported that there was need for improvement of coverage for prescription drugs and home-based healthcare and for reform of primary care delivery.

In response to growing public concerns and provincial/territorial claims on Canada's publicly funded healthcare system, the House of Commons in 2001 established the Royal Commission on the Future of Health Care (known as the Romanow Commission because it was chaired by Roy Romanow, former Premier of Saskatchewan), and the Senate created the standing committee on social affairs, science and technology, chaired by Senator Michael Kirby. In the fall of 2002, the commission and the committee each released a federal report, known as the Romanow Report and the Kirby Report. The Romanow Report stressed the importance of maintaining and expanding universal publicly funded healthcare delivery, improving access to healthcare for rural and remote communities, expanding provincial/territorial health insurance plans so they would cover home-based healthcare services and prescription drugs, and reforming primary care. Although the Kirby Report generally supported the Romanow

Report, it proposed expanding the role of the private sector by allowing for more healthcare services to be contracted out to investor-owned agencies and institutions, including private hospitals and clinics, within a single-payer framework.

Following the two federal reports, the Prime Minister and all first ministers from Canada's provincial/territorial governments met in 2003; the meeting led to "the Accord on Health Care Renewal," which provided for reforms to enhance the accessibility, quality, and long-term survivability of Canada's healthcare system. Under the accord, the federal government's cash transfers in support of provincial/territorial healthcare programs were generally increased, but cash and tax transfers under the CHST were divided into the Canada Health Transfer for health and the Canada Social Transfer for post-secondary education, social services, and social assistance. This implied that provincial/territorial governments could obtain more financial support from the federal government, but the federal government could reduce provincial/territorial authority and discretion in regard to healthcare through its management of cash transfers.

In 2004, the first ministers announced another reform plan entitled "A 10-Year Plan to Strengthen Health Care."[74] Under this plan, the federal government would focus on improving access to quality care and reducing wait-times. Specific areas of concern listed in the plan include human resources for adequate supply of healthcare professionals, aboriginal health, home care, primary healthcare, prescription drug coverage and other elements of a national pharmaceutical strategy, healthcare services in the northern communities, medical equipment, prevention of disease and injury, and promotion of public health.

The 1984 Canada Health Act[75]

Since 1984, Canadian healthcare policy and nationwide universal standards for healthcare delivery have been based on the Canada Health Act. Given the centrality of the CHA in Canada's healthcare system, it is important that we take a closer look at the CHA's principles, eligibility criteria, and penalty provisions.

Principles   According to the CHA, healthcare in Canada is guided by five principles reflecting the values of equality and solidarity in Canada. Although we mentioned these principles before, we now present them in more detail:

1. *Universality of coverage:* All insured provincial/territorial residents are entitled to the same insured healthcare services under provincial/territorial healthcare insurance plans.
2. *Comprehensiveness of insured services:* All insured healthcare (hospital, physician, or surgical-dental) services must be insured by provincial/territorial healthcare insurance plans.
3. *Portability of benefits across provincial/territorial boundaries:* Residents who move from one province/territory to another remain entitled to insured healthcare services covered by their home provinces/territories during a minimum waiting period determined by their new provinces/territories of residence.

4. *Public administration by provincial/territorial agencies:*   All administration and operation of provincial/territorial healthcare insurance plans must be carried out on a nonprofit basis by public authorities that are held accountable to provincial/territorial governments and whose records and accounts are subject to audits.
5. *Accessibility to insured services on uniform terms and conditions:*   All insured persons in provinces/territories have reasonable access, on uniform terms and conditions, to insured healthcare (hospital, medical, or surgical-dental) services. Furthermore, provincial/territorial healthcare insurance plans must reasonably compensate physicians and dentists for services rendered by them and pay hospitals for costs of insured healthcare services.

Eligibility Criteria   The Canada Health Act stipulates that the primary objective of Canadian healthcare policy is "to protect, promote and restore the physical and mental well-being of residents of Canada and to facilitate reasonable access to health services without financial or other barriers." On the basis of the CHA, Medicare in Canada, unlike Medicare in the United States, is a national universal health insurance plan.

Under the CHA, insured healthcare services include medically necessary hospital, physician, and surgical-dental services. The CHA is comprehensive and universal but does not cover all Canadian residents or all healthcare services. Although it is not intended to create differences in access to publicly insured healthcare, there are criteria for exclusion from insured healthcare services predating adoption of the CHA. Specifically, the CHA excludes members of the Canadian Forces, persons appointed to a position of rank within the Royal Canadian Mounted Police, persons serving a prison term in a federal penitentiary, and persons who have not completed a minimum period of residence in one of Canada's provinces/territories. Furthermore, the CHA excludes healthcare services to persons provided under any other Act of Parliament (e.g., services to foreign refugees) or under provincial/territorial workers' compensation legislation.

In addition to medically necessary hospital, physician, and surgical-dental services insured under the CHA, provinces/territories have discretion in providing a range of healthcare services outside the scope of the CHA, on terms and conditions that vary from one province/territory to another. Provinces/territories may provide additional healthcare services, which may include pharmacare, ambulance services, and optometric services, to specific population groups (e.g., children, seniors, or recipients of social assistance); these services may be partially or fully covered by provincial/territorial health insurance plans. Various healthcare services are not considered medically necessary and thus not insured under provincial/territorial health insurance legislation. Uninsured health care services for which patients may be charged include hospital services, such as preferred but not physician-prescribed hospital accommodation; private-duty nursing services as well as telephones and televisions; and physician services, such as telephone advice and medical certificates required for work, school, insurance purposes, fitness clubs, testimony in court, and cosmetic services.

Penalty Provisions According to the Canada Health Act, the federal government can impose financial sanctions to penalize provinces/territories for violations of the CHA. There are mandatory and discretionary penalty provisions. Under mandatory penalty provisions, provinces/territories that allow extra billing and user charges are subject to mandatory dollar-for-dollar deductions from federal transfer payments under the Canada Health Transfer. For example, if it was determined that a province/territory allowed $500,000 in extra billing by physicians, federal transfer payments to that province/territory would be reduced by that amount. Under Discretionary Penalty Provisions, provinces/territories that do not comply with any of the five CHA principles (mentioned) earlier are subject to discretionary deductions from federal transfer payments under the Canada Health Transfer determined by the gravity of noncompliance. The CHA provides for a consultation process before discretionary penalties can be levied against a province/territory.

Provincial/Territorial Health Insurance

Health insurance is handled by individual provinces/territories.[76] New provincial/territorial residents must apply for healthcare coverage. After healthcare coverage has been granted, a health card is issued as proof of provincial/territorial health insurance. For new residents, there are typically wait periods before healthcare coverage will be granted. This can vary but cannot exceed three months. Certain provinces (British Columbia, Alberta, and Ontario) require healthcare premiums for services. Under the CHA, however, healthcare services cannot be denied due to financial inability to pay premiums. In addition to standard healthcare services covered under the CHA, provinces/territories usually provide additional services such as physiotherapy, dental coverage, and prescription medicines. Provinces/territories have no obligation to provide healthcare services outside the scope of the CHA, and such services may be affected by changing government policies.

Problems and Challenges

Many Canadians have expressed dissatisfaction with healthcare delivery and treatment, so the federal government and provincial/territorial governments have undertaken reforms of Canada's healthcare system under the CHA.

According to the *OECD Health Data 2011*, the Canadian healthcare system is relatively expensive, and only five other countries (the United States, the Netherlands, France, Germany, and Denmark) spend more on healthcare than Canada.[77] In a detailed comparison of the Organization for Economic Cooperation and Development (OECD) countries with universal access and publicly funded healthcare systems, the Fraser institute's *How Good Is Canadian Healthcare? 2008 Report* concludes that "the Canadian health care model is inferior to those that are in place in other countries of the OECD."[78] There are major problems of the contemporary Canadian healthcare system mentioned in various reports.[79] The wait-time between seeing a family physician and actually receiving needed treatment almost doubled between 1993 and 2007. There is uneven health insurance coverage regarding prescription drugs. Private health insurances are allowed only in limited areas, and private care and hospital services are not covered by national health insurance. Overall, the system sometimes delivers low-quality healthcare and can be slow to implement new technology.

One of the most controversial healthcare reform issues in Canada has been whether Canadians can have some sort of private insurance instead of, or in addition to, a publicly funded health insurance program in order to gain increasing access to quality health services beyond some basic treatment.[80] Although they have been paying high taxes, Canadians have been increasingly willing to pay out of their own pockets to enjoy private physician and hospital services.[81] In June 2005, with regard to the legal case of long wait times in public health services violating individuals' rights to preserve their own health, the Supreme Court of Canada ruled that "the Quebec government cannot prevent people from paying for private insurance for healthcare procedures covered under Medicare."[82] Although the ruling applies only in the province of Quebec, it could greatly influence other provincial decisions and policy changes on public healthcare delivery under the CHA. Indeed, patients in Alberta and Ontario have been challenging their provincial governments' monopoly on health insurance in court.

Another question is whether Canada's publicly funded universal health insurance is sustainable without private funding. As we discussed earlier with regard to the history of Canadian healthcare policy, concern about the sustainability of Canada's publicly funded healthcare system is at the top of the country's healthcare reform agenda. As of 2014, there is continued debate over alternative funding through private insurance options.[83]

Among notable features of the Canadian healthcare system are *cost-sharing* and *no user fees* for all Canadians. Although universal access to healthcare is one of the major principles of the CHA, Canada does not succeed in actually delivering access to necessary medical care. Government data show that an estimated 1.7 million Canadians were unable to access a regular family physician in 2007.[84] If patients cannot have access to any single family doctor under CHA practice, none of them can receive either regular primary care or referrals for selected specialists and other elected medical services, including hospitalization. An even more important consideration here is that 1.7 million does not include Canadians who have access to a regular family doctor but who are on a long waiting list for specialist treatment, including MRI diagnostics. Although patients can obtain desired health treatment by paying for it through the fee-for-service plan, there is no private insurance or tax benefit (deduction), and there is no reimbursement or local government subsidy.

Whenever policy alternatives for healthcare reform are suggested to Americans, policymakers seem to hesitate to enact fundamental reform out of concern that people might lose their current health benefits. This applies to Canadians as well. Whenever healthcare reform proposals emerge, Canadian policymakers seem to hesitate to fundamentally reform the Canadian healthcare system beyond the CHA. Although healthcare effectiveness, efficiency, and accessibility in other OECD countries may point to some combination of other OECD models as a promising blueprint for Canadian healthcare reform, many Canadians still hold on to the healthcare system under the CHA.[85]

Comparison

An essential goal of healthcare policy is to provide affordable and accessible healthcare services to all citizens. No matter whether we look at the United States or Canada, or many other countries, healthcare policy exists to maintain not only individual health but also public health. Under the managed care system in the United States and the publicly funded single-payer system in Canada, citizens in both countries receive high-quality healthcare services if they are able to afford such services; nonetheless, health insurance coverage and the quality of healthcare services vary from country to country. Our investigation of healthcare policy in the United States and Canada unveiled different types of healthcare systems (plural- and single-payer models), with demands for reform to reduce rising healthcare costs and to ensure fair access to high-quality healthcare services. As we saw earlier, in statistical comparison, healthcare appears to cost less in Canada than in the United States. However, it is likely that Canadian health insurance does not cover many advanced medical treatments, including new medicines and technologies that are commonly available to Americans. If Canadians had access to the same quality and quantity of healthcare services that Americans enjoy, Canadian health insurance would cost more than it currently does.[86]

In this concluding comparison, we look at some differences and similarities between the American and Canadian healthcare systems. We then consider the extent to which the two healthcare systems may be moving closer to one another.

One of the differences between the American and Canadian healthcare systems lies in their administration. With few exceptions—most notably publicly funded insurance such as Medicare and Medicaid—the American healthcare system is private and for-profit. The majority of Americans have tax-subsidized employer-based or other individual-paid private health insurance. Private health insurance is very expensive and may not cover various forms of healthcare, such as eye care, dental care, or specialist services. Americans must pay premiums to insurance companies but must also pay for many other health-related expenses. As we saw in the example of a United Auto Workers employee, a co-payment must be made when coming into contact with a primary care physician.

The Canadian healthcare system is mostly public and not-for-profit. When people need healthcare, it is possible for them to receive treatment from a family practitioner or local health clinic without any fees, co-payments, or deductibles, and there is no dollar limit on annual coverage. Expenses are paid through national health insurance. Some doctors operate private practices, in which case a fee-for-service must be paid, but Canadians can submit a claim to their health insurance company for reimbursement. Yet, there is dissatisfaction with the Canadian healthcare system expressed among Canadians for reasons that include longer wait-times to see a physician and receive treatment.

Another difference between the American and Canadian healthcare systems can be found in their organization. The American healthcare system is rather fragmented, with several health insurance options, including tax-subsidized employer-paid insurance, individual-paid private insurance, as well as publicly funded insurance such as Medicare and Medicaid. In addition, Title I of the Patient Protection and Affordable Care Act (PPACA) creates state-based community health insurance options. Yet, since states can choose not to provide these options if they pass legislation to that extent, they may be available in some states but not in others. Thus, the PPACA may increase the discrepancies between states that already exist in healthcare coverage (e.g., Medicaid). The fragmentation of the U.S. system is not only because it includes several health insurance options but also because it is based on a patchwork of legislative acts, the most recent one being the PPACA.

The Canadian healthcare system is rather unified, with publicly funded single-payer insurance providing most coverage and with private insurance as well as out-of-pocket payments for healthcare services that are not covered otherwise. Since 1984, the Canadian healthcare system has been based on the Canada Health Act, a single legislative act with five principles: (1) universality of coverage, (2) comprehensiveness of insured services, (3) portability of benefits across provincial/territorial boundaries, (4) public administration by provincial/territorial agencies, and (5) accessibility to insured services on uniform terms and conditions.

One of the similarities between the American and Canadian health care systems is that both are confronted with rising healthcare costs that need to be paid for under fiscal constraints and economic challenges. The United States has the most expensive healthcare system in the world, and Canada's healthcare system is not far behind in terms of costs. In comparison with five other countries (Australia, Germany, the Netherlands, New Zealand, and the United Kingdom), the United States and Canada have the highest and second-highest, respectively, health expenditures per capita but rank second-lowest and lowest, respectively, in quality care.[87] This raises serious questions about the cost-effectiveness of healthcare in both countries, even though the American and Canadian healthcare systems are administered and organized very differently.

Another similarity between the American and Canadian healthcare systems is that there are concerns over access to high-quality healthcare. In both countries, access to high-quality healthcare depends on one's economic status or adequate health insurance. In the United States, millions of people are uninsured; without personal funds to pay for expensive health services, they cannot access high-quality healthcare even though it is available. Furthermore, although people have health insurance, coverage of high-quality health services may depend on specific health insurance plans. Since the Canadian healthcare system is a nonprofit, there are reduced incentives for physicians to provide high-quality health services. So, while Canada's publicly funded single-payer insurance provides universal coverage, many Canadians think that some sort of private insurance will give them greater access to quality health services beyond some basic treatment.

Due to rising healthcare costs and concerns over access to high-quality healthcare, healthcare reform has been high on the agenda of policymakers in both the United States and Canada, and it is through reform that the two countries' healthcare systems may be moving closer to one another. In the United States, the need for healthcare reform has found a response in the PPACA, a far-reaching legislative act that seeks to reduce steeply rising healthcare costs, enhance the quality of healthcare, and make quality healthcare coverage available and affordable for all Americans. The PPACA is an important step toward a universal healthcare system in the United States. Goals and titles of the PPACA bring the American healthcare system closer to the Canadian healthcare system under the CHA and its principles. Although state-based community health insurance options under the PPACA in the United States do not replace private insurance, and states can choose not to provide them through legislation in that regard, they are, to some extent, similar to provincial/territorial health insurance under the CHA in Canada.

Since the CHA was passed in 1984, the need for healthcare reform in Canada has led to demands for more privatization of Canada's healthcare system so that Canadians can rely on private health insurance to gain more unlimited access to high-quality private physician and hospital services. It is through more privatization that the Canadian healthcare system would move closer to the largely private and for-profit American healthcare system.

In order to better evaluate healthcare policy and its outcomes, more comprehensive and systematic policy-evaluation tools need to be established. Nonetheless, according to our inquiry, the American and Canadian healthcare systems have advantages and disadvantages under a variety of criteria (e.g., insurance coverage, quantity and quality of doctors and services, delivery, and financing). Differences between the American and Canadian healthcare systems are related to differences in political, economic, and cultural settings. Many Americans still believe that market competition is a more effective way to implement healthcare policy. By contrast, many Canadians still favor governmental intervention in various policy areas, including healthcare.

There are demands for healthcare reform in both the United States and Canada. But before concluding whether universal health insurance is or is not better for all, both countries need to be able to effectively evaluate such fundamental issues as accessibility, quality, costs, and accountability of healthcare delivery in the context of demographic changes as well as fiscal constraints and economic challenges. Each healthcare system needs a model that best fits its needs, perhaps combining alternative models adopted by countries of the OECD.[88]

Key Terms

- American Association of Retired Persons (AARP)
- American Medical Association (AMA)
- Canada Health Act (CHA)
- Canadian Medical Association (CMA)
- Decentralized healthcare system
- Department of Health and Human Services (DHHS)

- Department of Veterans Affairs (DVA)
- Fee-for-service (FFS)
- Health Canada
- Health Care Fraud and Abuse Control (HCFAC) program
- Health maintenance organizations (HMOs)
- Health Maintenance Organization (HMO) Act
- Independent practice associations (IPAs)
- Individual-paid private insurance
- Managed healthcare
- Medicaid
- Medical Care Insurance Act (MCIA)
- Medicare

- Patient Protection and Affordable Care Act (PPACA)
- Pharmaceutical Research and Manufacturers of America (PhRMA)
- Preferred provider organizations (PPOs)
- Primary care physician (PCP)
- Provincial/territorial health insurance plan
- Publicly funded insurance
- Single-payer healthcare system
- Social Union Framework Agreement (SUWA)
- State Children's Health Insurance Program (SCHIP)
- Tax-subsidized, employer-based insurance
- TRICARE

Critical Thinking Questions

- To what extent and in what ways do people have access to healthcare in the United States and Canada?
- What policy actors are involved in healthcare policy making in the United States and Canada?
- What healthcare programs have been developed in the United States and Canada?
- How is healthcare policy implemented under federalism in the United States and Canada?
- What are some similarities and differences between the Patient Protection and Affordable Care Act and the Canada Health Act?
- What are the most important problems and challenges related to healthcare policy in the United States and Canada?

Recommended Resources for U.S. Healthcare Policy

Peter R. Kongstvedt, ed., *Essentials of Managed Health Care* (5th ed.) (Sudbury, MA: Jones & Bartlett, 2007).

James Morene, Theodor J. Litman, and Leonard S. Robins, eds., *Health Politics and Policy* (4th ed.) (Albany: Delmar Cengage Learning, 2008).

Kant Patel and Mark E. Rushefsky, *Health Care Politics and Policy in America* (3rd ed.) (Armonk, NY: M. E. Sharpe, 2006).

Mark E. Rushefsky and Kant Patel, *Politics, Power and Policy Making: The Case of Health Care Reform in the 1990s* (Armonk, NY: M. E. Sharpe, 1998).

Harry A. Sultz and Kristina M. Young, *Health Care USA* (7th ed.) (Sudbury, MA: Jones & Bartlett, 2010).

Carol S. Weissert and William G. Weissert, *Governing Health: The Politics of Health Policy* (3rd ed.) (Baltimore: Johns Hopkins University Press, 2006).

Useful Web Sources for U.S. Healthcare Policy

Department of Health and Human Services: http://www.hhs.gov/
Center for Medicare and Medicaid Services: http://www.cms.gov/
The Henry J. Kaiser Family Foundation: http://www.kff.org/
The Commonwealth Fund: http://www.commonwealthfund.org/

Suggested Readings for Canadian Healthcare Policy

Duane Adams, ed., *Federalism, Democracy, and Health Policy in Canada* (Montreal and Kingston: McGill-Queen's University Press, 2001).

Keith G. Banting and Stan Corbett, eds., *Health Policy and Federalism: A Comparative Perspective on Multi-Level Governance* (Montreal and Kingston: McGill-Queen's University Press, 2001).

Nadeem Esmail and Michael Walker. *How Good Is Canadian Healthcare? 2008 Report* (Vancouver, BC: Fraser Institute, 2008).

Katherine Fierlbeck, *Health Care in Canada: A Citizen's Guide to Policy and Politics* (Toronto: University of Toronto Press, 2011).

Malocolm G. Taylor, *Health Insurance and Canadian Public Policy: The Seven Decisions That Created the Canadian Health Insurance System and Their Outcomes* (2nd ed.) (Kingston and Montreal: McGill-Queen's University Press, 2009).

Carolyn Hughes Tuohy, *Accidental Logics: The Dynamics of Change in the Health Care Area in the United States, Britain, and Canada* (New York and Oxford: Oxford University Press, 1999).

Useful Web Sources for Canadian Healthcare Policy

Health Canada
Canadian Institute for health Information
Canadian Health Services Research Foundation
The Fraser Institute

Notes

1. See Pablo Gottret and George Schieber, *Health Financing Revisited: A Practitioner's Guide* (Washington DC: World Bank, 2006), available at http://siteresources.worldbank .org/INTHSD/Resources/topics/Health-Financing/HFRFull.pdf (accessed May 31, 2012).

2. For a good summary of different health policy concerns in the United States and Canada, see Theodore R. Marmor and Antonia Maioni, "Health Care in Crisis: What's Driving Health Reform in Canada and the United States?," *One Issue, Two Voices,* Issue 9 (April 2008) (Washington, DC: Woodrow Wilson International Center for Scholars), available at http://www.wilsoncenter.org/sites/default/files/ CI_OneIssue_9.pdf (accessed May 31, 2012).

3. The 2012 figures were obtained from "Health Expenditures per Capital (Current US$)," The World Bank, 2014 (accessed April 23, 2014). The 2009 figures were obtained from the Organization for Economic Cooperation and Development (OECD), *OECD Health Data,* 2011 (Paris: OECD, 2011), available at http://www.oecd.org/document/3 0/0,3746,en_2649_37407_12968734_1_1_1_37407,00.html (accessed May 31, 2012).

4. The 30 OECD countries are Australia, Austria, Belgium, Canada, the Czech Republic, Denmark, Finland, France, Germany, Greece, Hungary, Iceland, Ireland, Italy, Japan, South Korea, Luxembourg, Mexico, the Netherlands, New Zealand, Norway, Poland, Portugal, the Slovak Republic, Spain, Sweden, Switzerland, Turkey, the United Kingdom, and the United States.

5. See Victor R. Fuchs and Ezekiel J. Emanuel, "Health Care Reform: Why? What? When?" *Health Affairs* 24(6) (2005): 1399–1414. For a summary of the philosophical considerations of equality, equity, and fairness in extending access to healthcare for all Americans, see Kant Patel and Mark Rushefsky, *Health Care Politics and Policy in America* (3rd ed.) (Armonk, NY: M. E. Sharpe, 2006), Chapter 6.

6. See the CBS News/New York Times Poll, "The Debate over Health Care," released June 20, 2009, available at http://www.cbsnews.com/htdocs/pdf/CBSPOLL_June09a_health_care.pdf?tag=contentMain;contentBody (accessed May 31, 2012).

7. See Carmen DeNavas-Walt, Bernadette D. Proctor, and Jessica C. Smith, U.S. Census Bureau, *Income, Poverty, and Health Insurance Coverage in the United States: 2010* (Washington, DC: U.S. Government Printing Office, 2011), available at http://www.census.gov/prod/2011pubs/p60-239.pdf (accessed May 31, 2012).

8. See Harris Poll, "Americans Rate Canadian Health Care System Better than U.S. System," *Health Care News* 4(14) (2004), available at http://www.harrisinteractive.com/news/newsletters/healthnews/HI_HealthCareNews2004Vol4_Iss14.pdf (accessed May 31, 2012).

9. See Marmor and Maioni, "Health Care in Crisis: What's Driving Health Reform in Canada and the United States?" (2008); Matthew Mendelsohn, *Canadian's Thoughts on Their Health Care System: Preserving the Canadian Model Through Innovation*, the Commission on the Future of Health Care in Canada, Queen's University, June 2002, available at http://www.queensu.ca/cora/_files/MendelsohnEnglish.pdf (accessed May 31, 2012); and Nadeem Esmail and Michael Walker, *How Good Is Canadian Healthcare? 2008 Report* (Vancouver, BC: Fraser Institute, December 2008), available at http://www.fraserinstitute.org/research-news/display.aspx?id=13104 (accessed May 31, 2012).

10. See the Canadian Prime Minster office's information, available at http://www.pm.gc.ca/eng/feature.asp?pageId=40 (accessed May 31, 2012).

11. For a summary of contemporary healthcare policy issues in Canada, see Antonia Maioni "Canadian Health Care," in Kenneth G. Pryke and Walter C. Soderlund, eds., *Profiles of Canada* (3rd ed.) (Toronto: Canadian Scholars' Press, 2003), pp. 307–323; Allan S. Detsky and C. David Naylor, "Canada's Health Care System—Reform Delayed," *New England Journal of Medicine* 349(8) (2005): 804–810; and Pat Armstrong and Hugh Armstrong, *Wasting Away: The Undermining of Canadian Health Care* (2nd ed.) (Oxford: Oxford University Press, 2002).

12. For a historical analysis of the development of different health insurances in the United States and Canada, see Antonia Maioni, *Parting at the Crossroads: The Emergence of Health Insurance in the United States and Canada* (Princeton, NJ: Princeton University Press, 1998).

13. For a good discussion of the development of the managed healthcare system in the United States, see Peter R. Kongstvedt, ed., *Essentials of Managed Healthcare* (5th ed.) (Sudbury, MA: Jones & Bartlett, 2007); Peter R. Kongstverdt, *Managed Care: What It Is and How It Works* (2nd ed.) (Sudbury, MA: Jones & Bartlett, 2002); and Arnold Birenbaum, *Managed Care: Made in America* (Westport, CT: Prager, 1997).

14. See Theodor J. Litman, "Appendix: A Chronology and Capsule Highlights of the Major Historical and Political Milestones in the Evolution of the Relationship of

Government Involvement in Health and Health Care in the United States," in James Morone, Theodor J. Litman, and Leonard S. Robins, eds., *Health Politics and Policy* (4th ed.) (Albany: Delmar Cengage Learning, 2008), and Fuchs and Emanuel, "Health Care Reform: Why? What? When?" (2003).

15. The figure was reported in Christopher A. Simon, *Public Policy: Preferences and Outcomes* (New York: Pearson-Longman, 2007), p. 65.

16. See CBS News/New York Times Poll, "The Debate over Health Care," released June 20, 2009, available at http://www.cbsnews.com/htdocs/pdf/CBSPOLL_June09a_health_care.pdf?tag=contentMain;contentBody (accessed May 31, 2012), p.1.

17. For example, see Elizabeth Mendes, "More Americans Uninsured in 2011: However, More Adults Aged 18 to 26 Now Covered," January 24, 2012, available at http://www.gallup.com/poll/152162/americans-uninsured-2011.aspx (accessed May 31, 2012).

18. For a good overview of actors in healthcare policy making, see Weissert and Weissert, *Governing Health* (2006) and Rushefsky and Patel, *Politics, Power, and Policy Making* (1998).

19. See Woodrow Wilson, *Congressional Government* (Boston: Houghton Mifflin, 1885 [1913]), p. 79.

20. See Michael T. Heaney, "Outside the Issue Niche: The Multidimensionality of Interest Group Identity," *American Politics Research* 32(6) (2004): 611–651.

21. Quoted in Weissert and Weissert, *Governing Health* (2006), p. 129.

22. See http://www.hhs.gov/about/index.html (accessed May 31, 2012).

23. See http://www.ssa.gov/history/ssa/ssa2000chapter4.html (accessed May 31, 2012).

24. See http://www.cms.gov (accessed May 31, 2012).

25. See http://www.fda.gov (accessed May 31, 2012).

26. See http://www.nih.gov (accessed May 31, 2012).

27. See http://www.cdc.gov (accessed May 31, 2012).

28. See http://www.va.gov/health/aboutVHA.asp (accessed May 31, 2012).

29. See http://www.health.mil/default.aspx (accessed May 31, 2012).

30. See http://www.tricare.mil/ (accessed May 31, 2012) and M. Nicholas Coppola, Jeffrey P. Harrison, Bernie Kerr, and Dawn Erckenbrack "The Military Managed Healthcare System," in Kongstvedt, ed., *Essentials of Managed Healthcare* (2007), Chapter 28.

31. For a good discussion of the role of state governments in healthcare policy, see Weissert and Weissert, *Governing Health* (2006), Chapter 5, and Debra J. Lipson, "State Roles in Health Care Policy: Past as Prologue?" in Litman and Robins, eds., *Health Politics and Policy* (1997).

32. See Robert E. Moffit, "State Health Reform: Six Key Tests," *WebMemo* No. 1900 (April 23, 2008), available at www.heritage.org/Research/HealthCare/wm1900.cfm (accessed May 31, 2012).

33. See Heaney, "Outside the Issue Niche" (2004).

34. See http://www.ama-assn.org/ (accessed May 31, 2012).

35. See http://www.aarp.org (accessed May 31, 2012).

36. See http://www.phrma.org (accessed May 31, 2012).

37. For a good discussion of the development of Medicare and Medicaid, see Theodore R. Marmor, *The Politics of Medicare* (2nd ed.) (New York: Aldine Transaction, 2000); Rashi Fein, *Medical Care, Medical Costs* (Cambridge, MA: Harvard University Press, 1986); Jonathan Oberlander, *The Political Life of Medicare* (Chicago: University of Chicago Press, 2003); and Weissert and Weissert, *Governing Health* (2006).

38. See DeNavas-Walt et al., *Income, Poverty, and Health Insurance Coverage in the United States: 2010*, available at http://www.census.gov/prod/2011pubs/p60-239.pdf (accessed May 31, 2012).

39. The following description of Medicare is based on the official Medicare booklet (SSA Publication No. 05-10043, May 2008, ICN 460000), available at http://www. socialsecurity.gov/pubs/10043.pdf (accessed May 31, 2012).

40. See the US Census, *The 2012 Statistical Abstract,* Table 151. *Medicaid—Beneficiaries and Payments: 2000 to2009,* available at http://www.census.gov/compendia/statab/2012/ tables/12s0152.pdf (accessed May 31, 2012).

41. The following information is based on "Medicare Program: General Education," available at http://www.cms.gov/Medicare/Medicare-General-Information/MedicareGenInfo/ index.html (accessed May 31, 2012).

42. See the U.S. Census, *The 2012 Statistical Abstract,* Table 152. *Medicaid—Summary by State: 2000 and 2009,* available at http://www.census.gov/compendia/statab/2012/ tables/12s0152.pdf (accessed May 31, 2012).

43. See the U.S. Census, *The 2012 Statistical Abstract,* Table 145. Children's Health Insurance Program *CHIP—Enrollment and Expenditures by State: 2000 and 2010,* available at http:// www.census.gov/compendia/statab/2012/tables/12s0145.pdf (accessed May 31, 2012).

44. See Kongstvedt, ed., *Essentials of Managed Healthcare* (2007); Birenbaum, *Managed Care* (1997); and Weissert and Weissert, *Governing Health* (2006).

45. See Jonathan P. Weinder and Gregory de Lissovoy, "Razing a Tower of Babel: A Taxonomy for Managed Care and Health Insurance Plans," *Journal of Health Politics, Policy, and Law,* 18(1) (1993): 75–103, and R. A. Dudley and H. S. Luft, "Managed Care in Transition," *New England Journal of Medicine* 334(14) (2001): 1087–1092. For a summary of issues regarding the managed healthcare system, see Paul Krugman and Robin Wells, "The Health Care Crisis and What to Do about It," *The New York Review of Books* 53(5) (March 23, 2006), available at http://www. nybooks.com/articles/18802 (accessed May 31, 2012).

46. See Patel and Rushefsky, *Health Care Politics and Policy in America* (2006).

47. For the Senate's action, see GovTrack.us. S. 2083—108th Congress (2004): Bipartisan Patient Protection Act of 2004, GovTrack.us (database of federal legislation), available online at http://www.govtrack.us/congress/bill.xpd?bill=s108-2083) (accessed May 31, 2012). For the House of Representatives' action, see GovTrack.us. H.R. 4628—108th Congress (2004): Patients' Bill of Rights Act of 2004, available online at http://www.govtrack.us/congress/bill.xpd?bill=h108-4628) (accessed May 31, 2012).

48. For the COBRA, see http://www.dol.gov/dol/topic/health-plans/cobra.htm (accessed May 31, 2012).

49. For the HIPAA, see http://www.dol.gov/dol/topic/health-plans/portability.htm (accessed May 31, 2012).

50. For a good discussion of why and how the Clinton healthcare proposal was not passed by Congress in the 1990s, see Rushefsky and Patel, *Politics, Power, and Policy Making* (1998). For a critical view on the Clinton Health Reform Plan, see Robert E. Moffit, "A Guide to the Clinton Health Plan," *Talking Points,* November 19, 1993 (the Heritage Foundation), available at http://thf_media.s3.amazonaws.com/1993/ pdf/tp_00.pdf (accessed May 31, 2012).

51. See Moffit, "A Guide to the Clinton Health Plan," p. 2.

52. See Moffit, "A Guide to the Clinton Health Plan," p. 2 and footnote 2 on p. 26.

53. See Weissert and Weissert, *Governing Health* (2006) and Kongstvedt, ed., *Essentials of Managed Healthcare* (2007).

54. See Karen Davis, Cathy Schoen, and Kristof Stremikis, *Mirror, Mirror on the Wall: How the Performance of the U.S. Health Care System Compares Internationally, 2010 Update,* the Commonwealth Fund, June 2010, available at http://www.

commonwealthfund.org/~/media/Files/Publications/Fund%20Report/2010/ Jun/1400_Davis_Mirror_Mirror_on_the_wall_2010.pdf (accessed June 1, 2012).

55. For the problems of fraud and abuse of Medicare and Medicaid, see the testimony on the *False Claims Act* by Lewis Morris before the Committee on the Judiciary Subcommittee on Immigrations and Claims, April 28, 1998, available at http://www. hhs.gov/asl/testify/t980428b.html (accessed May 31, 2012).

56. See http://www.oig.hhs.gov/publications/hcfac.asp (accessed May 31, 2012).

57. For more information on preventive care initiatives by the DHHS, see http://www. hhs.gov/safety/index.html (accessed June 1, 2012).

58. See DeNavas-Walt et al., *Income, Poverty, and Health Insurance Coverage in the United States: 2010*, available at http://www.census.gov/prod/2011pubs/p60-239. pdf (accessed May 31, 2012).

59. See Keith G. Banting and Stan Corbett, eds., *Health Policy and Federalism: A Comparative Perspective on Multi-Level Governance* (Montreal and Kingston: McGill-Queen's University Press, 2002).

60. This description is based on 'How Health Care Services Are Delivered' in Canada's Health Care System, available at http://www.hc-sc.gc.ca/hcs-sss/pubs/system-regime/2011-hcs-sss/index-eng.php (accessed May 31, 2012).

61. See *OECD Health Data, 2011* (Paris: OECD, 2011), available at http://www.oecd.org/docum ent/30/0,3746,en_2649_37407_12968734_1_1_1_37407,00.html (accessed May 31, 2012).

62. See the Canadian Institute for Health Information, *National Health Expenditure Trend, 1975–2011*, available at https://secure.cihi.ca/free_products/nhex_trends_report_2011_ en.pdf (accessed May 31, 2012).

63. For a good summary of issues in reforming the Canadian healthcare system, see John K. Iglehart, "Revisiting the Canadian Health Care System," *New England Journal of Medicine* 342(26) (2000): 2007–2112; Allan S. Detsky and C. David Naylor, "Canada's Health Care System—Reform Delayed," *New England Journal of Medicine* 349(8) (2003): 804–810; and Esmail and Walker, *How Good Is Canadian Healthcare? 2008 Report* (2008).

64. See Davis et al., *Mirror, Mirror on the Wall* (2010).

65. See Esmail and Walker, *How Good Is Canadian Healthcare? 2008 Report* (2008), and Antonia Maioni, "Canadian Health Care" (2003).

66. The following description is based on James Bickerton and Alain-G. Gagnon, eds., *Canadian Politics* (4th ed.) (Peterborough, Ontario: Broadview Press, 2004) and Eugene A. Forsey, *How Canadians Govern Themselves* (6th ed.), revised on August 2005, updated by the Canadian Library of Parliament Information Service, available at http://www.parl.gc.ca/About/Parliament/SenatorEugeneForsey/Home/Index-e.html (accessed May 31, 2012).

67. For example, see Antonia Maioni, "Roles and Responsibilities in Health Care Policy," in Tom McIntosh, Pierr-Gerlier Forest, Gregory P. Marchildon, eds., *The Governance of Health Care in Canada: The Romanow Papers*, Volume 3 (Toronto: University of Toronto Press, 2004), pp. 169–198.

68. See Tuohy, *Accidental Logics* (1999), pp. 203–237.

69. For an organizational chart and further information regarding Health Canada, see http:// www.hc-sc.gc.ca/ahc-asc/branch-dirgen/index-eng.php#list (accessed June 1, 2012).

71. Health Canada, "About Mission, Values, Activities," see www.hc-sc.gc.ca/ahc-asc/ activitabout-apropos/index (accessed April 28, 2014).

70. For the CMA, see http://www.cma.ca/ (accessed June 1, 2012).

71. The following discussion of the evolution of Canada's single-payer Medicare system is based mostly on "Making Medicare: The History of Health Care in Canada,

1914–2007," available at http://www.civilization.ca/cmc/exhibitions/hist/medicare/ medic00e.shtml (accessed May 31, 2012); Antonia Maioni, "Key Events" of *Public Health Insurance Through History-Virtual Exhibit* at the McGill Institute for the Study of Canada (retrieved August 19, 2006); and Malcolm G. Taylor, *Health Insurance and Canadian Public Policy: The Seven Decisions That Created the Canadian Health Insurance System and Their Outcomes* (2nd ed.) (Kingston and Montreal: McGill-Queen's University Press, 2009).

72. See Detsky and Naylor, "Canada's Health Care System—Reform Delayed" (2003), p. 805.

73. For a discussion of the role of the National Forum on Health in reforming Canada's healthcare system, see Tuohy, *Accidental Logics* (1999), pp. 95–97. See the text of the report, available at http://www.hc-sc.gc.ca/hcs-sss/com/fed/nfh-fns-eng.php (accessed June 2, 2012).

74. See the full document and action plan, available at http://www.hc-sc.gc.ca/hcs-sss/ delivery-prestation/fptcollab/2004-fmm-rpm/index-eng.php (accessed May 31, 2012).

75. See the text of the Canada Health Act (CHA), available at http://laws-lois.justice. gc.ca/PDF/C-6.pdf (accessed May 31, 2012). For a brief discussion of the Canadian healthcare system under the CHA, see Canada's Health Care System, available at http://www.hc-sc.gc.ca/hcs-sss/pubs/system-regime/2011-hcs-sss/index-eng.php (accessed May 31, 2012).

76. For each provincial and territorial health plan, see the online resource section "Provinces and Territories," available at http://www.hc-sc.gc.ca/hcs-sss/pubs/system-regime/2011-hcs-sss/index-eng.php (accessed June 2, 2012).

77. See *OECD Health Data,* 2011 (Paris: OECD, 2011), available at http://www. oecd.org/document/30/0,3746,en_2649_37407_12968734_1_1_1_37407,00.html (accessed May 31, 2012) and The Organization for Economic Cooperation and Development, *OECD Health Data,* 2008 (Paris: OECD, 2008), available online at http://www.oecd.org/els/health/data.

78. See Esmail and Walker, *How Good Is Canadian Healthcare? 2008 Report* (2008), p. 86.

79. See Skinner et al., "The Hidden Costs of Single Payer Health Insurance" (2008), pp. 4–5.

80. See Esmail and Walker, *How Good Is Canadian Healthcare?* (2008), pp. 56–61, and Marmor and Maioni, "Health Care in Crisis: What's Driving Health Reform in Canada and the United States?"(2008).

81. See Marmor and Maioni, "Health Care in Crisis: What's Driving Health Reform in Canada and the United States?"(2008), and Steinbrook, "Private Health Care in Canada" (2006).

82. See CBC News, "Top Court Strikes Down Quebec Private Health-Care Ban," June 9, 2005, available at http://cbc.ca/news/canada/top-court-strikes-down-Quebec (accessed April 28, 2014).

83. See Brett J. Skinner and Mark Rovere, *Canada's Medicare Bubble: Is Government Health Spending Sustainable without User-Based Funding?* Fraser Institute, April 2011, available at http://www.fraserinstitute.org/uploadedFiles/fraser-ca/Content/research-news/research/publications/canadas-medicare-bubble.pdf (accessed June 1, 2012).

84. See Skinner et al., "The Hidden Costs of Single Payer Health Insurance" (2008), p. 7, and Marmor and Maioni, "Health Care in Crisis: What's Driving Health Reform in Canada and the United States?"(2008), pp. 24–25.

85. See Mark Rovere and Brett J. Skinner, "Value for Money from Health Insurance Systems in Canada and the OECD, 2012 edition," *Fraser Alert*, April 2012, available at

http://www.fraserinstitute.org/uploadedFiles/fraser-ca/Content/research-news/research/publications/value-for-money-from-health-insurance-systems-2012.pdf (accessed June 1, 2012).

86. See Skinner et al., "The Hidden Costs of Single Payer Health Insurance: A Comparison of the United States and Canada" (2008).
87. See Davis et al., *Mirror, Mirror on the Wall* (2010).
88. See Esmail and Walker, *How Good s Canadian Healthcare? 2008 Report* (2008).

CHAPTER 7

Social Welfare Policy

LEARNING OBJECTIVES

- Define social welfare policy and its purpose.
- Understand the differences between the United States and Sweden as welfare states.
- Understand different types of social welfare policies

implemented by the United States and Sweden.
- Explain how the United States and Sweden deal with demographic, economic, and societal challenges through social welfare programs.

Social welfare, or the well-being of society at large, has been the biggest public policy concern of many governments in the contemporary world.[1] In this chapter, we define social welfare policy in terms of government efforts to alleviate economic inequality by providing economic benefits directly to individuals who are having a hard time escaping from economic difficulty. Social welfare programs cover a wide range of benefits, such as Social Security, public assistance, job training, public health, unemployment compensation, and disability support. These benefits are for the protection and improvement of living standards of targeted citizens, specifically children, the elderly, people with disabilities, those who are unemployed, and working women with children. Social welfare measures can be divided into three categories. The first category encompasses **social insurance programs**, such as Social Security, unemployment insurance, worker's compensation, and disability insurance. The second category comprises **public assistance programs** to alleviate poverty for those not covered by social insurance. The third category includes **employment programs** to provide jobs, job training, and other assistance to those needing help to lift themselves out of poverty. In addition, many governments provide healthcare and education programs under social welfare policy.

In the late twentieth century and the early twenty-first century, many governments devoted a large portion of their budgets to social welfare spending. On average, the world's wealthiest states, the members of the Organization of Economic Cooperation and Development (OECD), have expanded their social welfare spending, relative to their gross domestic product (GDP), from

15.6 percent in 1980 to 19.3 percent in 2007.[2] The United States, with the world's largest economy and a population of more than 300 million people, allocated 16.2 percent of its GDP, or $6,145 per capita, to public social spending in 2007. In comparison, Sweden, which is known as a generous social welfare state with a population of about 9 million people, allocated 27.3 percent of its GDP, or $9,108 per capita, to public social spending in 2007. The costs of social welfare will increase because a growing aging population will need to be covered by social insurance, and entitlement programs will be required to help a growing number of poor single-parent households. Many contemporary governments, including the governments of the United States and Sweden, have been confronted with challenges to cut the costs of social welfare without reducing social welfare benefits and increasing taxation.

Social welfare policy, which is usually associated with a welfare state, is often confused with socialism. What is a welfare state? How does social welfare policy differ from socialism? According to Harold L. Wilensky, the essence of a **welfare state** is "government-protected minimum standards of income, nutrition, health, and housing and education, assured to every citizen as a political right, not charity."[3] Welfare states (e.g., Canada, Japan, Sweden, and the United States) are foremost democratic states that guarantee social protection as a right of citizenship. By contrast, **socialist states** (e.g., China and Cuba) grant no individual political, social, and economic rights, and their governments determine standards of income, nutrition, health, housing, and education. Welfare states operate under democratic political rules and market economic principles, such as respect for economic freedom and property rights, and their governments have regulations and institutions to provide social welfare.

According to Gøsta Esping-Andersen, before 1990, the United States and Sweden exemplified two models of welfare states in terms of the following characteristics: (1) benefit generosity, (2) social rights, (3) welfare provision, (4) benefits, (5) funding, and (6) the role of government. The United States exemplified a *liberal welfare model,* which is characterized by (1) low benefit generosity, with relatively few entitlement programs; (2) social rights based on need, as determined by minimum income; (3) welfare provision through mixed public and private services for eligible citizens; (4) flat benefits; (5) funding through income taxes and private sources; and (6) a minimum role of government. Sweden exemplified a *social democratic welfare model,* which is characterized by (1) high benefit generosity, with evenly distributed entitlement programs; (2) universal social rights; (3) welfare provision through public services for all residents regardless of their contributions; (4) redistributive benefits; (5) funding through income taxes; and (6) a maximum role of government. Both the United States and Sweden have undertaken social welfare reforms since the 1990s. Therefore, their current social welfare programs may differ from Esping-Andersen's models of welfare states before 1990.[4]

Although the United States and Sweden differ in their welfare models, their social welfare policy has been confronted with similar demographic, economic, and societal challenges. Demographic challenges include demographic changes (e.g., aging populations) and labor market changes, which could cause more unemployment and part-time employment, necessitating an expansion of social welfare benefits and/or a reevaluation of employment-based social insurance. Economic challenges include economic shifts, thus creating pressure on national economies from increasingly competitive global markets and pressure on national budgets from economic recession, higher interest rates, and increased national debt. Societal challenges include changes in family structure (e.g., higher teen pregnancy rates and more single-parent families) as well as continued immigration of unskilled legal and/or illegal workers. Other challenges include people following economic liberalization through the North American Free Trade Agreement (NAFTA) in the case of the United States and the European Union (EU) in the case of Sweden. These challenges have been significant forces requiring social welfare reforms and generating new dynamics in the process of social welfare policy making.

We chose Sweden as a comparison for the United States because it faces similar challenges. Also, both countries have advanced highly institutionalized democracies. The major difference between the two countries is that the United States is a constitutional democracy that uses a presidential system, whereas Sweden is a constitutional monarchy that uses a parliamentary system. These similarities and one major difference lend themselves to using both the historical and institutional approaches for comparing the United States and Sweden.

How do the United States and Sweden, two very different welfare states, deal with demographic, economic, and societal challenges through social welfare programs? How have these challenges shaped the liberal welfare model developed in the United States and the social democratic welfare model developed in Sweden? Motivated by these questions, this chapter will look at issues, government agencies and other actors, policy initiatives, contemporary programs, as well as challenges and problems related to social welfare policy in the United States and Sweden.

The United States

Since the onset of the Great Depression that followed the 1929 crash of the U.S. stock market, presidents of the United States have promoted and implemented social welfare programs to reduce economic inequality among citizens. Created in response to the Great Depression, the first major social welfare policy initiative in the United States was President Franklin Roosevelt's **New Deal**, a set of programs and legislation that included the 1935 Social Security Act. Before the 1930s, the United States had no nationwide social welfare program because many Americans believed that problems related to hunger, unemployment, poverty, aging, and disability were handled by families, churches, private charities, as well as state and local governments.[5] Since the federal government assumed responsibility for social welfare, federal spending on Social Security and anti-poverty programs has increased. Federal spending to fight poverty through programs providing healthcare, food, housing, cash, and other forms of assistance increased by 89 percent from $342,453 million in 2000 to $647,505 million in 2010.[6] Yet, in 2009, 43.6 million people lived in poverty, and the official poverty rate was 14.3 percent. The 2009 poverty rate was above 15 percent for children (20.7 percent), blacks (25.8 percent), and Hispanics (25.3 percent).[7]

Social welfare programs in the United States are based on philosophical assumptions that are different from social welfare programs in European welfare states. Many European welfare states see any government-sponsored social welfare program as a political right of all citizens, but the United States relies on social welfare programs with a focus on making opportunities for success available to most citizens by providing financial stability. The United States is sometimes called an "opportunity-insurance state."[8] Historically, many Americans believe that, although some individuals may rely heavily on social welfare programs, there are a great many more people who simply need temporary assistance and use social welfare programs only as needed. Whereas people in many European welfare states enjoy universal entitlement programs funded by high income taxes, Americans often debate the merits of social welfare, wondering about the nature and causes of poverty and inequality, the role of government, the taxpayer's burden, and appropriate strategies for coping with social problems.

A primary goal of social welfare programs is to improve the quality of life and living standards for the poor and underprivileged members of society, such as the elderly, people with disabilities, students, unpaid workers, mothers, and children. Contemporary social welfare programs available in the United States include Medicare (health insurance for the elderly), Medicaid (health insurance coverage for low-income families), the Supplemental Nutrition Assistance Program (SNAP), Supplemental Security Income (SSI), Housing and Urban Development (HUD) programs, Temporary Assistance for Needy Families (TANF), Head Start, Work Study, Child Nutrition Programs, the State Children's Health Insurance Program (SCHIP), Women, Infants and Children (WIC), child-care programs, as well as the Earned Income Tax Credit (EITC). The United States also operates a nationwide Social Security program, also known as the Old Age, Survivors, and Disability Insurance (OASDI) program.

Similar to other OECD countries, the United States faces increasing dependency on government entitlement programs, which raises social welfare costs and long-term budget deficits. The costs of Medicare, Medicaid, Social Security, and other government-entitlement programs, which were 10.2 percent of GDP in 2008, are expected to rise to 15.6 percent of GDP in 2020.[9] Hence, social welfare and security reforms are high on the agenda of Congress and the executive branch. One attempt to reform social welfare was the 1996 **Personal Responsibility and Work Opportunity Reconciliation Act (PRWORA)**. Renewed in 2005 and 2009, this act changed provisions of social welfare/entitlement programs established by the 1935 Social Security Act. In an attempt to reform Social Security, President George W. Bush proposed a partial privatization of social security in 2005; the majority of Americans overwhelmingly disapproved of this reform proposal, and it was not successful.

Government Agencies and Other Actors

The Legislative Branch Social welfare policy in the United States is based on acts of Congress. In the Senate, the primary committees in charge of social welfare are the Committee on Finance and its Subcommittee on Social Security, Pensions, and Family Policy.[10] The Committee on Agriculture, Nutrition, and Forestry deals with food stamps. In 1961, the Senate also established the Special Committee on Aging as a temporary committee to deal with an aging population and Social Security; this committee has been a permanent committee since 1977.[11] In the House of Representatives, the primary committees in charge of social welfare are the Committee on Ways and Means as well as its Subcommittee on Income Security and Family Support, its Subcommittee on Social Security, and its Subcommittee on Health.[12]

The Subcommittee on Income Security and Family Support deals with unemployment compensation, temporary assistance for needy families (TANF), child care, child support enforcement, child welfare, social services grants, and supplemental security income. The Subcommittee on Social Security deals with the Old-Age, Survivors, and Disability Insurance (OASDI) program, the Railroad Retirement program, as well as employment taxes and trust fund operations related to these programs. The Subcommittee on Health deals with healthcare programs under the Social Security Act (SSA). In addition to the Committee on Ways and Means, the Committee on Economic and Educational Opportunities as well as the Committee on Agriculture are in charge of social welfare by dealing with child services and food stamps.

The Executive Branch Although presidents need to communicate with key members of Congress about social welfare policy making, they may take the lead in setting economic and social policy agendas, as President Roosevelt did with regard to the New Deal, as President Johnson did with regard to the Great Society, and as President George W. Bush did with regard to Social Security reform.

In order to enhance the efficiency of policy making in the executive branch, several organs have been created in the Executive Office of the President (EOP). Among these organs, the Domestic Policy Council (DPC), the National Economic Council (NEC), the Council of Economic Advisers (CEA), and the Office of Management and Budget (OMB) have various forms of influence on social welfare policy making.

The Domestic Policy Council (DPC) The DPC has influence on social welfare policy through its coordination and supervision of and advice to the President on matters of domestic policy, except economic policy.[13]

The National Economic Council (NEC) and the Council of Economic Advisers (CEA) The NEC and the CEA have influence on social welfare policy related to domestic and international aspects of economic policy.[14]

The Office of Management and Budget (OMB) The OMB has influence on social welfare policy through its involvement in legislative clearance and regulatory review processes regarding social welfare policy proposals and programs presented by government agencies in accordance with the president's social welfare policy agenda.[15]

Authorized and monitored by Congress, social welfare policy is implemented and administrated through social welfare policy programs created by the executive branch. Let us now take a closer look at some departments and agencies that deal with social welfare issues.

The Department of Health and Human Services (HHS)   The HHS implements and monitors programs related to the protection of health and the provision of human services.[16] This department supervises Medicare and Medicaid, and HHS divisions operate federal social welfare programs for children and families as well as for the elderly and people with disabilities. The Administration for Children and Families (ACF), one of the HHS divisions, is responsible for family assistance, child support, child care, Head Start, child welfare, and various other programs for children and families.[17] Various tasks of the ACF are handled by specific administrative bodies, such as the Administration for Children, Youth, and Families (ACYF), the Office of Head Start, and the Office of Family Assistance (OFA). Since 2006, the OFA has administered the Temporary Assistance for Needy Families (TANF) program.[18] In addition to the ACF, another division within HSS is the Administration on Aging (AoA), whose mission is to help elderly individuals maintain their health and independence in their homes and communities.[19]

The Social Security Administration (SSA)   The SSA operates nationwide Social Security programs providing retirement benefits, benefits for surviving spouses and children of income earners, and benefits for people with disabilities, as well as Supplemental Security Income (SSI) and Medicare benefits. The SSA has over 64,000 employees, 10 regional offices, 6 processing centers, and more than 1,260 field offices providing local Social Security services.[20]

The Department of Labor (DOL)   Within the DOL, the Employment and Training Administration (ETA) provides and supervises unemployment insurance and job training programs largely administered by state and local governments.[21]

The Department of Agriculture (DOA)   The DOA is involved in social welfare policy through the Food and Nutrition Service (FNS). The FNS is responsible for the Supplemental Nutrition Assistance Program (SNAP).[22]

The Department of Housing and Urban Development (HUD)   This department administers Housing and Urban Development (HUD) programs, providing senior citizens and people with low or moderate incomes with access to affordable housing.[23] Within HUD, specific responsibility for programs that focus on decent housing, a suitable living environment, and expanded economic opportunities for people with low and moderate incomes is assigned to the Office of Community Planning and Development, which manages these programs in partnership with state and local governments as well as the private sector, including profit and nonprofit organizations.

State Governments With passage of the 1996 Personal Responsibility and Work Opportunity Reconciliation Act (PRWORA), state governments were given more responsibility for designing and implementing social welfare programs largely funded through **federal block-grants** (i.e., federal grants-in-aid that state governments can spend as they wish on specific social welfare programs under federal government guidelines). As a result, the design and implementation of social welfare programs vary from state to state.[24]

Interest Groups Since social welfare involves a wide range of issues and interests, there are numerous interest groups that seek to influence social welfare policy making.[25] Among interest groups that lobby members of Congress and testify before congressional committees and subcommittees in regard to social welfare are the American Federation of Labor and Congress of Industrial Organizations (AFL-CIO), the National Association of Chambers of Commerce (NACC), the National Association for the Advancement of Colored People (NAACP), the American Association of Retired Persons (AARP), the National Council of Senior Citizens (NCSC), the Children's Defense Fund (CDF), and the Child Welfare League of America (CWLA). Since the 1996 Personal Responsibility and Work Opportunity Reconciliation Act gave state governments more responsibility for designing and implementing social welfare programs, numerous profit and nonprofit interest groups have sought to influence state social welfare policy making.

Policy Initiatives

Current U.S. social welfare policy is based on the 1996 Personal Responsibility and Work Opportunity Reconciliation Act. This act brought about significant change to the social welfare system established mainly through President Franklin Roosevelt's New Deal in the 1930s and developed further through President Lyndon Johnson's Great Society in the 1960s.

The New Deal Program and the 1935 Social Security Act The first major policy initiative to establish a national social welfare system in the United States was President Franklin Roosevelt's New Deal, a set of programs designed and implemented in response to massive unemployment, poverty, and hunger affecting millions of Americans during the Great Depression. Under the New Deal, the Roosevelt Administration created unprecedented programs that promoted government–industry cooperation, stimulated agricultural revitalization, generated welfare for millions of unemployed, created massive public works, provided for strict federal regulation of securities and exchange markets, and made available billions of federal dollars to prevent home and farm foreclosures. Of all New Deal legislation, probably the most significant act was the 1935 Social Security Act. The SSA and amendments to it in 1939 and 1956 created the foundation for the current nationwide Social Security program, also known as the Old-Age, Survivors, and Disability Insurance (OASDI) program.[26] The SSA also initiated unemployment compensation as well as Aid to Dependent Children, which became Aid to Families with Dependent Children (AFDC). The AFDC guaranteed income assistance to poor single mothers unable to work and partake in federal job programs; it was the most important social welfare measure to support low-income families with children before Temporary Assistance for Needy Families (TANF) was introduced in 1996.

The Great Society and the War on Poverty   The national social welfare system established in the United States through the New Deal in the 1930s was developed further in the 1960s through President Lyndon Johnson's Great Society, a series of programs intended to stop racial injustice and bring an end to poverty. The War on Poverty launched by the Great Society was fought with various entitlements and social services. The Great Society and its War on Poverty expanded the national social welfare system in the United States by creating programs such as Medicare and Medicaid, Head Start, and the food stamp program. Medicare and Medicaid were introduced under the 1965 Social Security Amendments. Head Start was launched in 1965 by the Office of Economic Opportunity (OEO), which had been established by the 1964 Economic Opportunity Act to monitor Great Society programs. Administered by local nonprofit social service organizations and school systems, Head Start provides pre-school children from low-income families with resources to meet their social, educational, health, and psychological needs.[27] The food stamp program was established by the 1964 Food Stamp Act. Administered by the Department of Agriculture (DOA), the Food Stamp program, now called the Supplemental Nutrition Assistance Program (SNAP), was designed to assist people who have little or no income with food stamps that are distributed by states and can be exchanged for food at grocery stores. The Food Stamp program was expanded through new programs such as the Special Supplemental Food Program for Women, Infants, and Children (WIC), which was launched in 1974 to provide pregnant and nursing women as well as infants and children under age 5 with nutritious supplements to their diets as well as education and access to health services.[28]

The 1996 Personal Responsibility and Work Opportunity Reconciliation Act (PRWORA)   The PRWORA, signed by President William Clinton in 1996, was designed as a comprehensive welfare reform plan to change the U.S. entitlement system into one that would require work in exchange for time-limited assistance.[29] There had been prior efforts to expand social welfare programs, but the main idea of the PRWORA was to move millions of Americans from being dependent on entitlement programs to being self-sufficient through the Welfare-to-Work initiative. The PRWORA created Temporary Assistance for Needy Families,[30] which replaced several federal entitlement programs, including Aid to Families with Dependent Children, the Job Opportunities and Basic Skills (JOBS) training program, and the Emergency Assistance (EA) program.

Contemporary Programs

The Pension System   The United States has a unique hybrid public–private pension system composed of (1) the public sector Old-Age, Survivors, and Disability Insurance program, commonly known as the Social Security program; and (2) private sector retirement plans, such as the 401k plan.

The public sector Old-Age, Survivors, and Disability Insurance program provides monthly payments to retired people, surviving spouses and children of income earners, and people with disabilities. The OASDI is a public sector program funded through what is called the Social Security Trust Fund. Contributions to this fund come from the payroll tax levied on employees and employers as well as from government spending on behalf of people with little or no income as determined by means tests. In 2009, each employee and employer contributed 6.2 percent of the employee's payroll to the Social Security Trust Fund. While the full retirement age then was 66, expectations are that it will to rise to age 67 by 2027. In 2009, more than 46 million Americans received OASDI benefits, with a maximum monthly payment of $2,323 for a retired worker and $4,065 for his or her family. For surviving spouses and children of income earners, benefits amounted to 100 percent of what the deceased would have received in primary insurance benefits at full retirement age. For people with permanent disabilities who are unable to perform substantial gainful activities due to physical or mental impairments expected to last at least a year or result in death, the maximum monthly payment at the age of 50 was $2,453 for an insured person and $3,679 for his or her family.[31]

Private sector retirement plans, such as the 401k plan, were created under the 1974 Employee Retirement Income Security Act (ERISA). Paid by employers, these plans vary in their coverage across employment agreements.[32]

Public Assistance Programs   In the United States, there are two types of public assistance programs: cash-benefit programs and in-kind benefit programs. **Cash-benefit programs** include Temporary Assistance for Needy Families, Supplemental Security Income (SSI), the Earned Income Tax Credit (EITC), the Child Tax Credit (CTC), as well as family and medical leave coverage. **In-kind benefit programs** include the Supplemental Nutrition Assistance Program, also known as the food stamp program, and housing programs.

Temporary Assistance for Needy Families (TANF) requires beneficiaries to work as soon as they are job-ready or no later than two years after receiving assistance, and it puts a five-year limit on eligibility for cash assistance. Administered by the Office of Family Assistance (OFA) under the Administration for Children and Families (ACF), one of the divisions of the Department of Health and Human Services, TANF is a federal block-grant program that allocates federal funds to specific programs designed and implemented by state governments. Four major goals of TANF are to (1) assist needy families so that children can be cared for in their own homes; (2) reduce the dependency of needy parents on entitlement programs by promoting job preparation, work, and marriage; (3) prevent out-of-wedlock pregnancies; and (4) encourage the formation and maintenance of two-parent families. The TANF program was reauthorized under the 2005 Deficit Reduction Act and, again, under the 2009 American Recovery and Reinvestment Act.[33]

Supplemental Security Income (SSI), which is administered by the Social Security Administration, assists the elderly and people with disabilities who have little or no income. Eligibility for SSI benefits is determined by means tests. The maximum monthly benefit is $674 for an individual and $1,011 for a couple.[34]

The **Earned Income Tax Credit (EITC)** is a refundable federal income tax credit for working people with little or moderate income. Eligibility is based on income thresholds determined annually by means tests.[35] In 2013, those who qualify for EITC for tax year 2013 can get a credit from:

- $2 to $487 with no qualifying children
- $9 to $3,250 with one qualifying child
- $10 to $5,372 with two qualifying children
- $11 to $6,044 with three or more qualifying children.[36]

What is a "qualifying child" in regard to the EITC? This depends on relationship, age, and residency. Regarding *relationship,* a qualifying child must be a tax-return filing person's son, daughter, adopted child, stepchild, foster child, or a descendant of any of them, such as a grandchild, or a qualifying child must be a tax-return filing person's brother, sister, stepbrother, stepsister, or a descendant of any of them, such as a niece or nephew. Regarding *age,* at the end of a tax year, a qualifying child must be the child of a tax-return filing person who is older than the child; if a person files a tax return jointly with his or her spouse, the spouse must be older than the child. Additionally, a qualifying child must be under age 19 or under age 24 if the child is a full-time student. A qualifying child may be of any age if he or she is a child with a permanent disability who is unable to perform substantial gainful activities due to a physical or mental impairment. Regarding *residency,* a qualifying child must live with a tax-return filing relative in the United States for more than half of a tax year.[37] In addition to the federal EITC, there are state and local EITCs. Currently, 22 state governments and 3 local governments provide their own EITCs based on eligibility criteria established by those state and local governments.[38]

The **Child Tax Credit (CTC)** is a refundable federal income tax credit for working people who raise children and whose earned income is below $75,000, or below $110,000 if they are married and file their tax returns jointly with their spouses. The maximum CTC is $1,000 for each qualifying child. A qualifying child must be under the age of 17 and be a tax-return filing person's son, daughter, stepchild, foster child, brother, sister, stepbrother, stepsister, or a descendant of any of them, such as a grandchild, niece, or nephew. In addition, a qualifying child must not have provided more than half of his or her own support, must be claimed as a dependent on a person's federal tax return, must be a U.S. citizen, U.S. national, or U.S. resident alien, and must live with a tax-return filing relative for more than half of a tax year.[39]

Family and medical leave coverage, established under the 1993 Family and Medical Leave Act (FMLA), provides each qualified employee with unpaid and job-protected leave for up to 12 weeks per year while maintaining his or her employer-paid medical healthcare benefits. Reasons for such leave include birth of and care for an employee's newborn child, placement of a child with an employee for adoption or foster care, care for an employee's immediate family member (spouse, child, or parent) with a serious health condition, and an employee's inability to work due to a serious health condition.[40]

The **Supplemental Nutrition Assistance Program (SNAP)**, which used to be known as the food stamp program, is administered by the Department of Agriculture through the Food and Nutrition Service. The SNAP provides food and nutrition services to U.S. households with little or no income. The program's benefits apply only to the purchase of food items at grocery stores. This includes processed foods such as potato chips and soft drinks. Eligibility for SNAP benefits is determined by means tests. In 2010, a household of four people would be eligible for SNAP benefits if their net monthly income was not more than $1,838.[41]

Housing programs are federal government programs that guarantee decent shelter for people (individuals and single-household families) with little or no income as well as for homeless people with or without families. Administered by the Department of Housing and Urban Development, housing programs include public housing programs, rural farm labor housing programs, homeless programs, rent and mortgage subsidy programs, as well as federal programs for local community development and neighborhood rehabilitation.[42] Under *public housing programs,* local housing authorities and nonprofit social service organizations with funding through federal grants build and maintain subsidized public housing units for low-income individuals and families, including senior citizens and/or children who live in single-parent households.[43] Under *homeless programs,* local organizations in collaboration with the federal government provide a range of services, including shelter, food, counseling, and job skills programs.[44]

Unemployment Insurance (UI) Programs   Administered by the Department of Labor, UI programs "provide unemployment benefits to eligible workers who are unemployed through no fault of their own, and meet other eligibility requirements."[45] One of these programs is the Federal-State Unemployment Insurance Program, which operates under federal guidelines and provides unemployed workers with unemployment insurance if they meet certain conditions established under state law. Unemployment benefits are funded through federal and state payroll taxes paid by employers. The federal tax is 0.8 percent. Although the state tax is usually 5.4 percent, it varies across states from 0 percent to 10 or more percent. Funds generated by the federal tax are used to administer state unemployment compensation programs and to support states with loans to pay for unemployment benefits, which are also covered by funds generated by the state tax. Although unemployment benefits vary across states, they are paid to eligible workers based on a percentage of an insured worker's earnings for a maximum of 26 weeks in most states; the percentage is capped at around 50 percent of a state's average weekly wage.[46]

Problems and Challenges

Similar to many OECD countries, the United States is under pressure to cut public social spending and reduce government budget deficits while maintaining the quality and benefits of its social welfare system. An important issue on the agenda of U.S. public policymakers has been Social Security reform.[47] According to a projection by the Congressional Budget Office, the annual costs of the Old-Age, Survivors, and Disability Insurance program will exceed Social Security tax revenues in 2016, and the Social Security Trust Fund will be exhausted in 2039.[48]

There are over 30 Social Security reform plans that, in some combination or another, seek to (1) increase the Social Security payroll tax, (2) trim people's initial benefits, (3) increase returns to trust fund investments by modifying investment options, (4) increase the full retirement age, and (5) reduce the cost-of-living adjustment applied to continued benefits. A major plan for Social Security reform was President George W. Bush's individual account proposal in 2005. The primary goal of the plan was to revamp Social Security by allowing workers to transfer part of the payroll tax paid by themselves and their employers to individual investment accounts.[49] The majority of Americans as well as interest groups such as the American Association of Retired Persons (AARP) and trade unions rejected the plan. Among their concerns were whether the plan would provide insurance against downturns in the stock market, whether it would give subsidies to people with low income and interrupted work histories, how it would handle benefits, how it would be regulated, and how investors would be informed. Social Security reform continues to be a major topic of debate.[50]

Another important issue on the agenda of U.S. policymakers has been the alleviation of poverty. In 2009, almost 44 million people lived in poverty; many of them children.[51] Temporary Assistance for Needy Families was created under the 1996 Personal Responsibility and Work Opportunity Reconciliation Act to alleviate poverty while reducing the number of people dependent on entitlement programs and assisting them in efforts to become self-sufficient through the Welfare-to-Work initiative.[52] The economic downturn of the late 2000s expanded the income gap between rich and poor, and the loss of jobs due to outsourcing overseas has undermined the goal of the PRWORA to change the U.S. entitlement system into one that would require work in exchange for time-limited assistance. Because people who are eligible for TANF are largely unskilled, they are competing for jobs not only with similar people abroad but also with unskilled immigrants and unauthorized workers in the United States. Despite these circumstances, TANF continues alongside other public assistance programs, such as the Earned Income Tax Credit and the Child Tax Credit.[53] Alleviating poverty while reducing dependence on entitlement programs remains a challenge to U.S. social welfare policy, especially during an economic downturn in an age of globalization. This challenge is exacerbated by the problem of wasteful spending on ineffective public social programs designed and implemented by federal and state governments.

Although economic liberalization is associated with opportunities for economic success, it comes with social problems that increase government budget deficits due to increased demands for entitlement programs, along with demands for lower taxes to stimulate or sustain economic growth. Under these conditions, U.S. policymakers are challenged to review entitlement programs and to reform not only social welfare policy but also several other policies, including economic and immigration policies, affecting social welfare in the United States.

Sweden

Sweden, a prime example of a social democratic welfare state, has one of the world's most generous comprehensive social welfare systems. Although Sweden has a capitalist economy with private property as well as open and competitive markets, the country's political regime is a **social democracy**. Proponents of social democracy argue that, because unchecked economic activities in open and

BOX 7.1

Country Profile of Sweden

Name of Country: Sweden

Conventional Long Form: Kingdom of Sweden

Type of Government: Constitutional monarchy

Executive Branch:

Chief of State: King CARL XVI GUSTAF (since 19 September 1973); Heir Apparent Princess VICTORIA Ingrid Alice Desiree, daughter of the monarch (born 14 July 1977)
Head of Government: Prime Minister Fredrik REINFELDT (since 5 October 2006); Deputy Prime Minister Jan BJORKLUND (since 5 October 2010)

Legislative Branch:

Unicameral Parliament or Riksdag (349 seats; members are elected by popular vote on a proportional representation basis to serve four-year terms)

Judicial Branch:

Supreme Court or Högsta domstolen (judges are appointed by the prime minister and the cabinet)

Administrative Divisions:

21 counties (lan, singular and plural); Blekinge, Dalarna, Gavleborg, Gotland, Halland, Jamtland, Jonkoping, Kalmar, Kronoberg, Norrbotten, Orebro, Ostergotland, Skane, Sodermanland, Stockholm, Uppsala, Varmland, Vasterbotten, Vasternorrland, Vastmanland, Vastra Gotaland

Economic Indicators:

GDP (purchasing power parity): $395.8 billion (2012 estimation)
GDP Real Growth Rate: 1.2 percent (2012 estimation)
GDP per capita (purchasing power parity): $41,700 (2012 estimation)
Economic Structure: Agriculture 1.8 percent; Industry 27.3 percent; Services 70.9 percent (2012 estimation)

Demographic Indicators:

Population: 9,119,243 (2013 estimation)
Population Growth: 0.16 percent (2013 estimation)

Birth Rate: 10.33 births/1,000 population (2013 estimation)

Infant Mortality Rate: 2.73 deaths/1,000 live births (2013 estimation)

Life Expectancy at Birth: 81.28 years (2013 estimation)

Literacy (age 15 and over can read and write): 99 percent (2010 estimation)

Ethnic Groups: indigenous population (Swedes with Finnish and Sami

minorities); foreign-born or first-generation immigrants (Finns, Yugoslavs, Danes, Norwegians, Greeks, Turks)

Religion: Lutheran 87 percent, other (includes Roman Catholic, Orthodox, Baptist, Muslim, Jewish, and Buddhist) 13 percent

Source: CIA, *The World Factbook*, https://www.cia.gov/library/publications/the-world-factbook/geos/sw.html (accessed March 24, 2012).

competitive markets are likely to generate greater inequality between economic winners and losers, it is the state's responsibility to ensure economic equality, protect social rights, regulate free economic enterprise, and spend tax revenue on basic social welfare benefits.[54] In order to meet this responsibility, social democracies rely on **neo-corporatism**, a consensual policy-making arrangement between governments and a small number of associations that represent large sections of businesses and labor (i.e., business associations and trade unions). Since this arrangement emphasizes consensus among key actors in society, it reduces the chance of conflict in economic and social welfare policy making. According to Peter Katzenstein, social democracy tends to be associated with a small population size and a culturally homogeneous society.[55] This describes Sweden, and it is unlike the United States with its large culturally diverse population.

Sweden's social democracy is seen as a People's Home (Folkhemmet). In a speech to Sweden's parliament, the Riksdag, in 1928, Social Democrat Per Albion Hansson, Sweden's prime minister between 1932 and 1946, said that "the good society is a society which functions like a good home."[56] The idea of the People's Home is about **social solidarity**, which rests on equality and social responsibility. According to Henry Milner, social solidarity "links individuals with their communities through reciprocal rights and obligations over and above the right of all human beings to be treated fairly, without distinctions as to race, sex, disability, etc."[57] Social solidarity in Sweden has been institutionalized through various social welfare programs.

Although there is disagreement over why and how the Swedish welfare state took its present form, it is clear that governments led by the Swedish Social Democratic Party, or the *Sveriges socialdemokratiska arbetare parti (SAP)*, and the Swedish-style neo-corporatism (i.e., rational, pragmatic, and consensual policy making among government, businesses, and labor) have created a widely recognized social welfare system, which is now a significant part of Swedish lifestyle.[58] Whether the SAP or a conservative party is in government, there is consistent support for Sweden's social welfare system because Swedes enjoy very generous public services and benefits. For instance, although the center-right government led by the Moderate Party, which replaced a government led by the SAP in 2006, is committed to tax cuts and privatization of state-owned businesses, it is still largely supportive of Sweden's social welfare system.

After joining the European Union (EU) in 1995, Sweden has adjusted domestic regulations to rules among EU member states regarding social security (i.e., social insurance, healthcare, and unemployment benefits). In 1999, Sweden enacted social security reform when the Riksdag passed the Social Insurance Act to regulate the fundamentals of entitlements to be covered by the country's social insurance system.[59] Since the 1990s, reforms of Swedish social welfare programs have been driven not only by Sweden's EU membership but also by economic recession, demographic changes associated with an aging population, labor market changes, changes in family structure (e.g., an increase in single-parent households with children), as well as social changes due to immigration under economic liberalization. A primary issue of concern to Swedish policymakers is how to reduce unemployment and decrease budget deficits without cutting social welfare benefits.

Government Agencies and Other Actors

The Constitution   Sweden's current constitution, which was enacted in 1974 and came into force on January 1, 1975, is composed of four fundamental laws: (1) the Instrument of Government, (2) the Act of Succession, (3) the Freedom of the Press Act, and (4) the Fundamental Law on Freedom of Expression.[60] According to the Instrument of Government, Sweden is a constitutional monarchy with a parliamentary system. Sweden's current constitution includes an extensive bill of rights.

The Legislative Branch   Sweden's legislature is the Riksdag,[61] a unicameral parliament with 349 members elected for four-year terms by popular vote based on **proportional representation (PR)**, which means that voters choose between political parties competing in multimember districts, and parties win seats representing districts in proportion to the percentage of votes for them. In order to gain a seat in the Riksdag, each party's share of a national vote must be at least 4 percent.

The Riksdag can enact laws, amend the Swedish constitution, and appoint a government. Each legislator can submit a policy proposal to the Speaker of the Riksdag. The Speaker and three Vice Speakers, who are elected by a majority of legislators, preside over parliamentary debates and, after consultation with committee chairs, determine the order in which bills and committee reports will be submitted to a session of the full Riksdag. The Riksdag has 15 standing committees. Although a committee can scrutinize and amend bills under its jurisdiction, it cannot reject bills.

The primary committees of the Riksdag responsible for social welfare in Sweden are the Committee on Health and Welfare and the Committee on Social Insurance. The Committee on Health and Welfare prepares appropriations related to healthcare, medical care, and social services. The Committee on Social Insurance deals with matters related to national insurance, national pensions, occupational injury insurance, financial support for families with children, as well as Swedish citizenship and migration.[62]

The Executive Branch   According to Chapter 1, Article 6, of the Instrument of Government of Sweden's current constitution, "The Government governs the Realm. It is accountable to the Riksdag." Although Sweden has a monarch as its symbolic head of state, its head of government is a prime minister appointed by the Riksdag. Sweden's chief executive body is a cabinet, the Regeringen, which is headed by the prime minister and is accountable to the Riksdag. The prime minister appoints approximately 20 cabinet members in charge of government ministries and agencies. The cabinet makes collective decisions with a quorum of at least five of its members after a report from each member. In practice, reports are written, and discussions are rare during formal cabinet meetings.

Sweden's government submits most legislative proposals to the Riksdag.[63] Before the government formulates a legislative proposal to be submitted to the Riksdag, the proposal goes through an inquiry stage and a referral process. At the inquiry stage, the matter addressed by the proposal is examined by an inquiry body that is independent of the government and may be composed of politicians, public officials, and experts. Recommendations from the inquiry body appear in a report that is published in the Swedish Government Official Reports series, the *Statens Offentliga Utredningar (SOU)*. In the referral process, the inquiry body's report is submitted for consideration to referral bodies, such as central government agencies, local government authorities, or special-interest groups, whose actions could be influenced by a specific legislative proposal. Through the referral process, the government obtains feedback as well as an estimate of how much support it can expect. If there is not enough support for recommendations from the inquiry body among referral bodies, the government may attempt to formulate an alternative legislative proposal. After a legislative proposal passes the inquiry stage and the referral process, the ministry responsible for the proposal drafts it as a bill to be introduced in the Riksdag.[64]

The Judicial Branch   Sweden has two parallel court systems: (1) a general court system, which includes the Supreme Court, courts of appeal, and district courts; and (2) a general administrative court system, which includes the Supreme Administrative Court, administrative courts of appeal, and county administrative courts. General courts are in charge of civil and criminal cases, and general administrative courts are in charge of cases pertaining to public administration. Furthermore, there are numerous special courts and tribunals as well as the National Courts Administration, a central agency for the administration of Swedish courts.[65]

Political Parties   Sweden's social democracy is closely associated with the Social Democratic Party or the *Sveriges socialdemokratiska arbetare parti*. Although the SAP has been in government and the largest party in the Riksdag since Social

Democrat Per Albion Hansson mentioned the People's Home (Folkhemmet) in 1928, Sweden has a multiparty system. Since elections to the Riksdag are based on proportional representation (PR), not only the largest parties but also numerous smaller parties may gain seats in the Riksdag provided that they get at least 4 percent of a national vote. As a result of the 2010 general Riksdag election, 8 parties gained seats in the Riksdag: the Social Democratic Party (112 seats), the Moderate Party (107 seats), the Green Party (25 seats), the Liberal Party (24 seats), the Centre Party (23 seats), the Sweden Democrats (20 seats), the Christian Democrats (19 seats), and the Left Party (19 seats). The election resulted in a center-right government formed by the Moderate Party in a coalition, the Alliance for Sweden, with the Liberal Party, the Centre Party, and the Christian Democrats, with the main opposition being a Red-Green coalition between the Social Democratic Party, the Green Party, and the Left Party. The Sweden Democrats, a nationalist movement, won seats in the Riksdag for the first time in Sweden's history.

The Ministry of Health and Social Affairs, or Socialdepartementet (MHSA)   The MHSA has primary responsibility for administrating Swedish social welfare programs.[66] Within the MHSA, the Swedish Pensions Agency, or *Pensionsmyndigheten*, and the Swedish Social Insurance Agency, or *Försäkringskassan*, deal specifically with pension and social insurance programs. The Swedish Pensions Agency is in charge of income pensions, premium pensions, guaranteed pensions, supplementary pensions, housing supplements for pensioners, maintenance support for the elderly, and survivor's pensions.[67] The Swedish Social Insurance Agency is in charge of benefits for families with children, housing allowance, benefits for people who are ill or people with disabilities, and benefits for the elderly.[68]

The Ministry of Employment, or Arbetsmarknadsdepartementet (ME)   The ME is responsible for administrating unemployment insurance, job training, and labor market programs.[69] Within the ME, the Unemployment Insurance Board, or *Inspektionen för arbetslöshetsförsäkringen (IAF)* supervises unemployment insurance funds as well as the Public Employment Service.[70]

Interest Groups   As noted earlier, Sweden's social welfare system is rooted in Swedish-style neo-corporatism (i.e., rational, pragmatic, and consensual policy making among government, businesses, and labor). Within this context, the most influential interest groups regarding social welfare policy making include the Swedish Trade Union Confederation, or *Landsorganisationen i Sverige (LO)*, the Swedish Confederation of Professional Employees, or *Tjänstemännens Centralorganisation (TCO)*, and the Swedish Confederation of Professional Associations, or *Sveriges Akademikers Centralorganisation (SACO)*. The LO is a central union of blue-collar workers; it has more than 2.1 million members in 19 unions. The TCO is composed of 19 trade unions with almost 1.3 million white-collar workers in the public and private sectors. The SACO consists of 25 trade unions and professional organizations with about 350,000 active members.[71]

The European Union   In 1995, following a nationwide referendum, Sweden became a member of the European Union. Since then, Sweden's social welfare system has been adapted to rules among EU member states regarding the coordination of social security regulations so that their people can move to live and work in any EU member state without losing their social insurance protection or entitlement to social security benefits.[72]

Policy Initiatives

Institutionalization of a universal social welfare system in Sweden began in the late nineteenth century and the early twentieth century. It was a response to demand for protection of a new industrial working class in Sweden's iron and timber industries at a time of rapid industrialization. The first universal social welfare programs were created by the **Poor Law in 1882** and the **National Pension Act in 1913**. During World War I and the interwar period between 1917 and 1939, the National Unemployment Commission under the Riskdag examined and debated possible extensions of work-related and unemployment benefit programs to include substantial supplements to retired workers, social services, and benefits for victims of accidents as well as for the sick and unemployed, all of which were then provided by local governments, private charities, churches, and families.

In the 1930s, the Swedish government created a medical benefit program to support people in cases of sickness and maternity as well as a benefit program to help people in case of unemployment. In the 1940s, it introduced a family allowance for children as well as a basic pension for people of old age, people with disabilities, and surviving spouses and children of income earners. In 1960, an earnings-related supplement to the basic pension took effect with a nationwide general supplementary pension scheme, or *allmän tilläggspension (ATP)*. An earnings-related supplementary pension was considered necessary to meet public demand for a more generous pension while reducing costs of public-funded social insurance benefits.[73]

The 1962 National Social Insurance Act   In 1962, the Riksdag passed the National Social Insurance Act, which unified health and maternity insurance as well as basic and supplementary pensions into one single coordinated social insurance system. Under this system, all Swedish citizens and residents can receive "payments in case of childbearing, illness, disability, old age and death of the family breadwinner."[74]

The 1982 Social Services Act and the 1983 Health and Medical Services Act   According to the 1982 Social Services Act, which combined programs in one legal framework, social services have four objectives: (1) economic security, (2) equality in living conditions, (3) promoting participation in community life, and (4) self-determination and respect for personal privacy. Especially under the fourth objective, care has become increasingly deinstitutionalized, allowing care recipients to live at home—in other words, in a setting that they can manage.

A major point of the 1982 Social Services Act is that "over and above the specific services public agencies are obliged to provide under the various programmes, there exists a general obligation upon all of them to assist anyone in need."[75] According to the 1983 Health and Medical Services Act, the goal of healthcare and medical services is to maintain a good standard of health and provide care on equal terms for the entire Swedish population. Under the 1983 Health and Medical Services Act, county councils have primary responsibility for providing healthcare and medical services.[76]

The 1999 Social Insurance Act   Under the 1999 Social Insurance Act, social insurance in Sweden is divided into a residence-based insurance and a work-based insurance. Any person who lives or works in Sweden qualifies for social insurance, which is under administration of the Swedish Pensions Agency, or *Pensionsmyndigheten,* and the Swedish Social Insurance Agency, or *Försäkringskassan.* Social insurance provides (1) universal benefits (e.g., child allowance) for everyone at an equal rate, (2) means-tested benefits (e.g., housing allowance), and (3) taxable income-related benefits.[77] The 1999 Social Insurance Act is the foundation of Sweden's contemporary social welfare programs, which include the Swedish pension system, public assistance programs, and unemployment insurance programs.[78]

Contemporary Programs

The Pension System   Sweden's current pension system, which took effect in 2000, is composed of (1) a national basic pension and insurance plan, (2) an occupational-based pension and insurance plan, and (3) a private pension and insurance plan. The national basic pension and insurance plan offers benefits to all Swedish residents. The occupational-based pension and insurance plan involves benefits that employers, in occupational-based agreements with their employees, agree to pay for in order to supplement their employees' benefits from the basic national insurance plan. The private pension and insurance plan allows employees to choose additional benefits with private insurance.[79]

Sweden's national basic pension and insurance plan is a public pension system that provides an income-related pension as well as a top-up guarantee pension. The **income-related pension,** which is linked to Sweden's economy through an income index that gauges change in Swedes' average income, is funded through contributions from insured individuals and their employers and, sometimes, from the state. Contributions that pay for the income-related pension amount to 18.5 percent of gross income. Out of the 18.5 percent, 16.0 percent supports a pay-as-you-go (PAYG) system, while the remaining 2.5 percent is put in an individual premium pension account. The PAYG system, also known as an *income pension,* uses a year's contributions to pay for that year's pensions so that the retired generation obtains income from the working population. Money in the individual premium pension account, also known as a *premium pension,* is available for people to invest in funds of personal choice.

The **top-up guarantee pension** is funded by the Swedish government. People are paid this guarantee pension if they receive an insufficient or no income-related pension, if they are at least age of 65 or were born in or after 1938, and if they have been Swedish residents for at least 3 years; full payment of this guarantee pension requires Swedish residence for at least 40 years. Elderly people with little or no guarantee pension can receive maintenance support, and pensioners with little pension can obtain housing supplements.[80]

Public Assistance Programs   Swedish public assistance programs provide universal cash transfer benefits administered by Sweden's Social Insurance Agency. There is a wide range of cash transfer benefits to support families with children, including parental benefits, temporary parental benefits, pregnancy benefits, child allowance, maintenance support, housing allowance, child-care allowance, and adoption allowance.

Parental benefits are paid for a total of 480 days for each child. Payments are made at the earliest 60 days before the expected birth of a child and until the child is 8 years old. Parental benefits come in two parts. The first part, which amounts to about 80 percent of an insured person's lost income, is paid for 390 days. Parents with little or no income get a basic amount of 180 kronor (about $25) per day. The second part, which is a basic amount of 180 kronor (about $25) per day or 60 kronor (about $8) per day for children who were born before July 2006, is paid for another 90 days.

Temporary parental benefits are paid for a total of 60 days per year for a sick child less than 12 years old or, in some situations, less than 16 years old, with a possible extension of another 60 days. Temporary parental benefits amount to 80 percent of an insured person's lost income.

Pregnancy benefits, which amount to 80 percent of an insured person's lost income, are paid to women in the later stages of pregnancy who cannot continue a physically demanding or dangerous job, and who cannot be transferred to a different job. Pregnancy benefits for women in physically demanding jobs are paid for up to 50 days. Payments start at the earliest 60 days and at the latest 11 days before the expected birth of a child. Pregnancy benefits for women in dangerous jobs are paid throughout a woman's entire pregnancy until 11 days before the expected birth of a child.

Child allowance amounts to 1,050 kronor ($147) per month paid for a child until the age of 16 or until the age of 21 if the child is a student; there is no age limit for a child who attends school and has learning difficulties.

Maintenance support is paid for a child whose parents do not live together. Payment is made to the parent living with the child. Entitlement to maintenance support requires that a child is younger than age 18 or younger than 21 years old if the child is a student. It also requires that the child lives permanently with only one parent and that the parent responsible for the child pays no child support or less than the amount of maintenance support, which can be a maximum of 1,273 kronor (about $179) per month. There may be special maintenance support for a child who moves between households.

Housing allowance is available to households that have children living at home and access rights to children. Amounts of housing allowance are determined by a household's number of children as well as by household income, housing space, and housing costs.

Child-care allowance, which amounts to 8,833 kronor (about $1,241) per month, is paid to a parent who takes care at home of a child who is sick or has a disability. Eligibility for child-care allowance requires that the child is in need of special care and supervision for a minimum of 6 months or that the child has an illness or a disability that involves considerable added costs.

Adoption allowance amounts to 40,000 kroner (about $5,618) paid for the adoption of a child who is younger than 10 years old and who is neither a Swedish citizen nor a Swedish resident. It is required that the child is adopted through an authorized adoption agency.[81]

The Unemployment Insurance System   Sweden has a unified unemployment insurance system that is part of Swedish labor-market policy and consists of legally independent unemployment insurance funds in often close cooperation with trade unions. Administered by the Swedish Unemployment Insurance Board, there are 32 unemployment insurance funds divided into programs that provide basic unemployment benefits and programs that provide voluntary income-related unemployment benefits.

Basic unemployment benefits cover employees and employment seekers who are older than the age of 20 and younger than the age of 65 and who do not qualify for voluntary income-related unemployment benefits. Basic unemployment benefits amount to 320 kronor (about $45) per day provided to insured people for a maximum of 300 days per benefit period, with a possible extension of another 150 days for insured people who have at least one child younger than age 18. For insured people to receive this amount, they must have worked 40 hours a week before being unemployed; for insured people who worked less than 40 hours a week before being unemployed, the amount is reduced proportionately to the reduced number of hours worked per week. Basic unemployment benefits are subsidized by the Swedish government.

Voluntary income-related unemployment benefits cover employed and self-employed people who are under the age of 65 and are members of an unemployment insurance fund as employees in a particular occupation or industry. Voluntary income-related unemployment benefits provided to an insured person in a benefit period of 300 days amount to 80 percent of the insured person's previous income for the first 200 days and 70 percent of the insured person's previous income for the next 100 days. The maximum amount is 680 kronor (about $96) per day. Insured people who have at least one child younger than 18 years old may receive payments for another 150 days beyond the 300-day benefit period. Voluntary income-related unemployment benefits are funded by a membership fee paid by insured people, by a membership fee paid by self-employed people, and with unemployment insurance that employers pay for out of a labor-market contribution based on a payroll percentage.[82]

Problems and Challenges

A primary issue of concern to Swedish social welfare policy is to maintain one of the world's most generous comprehensive social welfare systems under pressure to reduce government deficits by cutting public spending and/or raising tax revenue. As in other EU member states, this fiscal pressure comes from increased demands for social welfare benefits that need to be paid for with increasingly limited resources. An aging population, low birth rates, changes in family structure, and immigration are demographic challenges to Sweden's social welfare system as more people become eligible for public services and benefits that need to be financed with more revenue from a declining population of working age.

In order to deal with fiscal problems associated with the need to maintain its social welfare system within a changing demographic environment, Sweden has been working on social security reforms in coordination with its partners in the European Union.[83] Under the EU's commitment to social protection and social inclusion, national governments are encouraged to (1) reduce poverty and social exclusion, (2) change their social welfare systems (3) examine and react to future demographic changes and (4) regularly report with facts that are comparable across the EU.

Of particular importance to Swedish social welfare reforms has been the EU's Social Protection Committee, which was created to foster cooperation in regard to social protection policies between EU member states and the EU Commission. The major goals of this committee are to (1) "make work pay and provide secure income," (2) "make pensions safe and pension systems sustainable," (3) "promote social inclusion," and (4) "ensure high-quality and sustainable health care."[84]

Guided by the EU's commitment to social protection and social inclusion and the major goals of the EU's Social Protection Committee, the Swedish government has developed a national strategy to improve Sweden's social welfare programs. According to Sweden's strategy report for social protection and social inclusion 2008–2010, universal welfare is essential to promoting equal opportunities and social cohesion. Specifically,

> The general pension system, like health care and long-term care, covers the whole population on equal terms. Universal welfare policy creates the basis on which to prevent poverty and social exclusion and is therefore the foundation on which the Swedish action plan for social inclusion is built. Universal welfare contributes to reducing the gaps between different groups in society, but it must be supplemented by support targeted at the most vulnerable groups in society so that social inclusion that covers everyone is attained.[85]

Furthermore, the report sees a close connection between Sweden's social welfare system and participation in the labor market. As the report points out,

> High employment is essential if a generous and financially sustainable welfare system is to be maintained. Activation is therefore an important aspect in universal welfare policy. Having a job is the best way of influencing one's own economic situation. Work and education are the basis of people's personal and social development and are important factors underlying participation in society. [86]

It is clear that reducing social exclusion and increasing employment are key objectives of Swedish social welfare policy. In pursuit of these objectives, the Swedish government has created various incentives for people to stay in the labor force. Among such incentives are increased occupational-based pension and insurance plan benefits, increased private pension and insurance plan benefits, as well as increased benefits through the income-related pension provided under Sweden's national basic pension and insurance plan.

The Swedish government realizes that it is necessary not only "to get more people into work and to get more people to work longer, create more flexible jobs and reduce sick leave levels" but also to provide more effective healthcare. Furthermore, the Swedish government encourages people to have children through better opportunities to combine work and family and more support for parents of young children. Incentives in this regard include a child-raising allowance for caregivers registered and living with a child who is between 12 months and 3 years old as well as a gender-equality bonus to motivate parents to share their parental leave as equally as possible.[87]

Comparison

An essential goal of social welfare policy is to reduce economic inequality by distributing and/or redistributing certain goods and services through government measures. Social welfare benefits are public goods intended to help poor and underprivileged people, especially children, the elderly, people with disabilities, those who are unemployed, and working women with children. Among social welfare benefits are social security, public assistance, job training, public health, unemployment compensation, and disability support. Many governments allocate a large part of their budgets to social welfare spending, and the costs of social welfare will rise due to growing demands for social welfare benefits, especially from an increasingly aging population and an increasing number of poor single-parent households.

The United States and Sweden are highly institutionalized democracies with highly advanced open economic systems. They are two of the world's wealthiest democratic welfare states whose social welfare policy has been confronted with similar demographic, economic, and societal challenges. Both the United States and Sweden have growing aging populations and need to deal with significant demographic and labor market changes. Both countries have experienced economic shifts that create pressure on their national economies from increasingly competitive global markets and pressure on their national budgets from economic recession, higher interest rates, and increased national debt. Both countries are also affected by changes in family structure and by immigration of unskilled legal and/or illegal workers and their families following economic liberalization through the North American Free Trade Agreement (NAFTA) in the case of the United States and the European Union (EU) in the case of Sweden.

Although both the United States and Sweden provide social welfare benefits through a pension system, public assistance programs, and an unemployment insurance system, their social welfare programs are based on different welfare models. In the United States, social welfare programs are based on a liberal welfare model, with emphasis on self-sufficiency and individual freedom; social protection comes into play after breakdowns of the private market and the family as natural channels for the fulfillment of social needs. In Sweden, social welfare programs are based on a social democratic welfare model, with emphasis on social responsibility and equality; social welfare benefits are granted because all people have a political right to social protection within a generous comprehensive social welfare system. This difference means that in the United States, individuals needing social welfare may have to experience hardship before receiving assistance that the poor or needy in Sweden need not face.

Sweden is widely recognized for its generous social welfare benefits, but its traditionally public pension system has been transformed into a hybrid public–private pension system that combines a national basic pension and insurance plan with an occupational-based pension and insurance plan and a private pension and insurance plan. Sweden's current partially privatized pension system operates not only with funds from the Swedish government but also with a pay-as-you-go (PAYGO) system and an individual premium pension account funded by contributions from insured individuals and their employers. President George W. Bush's individual account proposal in 2005 to reform Social Security in the United States was rejected by most Americans and several interest groups. Thus, in regard to its individual premium pension account, Sweden's current pension system is more market-oriented than the U.S. Social Security system.

Pension reform was necessary for Sweden to meet rising demands for pensions from a growing aging population with increasingly limited resources. In other words, pension reform was driven by serious concerns about the sustainability of Sweden's pension system. There are similar concerns about the sustainability of the U.S. Social Security system for a growing aging population under increased national debt and government budget deficits. Arguably, Sweden's individual premium pension account may find new advocates of individual investment accounts regarding U.S. Social Security reform in order to deal with demographic and economic challenges facing the United States, Sweden, and other advanced democratic welfare states today and tomorrow.[88]

Rising costs of government-funded entitlements have led both the United States and Sweden to take steps to reform their public assistance programs. The United States created Temporary Assistance for Needy Families (TANF) under the 1996 Personal Responsibility and Work Opportunity Reconciliation Act (PRWORA) in order to alleviate poverty while moving millions of Americans from dependence on entitlement programs to self-sufficiency through the Welfare-to-Work initiative. Although the economic downturn that started in 2006 and outsourcing overseas have undermined the PRWORA in its objective to transform the U.S. entitlement system into one that would require work in exchange for time-limited assistance, TANF continues alongside other public assistance programs. Some of these programs do not provide payments but tax credits, such as the Earned Income Tax Credit (EITC) and the Child Tax Credit (CTC).

Reforms of public assistance programs focused on encouraging people to work have been pursued not only in the United States but also in Sweden. As a member of the European Union, Sweden has adopted a national strategy to improve its universal social welfare programs with emphasis on a close connection between Sweden's social welfare system and participation in the labor market. Sweden is committed to social protection and social inclusion. Universal welfare is seen as essential to promoting equal opportunities and social cohesion, and high employment is considered essential to sustaining Sweden's generous social welfare programs.

There are demands for social welfare reforms in the United States as well as in Sweden. Yet, there is no agreement on what reforms are economically most efficient, socially most acceptable, and politically most feasible. One of the major differences between the United States and Sweden regarding the politics of social welfare policy making is that the United States retains more sovereignty over social welfare policy than does Sweden. Since Sweden joined the EU, its social welfare programs have been guided by rules of the EU, perhaps most notably by the EU's commitment to social protection and social inclusion and the major goals of the EU's Social Protection Committee.

Accessibility, quality, costs, and accountability are all concerns affecting debates over social welfare policy. When evaluating social welfare programs subject to debate, we must keep in mind what concerns and objectives we have and what indicators, data, and statistics we rely on for informed assessments. According to recent research, greater economic prosperity and higher social welfare spending do not guarantee social satisfaction and happiness.[89]

Key Terms

- Social insurance programs
- Public assistance programs
- Employment programs
- Welfare state
- Socialist state
- New Deal
- Personal Responsibility and Work Opportunity Reconciliation Act (PRWORA)
- Federal block-grants
- Cash-benefit programs
- In-kind benefit programs
- Temporary Assistance for Needy Families (TANF)
- Supplemental Security Income (SSI)

- Earned Income Tax Credit (EITC)
- Child Tax Credit (CTC)
- Family and medical leave coverage
- Supplemental Nutrition Assistance Program (SNAP)
- Social democracy
- Neo-corporatism
- Social solidarity
- Proportional representation
- Poor Law in 1882
- National Pension Act in 1913
- Income-related pension
- Top-up guarantee pension

Critical Thinking Questions

- What are the three categories of social welfare programs?
- What is a welfare state? How does social welfare differ from socialism?
- What are the philosophical assumptions behind European and U.S. welfare? How do the United States and Sweden differ in the primary concerns regarding social welfare programs?
- Why are Social Security reforms in the United States a major topic of debate?
- What are the problems caused by economic liberalization?
- How does Sweden's social democracy political regime affect its social welfare programs? In other words, what do social democrats believe about competitive markets that impact how they view social welfare?
- What factors have driven reforms to Sweden's social welfare since the 1990s?
- What are the challenges Sweden faces to maintain its social welfare system?

Recommended Resources for the United States

Congressional Budget Office, *Social Security: A Primer*, Congressional Budget Office, released on September 2001.

Andrew Dobelstein, *Understanding the Social Security Act: The Foundation of Social Welfare for America in the Twenty-First Century* (Oxford: Oxford University Press, 2009).

Martin Gilens, *Why Americans Hate Welfare: Race, Media, and the Politics of Antipoverty Policy* (Chicago: University of Chicago Press, 1999).

Jeffrey Grogger and Lynn Karoly, *Welfare Reform: Effects of a Decade of Change* (Cambridge, MA: Harvard University Press, 2005).

Christopher Howard, *The Hidden Welfare State: Tax Expenditures and Social Policy in the United States* (Princeton, NJ: Princeton University Press, 1997).

Mary Reintsma, *The Political Economy of Welfare Reform in the United States* (Cheltenham, UK: Edward Elger, 2007).

Theda Skocpol, *Social Policy in the United States: Future Possibilities in Historical Perspective* (Princeton, NJ: Princeton University Press, 1995).

Useful Web Sources for U.S. Social Welfare Policy

Department of Health and Human Services
Social Security Administration
Social Security Administration (SSA) and the International Social Security Association (ISSA). *Social Security Programs throughout the World: Americans 2008–09: The United States*

Recommended Resources for Sweden

Gøsta Esping-Andersen, *The Three Worlds of Welfare Capitalism* (Cambridge: Polity Press, 1990).

Arthur Gould, *Capitalist Welfare Systems: A Comparison of Japan, Britain, and Sweden* (London and New York: Longman, 1993).

Matti Heikkila, Bjorn Hvinden, Mikko Kautto, Staffan Marklund, and Niels Plough, eds., *Nordic Social Policy: Changing Welfare States* (London: Routledge, 1999).

Ministry of Health and Human Affairs and National Social Insurance Board, *Swedish National Pension System*, released 2003.

Subhash Thakur, Michael Keen, Balazs Hrvath, and Valerie Cerra, *Sweden's Welfare State: Can the Bumblebee Keep Flying?* (Washington, DC: International Monetary Fund, 2003).

Virpi Timonen, *Restructuring the Welfare State: Globalization and Social Policy Reform in Finland and Sweden* (Cheltenham, UK: Edward Elgar, 2003).

Useful Web Sources for Sweden Social Welfare Policy

Ministry of Health and Social Affairs
Social Insurance Agency
Sweden Pensions Agency
Social Security Administration (SSA) and the International Social Security Association (ISSA). *Social Security Programs throughout the World: Europe 2010*

Notes

1. For more general information on social welfare policy and programs, see Diana M. DiNitto, *Social Welfare: Politics and Public Policy* (7th ed.) (Upper Saddle River, NJ: Prentice-Hall, 2010); Howard Jacob Karger and David Stoesz, *American Social Welfare Policy* (6th ed.) (Boston: Allyn and Bacon, 2009); Elizabeth A. Segal, *Social Welfare Policy and Social Programs: A Values Perspective* (2nd ed.) (Belmont, CA: Brooks/Cole-Cengage Learning, 2009); and Paul Spicker, *Social Policy: Themes and Approaches* (rev. and 2nd ed.) (Cambridge: Polity Press, 2008).

2. The OECD social expenditure statistics cover the years 1980 to 2007. The database is available at http://stats.oecd.org/Index.aspx?datasetcode=SOCX_AGG (accessed December 7, 2010).

3. Harold L. Wilensky, *The Welfare State and Equality: Structural and Ideological Roots of Public Expenditures* (Berkeley, CA: University of California Press, 1975), p. 1.

4. For a detailed discussion of various social welfare systems, see Gøsta Esping-Andersen, *The Three Worlds of Welfare Capitalism* (Cambridge: Polity Press, 1990). For a discussion of the evolution of welfare states in middle-income countries in Latin America, East Asia, and eastern Europe during the 1970s and 1980s, see Stephen Haggard and Robert R. Kaufman, *Development, Democracy, and Welfare States* (Princeton, NJ: Princeton University Press, 2006).

5. See Theodore R. Marmor, Jerry L. Mashaw, and Philip L. Harvey, *America's Misunderstood Welfare State: Persistent Myths, Enduring Realities* (New York: Basic Books, 1990). Theda Skocpol argues that the first pension system was a categorical plan of payments to soldiers injured in battle and to widows of soldiers killed in action established during the Civil War period (1861–1865) in the United States. Since then, the system has been transformed into a sort of discretionary old-age pension system. See Skocpol, *Social Policy in the United States: Future Possibilities in Historical Perspective* (Princeton, NJ: Princeton University Press, 1995).

6. See the Office of Management and Budget, *Historical Tables: Budget of the U.S. Government, FY 2011*, http://www.whitehouse.gov/sites/default/files/omb/budget/fy2011/assets/hist.pdf (accessed December 10, 2010) and Brian M. Riedl, "Federal

Spending by the Numbers, 2010" *Heritage Special Report* SR-78, released on June 1, 2010, http://report.heritage.org/sr0078 (accessed December 10, 2010).

7. See the U.S. Census website on poverty, http://www.census.gov/hhes/www/poverty/about/overview/index.html (accessed December 10, 2010).

8. Marmor et al., *America's Misunderstood Welfare State*, Chapter 2.

9. This budget projection is reported in Brian M. Riedl, "Federal Spending by the Numbers, 2010" *Heritage Special Report* SR-78.

10. See the U.S. Sentate Committee on Finance, http://finance.senate.gov/ (accessed December 7, 2010).

11. See U.S. Senate Special Committee on Aging, http://aging.senate.gov/ (accessed December 7, 2010). A special committee has no legislative authority, but it can study issues, conduct oversight of programs, and investigate reports of fraud and waste.

12. See U.S. House of Representatives, Committee on Ways and Means, *Committee Jurisdiction*, http://waysandmeans.house.gov/About/Jurisdiction.htm (accessed March 24, 2012).

13. See U.S. Domestic Policy Council, http://www.whitehouse.gov/administration/eop/dpc/ (accessed December 7, 2010).

14. For the NEC, see http://www.whitehouse.gov/administration/eop/nec (accessed December 7, 2010). For the CEA, see http://www.whitehouse.gov/administration/eop/cea/ (accessed December 7, 2010).

15. See U.S. Office of Management and Budget, http://www.whitehouse.gov/omb/ (accessed December 7, 2010).

16. See U.S. Department of Health and Human Services, http://www.hhs.gov/ (accessed December 7, 2010).

17. See U.S. Administration for Children and Families, http://www.acf.hhs.gov/index.html (accessed December 7, 2010).

18. See U.S. Administration for Children and Families, *Mission Statement*, http://www.acf.hhs.gov/programs/ofa/about.html (accessed January 29, 2011).

19. See U.S. Administration on Aging, http://www.aoa.gov/AoARoot/About/index.aspx (accessed December 8, 2010).

20. See U.S. Social Security Administration, http://www.ssa.gov/ (accessed December 7, 2010).

21. See U.S. Department of Labor, http://www.doleta.gov/etainfo/ (accessed December 8, 2010).

22. See U.S. Food and Nutrition Service, *Nutrition Assistance Programs*, http://www.fns.usda.gov/fns/ (accessed December 8, 2010).

23. See U.S. Department of Housing and Urban Development, http://www.hud.gov/ (accessed December 8, 2010).

24. For example, see the State of Michigan's Department of Human Services at http://michigan.gov/dhs (accessed December 8, 2010) and the State of Arizona's Department of Health Services at http://www.azdhs.gov/ (accessed December 8, 2010).

25. See Diana M. DiNitto, *Social Welfare: Politics and Public Policy* (7th ed.) (Upper Saddle River, NJ: Prentice-Hall, 2010) and Howard Jacob Karger and David Stoesz, *American Social Welfare Policy* (6th ed.) (Boston: Allyn and Bacon, 2009).

26. See Congressional Budget Office, *Social Security: A Primer*, http://www.cbo.gov/ftpdocs/32xx/doc3213/EntireReport.pdf (accessed December 6, 2010).

27. See Administration for Children and Families, *Legislation and Regulations for Head Start*, http://www.acf.hhs.gov/programs/ohs/legislation/index.html (accessed December 10, 2010).

28. See U.S. Department of Agriculture, *A Short History of Snap*, http://www.fns.usda. gov/snap/rules/Legislation/about.htm (accessed December 10, 2010).

29. For more information on the 1996 PRWORA, see Administration for Children and Families, *Fact Sheet*, http://aspe.hhs.gov/hsp/abbrev/prwora96.htm (accessed December 10, 2010).

30. For more information on TANF, see U.S. Temporary Cash Assistance for Needy Families, http://www.tanf.us/ (accessed December, 8, 2010).

31. For more information on OASDI eligibility, benefits, and funds in the United States, see the U.S. Social Security Administration (SSA) and the International Social Security Association (ISSA), *Social Security Programs throughout the World: Americans 2008–09: The United States*, at http://www.ssa.gov/policy/docs/progdesc/ssptw/2008-2009/ americas/united_states.pdf (accessed December 10, 2010).

32. For additional information on employer-paid private sector retirement plans, such as the 401k plan, see U.S. Department of Labor, *Retirement Plans, Benefits and Savings*, http://www.dol.gov/dol/topic/retirement/ (accessed December 10, 2010).

33. For more information on TANF, see US Temporary Cash Assistance for Needy Families, http://www.tanf.us/ (accessed December, 8, 2010).

34. For more information on SSI eligibility and benefits in the United States, see the U.S. Social Security Administration (SSA) and the International Social Security Association (ISSA), *Social Security Programs throughout the World: Americans 2008–09: The United States*, at http://www.ssa.gov/policy/docs/progdesc/ssptw/2008-2009/americas/ united_states.pdf (accessed December 10, 2010).

35. For more information, see U.S. Internal Revenue Service, *Earned Income Tax Credit*, http://www.irs.gov/individuals/article/0,,id=96406,00.html (accessed January 29, 2011).

36. See U.S. Internal Revenue Service, "Earned Income Tax Credit: Do I Qualify?" http:// www.irs.gov/uac/Newsroom/Earned-Income-Tax-Credit-Do-I-Qualify (accessed April 23, 2014).

37. See U.S. Internal Revenue Service, *Earned Income Tax Credit–Qualifying Child Rules,* http://www.irs.gov/individuals/article/0,,id=218779,00.html (accessed January 29, 2011).

38. See U.S. Internal Revenue Service, *States and Local Governments with Earned Income Tax Credit*, http://www.irs.gov/individuals/article/0,,id=177866,00.html (accessed January 29, 2011).

39. For more information, see U.S. Internal Revenue Service, *Ten Facts about the Child Tax Credit*, http://www.irs.gov/newsroom/article/0,,id=106182,00.html (accessed January 29, 2011).

40. For more information, see U.S. Department of Labor, *Leave Benefits–Family and Medical Leave*, http://www.dol.gov/dol/topic/benefits-leave/fmla.htm (accessed January 29, 2011).

41. For more information, see U.S. Food and Nutrition Service, *Supplemental Nutrition Assistance Program*, http://www.fns.usda.gov/snap/ (accessed January 29, 2011).

42. For more information on housing programs, see U.S. Department of Housing and Urban Development, http://portal.hud.gov/hudportal/HUD?src=/topics (accessed January 29, 2011).

43. For more information on public housing programs, see U.S. Department of Housing and Urban Development, *Public Housing,* http://www.hud.gov/offices/pih/programs/ ph/ (accessed January 29, 2011).

44. For more information on homeless programs, see U.S. Department of Housing and Urban Development, *Homeless Assistance,* http://portal.hud.gov/hudportal/ HUD?src=/topics/homelessness (accessed January 29, 2011).

45. For more information, see U.S. Department of Labor, *Unemployment Insurance,* http://www.dol.gov/dol/topic/unemployment-insurance/ (accessed January 29, 2011).

46. For information on unemployment insurance eligibility and benefits, see the U.S. Social Security Administration (SSA) and the International Social Security Association (ISSA). *Social Security Programs throughout the World: Americans 2008–09: The United States,* at http://www.ssa.gov/policy/docs/progdesc/ssptw/2008-2009/americas/united_states.pdf (accessed December 10, 2010).

47. Congressional Budget Office, *Social Security: A Primer.*

48. See U.S. Congress Budget Office, *Social Security Policy Options* http://www.cbo.gov/ftpdocs/115xx/doc11580/SummaryforWeb_SSOptions.pdf (accessed December 6, 2010).

49. See Laura Haltzel, "Social Security Reform: President Bush's Individual Account Proposal," *CRS Report for Congress,* RL32879, http://www.policyarchive.org/handle/10207/bitstreams/2411.pdf (accessed February 2, 2011).

50. See The White House, *Seniors and Social Security,* http://www.whitehouse.gov/issues/seniors-and-social-security (accessed December 6, 2010).

51. See the U.S. Census website on poverty, http://www.census.gov/hhes/www/poverty/about/overview/index.html (accessed December 10, 2010).

52. For more information on the 1996 PRWORA, see U.S. Administration for Children and Families, *Fact Sheet,* http://aspe.hhs.gov/hsp/abbrev/prwora96.htm (accessed December 10, 2010). For more information on TANF, see U.S. Temporary Cash Assistance for Needy Families, http://www.tanf.us/ (accessed December, 8, 2010).

53. See Christopher Howard, *The Hidden Welfare State: Tax Expenditures and Social Policy in the United States* (Princeton, NJ: Princeton University Press, 1997).

54. See Esping-Andersen, *The Three Worlds of Welfare Capitalism.*

55. See Peter Katzenstein, *Small States in World Markets* (Ithaca, NY: Cornell University Press, 1985).

56. This quote is cited in Henry Milner, *Sweden: Social Democracy in Practice* (Oxford: Oxford University Press, 1989), p. 186.

57. Milner, *Sweden,* p. 186.

58. See Thomas J. Anton, "Policy-Making and Political Culture in Sweden," *Scandinavian Political Studies* 4 (1969): 88–102.

59. See the Ministry of Health and Social Affairs, *Social Insurance in Sweden: Fact Sheet,* December 2009, available at www.regeringen.se/content/1/c6/13/75/63/d1783aed.pdf (accessed December 9, 2010).

60. See Sveriges Riksdag, http://www.riksdagen.se/templates/r_page____6357.aspx (accessed December 6, 2010).

61. See Sveriges Riksdag, http://www.riksdagen.se/templates/R_Page____6429.aspx (accessed December 6, 2010).

62. See Sveriges Riksdage, http://www.riksdagen.se/templates/R_Page____4397.aspx (accessed December 7, 2010).

63. See Government Offices of Sweden, *How Laws Are Made,* http://www.sweden.gov.se/sb/d/2854/a/19197 (accessed December 6, 2010).

64. Ibid.

65. See Government office of Sweden, http://www.regeringen.se/content/1/c4/33/41/0feab306.pdf (accessed February 7, 2011).

66. See Government Offices of Sweden, *Ministry of Health and Social Affairs,* http://www.sweden.gov.se/sb/d/2061 (accessed December 7, 2010).

67. See Swedish Pensions Agency, http://www.pensionsmyndigheten.se/Welcome_en.html (accessed December 7, 2010).

68. See Swedish Social Insurance Agency, http://www.forsakringskassan.se/sprak/eng/ (accessed December 7, 2010).

69. See Ministry of Employment, http://www.sweden.gov.se/sb/d/8281 (accessed December 7, 2010).

70. See IAF, http://www.iaf.se/English/ (accessed December 7, 2010).

71. See Virpi Timonen, *Restructuring the Welfare State: Globalisation and Social Policy Reform in Finland and Sweden* (Cheltenham, UK: Edward Elgar, 2003), Chapter 4.

72. See EUROPA, http://eur-lex.europa.eu/en/index.htm (accessed December 10, 2010).

73. For the historical development of Sweden's universal social welfare system, see Albert Harold Rosenthal, *The Social Programs of Sweden: A Search for Security in a Free Society* (Minneapolis: University of Minnesota Press, 1967), Chapter 1.

74. See Rosenthal, *The Social Programs of Sweden*, Chapter 1, as well as Estelle Seldowitz and Agnes W. Brewster, "Sweden's Health and Cash Sickness Insurance Program," *Public Health Reports* 79 (9)(1964): 815–822. The quote appears in Rosenthal, p. 6.

75. See Milner, *Sweden*, p. 190.

76. See Health, Social Services and Social Insurance, http://www.sweden.gov.se/sb/d/15660 (accessed March 24, 2012).

77. The following description of Sweden's contemporary social insurance programs as of 2009 is based on the Swedish Ministry of Health and Social Affairs, *Social Insurance in Sweden: Fact Sheet*, December 2009, http://www.regeringen.se/content/1/c6/13/75/63/d1783aed.pdf (accessed December 9, 2010).

78. For a summary of eligibility, coverage, and funds regarding contemporary social insurance programs in Sweden, see the U.S. Social Security Administration (SSA) and the International Social Security Association (ISSA), *Social Security Programs throughout the World: Europe 2010: Sweden*, http://www.ssa.gov/policy/docs/progdesc/ssptw/2010-2011/europe/sweden.pdf (accessed December 10, 2010).

79. For Sweden's current pension system, see "Fact Sheet: Running a Business: Social Security and Pensions" released January 2010, http://www.investsweden.se/Global/Global/Downloads/Fact_Sheets/Social-security-and-pensions.pdf (accessed December 10, 2010).

80. For Sweden's public pension system, see the Swedish Ministry of Health and Social Affairs, *Social Insurance in Sweden: Fact Sheet*, December 2009, http://www.regeringen.se/content/1/c6/13/75/63/d1783aed.pdf (accessed December 9, 2010); the Swedish Ministry of Health and Social Affairs/National Social Insurance Board, *The Swedish National Pension System*, released 2003, http://www.regeringen.se/sb/d/2028/a/24221 (accessed December 9, 2010); as well as the U.S. Social Security Administration (SSA) and the International Social Security Association (ISSA), *Social Security Programs throughout the World: Europe 2010: Sweden*, http://www.ssa.gov/policy/docs/progdesc/ssptw/2010-2011/europe/sweden.pdf (accessed December 10, 2010).

81. For the public assistance programs discussed in this section and the exchange rate between the Swedish kronor and the U.S. dollar, see the U.S. Social Security Administration (SSA) and the International Social Security Association (ISSA), *Social Security Programs throughout the World: Europe 2010: Sweden*, http://www.ssa.gov/policy/docs/progdesc/ssptw/2010-2011/europe/sweden.pdf (accessed December 10, 2010). See also see the Swedish Ministry of Health and Social Affairs, *Social Insurance in Sweden: Fact Sheet*, December 2009, http://www.regeringen.se/content/1/c6/13/75/63/d1783aed.pdf (accessed December 9, 2010).

82. For Sweden's unemployment insurance system and the exchange rate between the Swedish kronor and the U.S. dollar, see the U.S. Social Security Administration (SSA) and the International Social Security Association (ISSA), *Social Security Programs throughout the World: Europe 2010: Sweden*, http://www.ssa.gov/policy/docs/progdesc/ssptw/2010-2011/europe/sweden.pdf (accessed December 10, 2010). See also the Swedish Ministry of Health and Social Affairs, *Social Insurance in Sweden: Fact Sheet*, December 2009, http://www.regeringen.se/content/1/c6/13/75/63/d1783aed.pdf (accessed December 9, 2010).

83. For more information on social security coordination within the EU, see http://ec.europa.eu/social/main.jsp?catId=26&langId=en (accessed December 10, 2010).

84. For more information on the EU's Social Protection Committee, see http://europa.eu/legislation_summaries/employment_and_social_policy/social_protection/c10119_en.htm (accessed February 16, 2011).

85. See the Swedish Ministry of Health and Social Affairs, *Sweden's Strategy Report for Social Protection and Social Inclusion 2008–2010*, 2008, http://www.sweden.gov.se/content/1/c6/11/42/69/1009c964.pdf (accessed December 20, 2010) p. 11.

86. Ibid., p.11.

87. Ibid., p.10.

88. OECD, *Pensions at a Glance 2009: Retirement-Income Systems in OECD Countries*, http://ww.oecd.org/els/social/pensions/PAG (accessed December 6, 2010).

89. OECD, *Society at a Glance 2009*, and Robert E. Lane, *The Loss of Happiness in Market Democracies* (New Haven, CT: Yale University Press, 2000).

CHAPTER 8

Air and Water Pollution
Control Policy

LEARNING OBJECTIVES

- Understand air and water pollution control policy in the United States and Brazil.
- Explain the main public policy debates regarding air and water pollution in the United States and Brazil.

- Evaluate the main air and water regulatory agencies in the United States and Brazil.
- Understand international efforts to abate air and water pollution in the United States and Brazil.

The first Earth Day in the United States in 1970 and the Earth Summit (formally called the United Nations Conference on Environment and Development) in Brazil in 1992 have dramatically changed our awareness of environmental problems. Indeed, the first Earth Day was the stepping-stone for a variety of environmental regulatory policy developments in many industrialized countries.

Although environmental policies have been implemented in industrialized countries, there is growing concern about the environment and policies to address environmental problems in developing countries. In recent years, hundreds of environmental lobby groups have sprung up in Asia and Latin America. Some of these are offshoots of rich global groups, such as Greenpeace, which has offices in 11 developing countries. Many groups are homegrown, drawing support from people who are increasingly worried about the effect of pollution on their health. Today, several governments—for example, Brazil and China, are passing increasingly tough environmental regulations, many of them modeled on green standards in the United States and Europe. Yet, there are countries that are unwilling or unable to enforce green regulations.

In this chapter, we will first examine air and water pollution control policy in the United States and Brazil. This will include looking at the policy debates, the policy-making process, relevant interest groups and agencies, as well and problems and challenges faced by both countries. The two countries have similar policy-making processes and institutions at the federal level. A combination of institutional and pluralist approaches is used to compare the policies in both countries because the United States and Brazil are federal systems of government and they have similar interest groups surrounding each issue. This makes a comparative approach appropriate. The development of air and water policies is examined in both countries in order to highlight the similarities and differences between the countries. Although Brazil began basing its policies on those in the United States, the country soon found that those policies were not a proper fit for the environmental problems that exist in Brazil and with its economic climate.

The United States is an industrialized country with relatively progressive air and water policies. Brazil, however, is a developing country that needs to further develop its air and water policies. Development of such policies is also of high priority with regard to the preservation of clean air and water due to the importance of the Amazon Rainforest in generating oxygen while absorbing carbon dioxide, a greenhouse gas. Consider, too, the significance of the Amazon River Basin as one of the world's largest sources of fresh water.

The United States

In the United States, a major public policy debate over air pollution control relates to the use of coal. The Department of Energy (DOE) states that "the energy content of the nation's coal resources exceeds that of all the world's known recoverable oil."[1] The United States holds one-quarter of the world's coal reserves. Coal supports the nation's electric power industry by supplying more than half the electricity consumed by Americans.[2] Rather than stop using coal as a source of energy, the DOE is attempting to develop "low-cost environmental compliance technologies and efficiency-boosting innovations" to help protect the environment, specifically air and water quality, and reduce the amount of greenhouse gases that are emitted by coal-fired plants.[3] The Environmental Protection Agency (EPA) implemented a partnership program—the Coal Combustion Products Partnership—that takes the by-products of burning coal in coal-fired plants and finds beneficial uses for these coal by-products, such as long-life road pavements.[4] Researchers at Massachusetts Institute of Technology believe "that coal will continue to be used to meet the world's energy needs in significant quantities," and they think that new technologies for carbon dioxide capture and sequestration (CCS) may significantly reduce carbon dioxide emissions while still using coal to produce energy.[5]

Yet, the Union of Concerned Scientists (UCS) cites enormous health risks and environmental damage due to the continued use of coal-fired plants. Used primarily in the industrial and electricity sectors, coal accounts for 49.8 percent and 83 percent of carbon dioxide emissions in each sector, respectively. The amounts of carbon dioxide being emitted into the atmosphere by coal-fired plants significantly contribute to air pollution and global warming.[6] Many

environmental, health, farm, and community organizations have actively petitioned to reduce or remove the use of coal-fired plants, and state governments
have heeded these petitions and refused to permit new coal power plants in
states such as Florida and Kansas.[7]

A major public policy debate over water pollution control relates to the
lack of standardization in measuring and reporting water pollution at state and
local levels. In 2003, the Ozark Chapter of the Sierra Club petitioned the EPA
to "set consistent and adequate water quality standards for defined portions
of the Mississippi and Missouri Rivers."[8] Essentially, the Sierra Club believed
that inconsistencies in different state water quality standards led to lapses in
monitoring by some states contributing to the overall impairment of water quality downriver. The Natural Resources Defense Council (NRDC) cites the lack
of national protocol in measuring water quality at beaches—some states and
localities test water quality at beaches; others do not. According to the NRDC,
even if water quality tests are performed and it is found that high bacteria levels
exceed health standards, the public is not notified, and beaches are not closed.[9]
Although environmental groups argue that the lack of standardization in water
quality testing is causing problems, the EPA found that the majority of states
"have designated water uses consistent with the Clean Water Act and the federal
regulations."[10] The EPA did agree with the Sierra Club that there are short-
comings with current state monitoring programs, and is looking to implement
"more consistent monitoring and assessment programs in the petition states."[11]
However, as a NRDC report on water quality at U.S. beaches suggests, the problems arising from a lack of standardization in measurement, monitoring, and
reporting involve much more than just the Mississippi and Missouri Rivers.

Government Agencies and Other Actors

Policy Making   In the United States, policy making for air and water pollution control begins when public interest groups, citizens, businesses, and government agencies contact Congress with concerns about unaddressed problems
with air and water pollution control. It is then the responsibility of Congress to
discuss these concerns and, if warranted, to hold hearings and draft a bill that
addresses the problems. If a bill for air and water pollution control is passed
by Congress and signed into a law by the president, the law is then sent to the
Environmental Protection Agency (EPA) for implementation of these regulatory
policies.[12]

For air and water pollution policy making, the U.S. government relies heavily on "sound science" when developing policies and regulations. In meeting its
responsibility for developing air and water pollution control regulations, the
EPA often relies on peer review by qualified independent experts who provide
critical assessments.[13] Air and water pollution control policy making differs
from other environmental policy making because clean air and water are an
immediate concern to human survival when considering other aspects of the
environment in need of regulation.

According to the Pacific Institute, there are four pressing issues that the United States faces with regard to water quality. First is the need to deal with a **global water crisis**. Second is the need to update the Clean Water Act and the Safe Drinking Water Act. Third is the need to address the consequences of **global climate change** (as it gets hotter, more people need access to water; yet, as it gets hotter, there will be more water shortages). Fourth is the need to protect the United States against national security threats to its water supplies.[14] Since the establishment of the **Department of Homeland Security (DHS)** with its mission to protect the United States against threats to its security, the water sector is classified as a critical infrastructure and key resource, which has figured into assessments of water monitoring and security post-9/11.[15] Let us now take a closer look at two government agencies that deal with the environment.

Environmental Protection Agency (EPA)   The **Environmental Protection Agency (EPA)** was created by an executive order of President Nixon in 1970. The formation of the agency moved the federal government from an advisory and educational role on air pollution toward enforcement of air pollution laws.[16] The EPA has been the largest federal regulatory agency in terms of budget and personnel; its annual budget is about $8 billion, and it has over 18,000 employees. Responsibilities of the EPA include monitoring an extraordinarily large and technical complex set of environmental programs, coordinating collaboration among states and local communities, and implementing regulations that outline critical technical, operational, and legal details necessary to implement laws.

Council on Environmental Quality (CEQ)   Another agency involved in environmental policy is the **Council on Environmental Quality (CEQ)**. Congress created the CEQ in 1969 as part of the National Environmental Policy Act (NEPA). The CEQ provides the president with an annual report on the state of the environment, and the Council's Chair acts as the president's principal environmental policy adviser. The CEQ also oversees various environmental assessments according to NEPA guidelines.[17]

State Governments   State governments are often responsible for the implementation of EPA regulations regarding air and water pollution control. For example, under the **Safe Drinking Water Act**, states are responsible for assessing and protecting all sources of drinking water within their boundaries, and for ensuring "that water systems acquire and maintain the technical, managerial, and financial capability" to provide safe drinking water to their customers.[18] However, through a number of grants, the federal government helps subsidize many air and water pollution control regulations.[19]

Interest Groups   There are many interest groups in the United States with a stake in air and water quality. Public interest organizations with an environmental focus, such as the Sierra Club, regularly lobby for improvements to air and water quality statutes. Additionally, business and commercial organizations across various sectors of the economy are affected by concerns over air and water quality: mining (the National Mining Association); the oil and natural gas sector (the American Gas Association, the American Petroleum Institute); the agricultural sector (the American Farm Bureau Federation); the service sector (the National Association of Water Companies, the National Solid Wastes Management Association); and the automotive industry (the American Trucking Association, the Manufacturers of Emission Controls Association).[20]

Current Policies

Air Pollution Control Policies   In the United States, air pollution control policies have been continually updated since 1955. The **Air Pollution Control Act of 1955** "was the first federal air pollution law, and it mandated federal research programs to investigate the health and welfare effects of air pollution," with states receiving technical assistance from the federal government.[21] In 1963, the first **Clean Air Act (CAA)** was passed to define air quality criteria based on scientific studies; it also provided for grants to state and local air pollution control agencies.

Following the creation of the EPA, Congress amended the Clean Air Act in 1970. The amendments directed the EPA to establish **National Ambient Air Quality Standards (NAAQS)** for specific pollutants and gave the EPA greater power over both research and enforcement of air pollution laws. The amendments left the states with most of the burden for achieving NAAQS, with the EPA providing technical support. The 1970 amendment of the CAA also established **National Emissions Standards for Hazardous Air Pollutants (NESHAPs)** and the **Federal Motor Vehicle Emission Standards**.

The CAA was amended two more times, in 1977 and in 1990. In 1977, the amendments **Prevention of Significant Deterioration (PSD)** and **Nonattainment Provisions** were added. These amendments gave states that had not attained NAAQS a much longer and realistic time frame to achieve them. The 1990 amendments "renewed emphasis on controlling emissions of hazardous air pollutants and introduced efforts aimed at controlling acid rain and ozone depletion in the atmosphere."[22]

Water Pollution Control Policies   There are three major water pollution control policies in the United States: the Clean Water Act, the Safe Drinking Water Act, and the Ground Water Rule. In 1972, the **Clean Water Act (CWA)** was passed and has continued to evolve over time. The aim of the CWA is to "sharply reduce direct pollutant discharges into waterways, finance municipal waste water treatment facilities, and manage polluted runoff."[23] Over the past decade, the CWA has shifted from a case-by-case practice to "more holistic watershed-based strategies. Under the watershed approach equal emphasis is placed on protecting healthy waters and restoring impaired ones."[24]

In 1974, the first Safe Drinking Water Act (SDWA) was passed in order to "protect public health by regulating the nation's public drinking water supply."[25] The SDWA was amended in 1986 and in 1996.[26] The 1986 amendments increased the number of contaminants that are regulated.[27] The 1996 amendments called for "source water protection, funding for water system improvements, and public information as important components of safe drinking water."[28]

The purpose of the 2006 **Ground Water Rule (GWR)** is to provide extra protection to "public water systems that use ground water sources."[29] The GWR applies to source water locations such as lakes, rivers, reservoirs, and ground water aquifers because ground water sources are susceptible to fecal contamination, which can cause diseases. The GWR requires sanitary surveys of critical components of the public water system, with the EPA in a monitoring role.[30]

Standards

The United States is involved in various efforts to set international standards for air and water pollution control. The International Joint Commission between the United States and Canada monitors and investigates air and water pollution along the U.S.–Canadian border. Both countries have agreements on air quality (the Canada–United States Air Quality Agreement) and water quality (the Great Lakes Water Quality Agreement).[31] The United States is a member of the Organization for Economic Co-operation and Development (OECD), which coordinates environmental policies among its members. Furthermore, the United States has ratified the **Montreal Protocol**, which seeks to protect the ozone layer by reducing the use of chlorofluorocarbons (CFCs) that enter the atmosphere.[32]

Problems and Challenges

Although the United States has taken steps to reduce air and water pollution, many environmental and health organizations believe that stronger regulations are warranted. The EPA revised the national air ambient quality standard for lead air pollution in 2008, but enforcing these standards requires the EPA to greatly expand monitoring capabilities.[33] The EPA looked at strengthening the NAAQS for fine particulate matter, but, in 2005, EPA Administrator Stephen Johnson overruled a nearly unanimous recommendation from scientific advisors and maintained the existing standard.

There are still problems with the monitoring of water quality across states. In its 2004 *National Water Quality Inventory: Report to Congress*, the EPA concluded that 44 percent of rivers, 64 percent of lakes, and 30 percent of estuaries are impaired. The EPA noted that there is a need to build the capacity of the states to administer water programs so that water throughout the nation is being monitored in a consistent manner.[34] According to the National Resources Defense Council (NRDC), the most recent data available show that "57 percent of beaches are monitored, and only 45 percent of those are monitored at least once a week."[35] Beach pollution is a serious problem. It caused 18,682 beaches either to be closed or to "swim under advisory" in 2009. This pollution in 2009 came from storm water (7,200 closing and health advisory days); miscellaneous sources, including wildlife and boat discharges (3,500 closing and health advisory days); and sewage spills and overflows (1,600 closing and health advisory days). The NRDC believes that testing procedures currently in use must be improved on because tests are "not designed to protect the public against the full range of waterborne illnesses or to protect sensitive populations."[36]

Brazil

Throughout Brazil water contamination is a major problem, which is caused mostly by a lack of urban effluent treatment. The problem is institutional, and it is "due to shortage of financial resources and lack of political will."[37] The **National Water Agency (ANA)** states that untreated domestic sewage as well as agricultural and industrial pollution of water are some of the main issues of concern in the basin regions of Brazil.[38] Although Brazil is a large country with abundant water resources, these resources are not evenly distributed throughout the country. In Brazil's south and southeast regions, which are densely populated, water scarcity is due to overuse and pollution. A number of Brazilian water policies have been enacted to attempt to deal with water pollution.

BOX 8.1

Country Profile of Brazil

Name of Country: Brazil
Conventional Long Form: Federative Republic of Brazil
Type of Government: Federal Republic

Executive Branch:

Chief of State: President Dilma Rousseff (since 1 January 2011); Vice President Michel Temer (since 1 January 2011); the president is both the chief of state and head of government

Head of Government: President Dilma Rousseff (since 1 January 2011); Vice President Michel Temer (since 1 January 2011)

Legislative Branch:

Bicameral National Congress or Congresso Nacional consists of the Federal Senate or Senado Federal (81 seats; 3 members from each state and federal district elected according to the principle of majority to serve eight-year terms; one-third and two-thirds elected every four years, alternately) and the Chamber of Deputies or Camara dos Deputados (513 seats; members are elected by proportional representation to serve four-year terms)

Judicial Branch:

Supreme Federal Tribunal or STF (11 ministers are appointed for life by the president and confirmed by the Senate); Higher Tribunal of Justice; Regional Federal Tribunals (judges are appointed for life); note: though appointed "for life," judges, like all federal employees, have a mandatory retirement age of 70

Administrative Divisions:

26 states (estados [singular: estado]) and 1 federal district (distrito federal); Acre, Alagoas, Amapa, Amazonas, Bahia, Ceara, Distrito Federal, Espirito Santo, Goias, Maranhao, Mato Grosso, Mato Grosso do Sul, Minas Gerais, Para, Paraiba, Parana, Pernambuco, Piaui, Rio de Janeiro, Rio Grande do Norte, Rio Grande do Sul, Rondonia, Roraima, Santa Catarina, Sao Paulo, Sergipe, Tocantins

Economic Indicators:

GDP (purchasing power parity): $2.362 trillion (2012 estimation)
GDP Real Growth Rate: 1.3 percent (2012 estimation)

GDP per capita (purchasing power parity): $12,000 (2012 estimation)

Economic Structure: Agriculture 5.4 percent; Industry 27.4 percent; Services 67.2 percent (2012 estimation)

Demographic Indicators:

Population: 199,321,413 (2012 estimation)

Population Growth: 0.86 percent (2012 estimation)

Birth Rate: 15.2 births/1,000 population (2012 estimation)

Infant Mortality Rate: 20.5 deaths/1,000 live births (2012 estimation)

Life Expectancy at Birth: 72.79 years (2012 estimation)

Literacy (age 15 and over can read and write): 88.6 percent (2012 estimation)

Ethnic Groups: White 53.7 percent, Mulatto (mixed White and Black) 38.5 percent, Black 6.2 percent, other (includes Japanese, Arab, Amerindian) 0.9 percent, unspecified 0.7 percent (2000 census)

Religions: Roman Catholic (nominal) 73.6 percent, Protestant 15.4 percent, Spiritualist 1.3 percent, Bantu/voodoo 0.3 percent, other 1.8 percent, unspecified 0.2 percent, none 7.4 percent (2000 census)

Source: Program of the United Nations for the Environment, "UNEP News: Deforestation in Brazil," http://www.pnuma.org/informacion_ing/penumanuevasing/index_feb08.html#20 (accessed May 3, 2012).

Industry is a primary source of water pollution in Brazil. In the northeast of Brazil, water pollution is associated with sugar cane plantations. These plantations are used in the production of biofuels, which are better than fossil fuels for the environment. However, in order to make biofuels, sugarcane plantations use large quantities of toxic chemicals, such as insecticides and pesticides—the cause water pollution. Also, procedures such as pre-harvest burning result "in the emission of ash, particulate matter, and gases into the atmosphere."[39] The economic importance of the sugarcane industry is hard to ignore since Brazil is one of the world's leading producers of sugar, sugarcane, and ethanol.[40] It still remains to be seen whether the Brazilian government is able and willing to enact serious environmental regulations on an economically important part of its agricultural sector.

Brazil is of significant interest with regard to climate change, specifically global warming, which is believed to be caused by the trapping of greenhouse gases in the atmosphere. Tropical deforestation causes almost "a fifth of annual, human-induced emissions of heat-trapping gases to the atmosphere."[41] Given the importance of Brazil's Amazon Rainforest in absorbing carbon dioxide, a greenhouse gas, Brazil is in a unique position to counteract global warming by reducing deforestation that is caused by the expansion of cattle ranching and agriculture. Since 2004, "Brazil has created more than 20 million hectares of parks, extractive reserve, and national forests in the Amazon region."[42] These protected areas can greatly prevent carbon dioxide emissions that would result from deforestation. Government intervention and economic trends have significantly decreased Brazil's deforestation rates. The Brazilian government needs to address the financial reasons for deforestation, which extend beyond logging, in order to successfully enact deforestation regulations.

Government Agencies and Other Actors

Policy Making   Let us first take a look at the legislative process through which bills are adopted as laws in Brazil. This will provide insight into the legislative part of Brazil's air and water pollution control policy making.

Brazil has a bicameral legislature (National Congress) composed of the Chamber of Deputies and the Senate. The Chamber of Deputies has 16 standing committees, and the Senate has 6 standing committees. The two houses (the Chamber of Deputies and the Senate) also have a joint budget committee. According to Brazil's 1988 constitution, the committees can approve or reject legislation. "To override a committee decision…requires a petition signed by a certain number of members. Once one house passes a bill, the other deliberates on it. If a different version of the bill is passed, it returns to the original house for a final vote on the differences."[43] After passing through the National Congress, a bill moves to the president to be either signed into law or vetoed.[44] This process is similar to that in the United States.

National Water Agency (ANA)   Although it is Brazil's **Ministry of Environment** that oversees environmental policy, most water initiatives are left to the National Water Agency. The ANA is uniquely focused on water issues, specifically sanitation and drinking water availability, policymaking for water quality control and pollution regulation therefore differs from other environmental policy making. The purpose of the ANA is to monitor water quality, supply, and use. The agency regulates water-use permits and can develop and oversee use and conservation programs where needed.

National Water Resources Management System and National Environment System   The ANA is part of the National Water Resources Management System, established in 1997.[45] Together with several other agencies, the **National Water Resources Council (NWRC)**, along with state water resources councils, river basin committees, water management agencies, and basin agencies, are responsible for implementing water resource policy directed by the ANA. The National Water Resources Management System and all of its associated agencies must work with the **National Environment System**. The National Environment System uses primarily environmental permits to "control environmental impacts that may be caused by potentially damaging activities." Although the National Environment System is operated by the Ministry of Environment, the issuing of permits is left to the **National Environmental Council**.[46]

Interest Groups   Interest groups in Brazil are varied and active in regard to air and water pollution control policy. Major industry interest groups tend to group together, forming larger coalitions such as the São Paulo State Federation of Industries (FIESP), which assembles 127 industrial associations.[47] Two major national interest groups are the National Confederation of Industry (CNI) and the Brazilian Aluminum Association (ABAL). All of these groups actively lobby the National Congress on behalf of their constituents to promote their interests in air and water issues. Environmental policy has also been affected by high grassroots activism among the poor in Brazil's urban areas.[48]

Current Policies

Air Pollution Control Policies   In 1976, Brazil passed its first attempt to set standards for air pollutant emissions with a government statute, NR 0231. Informed by U.S. standards, the statute set emission standards that "were used to establish the maximum permitted concentration levels"[49] of air pollutants. Standards in the United States ultimately did not suit Brazil's needs, however. So, in 1989, the Brazilian government created the **National Program for Air Quality Control (PRONAR)**.

The main goal of the PRONAR was to reduce the negative effects of air pollution on the environment, particularly in metropolitan areas. In order to achieve this, the PRONAR focused on restricting pollution at the source, limiting emissions, and setting national air quality standards. One feature of the PRONAR is that it set maximum emission limits for pollution sources. PRONAR, being stricter on emissions, would cause newer technologies to be cleaner.[50]

In 1986, the National Environmental Council (CONAMA) created the **Program for Control of Air Pollution from Mobile Sources (PROCONVE)**. The PROCONVE focused on reducing air pollutant emissions from mobile sources, especially new vehicles.[51] Emissions standards were further increased in 1990 with Resolution 3/90 in order to enhance air quality.[52] States were given the responsibility to monitor the emissions. Stationary sources of air pollution are covered under Resolution 8/90.[53]

Water Pollution Control Policies   Since the early 1970s, Brazil has implemented several plans to deal with water quality and control water pollution: the National Base Sanitation Plan, the National Urbanisation Programme, and the Catchment Restoration Programme. **The National Base Sanitation Plan (PLANASA)** was in effect from 1971 to 1989. It featured dominant state sanitation companies, with state participation, and it conducted global viability studies. PLANASA ended as a result of inflation and questioning of the plan. The Brazilian government then implemented the **National Urbanisation Programme (PRONURB)** in 1990. Although the PRONURB was the dominant water program from 1990 to 1994, it did essentially nothing for Brazil. At that time, Brazil was heavily in debt, partly as a result of an expansive government welfare program.[54] This left the government with little money to carry out PRONURB.

The **Catchment Restoration Programme (PRODES)** was launched by ANA in 2001. The purpose is "to restore the quality of water in rivers and lakes and to encourage the use of modern water resource management tools, such as pricing for the use of water and introducing river basin committees and agencies."[55] The PRODES offers financial assistance and invests in sewage treatment projects. PRODES has not been able to meet its objectives due to federal budget cuts, causing the sanitation sector to go "backwards in terms of water quality."[56]

Standards

Over time, Brazil's air and water pollution control policies have come in line with international standards. Brazil is a signatory of several major international treaties on the environment: the Kyoto Protocol, the Montreal Protocol, and the Law of the Sea. The Kyoto Protocol and the Montreal Protocol both aim at reducing air pollution, by decreasing (1) greenhouse gas emissions and (2) the use of CFCs and other chemicals, respectively. The **Kyoto Protocol** went into effect in Brazil in 2005,[57] and the Montreal Protocol has been in effect since 1990.[58] The Brazilian government ratified the **Law of the Sea** in 1988,[59] which regulates the oceans, including marine environments, which are subject to pollution regulation measures.

Problems and Challenges

Although Brazil has made great strides in reducing air pollutant emissions from its energy sector—with 40 percent of total energy consumption supplied by renewable resources—greenhouse gas emissions still remain high. Part of this is due to tropical deforestation and forest degradation that release greenhouse gases.[60] Many nations in the world have acted in concert through the United Nations Environment Programme to end deforestation in Amazonia. In February 2008, new regulations aimed at decreasing deforestation, including "livestock control, the creation of conservation units, blocking funds for activities that trigger deforestation, and the registration of properties located in deforested zones" were reviewed.[61] However, the agricultural sector is not addressed, especially soybean crops that have been partly responsible for deforestation.

The extent of water pollution in Brazil has made it difficult to combat. There are large sanitation companies belonging to states, which conflict with municipalities over who has the institutional authority ("entitlement") over large urban sprawls. Developing laws to regulate sanitation would go a long way toward improving water quality in Brazil; with laws to protect it, the sanitation sector would be less risky for private capital, which would expand Brazil's capabilities to improve water quality.

Comparison

This chapter has examined air and water pollution control policy in the United States and Brazil through an institutional perspective. Although both countries have similar concerns about air and water pollution, each deals with particular issues in addressing these concerns.

In the United States, the use of coal is subject to a major public policy debate over air pollution control. As mentioned earlier in this chapter, coal supplies more than half of the nation's energy. Thus, it is no surprise that the Union of Concerned Scientists points to enormous health risks and environmental damage from using coal to generate energy. Carbon dioxide emissions released when burning coal increase air pollution and add to global warming. Yet, since the world will continue to rely to a significant extent on coal for its energy needs, the EPA and Massachusetts Institute of Technology researchers argue that we should transform by-products of coal combustion for beneficial use rather than stop using coal as an energy source.

An issue subject to a major public policy debate over water pollution control in the United States is the lack of standardization in state and local measuring, monitoring, and reporting of water contamination. As a result, there are still concerns about impaired water quality of rivers and at beaches. The EPA does state that the majority of states have designated water uses consistence with the Clean Water Act and other federal regulations.

The United States also faces four issues regarding water quality. First, it must deal with the global water crisis. Second, it needs to update both the Clean Water Act and the Safe Drinking Water Act. Third, the country must address the consequences of global climate change. And fourth, the United States needs to protect against national security threats to its water supply.

Unlike in the United States, water contamination is a serious problem in Brazil due to untreated domestic sewage as well as agricultural and industrial pollution of water, especially in the country's most densely populated regions. Urban sewage treatment has usually been hampered by inadequate political will and inadequate funding. Of particular concern in Brazil are water pollution and emissions from pre-harvest burning associated with sugarcane plantations as well as deforestation and its contribution to global warming. Sugarcane plantations are used not only to produce sugarcane and sugar, but they are also used in the production of biofuels. Deforestation clears land to be used primarily for cattle ranching. Sugarcane, sugar, and biofuel production as well as cattle ranching are important components of Brazil's economy.

Air and water pollution control policy making in the United States and Brazil involves similar legislative processes. In both countries, a bill has to be passed by two houses (the House of Representatives and the Senate in the United States, the Chamber of Deputies and the Senate in Brazil) of a bicameral legislature (the Congress in the United States, the National Congress in Brazil) before it is signed into law or vetoed by a president.

The United States has the Environmental Protection Agency (EPA) and the Council on Environmental Quality (CEQ) to administer environmental policy. The EPA monitors environmental programs, coordinates collaboration on the environment among states and local communities, and implements environmental regulations, with state governments often responsible for implementing EPA regulations regarding air and water pollution control. The CEQ oversees environmental assessments according to guidelines provided by the National Environmental Policy Act (NEPA) and submits to the president an annual report on the state of the environment; its chair is the president's principal environmental policy adviser.

Brazil has the Ministry of the Environment to administer environmental policy as well as the National Environment System and the National Water Resources Management System. The National Environment System relies mostly on environmental permits to control harm to the environment. These permits are issued by the National Environmental Council (CONAMA) at the center of the National Environment System as well as by several state-level agencies. Given the importance of the Amazon River Basin as one of the world's largest sources of fresh water, combined with the severity of Brazil's water contamination problem, it is not surprising that Brazil has the National Water Resources Management System. The National Water Resources Management System, which must work closely with the National Environment System, includes the National Water Agency (ANA), the National Water Resources Council (NWRC), and the various state water resources councils, river basin committees, water management agencies, and basin agencies. Since the ANA is uniquely focused on water issues, specifically sanitation and drinking water availability, most water initiatives in Brazil are left to the ANA, whose monitoring efforts, regulations, and programs are based on information from the Brazilian Institute of Geography and Statistics (IBGE).

In both the United States and Brazil, there are several active interest groups seeking influence over air and water pollution control policy. Regarding the United States, this chapter referred to public interest organizations with an environmental focus as well as many business and commercial organizations across various sectors of the economy, such as mining, the oil and natural gas sector, the agricultural sector, the service sector, and the automotive industry. Regarding Brazil, this chapter mentioned industrial associations, with a tendency to group together and forming larger coalitions, as well as grassroots activism among the poor in Brazil's urban periphery. Brazil's grassroots activism differs from the larger public interest organizations that are found in the United States. Another difference involves the role and activity of international environmental nongovernmental organizations (IENGOs) in Brazil. Examples of IENGOs are the World Wildlife Fund, Greenpeace, and other active groups in Brazil that provide an international input (however small) to Brazilian politics and policy making that is largely absent in the U.S. policy-making process (with a few exceptions in areas dealing with U.S. foreign policy).

Both the United States and Brazil have a variety of policies to (1) regulate emissions of air pollutants and improve air quality and (2) protect clean water sources and improve water quality. Air pollution control policies in the United States include the 1955 Air Pollution Control Act and the 1963 Clean Air Act (CAA), which was amended in 1970, 1977, and 1990. U.S. water pollution control policies include the 1972 Clean Water Act (CWA), the 1974 Safe Drinking Water Act (SDWA), which was amended in 1986 and 1996, and the 2006 Ground Water Rule (GWR). Brazilian air pollution control policies include the 1989 National Program for Air Quality Control (PRONAR), the 1986 Program for Control of Air Pollution from Mobile Sources (PROCONVE), as well as two CONAMA resolutions issued in 1990. Brazilian water pollution control policies include the 1971 National Base Sanitation Plan (PLANASA), the 1990 National Urbanisation Programme (PRONURB), and the 2001 Catchment Restoration Programme (PRODES).

Both the United States and Brazil are committed to efforts to create international air and water pollution control standards. The United States has agreements with

Canada on air and water quality, and it is Canada's partner in the International Joint Commission that monitors and investigates air and water pollution along the U.S.–Canadian border. The United States has ratified the Montreal Protocol, and it is involved in international coordination of environmental policies as a member of the Organization for Economic Co-operation and Development (OECD). Brazil has ratified the Kyoto Protocol, the Montreal Protocol, and the Law of the Sea.

Although the United States and Brazil have made progress in controlling air and water pollution, more work needs to be done. In the United States, the Natural Resources Defense Council (NRDC) argued that EPA efforts to control lead air pollution require greatly expanded monitoring capabilities and a standard for lead air pollution that is lower than the standard adopted by the EPA. Also, standardization of monitoring water quality across states requires significant improvement. In Brazil, greater efforts are needed to reduce greenhouse gas emissions and deforestation in Amazonia. Also, there are still laws to be developed to reduce the extent of water pollution.

We have seen that there are many institutional and organizational similarities between Brazil and the United States. Both countries have similar legislative and executive arrangements. Policy formation in both countries is heavily influenced by interest groups representing major polluting industries. To date, Brazil has more serious water pollution problems than the United States. This is understandable, given the state of development that Brazil is in vis-à-vis the United States. We would anticipate that as the Brazilian economy develops further, the Brazilian environment will improve.[62]

Recommended Resources for American Air and Water Pollution Control Policy

Judith A. Layzer, *The Environmental Case: Translating Values into Policy* (2nd ed.) (Washington, DC: CQ Press, 2006).

Walter A. Rosenbaum, *Environmental Politics and Policy* (6th ed.) (Washington, DC: CQ Press, 2005).

Zachary A. Smith, *The Environmental Policy Paradox* (6th ed.) (Upper Saddle River, NJ: Prentice-Hall, 2004).

Recommended Resources for Brazilian Air and Water Pollution Control Policy

Antonio Herman Benjamín, Cláudia Lima Marques, and Catherine Tinker, "The Water Giant Awakes: An Overview of Water Law in Brazil," *Texas Law Review* 83(7) (2005): 2185–2244.

Benedito Braga, Monica Porto, and Luciano Meneses, "Integrated Water Quality Management in Brazil," in Asit Biswas, Cecilia Tortayada, Benedito Braga, and Diego J. Rodriguez, eds., *Water Quality Management in the Americas* (Berlin: Springer, 2006).

Jerson Kelman, "Evolution of Brazil's Water Resources Management System," in Valente Canali et al., eds. *Water Resources Management: Brazilian and European*

Trends and Approaches (Porto Alegre, Brazil: Brazilian Water Resources Association, 2000), pp. 19–36.

Lesley K. McAllister, *Making Law Matter: Environmental Protection and Legal Institutions in Brazil* (Stanford: Stanford University Press, 2008).

Antonio de Aguiar Patriota, "An Introduction to Brazilian Environmental Law," *George Washington International Law Review* 40(3) (2008): 611–617.

Rodrigo Sales et al. "Trends on Brazilian Legislation Regarding Air Pollution," http://www.docstoc.com/docs/22858370/Trends-on-Brazilian-Legislation-Regarding-Air-Pollution (accessed April 24, 2014).

Notes

1. U.S. Department of Energy, "Accomplishments: 2006," http://www.netl.doe.gov/publications/others/accomp_rpt/accomp_fy06.pdf. (accessed April 27, 2012).

2. U.S Department of Energy, "Secure and Reliable Energy Supplies—Realizing the Clean Energy Potential of Domestic Coal," http://www.netl.doe.gov/KeyIssues/secure_energy2a.html (accessed June 1, 2012).

3. U.S. Department of Energy, "Coal," http://www.energy.gov/energysources/coal.htm (accessed May 3, 2012).

4. U.S. Environmental Protection Agency, *Coal Combustion Products Partnership (C^{2}P^2)*, http://www.uswag.org/c2p2factsheet.pdf (accessed May 3, 2012).

5. Massachusetts Institute of Technology, *The Future of Coal: An Interdisciplinary MIT Study* (2007), http://web.mit.edu/coal/The_Future_of_Coal_Summary_Report.pdf (accessed May 3, 2012).

6. Union of Concerned Scientists, "The Costs of Coal," http://www.ucsusa.org/clean_energy/technology_and_impacts/impacts/the-costs-of-coal.html (accessed May 3, 2012).

7. Lester R. Brown, "U.S. Moving Toward Ban on New Coal-Fired Power Plants," Earth Policy Institute, http://www.earth-policy.org/index.php?/plan_b_updates/2008/update70 (accessed May 3, 2012).

8. U.S. Environmental Protection Agency, "EPA Response to Sierra Club Petition Regarding Defined Portions of the Mississippi and Missouri Rivers," http://water.epa.gov/scitech/swguidance/waterquality/standards/SierraClub.cfm (accessed May 3, 2012).

9. Natural Resources Defense Council, "Water Quality at U.S. Beaches," http://www.nrdc.org/water/oceans/ttw/guide.asp (accessed May 3, 2012).

10. U.S. Environmental Protection Agency, "EPA Response to Sierra Club Petition Regarding Defined Portions of the Mississippi and Missouri Rivers," http://water.epa.gov/scitech/swguidance/waterquality/standards/SierraClub.cfm (accessed May 3, 2012).

11. U.S. Environmental Protection Agency, "EPA Response to Sierra Club Petition Regarding Defined Portions of the Mississippi and Missouri Rivers," http://water.epa.gov/scitech/swguidance/waterquality/standards/SierraClub.cfm (accessed May 3, 2012).

12. U.S. Environmental Protection Agency, "Environmental Laws: The Origin of Regulations," http://www.epa.gov/lawsregs/brochure/origins.html (accessed May 3, 2012).

13. U.S. Environmental Protection Agency, "Using Sound Science," http://www.epa.gov/lawsregs/brochure/science.html (accessed May 3, 2012).

14. Peter H. Gleick, "Water: Threats and Opportunities, Recommendations for the Next President," Pacific Institute, http://www.pacinst.org/publications/essays_and_opinion/presidential_recommendations/water_threats_opportunities.pdf (accessed May 3, 2012).

15. U.S. Department of Homeland Security, "Water Sector: Critical Infrastructures and Key Resources," http://www.dhs.gov/files/programs/gc_1188399291279.shtm (accessed May 3, 2012).
16. U.S. Environmental Protection Agency, "Origins of Modern Air Pollution Regulations," http://www.epa.gov/apti/course422/apc1.html (accessed May 3, 2012).
17. U.S. Executive Office of the President, Council on Environmental Quality, "Council on Environmental Quality," http://www.whitehouse.gov/administration/eop/ceq/ (accessed May 3, 2012).
18. U.S. Environmental Protection Agency, *Safe Drinking Water Act (SDWA): Public Access to Information and Involvement, EPA 816-F-04-039,* http://www.epa.gov/ogwdw/sdwa/30th/factsheets/pubinvolve.html (accessed May 3, 2012).
19. U.S. Environmental Protection Agency, "Grants and Fellowship Information," http://www.epa.gov/epahome/grants.htm (accessed May 3, 2012).
20. Library of Congress, Congressional Research Service, *CRS Report for Congress: A Directory of Some Interest Groups and Governmental Organization Concerned with National Environmental Policies (93-831 ENR),.* http://ncseonline.org/NLE/CRSreports/General/gen-2.cfm (accessed May 3, 2012).
21. U.S. Environmental Protection Agency, "Origins of Modern Air Pollution Regulations," http://www.epa.gov/apti/course422/apc1.html (accessed June 1, 2012).
22. U.S. Environmental Protection Agency, "The Clean Air Act," http://www.epa.gov/apti/course422/apc3.html (accessed May 3, 2012).
23. U.S. Environmental Protection Agency, "Water: Laws and Executive Orders," http://water.epa.gov/lawsregs/lawsguidance/ (accessed April 27, 2012).
24. U.S. Environmental Protection Agency, "Introduction to the Clean Water Act," http://www.epa.gov/owow/watershed/wacademy/acad2000/cwa/ (accessed May 3, 2012).
25. U.S. Environmental Protection Agency, "Safe Drinking Water Act," http://water.epa.gov/lawsregs/rulesregs/sdwa/index.cfm (accessed April 27, 2012).
26. U.S. Environmental Protection Agency, "Safe Drinking Water Act (SDWA): Basic Information," http://www.epa.gov/ogwdw/sdwa/basicinformation.html (accessed May 3, 2012).
27. U.S. Environmental Protection Agency, "President Signs Safe Drinking Water Act Amendments," http://www.epa.gov/history/topics/sdwa/04.htm (accessed May 3, 2012).
28. U.S. Environmental Protection Agency, "Safe Drinking Water Act (SDWA): Basic Information," http://www.epa.gov/ogwdw/sdwa/basicinformation.html (accessed May 3, 2012).
29. U.S. Environmental Protection Agency, "Ground Water Rule (GWR)," http://www.epa.gov/safewater/disinfection/gwr/index.html (accessed May 3, 2012).
30. U.S. Environmental Protection Agency, "Ground Water Rule (GWR): Basic Information," http://www.epa.gov/safewater/disinfection/gwr/basicinformation.html (accessed May 3, 2012).
31. International Joint Commission: Canada & United States, "Who We Are," http://www.ijc.org/en/background/ijc_cmi_nature.htm (accessed May 3, 2012).
32. United Nations Development Programme, "20 Years of the Montreal Protocol," http://www.undp.org/chemicals/20yearsmontrealprotocol (accessed May 3, 2012).
33. Natural Resources Defense Council, "EPA Takes Big Step toward Protecting Children from Lead Poison," http://www.nrdc.org/media/2008/081016.asp (accessed May 3, 2012).
34. U.S. Environmental Protection Agency, *National Water Quality Inventory: A Reporting to Congress for the 2004 Reporting Cycle—A Profile,* http://www.epa.gov/owow/305b/2004report/factsheet2004305b.pdf (accessed May 3, 2012).

35. Natural Resources Defense Council, "Beach Pollution," http://www.nrdc.org/water/oceans/ttw/faq.asp (accessed May 3, 2012).

36. Ibid.

37. Raymundo Garrido, "Institutional Aspects of Water Quality Management in Brazil," in Asit Biswas and Cecilia Tortayada (eds.), *Water Quality Management in the Americas* (Berlin: Springer, 2006): 97.

38. Brazilian National Water Agency, "Current Conflicts and Aims for the Future," http://www.ana.gov.br/ingles/Portais/folder/EasternNortheast/04-Conflicts_Aims.html (accessed May 3, 2012).

39. Günter Gunkel et al., "Sugar Cane Industry as a Source of Water Pollution—Case Study on the Situation in Ipojuca River, Pernambuco, Brazil," *Water, Air, & Soil Pollution*, 180(1-4) (March, 2007): 262.

40. Christine Bolling and Nydia R. Suarez, "The Brazilian Sugar Industry: Recent Developments," http://www.ers.usda.gov/briefing/Brazil/braziliansugar.pdf (accessed May 3, 2012).

41. NASA, "News and Press: Brazil Demonstrating that Reducing Tropical Deforestation Is Key Win-Win Global Warming Solution," http://earthobservatory.nasa.gov/Newsroom/view.php?id=32748 (accessed April 27, 2012).

42. Daniel C. Nepstad, "Brazil Demonstrating that Reducing Tropical Deforestation Is Key Win-Win Global Warming Solution," Woods Hole Research Center, http://www.whrc.org/news/pressroom/pdf/PR-2007-05-15-Win-Win.pdf (accessed May 3, 2012).

43. David V. Fleischer, "A Country Study: Brazil, the Legislature," Library of Congress Federal Research Division, http://lcweb2.loc.gov/frd/cs/brtoc.html (accessed May 3, 2012).

44. David V. Fleischer, "A Country Study: Brazil, the Executive," Library of Congress Federal Research Division, http://lcweb2.loc.gov/frd/cs/brtoc.html (accessed May 3, 2012).

45. Benedito Braga, Monica Porto, and Luciano Meneses, "Integrated Water Quality Management in Brazil," in Asit Biswas and Cecilia Tortayada (eds.), *Water Quality Management in the Americas* (Berlin: Springer, 2006): 82.

46. Ibid.

47. São Paulo State Federation of Industries, "About São Paulo," http://apps.fiesp.com.br/sitecin/english.asp and http://noticias.bol.uol.com.br/tecnologia/2010/12/16/impopularidade-dos-eua-e-barreira-para-parceria-economica-leia-em-ingles.jhtm (accessed May 3, 2012).

48. Jamie E. Jacobs, "Community Participation, the Environment, and Democracy: Brazil in Comparative Perspective," *Latin American Politics and Society*, 44(4) (Winter, 2002): 63.

49. Marco Aurélio dos Santos and Manoel Gonçalves Rodrigues, "Air Quality Management in the Thermopower Generation in Brazil," International Virtual Institute of Global Change, http://www.ivig.coppe.ufrj.br/docs/gmi.pdf: p. 2 (accessed May 3, 2012).

50. Ibid., p. 3.

51. Flavio Cotrim Pinheiro, "Program for Control of Air Pollution from Mobile Sources (PROCONVE) Analysis—Part I, Introduction," http://www.epa.gov/ies/pdf/brazil/ies_proconve1_intro.pdf (accessed May 3, 2012).

52. Marco Aurélio dos Santos and Manoel Gonçalves Rodrigues, "Air Quality Management in the Thermopower Generation in Brazil," International Virtual Institute of Global Change. http://www.ivig.coppe.ufrj.br/docs/gmi.pdf: p. 4 (accessed May 3, 2012).

53. Ibid., p. 5.

54. Raymundo Garrido, "Institutional Aspects of Water Quality Management in Brazil," in Asit Biswas and Cecilia Tortayada (eds.), *Water Quality Management in the Americas* (Berlin: Springer, 2006), p. 99.

55. Ibid., p. 103.

56. Ibid., p. 104.

57. United Nations Framework Convention on Climate Change, "Brazil," http://maindb. unfccc.int/public/country.pl?country=BR (accessed May 3, 2012).

58. Admiral Marques de Leão Training Center, Brazilian Navy, *Naval Patrol: Helping to Maintain the Sovereignty in the Brazilian Jurisdictional Waters,* https://www.mar.mil.br/ caaml/Revista/2007/Ingles/07-Pag24.pdf (accessed May 3, 2012).

59. John P. Holdren, "Linking Climate Policy with Development Strategy in Brazil, China, and India," Woods Hole Research Center, http://www.whrc.org/news/pressroom/pdf/ PR-2007-12-07-Hewlett.pdf (accessed May 3, 2012)

60. Program of the United Nations for the Environment, "UNEP News: Deforestation in Brazil," http://www.pnuma.org/informacion_ing/penumanuevasing/index_feb08. html#20 (accessed May 3, 2012).

61. Ibid.

62. The Kuznet's Curve explains the concept between environmental quality and the economy in a country. Countries that are developing economically experience high levels of environmental degradation. However, environmental quality improves once they have economies that are well developed and are experiencing economic growth.

CHAPTER 9

Alternative Energy Policy

LEARNING OBJECTIVES

- Understand different alternative energy sources in the United States and the Netherlands.
- Explain the problems associated with alternative energy sources.
- Understand the interest groups' politics surrounding alternative energy in the United States and the Netherlands.
- Identify the significant agencies and policies involved with alternative energy in the United States and the Netherlands.

The global expansion of energy consumption increases dependence on finite energy sources. A finite energy resource base may mean limits to potential horizons for economic and social freedom. Thus, concerns about alternative energy resources have gradually grown in the United States and across the world. Specifically, because of continuously record-high prices of oil and gas in the United States, a Gallup's annual environmental survey found that 77 percent of respondents endorse increased government efforts to encourage energy production from alternative energy sources, such as wind and solar power, whereas 39 percent support increased government aid to produce energy from traditional energy sources, such as oil and gas.[1] The same Gallup poll also reported that 42 percent of respondents describe the energy situation in the United States as "very serious," and 46 percent of respondents consider the development of energy supplies as a greater priority than protection of the environment.[2] The American government, under President Obama, has listed renewable energy as one of its top policy priorities and set policy goals to cut carbon emissions and use clean-energy sources such as wind, solar, and nuclear power. Policy changes toward new alternative energy in the United States are consistent with energy policies adopted by other industrial countries, notably members of the Organization for Economic Cooperation and Development (OECD).

The Netherlands has also made renewable energy production a priority. As part of the European Union, it has a renewable energy target of meeting 20 percent of domestic energy needs by 2020.[3] As will be explained in this chapter, the Dutch government has delayed attempts to meet this target. One reason for this delay is that the Netherlands is a major producer and exporter of natural gas. However, within the country there is major support for increasing energy efficiency and reliance on renewable energy. The Dutch government is being forced to reconcile economic growth that largely depends on exporting natural gas with meeting the EU's renewable energy target.

Among many inter-governmental and nongovernmental advocates, the **International Energy Agency (IEA)** is a leading advocate for adoption and implementation of renewable energy and other alternative energy policy.[4] As for renewable energy, the IEA has established policy goals to increase the diversity of energy supplies, replace diminishing fossil fuel resources over the long run, and accelerate the market penetration and diffusion of renewable energies to both developed and developing countries. Both the United States and the Netherlands are part of the IEA.

The Netherlands was chosen as a comparison for the United States not only because it is part of the IEA, but also because the Netherlands has a similar policy-making process. Therefore, an institutional approach is used to compare the countries. Although the Netherlands is a constitutional monarchy with a parliamentary system of government, it has a bicameral legislature that is similar to the one in the United States.

In this chapter, we will begin with a discussion of growing demands for alternative energy sources in the United States. After considering key agencies in U.S. alternative energy policy making, we will look at current U.S. policy as well as some challenges to alternative energy policy. Following our focus on U.S. alternative energy policy, we will move on to examine alternative energy policy in the Netherlands, one of the leading countries in renewable and alternative energy sources. Following a review of the institutional setting for alternative energy policy making and current policy adopted by the Dutch government for alternative energy, we will discuss challenges to Dutch alternative energy policy.

The United States

When considering alternative energy sources for the United States, many Americans think of **nuclear energy.** Nuclear energy is being advanced by its advocates as a solution to increasing demand for energy in the United States. Unlike fossil fuels, nuclear energy is clean, emitting virtually no air pollution. Another benefit of nuclear energy is that it is reliable in its production of energy, and the uranium fuel rods can be recycled ("reprocessed"), which cuts down on the amount of waste produced by nuclear facilities.[5] The Nuclear Energy Advisory Committee adds that, in addition to minimal pollution associated with nuclear energy, this source of energy is relatively inexpensive after the costs of nuclear power plants are amortized. Also, nuclear fuel is reliable, plentiful, and relatively inexpensive.[6]

Opponents of nuclear energy cite two problems: (1) the storage of nuclear waste and (2) the possible proliferation of nuclear weapons. The proposed site for nuclear waste in Nevada, **Yucca Mountain**, has remained embroiled in controversy since it was named as the site of choice in 1987. Concerns about nuclear waste storage facilities range from technical engineering problems to possible dangers to the local environment to a fear of nuclear radiation.[7] As the use of nuclear energy spreads, so does uranium enrichment. A staff expert in planning and economic studies at the International Atomic Energy Agency (IAEA), Alan McDonald, is quoted as saying, "If the world sees a big increase in nuclear energy, there will be an increased risk of [nuclear arms] proliferation— all things being equal."[8]

Although the U.S. Department of Energy (DOE) believes that a gradual change to renewable and nuclear energy is inevitable, it is also working on research and development of more efficient and environmentally cleaner fossil fuel technology. Currently, 85 percent of U.S. energy consumption comes from fossil fuels, and the DOE forecasts an increase in fossil fuel use over the next 20 years. According to the DOE, even with an increase in **renewable energy** sources, fossil fuels will continue to supply the vast majority of U.S. energy needs.[9] In addition, although renewable energy is often seen as less expensive than fossil fuels, it is often heavily subsidized, as is the case with wind-generated energy, which so far has proved inefficient since "wind farms' average output is less than 30 percent of their theoretical capacity."[10] Hydroelectric power can also have a negative impact on the environment, due to re-routing of water supplies, which can damage ecosystems, and the breakdown of vegetation around hydroelectric power plants, which releases methane, a greenhouse gas, into the atmosphere.[11]

After assuming office in 2009, President Obama announced his goals for renewable energy sources. His long-term goal is that, by 2025, renewable sources should provide 25 percent of the nation's energy.[12] Advocates of renewable energy sources—such as geothermal, hydroelectric, solar, and wind power—argue that these alternative energy sources emit minimal amounts of air pollution and do not create solid wastes.[13] In addition to environmental benefits, increasing use of renewable energy sources means new jobs. "The renewable energy industry is hiring new workers every day to build wind farms, install rooftop solar arrays, and build solar thermal and geothermal power plants."[14] For every billion dollars invested in wind farms and solar cell installations, 3,350 and 1,480 jobs are created, respectively.[15]

Government Agencies and Other Actors

Policy Making   The roles of the executive and legislative branches of government are to propose new bills on alternative energy issues, and then to pass finalized bills into laws. Although bills are often introduced by members of Congress, the sources of bills may come from constituents and often from lobbyists.

Today, the U.S. government makes alternative energy policy largely from the top down, with the White House and the Obama administration leading the way on new policies,[16] with the help of relevant government agencies, such as the

Department of Energy, the Office of Energy Efficiency and Renewable Energy (EERE), and the Office of Nuclear Energy (NE). Some aspects of alternative energy policy are quite different from aspects of other energy policy. For example, nuclear energy requires an extremely high level of security and maintenance to guard against human error, accident, and terrorism.[17]

Department of Energy (DOE)   The U.S. **Department of Energy** is the primary governmental agency for alternative energy policy. There are two divisions within the DOE that deal with specific aspects of alternative energy: the Office of Energy Efficiency and Renewable Energy and the Office of Nuclear Energy. The DOE is responsible for security of energy production, particularly of nuclear energy, and for research and development of new science and technology.[18]

Office of Energy Efficiency and Renewable Energy (EERE)   The task of the U.S. **Office of Energy Efficiency and Renewable Energy** is to strengthen public–private energy sector partnerships. The EERE enhances energy efficiency and productivity, and it brings new technologies to the marketplace to increase the energy choices available to Americans.[19] Often, the EERE testifies before congressional committees/subcommittees on renewable energy sources.[20]

Office of Nuclear Energy (NE)   The U.S. **Office of Nuclear Energy** is responsible for research and development of nuclear energy, as well as the maintenance and security of nuclear facilities.[21] Like the EERE, the NE is often called on to report to congressional committees and subcommittees on matters pertaining to nuclear energy and security.[22]

Environmental Protection Agency (EPA)   The U.S. **Environmental Protection Agency** educates the public and officials on energy issues such as energy conservation, alternative fuels, alternative energy strategies, and green buildings.[23] Officials from the EPA collect and review **Environmental Impact Statements (EIS)**, which are required by the **National Environmental Policy Act (NEPA)** to describe environmental consequences of proposed federal undertakings, as well as alternatives.[24] Large-scale federal alternative energy sites, such as new nuclear plants, would be subject to review by EIS.

State and Local Governments   State and local governments are not as involved in energy policy making as the federal agencies are, but they are often responsible for implementing energy policy. For example, Government Purchase Programs of the EERE encourage state and local governments to invest in energy-efficient technologies. The EERE notes that state and local governments increasing energy-efficient technology in public use are leading by example in encouraging individual citizens to likewise invest in such technologies in their homes and businesses.[25]

Interest Groups   Several interest groups and one political party have major stakes in alternative energy policy. The **National Mining Association**

(NMA) lobbies for the continued research and development of technologies for clean coal energy.[26] The **American Coalition for Ethanol (ACE)** lobbies on behalf of the ethanol industry.[27] The **American Council on Renewable Energy (ACORE)** works to move "renewable energy into the mainstream of America's economy, ensuring the success of the renewable energy industry."[28] The political party that deals most explicitly with "green" issues is the **Green Party of the United States**. A key value on the Green Party's political platform is that U.S. "actions and policies should be motivated by long-term goals.... We must counterbalance the drive for short-term profits by assuring that economic development, new technologies, and fiscal policies are responsible to future generations who will inherit the results of our actions."[29] The Green Party supports "a sustainable society which utilizes resources in such a way that future generations will benefit and not suffer from the practices of our generation. To this end we must practice agriculture which replenishes the soil; *move to an energy efficient economy* [emphasis added]; and live in ways that respect the integrity of natural systems."[30] The United States, with its simple member districts, has never elected a member of the Green Party to the U.S. Congress. This is a disadvantage "Green Parties" in many parliamentary systems do not face.

Current Policies

Thus far, alternative energy policies in the United States have mostly involved fuel efficiency for motor vehicles, although the Energy Policy Act of 2005 goes expand this problem. Major alternative energy legislation in the United States is summarized here.

Alternative Motor Fuels Act of 1988 (AMFA)   The **Alternative Motor Fuels Act of 1988 (AMFA)** "created vehicle manufacturer incentives in the form of Corporate Average Fuel Economy (CAFE) credits for the production of motor vehicles capable of operating on certain alternative fuels (electricity, liquid petroleum gasoline, and biodiesel are not included)."[31]

Clean Air Act of 1990 (CAA)   As amended in 1990, the **Clean Air Act of 1990 (CAA)**, which was enacted in 1970, "created several initiatives to reduce mobile source pollutants" and established "standards and procedures for reducing human and environmental exposure to a range of pollutants generated by industry and transportation."[32]

Energy Policy Acts of 1992 and 2005   The **Energy Policy Act of 1992** "established regulations requiring federal, state, and alternative fuel provider fleets to build an inventory of alternative fuel vehicles."[33] The **Energy Policy Act of 2005** "emphasized the use of alternative fuels and the development of supporting infrastructure."[34] It set out a program for research and development of energy efficiency, as well as renewable, nuclear, hydropower, and geothermal energy, and it continued research and development of fossil fuels.[35]

Energy Independence and Security Act of 2007   The **Energy Indepen-dence and Security Act of 2007** "introduced provisions to increase the supply of renewable fuel sources and raise CAFE standards to reach 35 miles per gallon by 2020."[36]

Energy Improvement and Extension Act of 2008   The **Energy Improve-ment and Extension Act of 2008** extended tax credits for biodiesel, alternative fuel excise, plug-in hybrid electric vehicles, qualified idle reduction devices, and alterna-tive fuel infrastructure.[37]

International standards   The United States is a member not only of the Organization for Economic Cooperation and Development but also of the International Energy Agency within the OECD framework. The IEA is respon-sible for implementing an international energy program. Major IAE-promoted standards that directly impact U.S. alternative energy policy are standards for increasing energy efficiency, promoting collaborative work on energy technol-ogy, and integrating environmental and energy policies.[38]

Problems and Challenges

Today, the U.S. government makes alternative energy policy from the top down, with the White House under the Obama Administration leading the way on new alternative energy policies,[39] informed by advice from relevant governmental agencies such as the DOE, the EERE, and the NE. There are aspects of alternative energy policy that make it very different from other energy policy. For example, as we have noted, nuclear energy requires an extremely high level of security and maintenance to guard against human error, accident, and terrorism.[40] Also, the country does not yet know how to dispose of the hazardous waste produced by nuclear energy.

Although alternative energy is generally thought of as being better overall than fossil fuels, particularly in terms of climate change, this is not always the case. For example, bipartisan support for ethanol has increased in recent years, but ethanol has unresolved problems. Cars running on ethanol have overall lower fuel economy, which can negate original air quality benefits. Additionally, although ethanol does lower CO_2 emissions, there is an increase in volatile organic compounds (VOCs) and nitrous oxides (NO_x), which are components of smog.[41]

The Netherlands

Currently, the Netherlands has one operating nuclear power plant providing about 4 percent of total energy generation. As the Dutch government is slowly pursuing an expansion of the existing Borssele nuclear power plant, it is also considering the addition of another nuclear reactor to increase energy output. Following the Chernobyl meltdown disaster, popular support for nuclear energy

█████████████ **BOX 9.1** █████████████

Country Profile of the Netherlands[66]

Name of Country: The Netherlands

Conventional Long Form: Kingdom of the Netherlands

Type of Government: Constitutional Monarchy

Executive Branch:

Head of State: Queen Beatrix (since April 30, 1980); Heir Apparent Willem-Alexander (born April 27, 1967), son of the monarch

Head of Government: Prime Minister Mark Rutte (since October 14, 2010); Deputy Prime Minister Lodewijk ASSCHER (since 5 November 2012)

Legislative Branch: Bicameral States—General (or Staten Generaal) consists of the Senate, the First Chamber (or Eerste Kamer) with 75 seats (members elected indirectly by the country's 12 provincial councils to serve four-year terms) and the House of Representatives, the Second Chamber (or Tweede Kamer), with 150 seats (members elected directly by popular vote to serve four-year terms)

Judicial Branch:

Supreme Court (or Hoge Raad) with justices nominated for life by the monarch

Administrative Divisions:

12 provinces (or provinces) including Drenthe, Flevoland, Friesland (or Fryslan), Gelderland, Groningen, Limburg, North Brabant (or Noord-Brabant), North Holland (or Noord-Holland), Overijssel, South Holland (or Zuid-Holland), Utrecht, and Zealand (or Zeeland)

Economic Indicators:

GDP (purchasing power parity): $709.5 billion (2012 estimation)

GDP Real Growth Rate: –0.5 (2012 estimation)

GDP per capita (purchasing power parity): $42,300 (2012 estimation)

Economic Structure: Agriculture 2.8 percent, Industry 24.1 percent, Services 73.2 percent (2012 estimation)

Demographic Indicators:

Population: 16,805,037 (2013 estimation)

Population Growth: 0.44 percent (2013 estimation)

Birth Rate: 10.85 births/1,000 population (2013 estimation)

Infant Mortality Rate: 3.69 deaths/1,000 live births (2013 estimation)

Life Expectancy at Birth: 81.01 years (2013 estimation)

Literacy (age 15 and over can read and write): 99 percent (2003 estimation)

Ethnic Groups: Dutch 80.7 percent, EU 5 percent, Indonesian 2.4 percent, Turkish 2.2 percent, Surinamese 2 percent, Moroccan 2 percent, Caribbean 0.8 percent, other 4.8 percent (2008 estimation)

Religions: Roman Catholic 30 percent, Dutch Reformed 11 percent, Calvinist 6 percent, other Protestant 3 percent, Muslim 5.8 percent, other 2.2 percent, none 42 percent (2006 estimation)

Source: Clingendael International Energy Programme, "Clingendael Energy Lecture: Dutch Energy Policy in an International Perspective," http://www.clingendael/nl/ciep/events/20060321/ (accessed June 15, 2012).

in the Netherlands severely diminished, but increased safety standards and environmental benefits of nuclear energy have brought about renewed interest in this energy source.[42]

Opponents of increased nuclear energy in the Netherlands raise concerns over the storage of nuclear waste and the addition of greenhouse gases from uranium mining. Currently, there are no facilities for storing nuclear waste. Even with the plans to shorten the hazardous period of nuclear waste by converting long-living radioactive substances into short-living ones, nuclear waste will still have a radioactive life of 700 to 1,500 years. Although nuclear fission to produce nuclear energy emits virtually no air-polluting substances and greenhouse gases, there is still harm to the environment due to greenhouse gases emitted in the process of mining uranium.[43]

Another concern relates to energy efficiency. Although there is a wide-ranging consensus that energy efficiency is positive for the future of the Netherlands, problems arise with the implementation of energy efficiency policies. The Netherlands, and 19 other European Union (EU) countries, are not in compliance with the EU's **Energy Services Directive.** "This directive aims at strengthening and improving energy end-use efficiency by providing a framework for incentives and energy services."[44] The Dutch national government and municipal governments have facilitated delays of energy efficiency policy in the past. In 2004, the Dutch Presidency of the European Union removed the Commission's draft energy efficiency directive from the Energy Council's agenda in favor of electricity infrastructure.[45] At the municipal level, policy, outputs, and outcomes have both been subject to delays in regard to energy efficiency policy.[46] The transportation sector has been the most problematic for the Dutch government. One report concludes that "sustainability must be achieved by means of technological development" because behavioral changes of individuals in regards to transportation are not realistic.[47]

Although Dutch governments have facilitated foot-dragging relating to efficient energy programs, which can be commonplace when implementing new policies, there is widespread support for energy efficiency measures. In 2007, the Dutch government implemented the **Energy Efficiency Action Plan,** which uses primarily taxes on the residential and transportation sectors, as well as policies aimed at increasing awareness of energy use in the residential sector.[48] The residential and industrial sectors have responded well to energy efficiency measures. From 1990 to 2006, energy efficiency has increased by more than 25 percent in the residential sector and by 21 percent in the industrial sector.[49]

Government Agencies and Other Actors

Policy Making   The Netherlands is a constitutional monarchy. The monarch nominates for life the justices of the Supreme Court and presides over the Council of State, which is not only the chief advisory body for the government but also the highest administrative tribunal. Ministers who propose bills work closely with the monarch as part of the Cabinet. The Cabinet, led by the Prime Minister, has between 12 and 14 ministers, and its policies are coordinated by the Council of Ministers. The Council of Ministers includes all ministers and is chaired by the Prime Minister; together with the monarch, it makes up the government. The role of parliament, a bicameral legislature with a lower chamber, the House of Representatives, and an upper chamber, the Senate,[50] is to debate bills and then pass or quash them. Bills are debated in both houses of parliament, but may not be amended in the Senate.

Provinces (state-level jurisdictions) and municipalities (local-level jurisdictions) implement measures passed by central government, and they may develop local ordinances so long as these do not conflict with higher legislation (e.g., provincial and municipal ordinances cannot conflict with national legislation, and municipal ordinances cannot conflict with provincial ordinances).[51] This is similar to the law in the United States (i.e., the Supremacy Clause in the U.S. Constitution).

Dutch Council for Housing, Spatial Planning and the Environment (VROMRAAD) The **Dutch Council for Housing, Spatial Planning and the Environment (VROMRAAD)** is responsible for "advising government and parliament on the main aspects of policy on sustainability of the environment and on housing, spatial planning and environmental management."[52]

Netherlands Agency for Sustainability and Innovation (SenterNovem) The **Netherlands Agency for Sustainability and Innovation (SenterNovem)** is an agency of the Dutch Ministry of Economic Affairs, and it promotes sustainable development and innovation. This agency is responsible for implementing policy regarding innovation, energy and climate change, and the environment and spatial planning.[53]

Netherlands Office of Energy Regulation (Energiekamer) Charged with regulations provided by the Electricity Act of 1998 and the Gas Act of 1998, the **Netherlands Office of Energy Regulation** is under the Ministry of Economic Affairs and the Netherlands Competition Authority (NMa), which enforces fair competition in the Dutch economy.[54]

Interest Groups The main interest groups affected by alternative energy policy are groups that produce, trade, and sell energy, including natural gas companies. These groups have organized into **EnergieNed**, the **Federation of Energy Companies** in the Netherlands.[55] There are also two green political parties in the Netherlands: the **Netherlands Green Party** and the **Netherlands Green Left Party**. Both parties have been severely weakened in recent elections due to an upswing in right-wing sentiments and anti-immigrant statements (e.g., 2006 anti-Muslim cartoons that sparked riots in a number of predominantly Muslim countries). Green Left is the stronger of the two parties and is based on "livable environment and the recovery of the ecological balance" and the "protection of the position of the least paid through a drastic leveling of income."[56]

Current Policies

Electricity Act of 1998   The Electricity Act 1998 established "new regulations relating to the production, transmission and supply of electricity, taking into consideration the importance of the reliable, sustainable and efficient supply of electricity."[57] This act also provides incentives for the production of sustainable energy.[58]

Subsidies Duurzame Energie (SDE)   The Subsidies Duurzame Energie (SDE) program sets premium payments for extra costs on top of wholesale prices for renewable energy producers, with a maximum limit of 10 years to receive premiums. The SDE follows the previous Minimum Energy Performance (MEP) premium program, which operated in the same way but was abolished in 2006.[59]

International/European Union Standards   The Netherlands is a member not only of the Organization for Economic Cooperation and Development but also of the International Energy Agency within the OECD framework. The IEA is responsible for implementing an international energy program. Major IAE-promoted standards that directly impact Dutch alternative energy policy are standards for increasing energy efficiency, promoting collaborative work on energy technology, and integrating environmental and energy policies.[60] As a member of the European Union, the Netherlands also has to meet specific EU goals related to energy efficiency and renewable energy sources, with the EU striving to increase the proportion of renewable energy in the energy mix to 20 percent by 2020.[61]

Problems and Challenges

The Dutch government has steadily moved toward more sustainable energy practices. Yet, since the Netherlands is a major producer and exporter of natural gas, sustainable energy policies must be reconciled with economic realities.[62] In a joint publication, the Council for Housing, Spatial Planning and the Environment as well as the General Energy Council of the Netherlands acknowledge that a switch to more sustainable energy is both dangerous and opportune. They recommend that the Netherlands look past the considerable costs associated with establishing a sustainable energy economy, and look to opportunities. Moving toward alternative energy policy making is a drastic transition, whereas other energy policy making is more stable and has less effects on the status quo.[63]

There is no broad political consensus on the future of nuclear energy in the Netherlands. The IEA's Executive Director Nobuo Tanaka commended the Dutch government on its energy goals, but said that, in order to make these goals a reality, it needs to take a serious look at increasing nuclear energy, which is a main issue subject to political contention in regard to Dutch energy policy. According to Tanaka, expanded nuclear energy "could make a significant contribution to meeting greenhouse gas emissions targets in a cost-effective manner."[64]

Implementation of energy policies and EU directives for renewable energy has been slower than necessary to keep up with goals. The target for renewable energy as a percentage of overall energy consumption was 1.84 percent in 2004 and 5 percent in 2005. The current target is 10 percent by 2020, which requires a large increase in renewable energy technologies, specifically technologies to generate biomass and offshore wind energy.[65] A weakness of Dutch alternative energy policy lies in the Dutch government's inability to implement technologies that are necessary to keep up with renewable energy targets.

Comparison

This chapter compared the United States and the Netherlands in the area of alternative energy policy. Both countries have similar policy-making processes. For example, they have bicameral legislatures and bills must be passed in both houses and signed by the president in the United States and the constitutional monarch and relevant ministers in the Netherlands before becoming law. Although both countries are interested in newer and more efficient energy sources, each faces particular challenges.

When Americans saw gasoline prices increase to almost $5 per gallon in some areas, it was time for change. The increased price of a barrel of oil led to a decrease in the pocketbooks of many Americans, prompting greater awareness of our energy consumption and its sources. Along with record gas and heat prices, many Americans came to be more conscious of carbon emissions. With the election of President Obama came promises of change as well as promises to promote renewable energy.

Across the Atlantic Ocean, the Netherlands realized that their energy efficiency standards were not being met; with only one nuclear power plant, they have delayed being up to par with the EU's Energy Services Directive. The main objective of this directive is to ensure that members of the European Union receive incentives for finding energy resources that are held to a certain efficiency standard.

In the United States, some lawmakers and lobbyists have been pushing for renewable energy. Considering an ever-increasing need for clean reliable energy to sustain economic growth and prosperity while protecting the environment, renewable sources of energy must be found quickly as alternatives to nonrenewable energy sources before they run out. The Department of Energy is responsible for developing policies pertaining to alternative energy. The DOE has two divisions for specific aspects of alternative energy: the Office of Energy Efficiency and Renewable Energy and the Office of Nuclear Energy. The former seeks to create a healthy relationship between the private and public energy sectors, and the latter deals with research and development of nuclear energy and with the maintenance and security of nuclear facilities. The federal government also works with state and local governments to promote energy-efficient technologies. Not only government agencies but also interest groups play a major role in regard to alternative energy policy. An example of such an interest group is the National Mining Association, which seeks to promote the use of clean coal energy.

In the Netherlands, the Dutch Council for Housing, Spatial Planning and the Environment advises the government on environmental sustainability and environmental management linked to housing and spatial planning. In addition to government agencies such as the Netherlands Agency for Sustainability and Innovation (SenterNovem), which deals with sustainable development and innovation, and the Office of Energy Regulation (Energiekamer), which is responsible for regulations provided by the Electricity Act of 1998 and the Gas Act of 1998, there are interest groups with stakes in alternative energy policy. The main interest groups concerned about alternative energy policy are groups that produce, trade, and sell energy, which suggests that energy markets, business, and profit may exert significant influence on alternative energy policy from outside the government. Alternative energy policy may be more effective if it includes incentives for energy companies to profit from producing, trading, and selling alternative energy.

Currently, the United States follows the 1970 Clean Air Act, as amended in 1990. The CAA ensures that there are standards and procedures to reduce pollutants emitted by industry and transportation. The United States also has the 1992 Energy Policy Act, which is similar to the 1988 Alternative Motor Fuels Act in that it promotes alternative fuel vehicles, and the 2005 Energy Policy Act, which promotes research and development of fossil fuels, renewable energy, and energy efficiency. Additional acts adopted to move the United States toward an alternative fuel infrastructure with renewable fuel sources and greater energy efficiency include the 2007 Energy Independence and Security Act and the 2008 Energy Improvement and Extension Act.

The Netherlands promotes sustainable and renewable energy through regulations and incentives provided by the 1998 Electricity Act and through a premium program known as *Subsidies Duurzame Energie*. The future of alternative energy in the Netherlands is shaped not only by relevant Dutch government agencies, interests groups, and policies but also by EU directives for renewable energy, such as the EU's Energy Services Directive, and specific EU goals related to energy efficiency and renewable energy sources.

Both the United States and the Netherlands share some similar obstacles in achieving greater energy efficiency. Not a matter not to be taken lightly is the question of where to put radioactive waste as a result of nuclear energy generation. Citizens are concerned with radioactive material harming their natural resources and taking up too much space. Some research is being done to shorten the radioactive life of nuclear waste, which is still estimated to last at least 700 years. Furthermore, greenhouse gases are generated not only by burning of fossil fuels but also by mining uranium for nuclear energy. Although energy generated by wind turbines might be the cleanest of all energy, it may not be as efficient as needed to run a high-powered country such as the United States, and it could possibly harm wildlife in surrounding areas. These countries must overcome their obstacles before renewable energy is a viable option for meeting their energy needs.

Key Terms

- Alternative Motor Fuels Act of 1988 (AMFA)
- American Coalition for Ethanol (ACE)
- American Council on Renewable Energy (ACORE)
- Clean Air Act of 1990 (CAA)
- Dutch Council for Housing, Spatial Planning and the Environment (VROMRAAD)
- EnergieNed
- Energy Efficiency Action Plan
- Energy Improvement and Extension Act of 2008
- Energy Independence and Security Act of 2007
- Energy Policy Act of 1992
- Energy Policy Act of 2005
- Energy Services Directive
- Environmental Impact Statement
- Green Party of the United States
- International Energy Agency (IEA)
- National Environmental Policy Act (NEPA)
- National Mining Association (NMA)
- Netherlands Agency for Sustainability and Innovation (SenterNovem)
- Netherlands Office of Energy Regulation
- Nuclear energy
- Renewable energy
- U.S. Department of Energy (DOE)
- U.S. Environmental Protection Agency (EPA)
- U.S. Office of Energy Efficiency and Renewable Energy (EENR)
- U.S. Office of Nuclear Energy
- Yucca Mountain

Critical Thinking Questions

- What are the major problems with using nuclear energy as an alternative source of energy in the United States and the Netherlands?
- What are the obstacles faced by the United States and the Netherlands with achieving greater energy efficiency?
- What role do interest groups play in the policy-making process regarding alternative energy in the United States and the Netherlands?
- How does the European Union impact alternative energy policy in the Netherlands?
- What is the significance of the International Energy Agency?

Recommended Resources for American Alternative Energy Policy

Michael E. Kraft, *Environmental Policy and Politics* (4th ed.) (New York: Pearson-Longman, 2007).

Walter A. Rosenbaum, *Environmental Politics and Policy* (6th ed.) (Washington, DC: CQ Press, 2005).

Zachary A. Smith, *The Environmental Policy Paradox* (6th ed.) (Upper Saddle River, NJ: Prentice-Hall, 2012).

Recommended Resources for Dutch Alternative Energy Policy

Valentina Dinica, *Sustained Diffusion of Renewable Energy—Politically Defined Investment Contexts for the Diffusion of Renewable Electricity Technologies in Spain, the Netherlands, and United Kingdom* (Enschede, The Netherlands: Twente University Press, 2003).

International Energy Agency, *Energy Policies of IEA Countries: The Netherlands 2008 Review* (Paris, France: OECD/IEA, 2009).

IPB USA, *Netherlands Energy Policy, Laws and Regulation Handbook* (Washington, DC: International Business Publications, USA, 2009).

Danyel Reiche (ed.), *Handbook of Renewable Energies in the European Union* (2nd ed.) (Bern, Switzerland: Verlag Peter Lang, 2005).

Notes

1. Jeffrey M. Jones, "Americans on Energy: Promote Both New Sources and Old," March 13, 2009, http://www.gallup.com/poll/116713/Americans-Energy-Promote-New-Sources-Old.aspx (accessed May 31, 2012).
2. Ibid.
3. European Commission, "Renewable Energy: Targets by 2020," http://ec.europa.eu/energy/renewables/targets_en.htm (accessed June 15, 2012).
4. International Energy Agency (IEA), an inter-governmental organization consisting of 28 member countries, acts as energy policy advisor to ensure reliable, affordable, and clean energy for their countries' citizens. See the IEA website at http://www.iea.org/. The current members are Australia, Austria, Belgium, Canada, Czech Republic, Denmark, Finland, France, Germany, Greece, Hungary, Ireland, Italy, Japan, South Korea, Luxembourg, the Netherlands, New Zealand, Norway, Poland, Portugal, Slovakia, Spain, Sweden, Switzerland, Turkey, the United Kingdom, and the United States.
5. Ross Wingo and H. Sterling Burnett, "Nuclear Renaissance: Atoms to Power the Future," National Center for Policy Analysis, http://www.ncpa.org/pub/ba635/ (accessed May 31, 2012).
6. Nuclear Energy Advisory Committee, *Nuclear Energy: Policies and Technology for the 21st Century*, http://www.ne.doe.gov/neac/neacPDFs/NEAC_Final_Report_Web%20Version.pdf, p. 6 (accessed May 31, 2012).
7. Isaac J. Winograd and Eugene H. Roseboom, Jr., "Nuclear Waste: Yucca Mountain Revisited," *Science*, 320(5882) (June 13, 2008): 1426–1427.
8. Cited in W. Conrad Holton, "Power Surge: Renewed Interest in Nuclear Energy," *Environmental Health Perspectives*, 113(11) (November, 2005): A745.
9. U.S. Department of Energy, "Fossil Fuels," http://www.energy.gov/energysources/fossilfuels.htm (accessed May 31, 2012).
10. H. Sterling Burnett, "Wind Power: Red Not Green," National Center for Policy Analysis, http://www.ncpa.org/pub/ba/ba467/ (accessed May 31, 2012).
11. U.S. Environmental Protection Agency, "Hydroelectricity," http://www.epa.gov/cleanenergy/energy-and-you/affect/hydro.html (accessed May 31, 2012).

12. White House, "The Agenda: Energy and the Environment," http://www.whitehouse. gov/agenda/energy_and_environment/ (accessed May 31, 2012).

13. U.S. Environmental Protection Agency, "Non-Hydroelectric Renewable Energy," http:// www.epa.gov/cleanenergy/energy-and-you/affect/non-hydro.html#wind (accessed May 31, 2012); U.S. Environmental Protection Agency, "Hydroelectricity," http://www.epa. gov/cleanenergy/energy-and-you/affect/hydro.html (accessed May 31, 2012).

14. Lester R. Brown, "Creating New Jobs, Cutting Carbon Emissions, and Reducing Oil Imports by Investing in Renewable Energy and Energy Efficiency," Earth Policy Institute, http://www.earth-policy.org/plan_b_updates/2008/update80 (accessed May 31, 2012).

15. Ibid.

16. White House, "Energy and the Environment," http://www.whitehouse.gov/agenda/ energy_and_environment/ (accessed May 31, 2012).

17. U.S. Department of Energy, "Nuclear Security," http://www.energy.gov/nationalsecurity/nuclearsecurity.htm (accessed May 31, 2012).

18. U.S. Department of Energy, "About DOE," http://www.energy.gov/about/index.htm (accessed May 31, 2012).

19. Office of Energy Efficiency and Renewable Energy, U.S. Department of Energy, "Mission," http://www1.eere.energy.gov/office_eere/ (accessed June 2, 2012).

20. Office of Energy Efficiency and Renewable Energy, U.S. Department of Energy, "Congressional Testimony," http://www1.eere.energy.gov/office_eere/congressional_ test.html (accessed June 2, 2012).

21. Office of Nuclear Energy, U.S. Department of Energy, "Our Mission," http://www. ne.doe.gov/neMission.html (accessed June 2, 2012).

22. Office of Nuclear Energy, U.S. Department of Energy, "Public Information Center: Congressional Testimony," http://www.ne.doe.gov/publicInformation/nePICongressionalTestimony07.html (accessed June 2, 2012).

23. U.S. Environmental Protection Agency, "Energy Conservation Action Plan," http:// www.epa.gov/greenkit/q5_energ.htm (accessed June 2, 2012).

24. U.S. Environmental Protection Agency, "National Environmental Policy Act (NEPA): Basic Information," http://www.epa.gov/compliance/basics/nepa.html#eis (accessed June 2, 2012).

25. Office of Energy Efficiency and Renewable Energy, U.S. Department of Energy, "State Energy Alternatives: Government Purchase Programs," http://www.eere.energy.gov/ golden/ (accessed June 2, 2012).

26. National Mining Association, "Energy," http://www.nma.org/issues/energy.asp (accessed June 2, 2012).

27. American Coalition for Ethanol, "About ACE," http://www.ethanol.org/index. php?id=7&parentid=7 (accessed June 2, 2012).

28. American Council on Renewable Energy, "History," http://www.acore.org/about/ history/ (accessed June 3, 2012).

29. Green Party of the United States, "Ten Key Values of the Green Party," http://www. gp.org/tenkey.shtml (accessed June 3, 2012).

30. Ibid.

31. Office of Energy Efficiency and Renewable Energy, U.S. Department of Energy, "Key Alternative Fuel and Fuel Economy Legislation," http://www.afdc.energy.gov/afdc/ laws/key_legislation (accessed June 3, 2012).

32. Ibid.

33. Ibid.

34. Ibid.
35. U.S. Congress, House, *Energy Policy Act of 2005*, H.R.6, 109th Cong., 1st sess, http://
thomas.loc.gov/cgi-bin/bdquery/z?d109:HR00006:@@@L&summ2=m&   (accessed
June 3, 2012).
36. Office of Energy Efficiency and Renewable Energy, U.S. Department of Energy, "Key
Alternative Fuel and Fuel Economy Legislation," http://www.afdc.energy.gov/afdc/
laws/key_legislation (accessed June 3, 2012).
37. Ibid.
38. International Energy Agency, *International Standards to Develop and Promote Energy
Efficiency and Renewable Energy Sources*, http://www.iea.org/papers/2008/cd_energy_
efficiency_policy/7-Energy%20utilities/7-Standards.pdf (accessed June 3, 2012).
39. White House, "Energy and the Environment," http://www.whitehouse.gov/agenda/
energy_and_environment/ (accessed June 3, 2012).
40. U.S. Department of Energy, "Nuclear Security," http://www.energy.gov/nationalsecurity/
nuclearsecurity.htm (accessed June 3, 2012).
41. Max Borders and H. Sterling Burnett, "The Environmental Costs of Ethanol,"
National Center for Policy Analysis, http://www.ncpa.org/pub/ba591 (accessed June
15, 2012).
42. World Nuclear Association, "Nuclear Power in the Netherlands," http://www.world-
nuclear.org/info/inf107.html (accessed June 15, 2012).
43. Herman Damveld, "Nuclear Energy and Nuclear Waste in the Netherlands: A Short
Overview," Milieufederatie Groningen, http://www.mfgroningen.nl/handlers/i.aspx?/
id=2740-g=Nuclear-energy-in-short.pdf (accessed June 15, 2012).
44. Europa, "20 Member States Still Not in Compliance with Community Legislation
Promoting Energy Efficiency," http://europa.eu/rapid/pressReleasesAction.do?referen
ce=IP/09/182&format=HTML&aged=0&language=EN&guiLanguage=en (accessed
June 15, 2012).
45. EurActiv, "Energy Efficiency Gets Kicked Off Presidency Agenda," http://www.euractiv.
com/en/energy/energy-efficiency-gets-kicked-presidency-agenda/article-130244 (accessed
June 15, 2012).
46. Valentina Dinica, Hans Th. A. Bressers, and Theo de Bruijn, "The Implementation
of a Multi-Annual Agreement for Energy Efficiency in The Netherlands," *Energy
Policy*, 35(2) (2007): 1200.
47. R. Mourik, A. Kets, E. Van Thuijl, and C. Roos, *E-Magining Future Energy
Infrastructures in the Dutch Transport Sector: An Analysis of Stakeholder Perspectives
on Future Energy Infrastructures in the Transport Sector*, Energy Research Centre of
the Netherlands, http://www.ecn.nl/docs/library/report/2005/c05051.pdf (accessed
June 15, 2012).
48. International Energy Agency, "Energy Efficiency Action Plan," http://www.iea.org/
Textbase/pm/?mode=pm&id=3669&action=detail (accessed June 15, 2012).
49. Odyssee, "Energy Efficiency Profile: Netherlands," http://www.odyssee-indicators.
org/publications/country_profiles_PDF/nld.pdf (accessed June 15, 2012).
50. Dutch Ministry of Foreign Affairs, "The Dutch State," http://www.minbuza.nl/en
(accessed June 15, 2012).
51. Ibid.
52. VROMRAAD, "English Introduction," http://www.vromraad.nl/info.asp?id=eng
(accessed June 15, 2012).
53. SenterNovem, "Turning Policy into Reality," http://www.senternovem.nl/english/index.
asp (accessed June 15, 2012).

54. Netherlands Office of Energy Regulation, Netherlands Competition Authority, "Netherlands Competition Authority (NMa) and the Energiekamer," http://www.nma-dte.nl/engels/home/index.asp (accessed June 15, 2012).

55. EnergieNed, "Energy companies in the Netherlands adapt the structure of the energy sector representative EnergieNed," http://www.energiened.nl/_upload/bestanden/11926_Energiezaak_EN.pdf (accessed June 15, 2012).

56. European Green Party, "GroenLinks—Netherlands," http://www.europeangreens.org (accessed June 15, 2012).

57. Netherlands Competition Authority and the Energiekamer, *Act of 2 July 1998 Providing Rules in Relation to the Production, Transmission and Supply of Electricity (Electricity Act)*, http://www.energiekamer.nl/nederlands/home/index.asp (accessed June 15, 2012), p. 1.

58. Ibid., p. 25.

59. European Renewable Energy Council, "Renewable Energy Policy Review: The Netherlands," http://www.erec.org/policy.html (accessed June 15, 2012).

60. International Energy Agency, *International Standards to Develop and Promote Energy Efficiency and Renewable Energy Sources*, http://www.iea.org/papers/2007/Standards.pdf (accessed June 15, 2012).

61. Europa, "An Energy Policy for Europe," http://europa.eu/legislation_summaries/energy/european_energy_policy/l27067_en.htm (accessed June 15, 2012).

62. Clingendael International Energy Programme, "Clingendael Energy Lecture: Dutch Energy Policy in an International Perspective," http://www.clingendael.nl/ciep/events/20060321/ (accessed June 15, 2012).

63. Council for Housing, Spatial Planning and the Environment and the General Energy Council of the Netherlands, *Energy Transition: A Climate for New Opportunities*, http://www.energieraad.nl/Include/ElectosFileStreaming.asp?FileId=133 (accessed June 15, 2012), pp. 5–6.

64. International Energy Agency, "IEA Commends the Netherlands for Its Sound and Sustainable Energy Policy, But Calls for More Focus on Implementation to Reach Ambitious Policy Objectives," http://www.iea.org/Textbase/press/pressdetail.asp?PRESS_REL_ID=279 (accessed June 15, 2012).

65. Senter Novem, "The Energy Policy in the Netherlands," http://www.senternovem.nl/offshorewindenergy/index.asp (accessed June 15, 2012).

CHAPTER 10

Trade Policy

LEARNING OBJECTIVES

- Distinguish between economic liberalism and mercantilism (or economic nationalism).
- Evaluate an open trade policy in comparison with a managed trade policy.
- Identify government agencies and other actors involved in trade policy making.

- Explain how politics influences trade policy.
- Understand free trade agreements and economic partnership agreements.
- Examine problems and challenges related to trade policy.

In an age of economic globalization, all countries' domestic markets are no longer local, and numerous goods and services come daily from all over the world. Controlling cross-border economic activities is difficult, but governments have attempted to manipulate the degree of economic interaction and competition as well as access to goods and services within their borders. Governments may regulate trade relations between two or more countries by raising tariffs on particular goods or services to (1) generate revenue or (2) protect or stimulate domestic firms and industries. Trade regulation and trade promotion have been among the most important economic policies that contemporary governments undertake. Although foreign investment, exchange rates, and immigration arise as issues in relation to trade policy, this chapter focuses exclusively on the manipulation of exchange of goods and services between countries.

Advocates of **economic liberalism**, influenced by Adam Smith (1723–1790) and David Ricardo (1772–1823) in England, argue that international exchange of goods and services between two or more countries increases the welfare of societies, whereas trade restrictions such as tariffs and other forms of government involvement in markets are inefficient and costly for societies. In a purely economic sense (subtract costs from benefits of trade with foreign countries), **free trade** is ideal for all countries. In support of economic liberalism, a study estimates that, if the logic of **comparative advantage** is correct, international trade without any government involvement contributes approximately

$1 trillion a year to the U.S. economy, and benefits are five times higher than estimated costs from job and earning losses associated with free trade.[1] Another study supports economic liberalism regarding free trade by unveiling that U.S. citizens in 2001–2002 had to purchase domestic sugar that was twice or three times as expensive as on world markets due to the U.S. government's sugar protection policies.[2]

Challenging economic liberalism are advocates of **mercantilism (or economic nationalism)**, influenced by Jean-Baptiste Colbert (1619–1883) in France and Friedrich List (1789–1846) in Germany. According to mercantilists, exports are good because they create jobs through domestic production of goods that are sold to consumers abroad, whereas imports are bad because they reduce jobs by competing with domestic products for consumers at home. Therefore, mercantilists claim that a government must intervene in its country's domestic economy by restricting imports from other countries while promoting exports of domestic products to them. This argument endorses trade policies related to restriction of imports and promotion of exports. Mercantilists also argue that free international trade can work to the disadvantage of countries with nothing to contribute to international markets other than nonrenewable natural resources.

The debate between economic liberals and mercantilists has influenced trade policy for a long time.[3] Historically, the mercantilist view has always won the battle, and policies of trade restriction have been at the center of trade policy making since the eighteenth century. Why? Put simply, although open trade without any restrictions —we call it "free" trade— promotes the welfare and wealth of a country at large, imports of foreign goods tend to hurt some domestic firms and workers by diminishing their shares in a country's domestic markets. This is the case for U.S. domestic automobile makers and workers. Imports of economically more efficient foreign cars decrease the share of domestic automobile producers in America's domestic automobile market. As a result, automobile producers in the United States are likely to lay off at least some of their workforce. Even though U.S. workers may enjoy cheap foreign goods, losing their jobs harms their lives physically and emotionally. Therefore, U.S. automobile business elites and their employees are likely to criticize free trade and demand that their government protect their jobs and impose restrictions on imports of foreign automobiles. The more people who experience physical and emotional harm due to job losses associated with foreign competition in U.S. domestic markets, the more support there is for the mercantilist view. As Gallup's annual World Affairs Survey shows, "Since 2005, Americans have become more likely to perceive foreign trade as a threat to the U.S. economy."[4] In response, policymakers in the United States are likely to generate measures to restrict foreign imports and demand that other countries buy American goods to increase U.S. exports.

This logic explains trade policy not only of the United States but also of other countries, such as Canada, China, India, Japan, and Mexico. If the U.S. government restricts foreign access to U.S. domestic markets, other countries may restrict U.S. access to their domestic markets. Such reciprocal import restriction is likely to reduce wealth from trade worldwide. That was the case of the **Smoot-Hawley Tariff Act** passed by the U.S. Congress in 1930. The act raised U.S. tariffs on over 20,000 dutiable foreign goods.[5] The higher tariffs provoked a storm of foreign retaliation against U.S. exports in the form of increased tariffs on U.S. goods. As the U.S. economy, already hurt by the Great Depression, was further impoverished due to radically declining U.S. imports from and exports to other countries, it was clear that an extreme tariff policy had made Americans worse off.

In recent years, many policymakers have frequently referred to **free trade agreements (FTAs)** and **economic partnership agreements (EPAs)** as new tools of trade policy. In contrast to the goal of a global free trade regime facilitated by the **World Trade Organization (WTO)**, FTAs and EPAs, such as the North American Free Trade Agreement (NAFTA), are trade blocs whose members protect economic interactions among themselves with trade barriers against countries outside those blocs. Furthermore, in order to promote the exchange of goods and services within FTAs and EPAs, their members reduce trade barriers against one another. By creating restrictions on trade with countries outside FTAs and EPAs but removing restrictions on trade with countries inside FTAs and EPAs, their members expect to create jobs in their domestic markets.

Considering past and contemporary trade policy, we understand trade policy as a "series of official objectives, laws, and actions designed to influence the flow of imports and exports of goods and services in a manner different from what would otherwise occur in a free market."[6] Every government adopts a variety of measures to maintain and promote significant interests in regard to its country's exchange of goods and services with foreign countries along a spectrum from total inaction (free trade) to aggressive comprehensive intervention with import protection, export restraints, and industrial policy that supports targeted industries.

Countries use a variety of instruments of trade protection. There are **tariffs**, **import quotas**, and **nontariff barriers (NTBs)**, including food, environmental, and health standards, procurement codes, and many other laws and regulations.

We chose Japan as comparison for the United States. Not only do these two countries have similar historical stances toward trade but they also have both transitioned from mercantilism to economic liberalism. This transition, however, has occurred for different reasons. Although the United States and Japan have been economic superpowers and major trade partners for many years, their trade policy making and policy initiatives are quite different. They also have different institutional sources of trade policy initiatives. These similarities and differences lend these two countries to both the historical and institutional approaches for comparison.

Furthermore, although the United States and Japan are formal allies and security partners, they have been involved in numerous trade disputes. A 2011 study sponsored by the Japanese government finds that although Americans in general perceive Japan as a reliable partner (84 percent among the American public and 90 percent among American opinion leaders), 42 percent of the American public and 46 percent of American opinion leaders rank the area of economic/trade relations as the most important issue to be improved between the United States and Japan.[7] Why are many Americans concerned about U.S. trade relations with Japan? How much do Americans know about Japan's trade policy? Is Japanese trade policy different from American trade policy? Motivated by these questions, this chapter will look at issues, government agencies and other actors, policy initiatives, as well as challenges and problems related to trade policy in the United States and Japan.

The United States

Modern U.S. presidents have mentioned frequently that free trade is in this nation's interest and spirit. This vision of free trade was unpopular in U.S. history before Congress passed the 1934 **Reciprocal Trade Agreement Act (RTAA)**, which allowed the president to negotiate tariff reductions with foreign countries. Although President Woodrow Wilson pledged to dismantle U.S. trade barriers as part of his "fourteen points" for global peace after World War I, members of Congress supported higher tariffs on imported goods from foreign countries to generate increased revenues for the federal government and to protect constituent domestic industries. Many industries and farmers were in favor of protectionist measures. Attitudes toward trade changed dramatically in the aftermath of the 1930 Smoot-Hawley Tariff Act, which generated a trade war as other countries imposed retaliatory tariffs and other trade barriers against U.S. products. This trade war led to the 1934 RTAA, which changed U.S. trade policy from mercantilism to economic liberalism endorsed by Secretary of State Cordell Hull under President Franklin Roosevelt.

Secretary Hull, who dominated the Roosevelt Administration's trade policy, was the architect of the modern American spirit of free trade. According to Hull, "Unhampered trade dovetailed with peace; higher tariffs, trade barriers, and unfair competition with war. If we could get a freer flow of trade—freer in the sense of few discriminations and obstructions...we might have a reasonable chance of lasting peace."[8] Although Hull's view was not fully shared by all Americans, by the end of World War II, his spirit of free trade gradually gained popular support, even among those opposed to free trade.[9] A reason for this was that many American industries had a technological edge over foreign competitors, which encouraged them to become exporters and foreign investors. Many industries that had hitherto been protectionist saw vast business opportunities and profits through trade liberalization.

Since World War II, the United States has relied on an **open trade policy** to stimulate its domestic economy and create jobs. Still, debates continue between economic liberals and mercantilists, between free traders and protectionists. A recent example is the inclusion of a **Buy American provision** in the 2009 **American Recovery and Reinvestment Act (ARRA)**.[10] According to the ARRA, a Buy American provision requires that all public projects funded by stimulus money must use only iron and steel produced in the United States. Before the

ARRA was passed, an economist commented, "This Buy American momentum is bad economics, and by threatening to destabilize trade and capital flows, it risks turning a global recession into a 1930-style depression."[11] Others concluded,

> The negative job impact of foreign retaliation against Buy American provisions could easily outweigh the positive effect of the measures on jobs in the US iron and steel sector and other industries.... The difference is that jobs lost would be spread across the entire manufacturing sector, while jobs gained would be connected in iron and steel and a few other industries.[12]

In addition, critics fear that Buy American provisions invite retaliation from foreign countries and violate U.S. trade obligations to the World Trade Organization's Agreement on Government Procurement (GPA) and the procurement chapter of the North American Free Trade Agreement (NAFTA). To address employment disruptions directly attributable to trade policy, Congress passed the Trade and Globalization Adjustment Assistance Act of 2009 (TGAAA). The TGAAA authorized the president to expand Trade Adjustment Assistance (TAA) programs for unemployed workers by providing unemployed benefits and training options, and increasing the affordability of health insurance coverage.

Concerns about Buy American provisions and TAA programs highlight the reality and complexity of contemporary trade policy making in the United States. As stated earlier, the ARRA's Buy American provision is not a tariff; rather, it is a nontariff barrier designed to restrict imports of iron and steel from foreign countries and protect domestic iron and steel producers. As critics claim, however, although the provision might help iron and steel industries and other related industrial sectors, it might harm the principal goal of the ARRA, which is to stimulate the American domestic economy and create jobs across entire manufacturing and service sectors in the United States. Foreign retaliatory nontariff barriers against the ARRA's Buy American provision would hurt U.S. manufacturing and service sectors that rely on exports. Furthermore, although TAA programs assist people who lost their jobs because such jobs were sent "offshore" to other countries, they do not assist people who lost their jobs for other reasons.

While imposing protectionist measures at home, the U.S. government has been actively involved in negotiations of trade liberalization to dismantle tariffs and nontariff barriers across the world.[13] In order to promote U.S. exports of goods and services, and to ensure that U.S. farmers, ranchers, manufacturers, and service providers can pursue new economic opportunities, the United States has been involved in the WTO Doha Round of multilateral trade negotiations as well as in negotiations of specific free trade agreements to reduce tariffs and nontariff barriers.

Government Agencies and Other Actors

The Legislative Branch　The U.S. Constitution, Article 1, Section 8, gives Congress the power to "regulate Commerce with foreign Nations" and to "lay and collect Taxes, Duties, Imposts and Excises." Members of the Senate and the

House of Representatives can exercise congressional trade policy-making power through four formal legislative activities:[14]

- Passage of trade legislation (or refusal to pass trade legislation requested by the administration)
- Approval of agency and program budgets and appropriation of funds
- Confirmation of senior policymakers
- Oversight—general review and evaluation—of existing and evolving executive activities and programs

Although all members of Congress have power over trade policy making, not all members have influence on specific trade legislation. A notable example is the role that Representative Sander Levin (a Michigan Democrat) had in trade legislation concerning the automobile industry. When he was chair of the House Ways and Means Subcommittee on Trade, Representative Levin had significant influence on U.S. trade policy. He persistently supported trade legislation that met specific interests of the automobile industry and related industries as well as members of the United Auto Workers (UAW). Similarly, other members of Congress have supported trade legislation that meets specific interests of those involved in agriculture, textile manufacturing, iron and steel production, or advanced technology.

Primary responsibility for trade policy making in Congress is vested in the **Senate Committee on Finance** and the Subcommittee on International Trade, Customs, and Global Competitiveness as well as the **House Committee on Ways and Means** and the Subcommittee on Trade.[15] Yet, since trade policy often overlaps with numerous other policies on issues such as the environment, human rights, foreign relations, national security, food and product safety, finance, healthcare, and Social Security, trade policy making may be influenced by many other congressional committees and subcommittees.

The Executive Branch   According to the U.S. Constitution, the president has no formal power to make his or her own trade policy. Nonetheless, the executive branch has been involved in the formulation and administration of numerous trade policy programs. The foundation of presidential trade policy-making power is the 1934 Reciprocal Trade Agreement Act, which delegated tariff-setting authority to the president. According to many experts, the RTAA significantly altered the executive branch's role in trade policy making.[16]

The President of the United States is involved in formulating and implementing trade policy programs with the assistance of his or her cabinet. However, the complexity and importance of trade policy programs, with links to other policies on both domestic and international issues, has led post-WWII presidents to rely heavily on formal and informal policy advisory groups within the White House. Members of these advisory groups, unlike cabinet members, can be appointed by the president without Senate approval. The primary roles of these advisory groups are to strengthen the president's trade policy-making power and to increase the efficiency and consistency of trade restriction and promotion programs designed and implemented by various government agencies.

For advice on trade and related economic issues, the president relies primarily on the Office of the U.S. Trade Representative (USTR), the National Economic Council (NEC), and the Council of Economic Advisers (CEA), which are all part of the executive office of the president.

The Office of the U.S. Trade Representative (USTR)   Created as the Office of the Special Trade Representative (STR) by the 1962 Trade Expansion Act, the **U.S. Trade Representative (USTR)** is "responsible for developing and coordinating U.S. international trade, commodity, and direct investment policy, and overseeing negotiations with other countries." It is under the direction of the U.S. Trade Representative, a cabinet member who serves the president as "principal trade advisor, negotiator, and spokesperson on trade issues."[17]

The National Economic Council (NEC)   The NEC was created by a presidential executive order in 1993

> to coordinate policy-making for domestic and international economic issues,
> to coordinate economic policy advice for the President, to ensure that policy
> decisions and programs are consistent with the President's economic goals, and
> to monitor implementation of the President's economic policy agenda.

Members of NEC are "numerous department and agency heads within the administration, whose policy jurisdictions impact the nation's economy."[18]

The Council of Economic Advisers (CEA)   The CEA was created by the 1946 Employment Act. Staffed with economists, the CEA is "charged with offering the President objective economic advice on the formulation of both domestic and international economic policy" based on "economic research and empirical evidence, using the best data available."[19]

Ad-Hoc Inter-Agency Coordinating Groups   In addition to the Office of the U.S. Trade Representative, the National Economic Council, and the Council of Economic Advisers, there have been ad-hoc inter-agency coordinating groups set up by executive order. For instance, in 1993, the Clinton Administration set up the Trade Promotion Coordinating Committee (TPCC), chaired by the Commerce Secretary, in order to (1) generate coherent export programs among more than six agencies and (2) coordinate export control and promotion programs administrated by twenty departments and agencies.[20]

Departments and agencies in the U.S. executive branch have no constitutional authority over trade policy making but they receive specific administrative authority from Congress. Congress provides the legislative foundation and framework for U.S. trade policy, which is then implemented and administrated through trade policy programs created by the executive branch. In addition, Congress monitors all administrative activities. Let us now take a closer look at some departments and agencies that deal with trade and related issues.

The Department of Treasury (DOT)   The Department of Treasury manages federal finances; it collects taxes, duties, and monies paid to and due to the United States. It also pays all bills of the United States, manages government accounts and the public debt, produces currency and coinage, and supervises national banks and thrift institutions. Furthermore, the DOT provides advice on domestic and international financial, monetary, economic, trade and tax policy; enforces federal finance and tax laws; and investigates and prosecutes tax evaders, counterfeiters, and forgers.[21]

The Department of Commerce and the International Trade Administration (ITA)   The Department of Commerce promotes U.S. businesses domestically and internationally.[22] Within the Department of Commerce, the (ITA) "works to improve the global business environment and helps U.S. organizations compete at home and abroad." It also "strengthens the competitiveness of U.S. industry, promotes trade and investment, and ensures fair trade through the rigorous enforcement of our trade laws and agreements."[23]

The Department of State   The Department of State has responsibility for U.S. foreign policy and evaluates the probable effects of U.S. trade policy measures on other countries. Within the Department of State, regional bureaus, and the Bureau of Economic and Business Affairs are key actors in monitoring U.S. trade with other countries.[24] Through the Department of State, in coordination with the USTR and other departments, such as the Department of Treasury and the Department of Commerce, the United States conducts bilateral commercial negotiations with specific countries as well as multilateral negotiations through the World Trade Organization. The State Department also administers Trade Policy and Programs (TPP), whose goal is to advance U.S. trade policy objectives by opening new export opportunities for U.S. businesses, farmers, ranchers, and workers through global, regional, and bilateral trade initiatives, such as free trade agreements and the WTO Doha Development Agenda.[25]

Other Departments and Agencies   In addition to the Department of Treasury, the Department of Commerce, and the Department of State, there are other departments and agencies involved in trade policy making related to specific policy jurisdictions. These include the Department of Agriculture, the Department of Labor, the Department of Energy, the Department of Defense, the Food and Drug Administration (FDA), and the Environmental Protection Agency (EPA).

The Export-Import Bank   The Export-Import Bank of the United States is the official U.S. export credit agency. Its mission is to assist in financing the export of U.S. goods and services to international markets. The Export Import Bank supports large and small U.S. exporters by providing working capital guarantees (pre-export financing), export credit insurance, as well as loan guarantees and direct loans (buyer financing).[26]

The International Trade Commission (ITC)   The ITC contributes independently to trade policy making by investigating import relief petitions from U.S. domestic firms and industries.[27] Its decisions influence duties on foreign imports. There are six commissioners appointed by the resident with Senate approval.

Interest Groups   Trade policy, like any other public policy, is shaped not only by government agencies but also by many interest groups representing various sectors of the U.S. economy.[28] In agriculture, interest groups include farmers' associations whose demands on U.S. trade policy depend on whether they are import-sensitive or export-oriented. Import-sensitive farmers' associations lobby the government to support them with subsidies and to prevent the import of cheap foreign products, specifically meat and sugar. Export-oriented farmers' associations lobby the government to promote the export of their products, specifically soybeans, corn, and wheat. In the automobile industry, interest groups include the Big Three (General Motors, Ford, and Chrysler) and the United Auto Workers (UAW). There are interest groups in the steel industry, the textile industry, and many other industries. In retail, a major interest group is the Retail Trade Action Coalition (RTAC). In addition, there are business interest groups such as the Business Roundtable, the Chamber of Commerce, and the National Association of Manufacturers. Furthermore, there are many consumer interest groups, the largest of which is the Consumer Federation of America (CFA), formed by approximately 280 nonprofit organizations with more than 50 million members across the United States.

Policy Initiatives

Contemporary U.S. trade policy has been shaped by several policy initiatives for the protection and promotion of trade. In this section, we review some of these policy initiatives.[29]

The 1930 Smoot-Hawley Tariff Act (SHTA)   The best-known protectionist legislation in U.S. history was the 1930 Smoot-Hawley Tariff Act, which intended to (1) protect domestic markets and producers from foreign imports and (2) increase federal revenue from increased duties on imported goods. The SHTA raised U.S. tariffs on over 20,000 dutiable items to record-high levels; the average tariff on dutiable imports was raised to 52.8 percent. By the end of 1931, however, 26 countries, including Canada, France, Mexico, and Cuba, had enacted a variety of retaliatory trade measures against U.S. exports. As a consequence, U.S. imports from Europe fell from $1.334 billion in 1929 to $390 million in 1932, whereas U.S. exports to Europe fell from $2.341 billion in 1929 to $784 million in 1932.

The 1934 Reciprocal Trade Agreements Act (RTAA)   In 1934, Congress passed the RTAA in response to the SHTA. The RTAA was supposed to help legislators insulate themselves from protectionist pressures, and it authorized the

President to enter into trade negotiations with other countries to obtain reciprocal tariff cuts. Under the Reciprocal Trade Agreements Act, the United States reached 28 reciprocal tariff agreements, which steadily reduced tariffs between 1934 and 1945. In a series of reciprocal trade agreement expansion acts passed from 1934 to 1974, Congress renewed and extended the president's authority over trade negotiations to cut tariffs. Given this authority, President Harry Truman and his successors entered into tariff reduction agreements in five rounds of negotiations under the General Agreement on Tariffs and Trade (GATT) between the 1940s and 1960s.

The International Trade Organization (ITO) and the General Agreement on Tariffs and Trade (GATT)   In 1948, the United States and 53 other countries concluded the Havana Charter, which was expected to establish the International Trade Organization. The primary goal of the ITO was to promote free trade by reducing trade barriers and ensuring nondiscriminatory trade relations. Yet, the U.S. Senate never ratified the ITO Charter, and the ITO was never established.[30] Its place was filled by the General Agreement on Tariffs and Trade, which had been signed originally in 1947. Since the GATT was a trade agreement rather than an organization based on a formal treaty or charter, it did not require ratification by a two-thirds majority in the U.S. Senate. In 1949, the Truman Administration committed the United States to the GATT through an executive agreement approved by majority votes in both houses of Congress.[31]

The 1974 Trade Act   The 1974 Trade Act influenced U.S. trade policy by establishing (in Section 151 of the Act) fast-track authority for the president to engage in negotiations of trade agreements. Under fast-track authority, the president is required to (1) consult with appropriate congressional committees before and during bilateral and multilateral trade negotiations to cut tariffs and nontariff barriers and (2) notify Congress at least 90 days before entering into a trade agreement while Congress is required to vote on a negotiated trade agreement without any amendment.[32] The purpose of fast-track authority is to assure foreign governments that Congress will act expeditiously on a trade agreement that it negotiates with the U.S. government. Fast-track authority was renewed until 1994. It has been instrumental in the negotiation and implementation of several major trade agreements, including the North American Free Trade Agreement (NAFTA).

Fast-track authority extended (in Section 201 of the 1974 Trade Act) a so-called escape clause that appeared originally in the 1943 Reciprocal Trade Agreement with Mexico. The escape clause allows any domestic group representing a domestic industry in the United States to petition the International Trade Commission for protection against foreign imports when those imports cause "injury" (i.e., economic damage) to the import-competing domestic industry.

The 1974 Trade Act introduced (in Section 301) a new provision authorizing import-restrictive retaliatory measures against unfair foreign trade practices. This provision authorizes the president to impose retaliatory measures against imports from any country found to maintain unfair, unreasonable, or discriminatory trade practices—including tariffs, import restrictions, and import or export subsidies—that violate international trade agreements and harm U.S. commerce by restricting U.S. exports to their domestic markets.

It also established (in Section 221) the Trade Adjustment Assistance program (created originally under the 1962 Trade Expansion Act). This program is designed to provide retraining and financial benefits to workers and firms that are injured as a result of increased imports.

The 1988 Omnibus Trade and Competitiveness Act (OTCA)   The 1988 Omnibus Trade and Competitiveness Act modified prior trade legislation through a provision known as "Super 301," which strengthened trade retaliation measures authorized under Section 301 of the 1974 Trade Act. Additionally, the OTCA renewed fast-track authority for the president to enter into the General Agreement on Tariffs and Trade Uruguay Round of multilateral trade negotiations and to negotiate the North American Free Trade Agreement, and it enhanced the authority of the U.S. Trade Representative.[33]

The 1994 North American Free Trade Agreement (NAFTA)   Under fast-track authority renewed by the 1988 OTCA, the Reagan, Bush, and Clinton administrations negotiated the North American Free Trade Agreement as a free trade agreement to remove all trade barriers to the movement of goods, capital, and services between Canada, Mexico, and the United States. The United States entered into the NAFTA with a decision approved by majority votes in both houses of Congress in 1994.

The 1994 Uruguay Round Agreement Act (URAA) and the Creation of the World Trade Organization (WTO)   With renewal of fast-track authority for the president under the 1988 OTCA, the Reagan, Bush, and Clinton administrations entered into the General Agreement on Tariffs and Trade Uruguay Round of multilateral trade negotiations (1986–1993), which led to several trade liberalization agreements, including an agreement to create the World Trade Organization. In addition to issues such as tariffs, subsidies, dumping, government procurement policy, technical barriers to trade, dispute settlement, and institutional reform, the Uruguay Round covered a variety of new topics, including trade in services, trade-related intellectual property rights, and trade-related aspects of investment measures.[34] In 1994, Congress passed the Uruguay Round Agreements Act (URAA), which authorized the president to implement agreements that were reached in the Uruguay Round between 1986 and 1993. Under the URAA, the U.S. Trade Representative is required to consult with appropriate congressional committees concerning the implementation of multilateral trade agreements and WTO rulings that would require changes in U.S. federal or state laws. The WTO was established in 1995, with the United States as one of its original members.

The 2002 Trade Act   The 2002 Trade Act influenced trade policy by reshaping trade adjustment assistance programs (TAAPs). It renewed trade promotion authority[35]—previously known as fast-track authority—for the U.S. president to enter into the WTO Doha Round of multilateral trade negotiations and various negotiations of bilateral free trade agreements. Under trade promotion authority, the George W. Bush administration concluded seven free trade agreements, including the U.S.–Chile Free Trade Agreement, the U.S.–Singapore Free Trade Agreement, and the U.S.–Australia Free Trade Agreement. Also, the 2002 Trade Act required the president to (1) consult with congressional committees as well as a new Congressional Oversight Group during trade negotiations and (2) notify Congress at major stages of such negotiations.

The 2010 National Export Initiative   In 2010, President Barack Obama signed an executive order that established the National Export Initiative (NEI) to "double our exports over the next five years, an increase that will support two million jobs in America."[36] In order to achieve this goal, the president created an Export Promotion Cabinet composed of the Secretaries of State, Treasury, Commerce, and Agriculture, as well as heads of other federal agencies responsible for exports. The primary roles of the newly created Export Promotion Cabinet under the NEI are to hire trade experts to provide advice to potential U.S. exporters, to mobilize government officials to engage in advocacy of export promotion, to expand export counseling for small- and mid-sized businesses, to reduce trade barriers against U.S. businesses, and to open new markets for U.S. exports.

Problems and Challenges

In order to maintain its status as the world's leading economic power, the United States needs to reduce its trade deficits and stimulate its domestic economy while improving interagency coordination, reducing institutional redundancy and inefficiency, and resolving inconsistency due to the implementation of both trade restriction and promotion programs. Efforts to coordinate trade policy include ad-hoc inter-agency coordinating groups and policy advisory groups within the White House. One example of such efforts is the U.S. Trade Representative. Another example is President Obama's 2010 NEI, which created another executive organ, the Export Promotion Cabinet, in addition to existing departments and agencies dealing with U.S. trade policy. In order to fundamentally reform trade policy making and reduce institutional redundancy and inefficiency, however, trade policy experts argue that the United States needs to establish a single cabinet-level department for trade policy. Such a department would be in charge of designing, implementing, and monitoring a more consistent and unified trade policy in conjunction with domestic industrial policy as well as foreign commercial policy.[37]

In January 2012, in order to help American businesses, President Obama proposed merging six departments and agencies (the Small Business Administration, the Office of the U.S. Trade Representative, the Export-Import Bank, the Overseas Private Investment Corporation, and the Trade and Development Agency) into "one Department with one website, one phone number and one mission."[38] The reorganization, as of 2014, did not occur due, in large part, to the opposition of Republicans in the U.S. House of Representatives.

In an age of economic globalization, there are advantages and disadvantages for national economies far beyond the control of sovereign states. In such a global economic environment, national policymakers are expected to do what they can to promote their country's prosperity. All countries, including the United States, pursue a trade policy that is influenced in one way or another by some combination of economic liberalism and mercantilism. Confronted with challenges of a dynamic global economy and domestic economic problems, U.S. trade policy needs to balance international trade liberalization with protection of domestic economic interests.

Since World War II, the United States has been committed to free trade despite demands for protectionist measures. One of the most important trade policy challenges for the United States is to expand U.S. exports of agricultural products, manufactured goods, and services to foreign countries that would bring benefits in support of U.S. economic recovery and prosperity.[39] The United States needs open markets and supports free and fair trade as much as possible while facing protectionist pressures and competing demands from various interest groups.

Under trade promotion authority, both President George W. Bush and President Barack Obama entered into the WTO Doha Round of multilateral trade negotiations.[40] The United States remains committed to open, competitive markets, compliance under the World Trade Organization. The United States remains committed to the "maintenance of open, competitive markets, compliance with WTO obligations, and leadership in the multilateral trading system." The United States has been involved not only in the Doha Round but also in negotiations of specific free trade agreements to promote domestic economic growth and job creation.

Japan

Post–World War II Japanese prime ministers from Shigeru Yoshida to Yoshihiko Noda have referred to Japan as a **trading state**. This is because Japan's economy depends completely on imports of raw materials and energy resources as well as on exports of manufactured goods. For Japanese policymakers, trade policy is a

---

BOX 10.1

Country Profile of Japan

Name of Country: Japan

Conventional Long Form: None

Type of Government: Parliamentary government with a constitutional monarchy

Executive Branch:

Chief of State: Emperor AKIHITO (since 7 January 1989)

Head of Government: Prime Minister Shinzo ABE (since 26 December 2012); Deputy Prime Minister Taro ASO (26 December 2012)

Legislative Branch:

Bicameral Diet or Kokkai consists of the House of Councillors or Sangi-in (242 seats—members elected for fixed

Continued

Box 10.1 Continued

six-year terms; half reelected every three years; 146 members in multi-seat constituencies and 96 by proportional representation) and the House of Representatives or Shugi-in (480 seats—members elected for maximum four-year terms; 300 in single-seat constituencies; 180 members by proportional representation in 11 regional blocs); the prime minister has the right to dissolve the House of Representatives at any time with the concurrence of the cabinet.

Judicial Branch:

Supreme Court (chief justice is appointed by the monarch after designation by the cabinet; all other justices are appointed by the cabinet)

Administrative Divisions:

47 prefectures: Aichi, Akita, Aomori, Chiba, Ehime, Fukui, Fukuoka, Fukushima, Gifu, Gunma, Hiroshima, Hokkaido, Hyogo, Ibaraki, Ishikawa, Iwate, Kagawa, Kagoshima, Kanagawa, Kochi, Kumamoto, Kyoto, Mie, Miyagi, Miyazaki, Nagano, Nagasaki, Nara, Niigata, Oita, Okayama, Okinawa, Osaka, Saga, Saitama, Shiga, Shimane, Shizuoka, Tochigi, Tokushima, Tokyo, Tottori, Toyama, Wakayama, Yamagata, Yamaguchi, Yamanashi

Economic Indicators:

GDP (purchasing power parity): $4.525 trillion (2012 est.)

GDP Real Growth Rate: 0.2 percent (2012 est.)

GDP per capita (purchasing power parity): $36,200 (2012 est.)

Economic Structure: Agriculture 1.2 percent; Industry 27.5 percent; Services 71.4 percent (2012 est.)

Demographic Indicators:

Population: 127,253,075 (July 2013 est.)

Population Growth: -0.077 percent (2013 est.)

Birth Rate: 8.23 births/1,000 population (2013 est.)

Infant Mortality Rate: 2.17 deaths/ 1,000 live births

Life Expectancy at Birth: 84.19 years (2013 estimation)

Literacy (age 15 and over can read and write): 99 percent (2002 estimation)

Ethnic Groups: Japanese 98.5 percent, Koreans 0.5 percent, Chinese 0.4 percent, other 0.6 percent

Note: Up to 230,000 Brazilians of Japanese origin migrated to Japan in the 1990s to work in industries; some have returned to Brazil (2004).

Religions: Shintoism 83.9 percent, Buddhism 71.4 percent, Christianity 2 percent, other 7.8%

Note: total adherents exceeds 100 percent because many people belong to both Shintoism and Buddhism (2005)

Source: CIA, *The World Factbook on Japan,* available at https://www.cia.gov/library/publications/the-world-factbook/geos/ja.html (accessed March 15, 2012).

---

vital part of national security policy.[41] Trade means not only economic prosperity but also Japan's national survival.

Japan's post–World War II trade policy making began with economic recovery.[42] Japan's involvement in World War II resulted not only in defeat but also in devastation of the entire Japanese economy. When the war ended in 1945, Japan's production index was only one-fifth of what it had been at its pre-war peak, and Japan's international trade was severely restricted. American bombing campaigns had destroyed most major cities and industrial facilities. Most of the Japanese suffered from shortages of food, energy, and other essential goods for their daily lives. In the aftermath of World War II, successful economic recovery was at the top of Japan's policy agenda—as important as regaining Japan's sovereignty from U.S. and Allied occupation.

In this context, the Japanese government put great emphasis on industrialization and export promotion. Since Japan has almost no raw materials and energy resources, the Japanese government promoted exports of manufactured goods to earn foreign currency to pay for imports of food, raw materials, and energy to support the Japanese population. Through implementation of industrial development programs, combined with a government-driven policy in support of exports, Japan emerged as one of the largest exporting countries within 20 years after World War II. By 1968, Japan's gross domestic product (GDP) had become the third-largest in the world, surpassed only by the United States and the Soviet Union. Japan was the world's second-largest economic power behind the United States from the 1970s until 2010 when China's economy ($1.33 trillion) overtook Japan's ($1.28 trillion).[43]

Japan's trade policy is known as a **managed trade policy**; it combines Japan's international trade and industrial policies and restricts free and open competition in administratively managed domestic markets. In this context, Japan's automobile makers, such as Toyota, Nissan, and Mitsubishi, have obtained financial, logistical, and legislative support to limit foreign access to the Japanese automobile market while promoting Japanese automobile exports to foreign markets. During the 1980s and 1990s, American and European firms accused Japan's managed trade policy and its domestic business practices as **"unfair trade practices"** or illegitimate trade.[44]

For the Japanese, their country's managed trade policy, combined with government-administered industrial development programs, was necessary for economic recovery because it efficiently allocated limited national resources, such as financial and human capital, and imported raw materials to specific industrial sectors. Japan is a trading state that relies heavily on selling processed goods; therefore, promoting domestic manufacturing industries was a necessary condition for Japan's survival based on **export-oriented economic growth**. According to development economists, Japan's model of export-oriented economic growth stands in contrast to a model of import substituting industrialization (ISI) that intends to reduce imports and encourage domestic manufacturing industries through trade barriers, subsidies for manufacturers, and state ownership of basic industries.[45]

In the twenty-first century, Japan's trade policy is focused on two objectives.[46] The first objective is to maintain and strengthen a rule-based global free trade system under the WTO and the WTO Doha Round of multilateral trade negotiations. The second objective is to expand exports through free trade agreements and economic partnership agreements such as the East Asia Free

Trade Agreement (EAFTA), the Comprehensive Economic Partnership in East Asia (CEPEA), and the Free Trade Area of the Asia-Pacific (FTAAP).

Government Agencies and Other Actors

Japan is ruled under a constitution adopted in 1947. This constitution, which was written by American constitutional framers following Japan's defeat in World War II, provides for popular sovereignty and a parliamentary democracy, with universal suffrage and checks and balances between legislative, executive, and judicial branches of government.[47]

The Legislative Branch The legislature or Diet (Ko-kkai) is Japan's highest organ of state power and exclusive law-making authority. The Diet is a bicameral parliament with a House of Representatives (Shu-Gi-In) as its lower house and a House of Councillors (San-Gi-In) as its upper house. The Shu-Gi-In has 480 members elected for a four-year term. Following Japan's electoral reform of 1993, 300 members are elected directly in single-member districts (SDs) and 180 members are elected by proportional representation (PR) in 11 regional blocs. The government can dissolve the Shu-Gi-In prior to the expiration of its members' four-year term to call elections from a position of strength or due to a vote of no confidence.

The San-Gi-In has 242 members elected for a six-year term. While 96 members are chosen from party lists in a nationwide election based on proportional representation (PR), 146 members are elected from 47 multimember districts (MMD) matching Japan's 47 prefectures. The Shu-Gi-In is more powerful than the San-Gi-In. Specifically, the Shu-Gi-In can override with a two-thirds majority any decision made by the San-Gi-In. The Diet's regular session is about 80 days each year; the prime minister can call a special session. Given the limited length of the regular session, standing Diet committees have an enormous workload. Many veteran politicians, known as policy tribes (Zoku-giin), serve members of specific standing committees with expertise in specific policy areas.

The Executive Branch As a **parliamentary democracy**, Japan has an executive branch in which the roles of head or chief of state (representing and symbolizing the people) and head of government (making and implementing policy) are performed by two separate individuals. The head of state is an emperor, and the head of government is a prime minister. The prime minister is elected by a simple majority in each house of the Diet whose members are elected by the Japanese people.[48] A candidate for prime minister must be approved by his or her party and is usually the president/chairperson of a party represented in the Diet. The prime minister can appoint or dismiss cabinet (Nai-Kaku) members who serve as ministers or heads of government departments and agencies.

The Judicial Branch Japan's judicial branch has a unitary court system with a high degree of independence from the legislative and executive branches of government as well as from private interest groups.[49] At the top of this court system, which includes 8 high courts, 50 district courts, and 50 family courts, is the Supreme Court. The Supreme Court, whose 15 members are appointed by the cabinet, is Japan's constitutional court and its final court of appeal in civil and criminal cases. The Supreme Court is responsible for nominating judges to lower courts, determining judicial procedures, overseeing the court system, supervising activities of public prosecutors, and disciplining judges and other judicial personnel.

The Liberal Democratic Party (LDP), Bureaucrats, and Ministries

The **Liberal Democratic Party** (**LDP**) dominated Japanese policy making, including trade policy making, between 1955 and 1993, and from 1996 to 2009; it designed, planned, and proposed numerous bills to the Japanese cabinet, or directly to the Diet.[50] So long as the LDP had a parliamentary majority, its party president was Japan's prime minister, and all cabinet positions were held by the LDP. This meant that the LDP had enormous power to influence policy decisions until the Democratic Party of Japan (DPJ) replaced it as Japan's ruling party in 2009.[51]

The Liberal Democratic Party established within its party structure a well-organized policy planning program known as the Policy Research Council (PRC).[52] The PRC consists of 12 different divisions that correspond to each ministry and agency represented in the cabinet. Although the Japanese constitution allows any member of the Diet to introduce a bill with support from at least five other members of the Diet, LDP procedures stipulate that no LDP member—whether as a member of the Diet, as a cabinet minister, or even as prime minister—is allowed to submit a bill to the Diet without PRC approval. After a bill is approved by the PRC and then reviewed by the LDP's Policy Deliberation Commission, it is submitted for a final decision by the LDP's highest decision-making organ, which is known as the party's General Council. When the Liberal Democratic Party was Japan's ruling party, its policy review process was a primary source of LDP power and control over Japanese policymaking.

The LDP procedures provided senior bureaucrats from various ministries and agencies with significant opportunities to initiate policy proposals and present them to LDP members of the Diet or as participants in Policy Research Council meetings. Thus, as bills made it through the Policy Research Council, the Policy Deliberation Commission, and the General Council to finally reach the cabinet and get introduced in the Diet, they had the signature of senior bureaucrats. The point here is that, under LDP procedures, senior bureaucrats gained a lot of power over policy formation. In the case of trade policy, we are talking primarily about senior bureaucrats from the **Ministry of International Trade and Industry** (**MITI**) and its 2001 successor, the **Ministry of Economy, Trade and Industry** (**METI**), the most important government agencies involved in Japanese trade policy making.[53]

The Ministry of Economy, Trade and Industry is a central comprehensive body in charge of trade policy formation, implementation, and evaluation; it coordinates trade policy with industrial policy, energy policy, and economic policy. Specifically, the METI is responsible for trade promotion as well as trade

restriction related to manufactured goods. Trade in agricultural and food products is under the jurisdiction of the Ministry of Agriculture, Forest, and Fisheries.
Financial, tax, exchange rate, insurance services related to trade are handled by
the Ministry of Finance. International trade negotiations are conducted with
involvement of the Ministry of Foreign Affairs. Other departments and agencies
may participate in trade policy making to the extent that it relates to their specific policy domains.

Inter-ministerial coordination to resolve disagreements or adjust diverse interests among different government agencies has been at the center of Japanese policy
making. Such coordination is a bureaucratic practice whereby senior bureaucrats
agree on policies before their ministry or agency submits them in a memorandum
to Japan's ruling party.

Before the Ministry of Economy, Trade and Industry replaced the Ministry of
International Trade and Industry, the MITI's primary objective was to encourage
Japanese participation in the world economy by promoting the development of
domestic export-oriented industries. The MITI's senior bureaucrats frequently
relied on administrative guidance (gyousei-sidou), which means that the MITI
implemented its policies/programs and controlled/managed domestic industries
without legislative authorization.[54] As of 2012, the METI carries out its trade
policy, industrial policy, and related programs through a number of functional
and sectional bureaus, offices, and agencies,[55] including the Trade Policy Bureau,
Trade and Economic Cooperation Bureau, Recycling Promotion Divisions,
Industrial Science and Technology Policy and Environment Bureau, Agency for
Natural Resources and Energy, Nuclear and Industrial Safety Agency, and the
Small and Medium Enterprise Agency.

Under the METI's Trade Policy Bureau, the Japan External Trade Organization (JETRO), established originally as an external but government-related
organization under the MITI in 1958, promotes mutual trade and investment
between Japan and the rest of the world.[56] Furthermore, the Japan Fair Trade
Commission (kousei-torihiki-iinkai), created under the 1947 Antimonopoly Act
(Act on Prohibition of Private Monopolization and Maintenance of Fair Trade),
is an independent institution that monitors fair trade, enforces anti-dumping and
anti-trust regulations, and, under Japan's anti-monopoly law, objects to carteli-
zation of specific industries or business mergers despite MITI/METI support for
such practices.[57]

Interest Groups Japanese economic, industrial, and trade policy making
is influenced heavily by powerful interest groups (usually big-business executives) that are linked to veteran politicians and senior bureaucrats in "iron tri-
angles" as trade policy networks.[58] Besides, there are numerous other interest
groups—many of them newcomers in specific businesses—that independently
and informally lobby individual politicians and bureaucrats for benefits.[59]

Two of Japan's most powerful interest groups formed by business lead-
ers are the Federation of Economic Organizations (Keizai Dantai Rengokai,
Keidanren, or KDR) and the Japan Association of Corporate Executives (Keizai
Doyu Kai, or KDK). In 2002, the KDR merged with the Japan Federation of

Employers' Association (Nihon Keieisha-dantai Renmei, or Nikkeiren), which created the Japan Business Federation (Nippon Keidanren), a comprehensive economic organization with 1,609 members representing 1,295 companies, 129 industrial associations, and 47 regional economic organizations. The mission of the Nippon Keidanren is to promote sustainable economic growth driven by Japan's private sector.

The KDK is a private, nonprofit, and nonpartisan organization with approximately 1,400 executives representing more than 900 large corporations. The KDK provides a broad, long-term, and independent research-based perspective on government policy toward industry and society as a whole, and it pursues active dialogue with members of political parties, government officials, bureaucrats, and leaders of business and labor organizations.

Some of Japan's most powerful interest groups are organized in business circles (Zaikai) formed by major corporate executives from various industrial sectors. The majority of these corporate executives are commonly part of corporate networks (Keiretsu) that usually include a large bank as well as several big manufacturing, trading, shipping, construction, and insurance companies. Corporate executives who are part of such Keiretsu have significant influence on policy making, both publicly and privately through campaign contributions for individual Diet members and offers of post-retirement positions for senior bureaucrats.

In addition to what we have said about interest groups so far, it is important to mention the Japan Chamber of Commerce and Industry (Nihon Shoko Kaigisho or Nissho) and Japan's National Federation of Agricultural Co-operative Associations (Zen-Noh). The Nissho formally represents interests of small- and medium-sized firms in Japan's service and manufacturing sectors, whereas the Zen-Noh protects Japan's agricultural business practices. Furthermore, there are many other interest groups, such as consumer associations and environmental organizations, involved in specific issues related to Japanese trade policy making.

Policy Initiatives

Post–World War II Japanese trade policy has been shaped predominantly by legislation, cabinet orders, ministerial ordinances, rules, and notifications initiated by the MITI and the METI.[60] Between 1949 and 1960, the MITI initiated more than 120 laws, cabinet orders, and ministerial ordinances to promote Japanese exports; examples include the Foreign Exchange and Foreign Trade Control Law (1949), the Export Trade Control Ordinance (1949), the Import Trade and External Payments Control Order (1949), the Export and Import Transaction Law (1952), the Export Inspection Law (1957), the Export Credit Insurance Law (1950), and the Law concerning Japan External Trade Organization (1958).[61] In the following section, we review policy initiatives that have had a significant impact on Japan's export-oriented economic development strategy since the late 1940s and its move towards trade liberalization since the 1980s.[62]

The 1949 Foreign Exchange and Foreign Trade Control Law   In 1949, while Japan was still under foreign occupation, the Japanese government enacted the Foreign Exchange and Foreign Trade Control Law to protect its country's infant domestic industries from foreign competition and to promote Japanese exports based on the MITI's objectives regarding Japan's international trade and industrial policy. This law established the foundation of what became a government-driven export policy.

The 1950 Foreign Investment Law   Following the Foreign Exchange and Foreign Trade Control Law, a second landmark to protect emerging domestic industries while promoting exports was the Foreign Investment Law passed in 1950. This law was intended to (1) shield weaker domestic firms from foreign ones, (2) encourage foreign capital inflow to strengthen domestic industries, and (3) facilitate cooperation between foreign and domestic firms in regard to advanced technology.

Joining the Post–World War II Liberal Economic Order   In 1952, Japan not only regained its sovereignty but it also joined the liberal economic order created after World War II. After Japan became a member of the International Monetary Fund in 1952, it entered into the General Agreement on Tariffs and Trade and obtained most-favored-nation (MFN) status in 1955.

Voluntary Export Restraints (VERs)   In response to a sharp increase in imports of manufactured products, such as textiles, from Japan during the 1950s, the United States demanded that Japan impose **voluntary export restraints (VERs)** to restrict Japanese exports of selected manufactured products to the United States. These voluntary export restraints were established through bilateral administrative agreements between the United States and Japan and administered by the MITI in coordination with Japanese businesses.

The 1955 Five-Year Plan for Economic Independence (Keizai Jiritsu go-ka-nen-Keikaku)   This Five-Year Plan for Economic Independence was the first national economic plan adopted by the Japanese government; it was followed by the New Long-Run Economic Plan (Shin Keizai Keikaku) between 1958 and 1962 and the Doubling National Income Plan (Kokumin Shtolu Baizo Keikaku) between 1961 and 1970. The main objectives of the Keizai Jiritsu go-ka-nen-Keikaku were to (1) modernize industrial plants and equipment, (2) promote international trade, (3) increases self-sufficiency, and (4) curtail consumption. In pursuit of these objectives, the MITI implemented various export-promotion measures, including export subsidies, low-interest government loans for successful export-oriented industries, and preferential tax treatment of income from exports and exploration of new export markets.

The 1960 Master Plan for Trade and Foreign Exchange Liberalization (Boeki-Kawase-Jiyuka-Keikaku-Taiko)   Adopted by the Japanese government in 1960, this Master Plan for Trade and Foreign Exchange Liberalization was designed to change Japan's trade policy from mercantilism (protectionism) to economic liberalism (free trade) by removing import quotas, eliminating restrictions of foreign exchange transactions involving current accounts, and reducing controls of capital-account transactions. Implementing this plan, the Japanese government removed or relaxed import quotas on 1,837 commodities between 1960 and 1963.

IMF Article 8, GATT Article 11, and OECD Membership   In 1964, Japan signed on to the International Monetary Fund Article 8 and the General Agreement on Tariffs and Trade Article 11, both of which prohibit foreign exchange controls and import restrictions. In the same year, Japan joined the Organization for Economic Cooperation and Development (OECD). With these events, Japan's trade policy was transformed significantly from industrial protection to trade liberalization.

The 1974–1979 GATT Tokyo Round   Between 1974 and 1979, Japan hosted the General Agreement on Tariffs and Trade Tokyo Round of multilateral trade negotiations to reduce tariffs and nontariff barriers. On the basis of agreements reached in these negotiations, the Japanese government relaxed the Foreign Exchange and Foreign Trade Control Law and abolished the Foreign Investment Law. In 1982, the Japanese government reviewed numerous rules related to import procedures and testing standards that other countries criticized as nontariff barriers. In the same year, the Japanese government established the Office of Trade Ombudsman, which later became the Office of Trade and Investment Ombudsman, to investigate complaints about importing procedures and government regulations.

The Market Oriented Selective Sector (MOSS) Talks and the Structural Impediments Initiative (SII)   In the 1980s and 1990s, Japan experienced trade frictions with the United States, its most important trade partner. The Japanese government used what it perceived as external pressure (Gaiatsu) from the United States to open Japanese markets as justification to push for more trade liberalization against resistance in Japan.[63] In 1985, the United States and Japan entered into a series of bilateral negotiations, the **MOSS talks**, to remove regulations claimed to impede the sale of American products in Japan. Of particular concern to negotiators were telecommunications, medical equipment/pharmaceuticals, microelectronics, and forest products. In 1986, transportation machinery and automotive parts were added to the agenda. In 1987, the MOSS talks concluded with only modest achievements. Because Japan was quite recalcitrant and offered only limited concessions, the United States threatened Japan with sanctions based on the Super 301 provision of the 1988 Omnibus Trade and Competitiveness Act (OTCA). In order to avoid U.S. sanctions, the Japanese government entered into special negotiations with the U.S. Trade Representative over a wide range of economic issues under the 1989 **Structural Impediments Initiative (SII)**. This initiative required Japan to open its markets by ending business practices and regulations impeding foreign imports and investments.

Voluntary Import Expansions (VIEs)   In the late 1980s, Japan introduced and implemented **voluntary import expansions** (VIEs) in response to U.S. requests that Japan expand its quantity of imports of specific goods, such as automobiles and semiconductors.

The U.S.–Japan Framework Talks   Accusations by the Clinton administration that Japan engaged in illegitimate trade practices that contributed to U.S. trade deficits with Japan led to the U.S.–Japan Framework Talks. The primary objectives of these talks, which began in 1993, were to increase U.S. exports to Japanese markets, reduce a $50 billion U.S. trade deficit with Japan, and harmonize Japan's trade structure with that of other advanced industrialized economies, including the United States.[64] In order to increase Japanese purchases of U.S. goods—including automobiles, high-technology items, financial services, and agricultural products—the U.S. government asked for changes in Japan's domestic markets and business practices administered by the Japanese government.

The World Trade Organization (WTO) and Aggressive Legalism   As a result of the MOSS talks, the threat of U.S. sanctions based on the Super 301 provision of the 1988 **Omnibus Trade and Competitiveness Act (OTCA)**, and the SII, Japan's trade policy has come to embrace free and fair trade within a multilateral framework whose hub is the WTO. In order to resolve trade-related disputes with trade partners such as the United States, Japan has relied increasingly on aggressive legalism, which means that Japan has increasingly made it a practice to actively use the WTO's trade dispute settlement mechanism.[65]

Free Trade Agreements (FTAs) and Economic Partnership Agreements (EPAs)   Since the mid-1990s, in response to a new wave of bilateral, multilateral, and regional free trade arrangements, such as the North American Free Trade Agreement and the European Union, Japan's trade strategy has focused on expanding Japanese exports to other countries through FTAs and EPAs.[66] The Trade Policy Bureau at the METI and the Economic Affairs Bureau at the Ministry of Foreign Affairs (MOFA) were two advocates of this strategy. Both the METI's *White Paper on International Economy and Trade 2010* and the MOFA's *Diplomatic Bluebook 2010* point out that, as a trading state that benefits significantly from a multilateral trade system anchored in the WTO, Japan must proactively contribute to the promotion of multilateral trade negotiations.[67] According to the MOFA, free trade agreements "are generally agreements aimed at eliminating tariffs, etc. and liberalizing trade in goods and services among designated countries and regions." Economic partnership agreements "aim to harmonize various economic systems and reinforce economic relations in a broader range of fields by promoting investment and movement of persons, rule-making in government procurement, competition policy, intellectual property rights, etc., and cooperation in various fields."[68] From Japan's perspective, FTAs and EPAs complement the WTO in promoting free trade by strengthening trade relations and achieving trade liberalization beyond levels attainable under the WTO.

Japan entered into its first free trade agreement in 2002 with Singapore. Since then, Japan has entered into economic partnership agreements with nine countries as well as with the Association of Southeast Asian Nations (ASEAN). In late 2011, after deeply divided debates over economic policy among politicians, business elites, and the Japanese public, the Japanese government decided to participate in Trans-Pacific Partnership (TPP) negotiations with Australia, Brunei, Chile, Malaysia, New Zealand, Peru, Singapore, Vietnam, and the United States.[69] As of 2012, Japan is involved in ongoing negotiations of EPAs as well as in studies to explore the viability of regional economic partnerships, specifically in East Asia and the Asia-Pacific region.

Problems and Challenges

As Japan's trade policy has changed from mercantilism (protectionism) to economic liberalism (free trade) starting with the 1960 Master Plan for Trade and Foreign Exchange Liberalization (Boeki-Kawase-Jiyuka-Keikaku-Taiko), it has encountered and continues to encounter a number of problems and challenges at the intersection between a dynamic global economy and entrenched domestic economic interests. One of Japan's trade policy challenges is to promote Japanese exports in order to recover from a prolonged economic recession that began in 2002.[70] In response to this challenge, Japan has relied increasingly on a trade strategy that involves free trade agreements and economic partnership agreements in attempts to expand Japanese exports. Still, in comparison with the United States, Germany, and even South Korea, Japan lags far behind in negotiating such agreements, which is largely due to the Japanese government's hesitation to open Japan's agricultural sector and other areas to free trade against pressure from the National Federation of Agricultural Co-operative Associations (Zen-Noh) and related interest groups. Given Japan's dependence on food imports, agricultural trade liberalization would benefit Japanese consumers because it would increase imports of food products and thus alleviate concerns about rising food prices and scarcities. Yet, competing imports of food products would also depress the income of Japanese farmers who would prefer for Japan's food security to depend on domestic self-sufficiency rather than on foreign markets.

Another trade policy challenge for Japan is to end business practices and regulations that restrict access of foreign imports and investments to Japanese markets. If Japan wants to use the WTO's trade dispute settlement mechanism and rely on FTAs and EPAs to expand Japanese exports, it needs to truly adhere to free trade principles and reduce or remove tariffs and nontariff barriers, which include business practices and regulations that interfere with free trade. In response to this challenge, the Japanese government established the Council for the Promotion of Regulatory Reform (CPRR) in 2007 and adopted the Three-Year Program for Promoting Regulatory Reform in 2008.

Given the dependence of Japan's economy on imports of raw materials and energy resources as well as on exports of manufactured goods, combined with the dependence of Japan's food security on imports of food products, Japan needs open global markets. The Japanese government has taken various measures to expand Japanese exports through trade liberalization and economic partnerships. Japan has relied increasingly on aggressive legalism by using the WTO's trade dispute settlement mechanism, and it has entered into a number of FTAs and EPAs. Despite Japan's dependence on imports and demands from other countries, most notably the United States and Asia-Pacific countries, that Japan reduce or remove import barriers, protectionist demands for trade control from domestic interest groups continue to undermine Japan's commitment to reciprocal free trade.

Comparison

According to economic liberals, free trade (exports and imports) of goods and services between two or more countries leads to economic growth and prosperity. Reducing or removing trade restrictions is a primary goal of a trade policy rooted in economic liberalism. Although mercantilists would agree with economic liberals that a government should promote exports to increase its society's welfare and create jobs through domestic production of goods that are sold abroad, they differ from economic liberals in regard to imports. Because imports reduce jobs by competing with domestic products for consumers at home, mercantilists argue, it is a government's responsibility to protect domestic producers and their workforce from job losses by restricting imports from other countries. In order to restrict imports, countries use a variety of instruments of trade protection, such as tariffs, import quotas, and nontariff barriers, including food, environmental, and health standards; procurement codes; and many other laws and regulations.

Although free trade is of significant interest to both the United States and Japan, both countries have used instruments to protect domestic firms and jobs from foreign imports while promoting their exports to other countries. The most significant example of protectionism in the United States was the 1930 Smoot-Hawley Tariff Act. Passed after the 1929 crash of the U.S. stock market had led to the Great Depression, this act was meant not only to shield domestic markets and producers from foreign imports but also to raise federal revenue from increased duties on imported goods. In Japan, two significant examples of protectionism were the 1949 Foreign Exchange and Foreign Trade Control Law and the 1950 Foreign Investment Law. A major objective of both laws was to protect infant or emerging domestic industries from foreign competition. In both the United States and Japan, major protectionist measures were generated by severe economic distress. The U.S. economy around the time of the Smoot-Hawley Tariff Act suffered from the Great Depression, and the Japanese economy around the time of the Foreign Exchange and Foreign Trade Control Law and the Foreign Investment Law was still being rebuilt out of the ashes of World War II.

In both the United States and Japan, strong mercantilism had consequences that resulted in commitments to economic liberalism. Yet, there is a notable difference between the United States and Japan relating to the impetus for this change in trade policy.

As other countries reacted to the Smoot-Hawley Tariff Act with retaliatory trade measures against U.S. exports, a drastic decline in U.S. foreign trade (both imports and exports) worsened the Great Depression, and the U.S. economy was further impoverished. In response to the Smoot-Hawley Tariff and its pernicious consequences for U.S. foreign trade and the U.S. economy, the 1934 Reciprocal Trade Agreements Act was passed. This act, which was intended to help legislators insulate themselves from protectionist pressures, led to numerous reciprocal tariff agreements, a steady reduction of tariffs, and a series of reciprocal trade agreement expansion acts. The Reciprocal Trade Agreements Act changed U.S. trade policy from mercantilism to economic liberalism. Endorsed by Secretary of State Cordell Hull under President Franklin Roosevelt, this change in U.S. trade policy turned the United States from a powerful protectionist to a powerful advocate of free trade. Although the U.S. Senate never ratified the ITO Charter, and the ITO was never established, the United States entered into the General Agreement on Tariffs and Trade and, several decades later, became an original member of the WTO. In short, the impetus for change in U.S. trade policy from protectionism to free trade was the extent to which a protectionist act contributed to further domestic economic distress.

Japanese protectionist measures, such as the Foreign Exchange and Foreign Trade Control Law and the Foreign Investment Law, were part of a managed trade policy combining international trade and industrial policies to promote Japanese exports abroad while restricting foreign exports to Japan. Unlike the protectionist Smoot-Hawley Tariff Act in the United States during the early 1930s, Japanese protectionist measures were successful in that they contributed to Japan's post–World War II economic recovery and helped infant or emerging domestic industries become industrial giants, such as Toyota, for example. Administered by the Ministry of International Trade and Industry (MITI) and the Ministry of Economy, Trade and Industry (METI), Japan's managed trade policy with its protectionist measures created entrenched bureaucratic interests in its continuation. Thus, regulations and business practices to protect Japanese industries from foreign imports were still upheld even though those industries were no longer infants but powerful export-oriented adults. It is not surprising that American and European firms complained about "unfair trade practices" when their exports to Japan continued to face significant import restrictions, even though Japan had chosen a path toward trade liberalization with the 1960 Master Plan for Trade and Foreign Exchange Liberalization.

In response to Japanese reluctance to open its domestic markets to imports from the United States, which was evident in Japanese recalcitrance during the Market Oriented Selective Sector (MOSS) Talks, the United States threatened Japan with sanctions based on the Super 301 provision of the 1988 Omnibus Trade and Competitiveness Act. Given the importance of trade not only to Japan's economic prosperity but also to the country's national survival, the Japanese government tried to avoid U.S. sanctions by entering into negotiations under the Structural Impediments Initiative (SII). This initiative required Japan to open its markets by ending business practices and regulations impeding foreign imports and investments.

Further demands by the United States that Japan expand its quantity of imports and open its markets to increased U.S. exports led Japan to take further steps toward trade liberalization. In the late 1980s, Japan introduced and implemented voluntary import expansions reminiscent of voluntary export restraints that Japan had introduced and implemented in response to U.S. demands in the 1950s. Then, in the 1990s, the U.S.–Japan Framework Talks provided another forum in which Japan addressed U.S. concerns about illegitimate Japanese trade practices. In short, the impetus for change in Japanese trade policy from protectionism to free trade was the extent to which external pressure (Gaiatsu) from the United States to open Japanese markets provided the Japanese government with justification to push for more trade liberalization against resistance in Japan. Avoiding U.S. sanctions in retaliation for illegitimate Japanese trade practices had to be of top priority to the Japanese government entrusted with Japan's economic prosperity and national survival.

The United States and Japan differ not only with relation to the impetus for change in trade policy but also with reference to institutional sources of trade policy initiatives. In the United States, trade policy initiatives originate with legislative acts passed by Congress. As we mentioned before, the U.S. Constitution, Article 1, Section 8, gives Congress the power to "regulate Commerce with foreign Nations" and to "lay and collect Taxes, Duties, Imposts and Excises." Through trade legislation, Congress provides the president with trade policy-making power and authority (e.g., fast track or trade promotion authority) to formulate and implement trade policy programs under congressional oversight. Examples of significant trade legislation granting the president tariff-setting and trade-negotiation authority are the 1934 Reciprocal Trade Agreements Act, the 1974 Trade Act, the 1988 Omnibus Trade and Competitiveness Act, and the 2002 Trade Act.

Several departments and agencies are involved in trade policy making under the U.S. president, including the Department of Treasury, the Department of Commerce, and the Department of State. Furthermore, the president obtains advice on trade and related economic issues from the Office of the U.S. Trade Representative, the National Economic Council, and the Council of Economic Advisers, as well as from ad-hoc inter-agency coordinating groups. Trade policy making is also affected by decisions of the Export-Import Bank and the International Trade Commission, and it is shaped by numerous interest groups.

In Japan, trade policy initiatives typically originated within the Liberal Democratic Party and were submitted to the cabinet and then to the Diet only after they had been approved by the party's Policy Research Council, reviewed by its Policy Deliberation Commission, and endorsed by its General Council. Senior bureaucrats from ministries and agencies, such as the Ministry of International Trade and Industry and the Ministry of Economy, Trade and Industry, had significant opportunities to initiate trade policy proposals, which gave them a lot of power over trade policy formation. In other words, trade policy initiatives in Japan typically originated not with legislative acts and the activities of lobbyists active in the legislature as in the United States, but with policy proposals shaped by senior bureaucrats representing ministries and agencies within the Liberal Democratic Party. Examples of Japanese trade policy initiatives are the 1949 Foreign Exchange and Foreign Trade Control Law, the 1950 Foreign Investment Law, the 1955 Five-Year Plan for Economic Independence, and the 1960 Master Plan for Trade and Foreign Exchange Liberalization, as well as voluntary export restraints and voluntary import expansions.

As they are confronted with challenges of a dynamic global economy and domestic economic problems in an age of globalization, both the United States and Japan need to balance international trade liberalization with protection of domestic economic interests. Both countries are committed to free trade despite demands for protectionist measures. Both countries embrace economic liberalism under influence of mercantilism. And both countries are supportive of a rule-based global free trade system under the WTO. In order to open foreign markets and promote exports, both the United States and Japan have been involved in multilateral trade negotiations, such as the Doha Round, as well as in negotiations of specific free trade agreements and economic partnership agreements. Examples of such agreements are the North American Free Trade Agreement for the United States as well as the East Asia Free Trade Agreement, the Comprehensive Economic Partnership in East Asia, and the Free Trade Area of the Asia-Pacific for Japan. Furthermore, both the United States and Japan pursue bilateral free trade agreements and now also participate in Trans-Pacific Partnership negotiations. Still, it remains to be seen how future challenges to U.S. and Japanese efforts to promote domestic economic growth and job creation as part of other economic policies affect the extent to which trade policy is influenced more by economic liberalism or mercantilism, by the pursuit of free trade or the pursuit of protectionism.

Key Terms

- American Recovery and Reinvestment Act (ARRA)
- Buy American provision
- Comparative advantage
- Economic liberalism
- Economic partnership agreements (EPAs)
- Export-oriented economic growth
- Free trade
- Free trade agreements (FTAs)
- House Committee on Ways and Means

- Import quotas
- Liberal Democratic Party (LDP)
- Managed trade policy
- Mercantilism (or economic nationalism)
- Ministry of Economy, Trade and Industry (METI)
- Ministry of International Trade and Industry (MITI)
- MOSS Talks (Market Oriented Selective Sector)
- Nontariff barriers (NTBs)

- Omnibus Trade and Competitiveness Act (OTCA)
- Open trade policy
- Parliamentary democracy
- Reciprocal Trade Agreement Act (RTAA)
- Senate Committee on Finance
- Smoot-Hawley Tariff Act (SHTA)
- Structural Impediments Initiative (SII)
- Tariffs
- Trading state
- Unfair trade practices
- U.S. Trade Representative (USTR)
- Voluntary export restraints (VERs)
- Voluntary import expansions (VIEs)
- World Trade Organization (WTO)

Discussion Questions

- How does economic liberalism differ from mercantilism (economic nationalism) with respect to trade policy?
- How does an open trade policy differ from a managed trade policy?
- What government agencies and other actors are involved in trade policy making in the United States and Japan?
- To what extent does politics influence trade policy in the United States and Japan?
- What are the most important problems and challenges related to trade policy in the United States and Japan?
- Why do countries pursue trade policy through free trade agreements (FTAs) and economic partnership agreements (EPAs)?

Recommended Resources for U.S. Trade Policy

Stephen D. Cohen, *The Making of United States International Economic Policy* (5th ed.) (Westport, CT: Praeger, 2000).

Stephen D. Cohen, Robert A. Blecker, and Peter D. Whitney, *Fundamentals of U.S. Foreign Trade Policy: Economics, Politics, Laws, and Issues* (2nd ed.) (Boulder, CO: Westview, 2003).

I. M. Destler, *American Trade Politics* (4th ed.) (Washington, DC: Institute for International Economics, 2005).

I. M. Destler, "The Foreign Economic Bureaucracy," in Steven W. Hook and Christopher M. Jones (eds.), *Routledge Handbook of American Foreign Policy* (New York: Routledge, 2012), Chapter 6, pp. 217–230.

Gene M. Grossman and Elhanan Helpman, *Interest Groups and Trade Policy* (Princeton, NJ: Princeton University Press, 2002).

USTR, *Trade Policy Annual Report* (various years).

WTO, *Trade Policy Review reported by the United States* (various years).

Useful Web Sources for U.S. Trade Policy

The Office of U.S. Trade Representative

The U.S. National Export Initiative

The U.S. Department of State's Bureau of Economic and Business Affairs

Recommended Resources for Japanese Trade Policy

Charmers Johnson, *MITI and the Japanese Miracle: The Growth of Industrial Policy, 1925–1975* (Stanford, CA: Stanford University Press, 1982).

John Kunkel, *America's Trade Policy towards Japan: Demanding Results* (London: Routledge, 2003).

MITI/METI, *International Economy and Trade* (various years).

Saadia M. Pekkanen, *Japan's Aggressive Legalism: Law and Foreign Trade Politics beyond the WTO* (Stanford, CA: Stanford University Press, 2008).

Richard J. Samuels, *"Rich Nation, Strong Army": National Security and the Technological Transformation of Japan* (Ithaca, NY: Cornell University Press, 1994).

Mikio Sumiya (ed.), *History of Japanese Trade and Industry Policy* (Oxford: Oxford University Press, 2000).

J. A. A. Stockwin, *Governing Japan: Divided Politics in a Major Economy* (4th ed.) (London: Wiley-Blackwell, 2008).

WTO, *Trade Policy Review reported by Japan* (various years).

Useful Web Sources for Japanese Trade Policy

The Japanese Ministry of Economy, Trade and Industry's External Economic Policy

The Japanese Ministry of Foreign Affairs' Economic Affairs

The Japanese Ministry of Finance's Trade Statistics of Japan

Notes

1. See Scott C. Bradford, Paul L. Grieco, and Gary Clyde Hufbauer, "The Payoff to America from Global Integration" in C. Fred Bergsten and the Institute for International Economics (eds.), *The United States and the World Economy: Foreign Economic Policy for the Next Decade* (Washington, DC: Institute for International Economics, 2005).

2. See John Beghin, Barbara El Osta, Jay Cherlow, and Samarendu Mohanty, "The Costs of the U.S. Sugar Program Revisited," *Contemporary Economic Policy* 21 (2003): 1006–1116.

3. For a good overview of the debate between economic liberalism and mercantilism (economic nationalism), see Robert Gilpin, *The Political Economy of International Relations* (Princeton, NJ: Princeton University Press, 1987) and Jeffrey A. Frieden, *Global Capitalism: Its Fall and Rise in the Twentieth Century* (New York: Norton, 2006).

4. See Jeffrey M. Jones, "Americans More Negative Than Positive about Foreign Trade: Have Held More Negative Views since 2005," February 18, 2009, http://www.gallup.com/poll/115240/americans-negative-positive-foreign-trade.aspx (accessed March 12, 2012).

5. For a good discussion of the Smoot-Hawley Tariff Act, see I. M. Destler, *American Trade Politics* (4th ed.) (Washington, DC: Institute of International Economics, 2005) and Douglas A. Irwin, "From Smoot-Hawley to Reciprocal Trade Agreements: Changing the Course of U.S. Trade Policy in the 1930s," in Michael D. Bordo, Claudia Goldin, and Eugene N. White (eds.), *The Defining Moment: The Great Depression and the American Economy in the Twentieth Century* (Chicago: University of Chicago Press, 1998).

6. See Cohen, Blecker, and Whitney, *Fundamentals of U.S. Foreign Trade Policy*, p. 5.
7. The report, *Opinion Poll: 2011 U.S. Image of Japan*, is available from the Japanese Ministry of Foreign Affairs website at http://www.mofa.go.jp/region/n-america/us/survey/fulltext2011.pdf (accessed March 12, 2012).
8. The statement was quoted in Richard N. Gardner, *Sterling-Dollar Diplomacy in Current Perspectives: The Origins and Prospects of Our International Economic Order* (New York: Columba University Press, 1980), p. 9.
9. For a brief discussion in this regard, see Frieden, *Global Capitalism: Its Fall and Rise in the Twentieth Century*, Chapter 11.
10. The original text can be found at http://www.gpo.gov/fdsys/pkg/PLAW-111publ5/content-detail.html (accessed March 15, 2012).
11. Burton G. Malkiel ,"Congress Wants a Trade War: The President Should Veto 'Buy American' if He Doesn't Want to Be Remembered Like Herbert Hoover," *The Wall Street Journal*, February 5, 2009, p. A13, available at http://online.wsj.com/article/SB123380102867150621.html (accessed March 12, 2012).
12. Gary Clyde Hufbauer and Jeffrey J. Schott, "Buy American: Bad for Jobs, Worse for Reputation," *Policy Brief* no. PB09-2 (Washington, DC: Peterson Institute for International Economics), p. 4.
13. See WTO, *Trade Policy Review reported by the United States* submitted to the WTO Trade Policy Review Body on August 25, 2010 (WT/TRP/235), available at http://www.wto.org/english/tratop_e/tpr_e/tp335_e.htm (accessed March 15, 2012).
14. For a good discussion of legislative powers regarding trade policy making, see Cohen, Blecker, and Whitney, *Fundamentals of U.S. Foreign Trade Policy*.
15. For the Senate Committee on Finance, see http://finance.senate.gov/ (accessed March 12, 2012). For the House Committee on Ways and Means, see http://waysandmeans.house.gov/ (accessed March 12, 2012).
16. See I. M. Destler, *American Trade Politics* (4th ed.) (Washington, DC: Institute for International Economics, 2005) and Stephen D. Cohen, *The Making of United States International Economic Policy* (5th ed.) (Westport, CT: Praeger, 2000).
17. For the quotes and more detail, see the USTR website at http://www.ustr.gov/about-us/mission (accessed March 15, 2012).
18. For the quotes and more detail, see the NEC website at http://www.whitehouse.gov/administration/eop/nec (accessed March 15, 2012). For the role of the National Economic Council (NEC) in U.S. international and domestic economic policy making, see also Roger B. Porter, *Presidential Decision Making: The Economic Policy Board* (Cambridge: Cambridge University Press, 1980) and I. M. Destler, *National Economic Council* (Washington, DC: Institute of International Economics, 1996).
19. For the quote and more detail, see the CEA website at http://www.whitehouse.gov/administration/eop/cea/about (accessed March 15, 2012).
20. These departments and agencies are (a) the Department of Commerce, (b) the Department of State, (c) the Department of Treasury, (d) the Department of Agriculture, (e) the Department of Energy, (f) the Department of Transportation, (g) the Department of Defense, (h) the Department of Labor, (i) the Department of the Interior, (j) the Agency for International Development (AID), (k) the Trade and Development Agency (TDA), (l) the Environmental Protection Agency (EPA), (m) the United States Information Agency (USIA), (n) the Small Business Administration (SBA), (o) the Overseas Private Investment Corporation (OPIC), (p) the Export-Import Bank (EIB), (q) the Office of the United States Trade Representative (USTR), (r) the Council of Economic Advisers (CEA), (s) the Office of Management and

Budget (OMB), (t) the National Economic Council (NEC), (u) the National Security Council (NSC), and (v) other departments or agencies by discretion of the president.

21. For details, see the DOT website at http://www.treasury.gov/about/role-of-treasury/Pages/default.aspx (accessed March 12, 2012).

22. For details, see the DOC website at http://www.commerce.gov/ (accessed March 12, 2012).

23. For the quotes and more detail, see the ITA website at http://trade.gov/about.asp (accessed March 12, 2012).

24. For details, see the DOS website at http://www.state.gov/ (accessed March 12, 2012).

25. For details, see the TTP website at http://www.state.gov/e/eb/tpp/ (accessed March 12, 2012).

26. For the role of the Export-Import Bank of the United States, see the EIB website at http://www.exim.gov/ (accessed March 12, 2012).

27. For the roles of ITC, see the USITC website at http://www.usitc.gov/ (accessed March 12, 2012).

28. For an excellent treatment of the roles of various interest groups in U.S. trade policy making, see Gene M. Grossman and Elhanan Helpman, *Interest Groups and Trade Policy* (Princeton, NJ: Princeton University Press, 2002).

29. The following discussion is largely relied on Robert E. Baldwin, "U.S. Trade Policy Since 1934: An Uneven Path toward Greater Trade Liberalization," *NBER Working Paper 15397* (Cambridge, MA: National Bureau of Economic Research, 2009); William A. Lovett, Alfred E. Eckes, and Richard L. Brinkman, *U.S. Trade Policy: History, Theory, and the WTO* (Armonk, NY: M. E. Sharpe, 2004); Stephen D. Cohen, *The Making of United States International Economic Policy* (5th ed.); Nitsan Chorev, *Rethinking U.S. Trade Policy: From Protectionism to Globalization* (Ithaca and London: Cornell University Press, 2007); and I. M. Destler, *American Trade Politics*.

30. For a discussion of the failure of the ITO and U.S. trade policy in the early Cold War era, see Thomas W. Zeiler, "Managing Protectionism: American Trade Policy in the Early Cold War," *Diplomatic History* 22(3) (1998): 337–360.

31. For the statutory background and historical development of the roles of executive agreements in U.S. trade policy making, see Jeanne J. Grimmett, "Why Certain Trade Agreements Are Approved as Congressional-Executive Agreements Rather Than as Treaties," *CRS Report of Congress*, 97-896, April 5, 2002, available at http://www.fas.org/sgp/crs/misc/97-896.pdf (accessed March 15, 2012).

32. For a brief chronological overview of fast-track authority, see Carolyn C. Smith, "Fast-Track Negotiating Authority for Trade Agreements and Trade Promotion Authority: Chronology of Major Votes," *CRS Report for Congress*, RS21004, December 18, 2001, available at http://www.policyarchive.org/handle/10207/bitstreams/3502.pdf (accessed March 15, 2012).

33. For a brief treatment of the significance and politics of the 1988 OTCA, see Destler, *American Trade Politics*, pp. 84–96.

34. For an analysis of the Uruguay Round, see Ernest H. Preeg, *Traders in a New World: The Uruguay Round and the Future of the International Trading System* (Chicago: University of Chicago Press, 1995).

35. For a discussion of trade promotion authority, see Lenore Sek, "Trade Promotion Authority (Fast-Track Authority for Trade Agreements): Background and Developments in the 107th Congress," *Issue Brief for Congress, IB10084*, January 14, 2003, available at http://fpc.state.gov/documents/organization/16806.pdf (accessed March 15, 2012). Fast-track authority had expired in 1994.

238 CHAPTER 10 ▶ Trade Policy

36. For details of new initiatives and activities under the NEI, see the NEI website at http://export.gov/nei/ (accessed March 15, 2012).

37. For a discussion of such a department, see Cohen, *The Making of United States International Economic Policy*, pp. 280–287. Also see I. M. Destler, "The Foreign Economic Bureaucracy," in Steven W. Hook and Christopher M. Jones (eds.), *Routledge Handbook of American Foreign Policy* (New York: Routledge, 2012), Chapter 6, pp. 217–230.

38. President Obama's proposal can be found in "Government Reorganization Fact Sheet," available at http://www.whitehouse.gov/the-press-office/2012/01/13/government-reorganization-fact-sheet (accessed March 15, 2012).

39. For details, see a series of USTR Trade Policy Agenda and annual report, available at http://www.ustr.gov/about-us/press-office/reports-and-publications/2012-0 (accessed March 15, 2012).

40. The following discussion and quotes are from WTO Trade Policy Review Body, *Trade Policy Review: Report by the United States* (WT/TPR/G/235), pp. 5–6, August 2010, available at http://www.wto.org/english/tratop_e/tpr_e/tp335_e.htm (accessed March 15, 2012).

41. See Eric Heginbotham and Richard Samuels, "Mercantile Realism and Japanese Foreign Policy," *International Security*, 22(4) (1998): 171–203; Richard J. Samuels, *"Rich Nation, Strong Army": National Security and the Technological Transformation of Japan* (Ithaca, NY: Cornell University Press, 1994); and Kenneth B. Pyle, *Japan Rising: The Resurgence of Japanese Power and Purpose* (New York: Public Affairs, 2007). For the concept of the trading state, see Richard Rosencrance, *The Rise of the Trading State: Commerce and Conquest in the Modern World* (New York: Basic Books, 1987).

42. For an overview of the Japanese economy, see David Flath, *The Japanese Economy* (2nd ed.) (Oxford: Oxford University Press, 2005).

43. For example, see David Barboza, "China Passes Japan as Second-Largest Economy," *New York Times,* August 15, 2010, available at http://www.nytimes.com/2010/08/16/business/global/16yuan.html?pagewanted=all (accessed March 15, 2012).

44. For a summary of unfair trade allegations against Japan, see Gary R. Saxonhouse, "A Short Summary of the Long History of Unfair Trade Allegations against Japan," in Jagdish Bhagwati and Robert E. Hudec (eds.), *Fair Trade and Harmonization: Prerequisites for Free Trade? Vol. 1: Economic Analysis* (Cambridge, MA: MIT Press, 1997), pp. 471–513.

45. For example, see the World Bank, *Asian Miracle* (Washington, DC: World Bank, 1993) and Joseph E. Stiglitz, *Making Globalization Work* (New York: Norton, 2006). The World Bank's report concluded that the rapid growth of the Japanese economy was due to a combination of domestic factors, such as a very strong governmental control/management policy, the entrepreneurial talent and initiative of business leaders, and a hard-working, literate, and increasingly skilled workforce.

46. See WTO Trade Policy Review Body, *Trade Policy Review: Report by Japan* (WT/TPR/G/211), 14 January 2009, available at http://www.wto.org/english/tratop_e/tpr_e/tp311_e.htm (accessed March 15, 2012).

47. For a survey of Japanese politics and policy making, see J. A. A. Stockwin, *Governing Japan: Divided Politics in a Major Economy* (4th ed.) (London: Wiley-Blackwell, 2008); Gerald L. Curtis, *The Logic of Japanese Politics: Leaders, Institutions and the Limits of Change* (New York: Columbia University Press, 2000); Minoru Nakano (translated by Jeremy Scott), *The Policy-Making Process in Contemporary Japan* (New York: St. Martin's Press, 1997); and Thomas E. Mann and Takeshi Sasaki, eds.,

Governance for a New Century: Japanese Challenges, American Experience (Tokyo: Japan Center for International Exchange, 2002).

48. If the two houses of the Diet cannot agree on a joint candidate for prime minister, the candidate who is elected by the Shu-Gi-In becomes prime minister.

49. Japan's court system is considered unitary in the sense that there are no independent court systems at prefecture-levels, which is equivalent to the state court system of the United States.

50. For a brief discussion of Japan's formal law-making process, see http://www.clb. go.jp/english/process.html (accessed Mach 15, 2012).

51. For example, see "Lost in Transition: Japan's People Are Trapped in the Past: Their New Government Must Help Secure Them a Future," *The Economist*, September 3, 2009, available at http://www.economist.com/node/14363169 (accessed March 15, 2012).

52. For an overview of the LDP's institutional structure, see http://www.jimin.jp/english/ profile/chart/index.html (accessed March 15, 2012).

53. For a detailed discussion of the MITI's role in Japan's trade and industrial policy making, see Mikio Sumiya (ed.), *History of Japanese Trade and Industry Policy* (Oxford: Oxford University Press, 2000); Charmers Johnson, *MITI and the Japanese Miracle: The Growth of Industrial Policy, 1925–1975* (Stanford: Stanford University Press, 1982); and Samuels, *"Rich Nation, Strong Army."*

54. For details, see Johnson, *MITI and the Japanese Miracle*, specifically, Chapter 7.

55. See the METI website at http://www.meti.go.jp/english/org/index.html (accessed March 15, 2012).

56. For more information about JETRO, see the JETRO website at http://www.jetro. go.jp/ (accessed March 15, 2012).

57. For more information, see the JFTC website at http://www.jftc.go.jp/en/index.html (accessed March 15, 2012).

58. See T. J. Pempel, "Japanese Foreign Economic Policy: The Domestic Bases for International Behavior," *International Organization* 31(4) (1977): 723–774; Johnson, *MITI and the Japanese Miracle*; and Samuels, *"Rich Nation, Strong Army."*

59. For a brief description of a variety of interest groups in Japan, see "interest groups" in Ronald E. Dolan and Robert L. Worden (eds.), *Japan: A Country Study* (Washington, DC: GPO for the Library of Congress, 1994), available at http://countrystudies.us/ japan/120.htm (accessed March 15, 2012).

60. See the METI website at http://www.meti.go.jp/english/information/data/laws.html (accessed March 15, 2012).

61. See Mikio Sumiya (ed.), *History of Japanese Trade and Industry Policy* (Oxford: Oxford University Press, 2000), Chapter 6, p. 139.

62. The following discussion relies on Singiro Hagiwawa, *Trade and Industrial Policy* [Tsusho-Sangou-Seisaki], (Japan, Nihon-Keizai-Hyouron-Sha, 2003); Mikio Sumiya (ed.), *History of Japanese Trade and Industry Policy* (Oxford: Oxford University Press, 2000); Ryutaro Komiya and Motoshige Itho, "Japan's International Trade and Trade Policy, 1955–1984," in Takashi Inoguchi and Daniel I. Okimoto (eds.), *The Political Economy of Japan: Vol.2, The Changing International Context* (Stanford, CA: Stanford University Press, 1989), pp. 173–224; and Gary R. Saxonhouse, "A Short Summary of the Long History of Unfair Trade Allegation against Japan" in Jagdish Bhagwati and Robert E. Hudec (eds.), *Fair Trade and Harmonization: Prerequisites for Free Trade? Vol. 1: Economic Analysis* (Cambridge, MA: MIT Press, 1997), pp. 471–513.

63. For useful chronological description and assessments of U.S. trade policy toward Japan, see John Kunkel, *America's Trade Policy towards Japan: Demanding Results*

(London: Routledge, 2003) and Saxonhouse, "A Short Summary of the Long History of Unfair Trade Allegations against Japan."

64. For a good summary and assessment of the U.S.–Japan Framework Talks, see Saxonhouse, "A Short Summary of the Long History of Unfair Trade Allegations against Japan."

65. See Saadia M. Pekkanen, "Aggressive Legalism: The Rules of the WTO and Japan's Emerging Trade Strategy," *The World Economy* 24(5) (2001): 707–737.

66. See Saadia M. Pekkanen, "Bilateralism, Multilateralism, or Regionalism? Japan's Trade Forum Choices," *Journal of East Asia Studies* 5(1) (2005): 77–103.

67. The METI's *White Paper on International Economy and Trade 2010* is available at http://www.meti.go.jp/english/report/data/gIT2010maine.html (accessed March 15, 2012).

68. The MOFA's *Diplomatic Bluebook 2010* is available at http://www.mofa.go.jp/policy/other/bluebook/2010/index.html (accessed March 15, 2012)

69. See "Free Trade in the Pacific: A Small Reason to Be cheerful," *The Economist*, November 19, 2011. For an update on TPP negotiations, see the USTR website, available at http://www.ustr.gov/trade-agreements/free-trade-agreements/trans-pacific-partnership/tpp-negotiation-updates (accessed March 15, 2012).

70. See the WTO Trade Policy Review Body, *Trade Policy Review: Report by Japan* (WT/TPR/G/211), 14 January, 2009, available at http://www.wto.org/english/tratop_e/tpr_e/tp311_e.htm (accessed March 15, 2012).

CHAPTER 11

Conclusion

U.S. Public Policy in Comparison

We have provided an overview of public policies and policy-making processes in the United States and put them in an international context for a comparison between the United States and other countries in regard to the same policies. Seven core chapters looked at four sets of issues of concern to public policymakers: (1) political organization, (2) human well-being, (3) the environment, and (4) international economic relations. The first set was covered with a focus on election and criminal justice policies, the second set examined healthcare and social welfare policies, the third set investigated air and water pollution control and alternative energy policies, and the fourth set focused on trade policy.

The international context that we chose for comparison with the United States included India, China, Canada, Sweden, Brazil, the Netherlands, and Japan. These countries are quite varied in terms of political institutions, wealth, demographics, geography, and culture. None of these countries was selected randomly; we chose them because we thought they are of particularly strong interest to students of comparative public policy due to the media coverage and public exposure they have received regarding certain public policies. India is one of the world's most populous and culturally diverse democracies, and China has received frequent attention over its violation of human rights in attempts to enforce public order. Canada is often referred to in debates pertaining to healthcare, and Sweden is usually considered a prime example of a social welfare state. Brazil's Amazon Basin is of great importance to the world's balance of oxygen and carbon dioxide and as one of the world's largest sources of fresh water, and the Netherlands has been on the forefront in exploring and relying on alternative energy sources to promote efficient and environment-friendly use of energy. Japan, one of the most important trading partners of the United States and many other countries, has been of particular concern over unfair trade practices, especially in the 1990s.

Throughout the comparative core of this book, we relied mostly on a public policy-making process approach that incorporated elements of a variety of theoretical approaches, such as institutional, incremental, systems, and pluralist theories, and a variety of methodological approaches, such as process and historical methods. In each core chapter, we first examined a public policy from the United States and then in a country chosen for comparison with the United States with regard to the policy. Here, we focused on country-specific issues, government agencies and other actors involved in policy making, policy initiatives or current policies, as well as challenges and problems concerning the policy in the United States and the country chosen for comparison.

Political Culture, Institutional Settings, and Public Policy

Although the United States and other countries are confronted with similar issues of concern to public policymakers, there are some notable differences between the United States and other countries when considering their public policy-making processes and the policies that they create to deal with these issues. These policy-making and policy differences are, to a large extent, related to differences in political culture and institutional settings. Regarding political culture, for example, we argued in Chapter 3 ("Setting the Stage") that public policy may be a direct result of the Dominant Social Paradigm (DSP) in the United States. The DSP constitutes those clusters of beliefs, values, and ideals that influence the nation's thinking about society, government, and individual responsibility. In the United States, the DSP is defined in terms of laissez-faire capitalism, market economics, private property, individualism, freedom, growth, and progress, as well as faith in science and technology.

Both Chapter 5 ("Criminal Justice Policy") and Chapter 7 ("Social Welfare Policy") provided good examples of the extent to which different policies regarding similar issues are rooted in different political cultures. Reflecting the DSP that is characteristic of U.S. political culture, the U.S. criminal justice system is bound by the rule of law, specifically by the U.S. Constitution's Bill of Rights, to respect, uphold, and protect individual rights and liberty throughout criminal justice proceedings. According to Chinese political culture, however, individual rights and liberty tend to be of lesser importance than social order, the country's socialist system, and the Chinese Communist Party. Thus, most crimes identified by China's 1997 revised Criminal Law involve crimes against the collective (state security, public security, the socialist market economic order, social order and its administration, national defense, and military duties).

Reflecting again the DSP that is characteristic of U.S. political culture, U.S. social welfare programs are based on a liberal welfare model, with emphasis on self-sufficiency and individual freedom, where social protection comes into play after breakdowns of the private market and the family as natural channels for the fulfillment of social needs. But according to Swedish political culture, it is the state's responsibility to ensure economic equality, protect social rights, regulate free economic enterprise, and spend tax revenue on basic social welfare benefits. Thus, Swedish social welfare programs are based on a social democratic welfare model, with emphasis on social responsibility and equality, where social welfare benefits are granted because all people have a political right to social protection within a generous comprehensive social welfare system.

Regarding institutional settings, Chapter 3 ("Setting the Stage") distinguished between presidential and parliamentary democracies and between federal and unitary systems. Except for China, a communist state, all the countries that we looked at in this book are representative democracies. Among these representative democracies, two are presidential democracies (the United States and Brazil) and five are parliamentary democracies (India, Canada, Sweden, the Netherlands, and Japan); four have federal systems (the United States, India, Canada, and Brazil) and three have unitary systems (Sweden, the Netherlands, and Japan). In *presidential democracies,* the same individual, a president, is the head of state as well as the head of government. In *parliamentary democracies,* one individual, a president or a monarch, is the head of state, and another individual, a prime minister, is the head of government. The president in presidential democracies is elected directly and separately from members of the legislature, but the prime minister in parliamentary democracies is elected indirectly through elections of members of the legislature, a parliament. Furthermore, the president in presidential democracies has a fixed term and can be ejected from office only if charged with misconduct. However, the prime minister in parliamentary democracies has an unfixed term, which depends on the support of his or her ruling party or coalition of parties, and can be ejected from office through a vote of no confidence taken by the legislature.

The United States is an established presidential democracy based on the U.S. Constitution, which provides for a separation of powers with checks and balances between three branches of government: the legislature (the U.S. Congress), the executive (the U.S. president and the federal administration or bureaucracy), and the judiciary (the U.S. Supreme Court and various lower-level courts). The role of the legislature is to make laws, the role of the executive is to implement and administer laws, and the role of the judiciary is to interpret laws and to uphold the U.S. Constitution. As Chapter 10 ("Trade Policy"), for example, explained specifically with relation to trade policymaking, U.S. public policy is based on laws or legislative acts passed by Congress to be implemented and administered through policy programs of government departments and agencies under the president. Members of the Senate and the House of Representatives can exercise congressional power over public policy making not only through legislation but also through approval of agency and program budgets and appropriation of funds, confirmation of senior policymakers, as well as oversight of existing and evolving executive activities and programs.

Unlike the executive in presidential democracies, such as the United States, the executive in parliamentary democracies not only implements and administers public policy but also has significant influence on laws or legislative acts authorizing public policy programs. This is so because the prime minister, the head of government, is usually the head of the party with a majority of seats in the legislature, or the largest party in a coalition of parties with a majority of seats in the legislature. It is also possible that public policy is based on initiatives from within the ruling party or coalition of parties. According to Chapter 10 ("Trade Policy"), for example, trade policy initiatives in Japan, a parliamentary democracy, typically originated not with legislative acts but with policy proposals shaped by senior bureaucrats representing ministries and agencies within the Liberal Democratic Party. Significant opportunities to initiate trade policy proposals gave senior bureaucrats a lot of power over trade policy formation.

Public policy making varies not only between presidential and parliamentary democracies but also between federal and unitary systems. In *federal systems,* political power is shared between a central or national government and regional governments, as well as local governments. By contrast, in *unitary systems,* most political power is held by a central or national government while regional and/or local jurisdictions have only limited political power. Combined with a separation of powers between legislative, executive, and judicial branches of government, federalism provides for decentralization to check and balance the power of a central or national government. Decentralization also gives regional and local jurisdictions a voice and role in many policy areas.

According to the Tenth Amendment to the U.S. Constitution, "The powers not delegated to the United States by the Constitution, nor prohibited by it to the States, are reserved to the States respectively, or to the people." Thus, in the United States, *federalism* means that, in addition to policy decisions made by the federal government, there are many policy decisions that are made by 50 state governments and an even greater number of local governments. Also, in many policy areas, the federal government, state governments, and local governments have shared jurisdiction as well as multiple and overlapping responsibilities. Furthermore, state governments can establish or abolish local governments, and delegate to them a wide variety of functions and responsibilities, often in regard to the implementation of federal laws.

As we saw in Chapter 6 ("Healthcare Policy"), for example, healthcare policy in both the United States and Canada is made within federal systems. In the United States, state governments have responsibility for health departments, hospitals, and mental health institutions, and they have discretion in delivering Medicaid and the State Children's Health Insurance Program. State governments can set eligibility standards for prescription drug coverage under the 2003 Medical Modernization Act, and they have regulated managed care organizations to enhance healthcare provision for all working-age families. Also, every state has passed legislation to control and monitor the managed care system. In Canada, however, provincial/territorial governments administer most healthcare services, whose allocation they decide on in negotiations with healthcare providers. Primary responsibility for healthcare in each province/territory is vested in a provincial/territorial ministry of health headed by a health minister, and there is a conference where all provincial/territorial health ministers meet with Canada's Minister of Health to coordinate provincial/territorial healthcare programs. Although Canada has a publicly funded single-payer healthcare system with nationwide universal standards for healthcare delivery based on the 1984 Canada Health Act, its origins were provincial healthcare initiatives by Saskatchewan in 1947 and by British Columbia and Alberta in 1949.

According to prominent scholars such as Alexis de Tocqueville and Seymour Martin Lipset,[1] the United States is exceptional in its values and institutional design. Although there is a stereotype that U.S. public policies are exceptional in the sense that they are underdeveloped, this is a rather narrow perspective focused on only social spending and only public policies since World War II. [2]

Although public funding and government involvement in providing public goods and services are more widely accepted in other countries than in the United States, this does not necessarily mean that public policy programs in the United States are less effective and efficient than they are in other countries. As we mentioned in Chapter 6 ("Healthcare Policy"), Canadians, in comparison with Americans, are more supportive of government intervention than of market competition in regard to healthcare delivery, and healthcare seems to cost less in Canada than in the United States. Yet, Canadian health insurance may not cover many advanced medical treatments that are commonly available to Americans. In this regard, it is noteworthy that many Canadians prefer some sort of private insurance instead of, or in addition to, a publicly funded health insurance program in order to obtain greater access to quality health services beyond some basic treatment.

Furthermore, as we conveyed in Chapter 7 ("Social Welfare Policy"), Swedish social welfare programs are based on a social democratic welfare model, with emphasis on social responsibility and equality, whereas American social welfare programs are based on a liberal welfare model, with emphasis on self-sufficiency and individual freedom. Although Sweden is widely recognized for its generous social welfare benefits, serious concerns about the sustainability of Sweden's pension system led to reform that changed Sweden's traditionally public pension system into a partially privatized hybrid public–private pension system.

Differences between the United States and other countries regarding public policies and policy-making processes are, to a large extent, related to differences in political culture and institutional settings. Despite these differences, the United States and other countries are confronted with similar demographic, economic, and societal challenges as they try to maintain or increase public goods and services with increasingly limited resources. Public policies to deal effectively and efficiently with similar issues under growing fiscal constraints and economic challenges may benefit from more international learning and cooperation across political cultures and institutional settings.

Recommended Resources

Robert A. Dahl, *A Preface to Democratic Theory* (Chicago: University of Chicago Press, 1956).

Richard S. Katz, *Political Institutions in the United States* (New York: Oxford University Press, 2007).

Arend Lijphart, *Patterns of Democracy: Government Forms and Performance in Thirty-Six Countries* (New Haven, CT: Yale University Press, 1999).

Seymour Martin Lipset, *American Exceptionalism: A Double- Edged Sword* (New York: Norton, 1997).

Peter H. Schuck and James Q. Wilson (eds.), *Understanding America: The Anatomy of an Exceptional Nation* (New York: Public Affairs, 2008).

Alexis de Tocqueville, *Democracy in America* (1835, various translations are available).

Notes

1. See Alexis de Tocqueville, *Democracy in America*, vols. 1 and 2 (New York: Vintage Books, 1990) and Seymour Martin Lipset, *American Exceptionalism: A Double-Edged Sword* (New York: Norton, 1997).
2. Edwin Amenta and Theda Skocpol, "Taking Exception: Explaining the Distinctiveness of American Public Policies in the Last Century," in Francis G. Castles (ed.), *the Comparative History of Public Policy* (New York: Oxford University Press, 1989).

INDEX

247